THE
THIN GREEN
LINE

By the same author

*Wall of Steel: The History of 9th (Londonderry) HAA Regiment, RA (SR),*North-West Books, 1988

The Sons of Ulster: Ulstermen at war from the Somme to Korea, The Appletree Press, 1992

Clear the Way! A History of the 38th (Irish) Brigade, 1941–47, Irish Academic Press, 1993

*Irish Generals: Irish Generals in the British Army in the Second World War,*The Appletree Press, 1993

Only the Enemy in Front: The Recce Corps at War, 1940–46, Spellmount Publishers, 1994

Key to Victory: The Maiden City in the Second World War, Greystone Books, 1995

The Williamite War in Ireland, 1688–1691, Four Courts Press, 1998

A Noble Crusade: The History of the Eighth Army, 1941–1945, Spellmount Publishers, 1999

Irish Men and Women in the Second World War, Four Courts Press, 1999

Irish Winners of the Victoria Cross (with David Truesdale), Four Courts Press, 2000

Irish Volunteers in the Second World War, Four Courts Press, 2001

The Sound of History: El Alamein 1942, Spellmount Publishers, 2002

The North Irish Horse: A Hundred Years of Service, Spellmount Publishers, 2002

Normandy 1944: The Road to Victory, Spellmount Publishers, 2004

Ireland's Generals in the Second World War, Four Courts Press, 2004

THE
THIN GREEN
LINE

A history of
The Royal Ulster Constabulary GC
1922–2001

by

Richard Doherty

Pen & Sword
MILITARY

First published in Great Britain in 2004 by
Pen & Sword Military
an imprint of
Pen & Sword Books Ltd
47 Church Street
Barnsley
South Yorkshire
S70 2AS

ISBN 1 84415 058 5

A CIP catalogue record for this book is
available from the British Library

Typeset in Sabon

Printed and bound in England by
CPI UK

Pen & Sword Books Ltd incorporates the Imprints of Pen & Sword
Aviation, Pen & Sword Maritime, Pen & Sword Military, Wharncliffe
Local History, Pen & Sword Select, Pen & Sword Military Classics
and Leo Cooper.

For a complete list of Pen & Sword titles please contact
PEN & SWORD BOOKS LIMITED
47 Church Street, Barnsley, South Yorkshire, S70 2AS, England
E-mail: enquiries@pen-and-sword.co.uk
Website: www.pen-and-sword.co.uk

Take these men [and women] for your example.
Like them, remember that posterity can only
be for the free; that freedom is the sure
possession of those who have the
courage to defend it.

THE YOUNG MAY MOON
(March past of the RIC and RUC GC)

The young May moon is beaming love
The glow worm's lamp is gleaming love,
How sweet to rove,
Through Morna's grove,
When the drowsy world is dreaming love.

Then awake – the heavens look bright my dear,
'Tis never too late for delight, my dear,
And the best of all ways
To lengthen our days
Is to steal a few hours from the night, my dear.

Now all the world is sleeping love,
But the sage his star watch is keeping love
And I whose star
More glorious far,
Is the eye from that
Casement peeping love.

Then awake –
'Tis the rise of the sun,
My dear, the sage's glass we'll shun,
My dear,
Or if watching the flight,
Of bodies of light,
He may happen to take you
For one, my dear.

(Thomas Moore, 1779–1852)

Contents

Foreword

Many people and organizations helped in the research and writing of this book and I would like to express my thanks to all of them. Without their help and encouragement the book would not have been possible. I am, therefore, indebted to: Mrs Agnes Adair BEM; Mr Richard Byrnes; Mrs Catherine Campbell (neé Whitsitt); Mr Paul Clarke; Mr Tony Crowe; Mr Ivan Duncan; Mr Neil Falkingham QPM MIRSO; Sir Ronnie Flanagan GBE MA; Sam Foster CBE FIRSO (Hon.); Sir John Gorman; Mr Charles Graham; Mr Norman Hamill MA; Mr Bobby Hanvey; Mr Luke Hasson MBE; Mr Alan Hawthorne; Mr Jim Herlihy; Sir John Hermon; Mr Douglas S. Hogg BEM FIRSO (Hon.); Mr Peter Leslie; Mr Michael McAtamney OBE LlB; Mr Peter McCandless; Mr Alan McConnell; Mrs Breege McCusker; Mr Bernard McGrath; Mr Sam Mitchell; Mr Albert Nicholl; Mr Herbert Ross; Mr Reggie Semple QPM; Mr Robin Sinclair MBE; Mrs Karen Stewart; Mr Stewart Tosh MBE; Mr Sam Trotter; Mr Ronnie Trouton MBE FIRSO; Mr David Truesdale; Mr Jack Truesdale; Mr David and Mrs Florence Walker.

A word of thanks is also due to my good friend Joe McCready AFM for reading and commenting on parts of the draft. Several individuals also provided information or assistance but asked that their names should not be included in the book. Their request for anonymity is respected but I would like to express my special gratitude to them.

Among the organizations that helped me were: The RUC GC Foundation; The RUC GC Association; The RUC GC Historical Society and The RUC GC Widows Association from which I would like to thank Mr Jim McDonald LVO MBE KCSG KCHS JP DL, Chairman of the Foundation, Mr Hugh Forrester, Secretary and Mr Richard Abbott MBE, Treasurer, of the Historical Society and Mrs Iona Meyer MBE, Chairperson of the Widows' Association, for their support. In addition I would like to thank Mr Terry Spence of the Police Federation for Northern Ireland and the RUC GC Benevolent Fund for his assistance and advice.

Institutional assistance was provided by the Northern Ireland Police Museum, the curator of which, Mr Hugh Forrester, was enthusiastic and energetic in his support; The Linenhall Library, Belfast, which tracked down some obscure books for my research; the staff of the Reading Room and the Search Room at the National Archives who were, as ever, highly professional and friendly; the British Library Newspaper Library, Colindale, London and the Central Library, Foyle Street, Londonderry. Mr Bob Catterson QPM, editor of the *Police Service Gazette*, formerly *Constabulary Gazette*, was another valuable source of information.

A number of quotations appear throughout the book and I am grateful for permission to use these from: Ivan Duncan for quotations from his book *Insult to Injury*; Pen & Sword Books Ltd., Barnsley for quotations from *The Times of My Life* by Sir John Gorman and *A Testimony to Courage, The regimental history of The Ulster Defence Regiment* by John Potter; Gill and Macmillan Ltd., Dublin for quotations from *Holding the Line* by Sir John Hermon; The RUC GC Historical Society for quotations from *The Women in Green* by Margaret Cameron; *The Sunday Times* for quotations from Eoghan Harris; Blackstaff Press Ltd., Belfast for quotations from *A Straight Left* by Paddy Devlin and *A History of Ulster* by Jonathan Bardon. Every effort has been made to ensure that no infringement of copyright has occurred but if, in spite of these efforts, any copyright has been infringed the author would be pleased to make arrangements to rectify this at the earliest available opportunity.

Photographs appear by courtesy of the Police Museum; Mrs Agnes Adair BEM; J. J. McCauley; Mrs Evy McDonald; Mr Reggie Semple QPM; and Mr Bobby Hanvey.

Brigadier Henry Wilson of Pen & Sword Books was a stalwart support throughout the research and writing process as well as being very patient. My thanks are due to Henry and all the excellent team at Pen & Sword who made this book possible.

It would be most remiss of me not to mention a very special group of ladies who provided many cups of tea, friendship and support in what now seems to have been a very different age. Thank you to Vera, sadly gone from us, Agnes, Joan, Denise, Claire, Hazel and Mary, all of whom wore green with pride and brought much credit to the uniform.

Finally I thank my family – my wife Carol, children Joanne, James and Catríona and grandson Ciarán – for their constant support.

Richard Doherty
Co. Londonderry
September 2004

Introduction

There was a time, and not so very long ago, when the popular image of a police officer was of the local 'bobby' or 'peeler' patrolling his beat, chatting to children and adults, perhaps giving some timely advice to teenagers who might be in danger of going astray, or assisting families and communities at times of trauma. Much of that image was due, in some respects, to media representations of police officers – the long-running BBC television series 'Dixon of Dock Green' is often quoted in this respect – but it also owes much to the reality of policing over a long period in our history when the single police officer walking the beat was an accepted, and assuring, sign for society.

But that perception has changed and often for the worst. Popular images of police officers in more recent years tend to concentrate on the mistakes made by them: deaths caused in vehicle chases; individuals shot dead by armed police in disputed circumstances; corruption involving police officers; investigations that appear to be bungled. Further afield, the image of American police officers beating Rodney King is still powerful. And there can be no doubt that there have been, and will continue to be, police officers who make mistakes, inquiries that were bungled, and individuals who have lost their lives because of mistaken decisions made by police officers.

However, concentrating on those officers who have done wrong, or who have failed to handle an investigation as professionally as possible, or who have neglected their duty in any way, takes away from the credit that is due to the overwhelming majority of police officers who have carried out their duties to the best of their abilities, who have tried to uphold the law without fear or favour and who have earned the respect of those in whose communities they operate and with whom they work. Nowhere has this been more true than in Northern Ireland where the Royal Ulster Constabulary GC received more opprobrium than credit in spite of the fact that the force held the line that allowed most of us who

1

lived in Northern Ireland over the past three decades to live a life that was as normal as possible.

During the years between 1969 and 1996 more than 300 police officers, male and female, lost their lives and thousands more were injured in the course of what were euphemistically called 'the troubles'. The deaths alone – and there were 302 of them – represent one-tenth of the strength of the RUC in early 1969 while the toll of injured was more than twice that number. When the force was awarded the George Cross in 1999 that decoration was seen as a reward for duty nobly done; for the tremendous courage that the men and women of the force had shown over three decades; and for the pain and suffering that they, and their families, had endured throughout those years. In the sixty-year history of the George Cross there is only one parallel to the award made to the Royal Ulster Constabulary – that made to the island of Malta during the Second World War. That parallel provides a perspective to the achievements and courage of Northern Ireland's police officers and is a sure indication of the respect in which the Royal Ulster Constabulary was held – and continues to be held.

Of course, there are those who had, and continue to have, no respect for the force, with one prominent Sinn Fein member describing it as the most discredited police force in Europe, an allegation that is without any sound or logical basis since, throughout Europe and much farther afield, the RUC was respected by those who knew anything at all about the difficulties of policing against a background of civil commotion and terrorism; and it was respected especially by the force's peers in law enforcement. However, one would not expect Republicans to praise the work of the RUC: in the form of the IRA, Republicans spent thirty years trying to destroy the force and murdering its members while conducting a campaign of vilification in a vain effort to blunt the effectiveness of police operations against terrorists. While Republicans saw the award of the George Cross as a cynical exercise, it has to be said that this view is shared by some police officers who considered it a counterbalance to the proposed changes in the police force that would also see the name changing to the anodyne Police Service of Northern Ireland and the distinctively Irish badge and emblems, inherited from the Royal Irish Constabulary, being replaced by what this writer regards as one of the worst examples of badge design ever perpetrated in these islands.

The final thirty years of existence of the RUC GC were dangerous years during which those who had the courage to don the uniform of a police officer faced death and injury on a daily basis. Before that there had been other periods in the force's history in which it also faced considerable danger but never desisted from its duty. But there were also years when life was reasonably normal, when Northern Ireland society was much more law-abiding than is the case today, and when police officers were able to operate, as they wished, with the support and consent of the entire community, bar that small faction that did not respect the law. Even in those days, halcyon though they may now seem, there was always some element of risk: that is the nature of a police officer's life. This book is an attempt to reflect what life was like for members of the Royal Ulster Constabulary GC during the force's existence and to demonstrate how important the force was to Northern Ireland and the degree to which it succeeded in carrying out its primary tasks, especially in the years since 1969. It is also a tribute to those who served in the RUC GC and especially to those who gave their lives between 1922 and 2000.

Over the past four decades I have been fortunate to know many members of the Royal Ulster Constabulary GC and I count police officers amongst my friends; some of them I regard as among the finest people I have ever met. Sadly, I have also attended the funerals of too many friends who had the courage to wear the green uniform and who paid with their lives for that courage. Their memory deserves more than the criticism hurled at them from too many quarters and I hope that this book will go some small way towards righting that wrong.

Richard Doherty
Londonderry
July 2004

Chapter One

The Force is Born

Most accounts of policing in Ireland credit the development of the Irish police forces to Robert Peel in his time as Ireland's Chief Secretary. What is often overlooked is that the word 'police' was first used in legislation in its modern sense anywhere in these islands in an act passed by the Irish parliament in 1786. The Dublin Metropolitan Police Act created the Dublin Metropolitan Police District; the Dublin Police, established in 1787, was the first modern police force in the British Isles. From that Act, and the creation of the Dublin Police, the word 'police' takes its accepted modern definition of regulating public order and enforcing good government. Before that the word, which comes from the Greek 'polis', meaning city, through French, implied the protection of society from the disaffected; the two meanings are, therefore, complementary. Today, many, including police officers, would regard protecting society as the primary role of any police force. Interestingly, either interpretation implies that policing is a service to society, and that police officers are civil servants, in the true sense. In that light, the decision to rename the Royal Ulster Constabulary GC as the Police Service of Northern Ireland shows a lack of understanding of clear English on the part of the decision makers, since the new title uses two words to say the same thing: 'police' and 'service'. This modern infatuation with convoluted language is not peculiar to Northern Ireland; London's force has been rebranded the Metropolitan Police Service in the interests of political correctness.

Peel's creation was not the national police force he had wanted but the Peace Preservation Force (PPF), which came into being in 1814, as the Napoleonic Wars drew to an end. Among the reasons for the formation of the Force was the shortage of military personnel to assist parish constables.[1] Peel objected to using the Army in a civilian situation and said so in Parliament; this rationale later led him to form the London Metropolitan Police. In between, the killing of eleven demonstrators and wounding of about 400 during a political reformers' gathering of some 50–60,000 people at St Peter's Field, Manchester on 16 August 1819 seemed to support Peel's argument. Although there was no disorder, magistrates lost their nerve and ordered the arrest of the demonstration's organizer. When yeomanry troopers tried to arrest him, they were surrounded and forced to draw their sabres. At that point a troop of regular cavalry intervened; at this time Manchester was notorious for rioting and the soldiers may have feared that a major riot was imminent. As the hussars moved forward panic ensued in which the eleven, including two women, died. The incident became immortalized as the 'Peterloo Massacre'.

Although the Peace Preservation Force was a national organization it did not have permanent stations throughout the country but was a form of emergency reserve that could be sent anywhere in Ireland 'proclaimed' to be in need by the Lord Lieutenant. To save money, members were not permanent, being liable to call up when decreed. The PPF first deployed to the barony of Castlethird in Tipperary in September 1814. Almost immediately members were nicknamed 'Peelers', a soubriquet applied to police officers in Ireland ever since. Many were former cavalry NCOs and the use of horses lent mobility. It appears that these men also created a tradition that survived into the Royal Ulster Constabulary, by wearing their rank chevrons on the right forearm with the points upwards. Army NCOs wore, and still wear, their chevrons on the right upper arm; chevrons in the RUC manner are worn in the Army but only by certain 'appointments' rather than ranks, e.g., pipe majors.

The PPF gave way to the Constabulary of Ireland, or County Constabulary, in 1822, established under the Constabulary Act. Peel, now Home Secretary, was again the driving force. Ireland was suffering yet another spasm of unrest, which allowed him to reintroduce his national police force concept. But, as with the PPF, there were objections from local magistrates, who feared erosion of their power, and from Irish MPs at Westminster and so the new force was constituted on a provincial basis. Continuing local objections delayed its introduction in some counties. In each barony there was to be a permanent complement of sixteen constables commanded by a chief constable with each province commanded by an inspector general. Before long there was an extensive reorganization that unified the forces under a single inspector general, based in Dublin Castle. The force structure did not include Dublin, Belfast or Londonderry, each of which had its own police. The Dublin Police had been disbanded in 1795 to be replaced by an unarmed civic guard controlled by the lord mayor and corporation which, in 1836, was superseded by the Dublin Metropolitan Police (DMP). Londonderry city had its own Borough Police as had the town of Belfast.[2] The latter pair would be absorbed by the national force but the DMP survived until April 1925 when it became part of the Garda Síochána. It is interesting to note that the word police was used for urban forces with constabulary being reserved for the national force, in much the same way as France has a national police for urban areas while the gendarmerie covers rural areas. This was also the case in Britain.

The PPF wore a blue uniform with scarlet facings, similar to that of many cavalry regiments but the Constabulary took its uniform colour from another branch of the Army, the rifle regiments, a relatively recent innovation, regarded as elite soldiers and which wore green uniforms. The shade of green, so dark as to appear almost black, was known as rifle-green; it was introduced as a form of camouflage, making the fast moving riflemen more difficult to spot than if they had been garbed in traditional scarlet. Thus was born another tradition that would be carried forward into the RUC. Although the RIC/RUC uniform has been described as unique this is not so; at least two other forces used dark green. Lancashire Constabulary's first uniform was a dark-green frock coat with dark-green trousers, black buttons and black leather belt. This may have been modelled on the Irish uniform since the Lancashire force was not formed until 1840; in Lancashire the rank of sergeant was shown by a single chevron on the left forearm. The London, Birmingham and Liverpool Railway Police also adopted a green tunic.[3]

The new constabulary created in 1822 recruited many senior ranks from the Army. Military men would also provide most of the inspectors general over the next century while the RUC's first and second Inspectors General, Sir Charles Wickham and Sir Richard Pim, had armed service backgrounds. One of the new force's main duties was suppressing faction fights, an unfortunate tradition of men gathering in 'factions' at fairs throughout the country to fight over grievances, real or imagined. These resulted in many deaths and injuries and were a curse on Irish rural life.[4] In 1825 Sir Walter Scott wrote that the public peace in Ireland seemed to be 'secured chiefly' by armed police who were like soldiers, either mounted or on foot, and dressed in the manner of yeomen in Britain. But he also noted that the constabulary behaved well and operated under strict discipline. Nonetheless, the Constabulary's provincial structure came to be considered a weakness, which led to the amalgamation of the provincial forces under the Irish Constabulary Act (1836). Also known as the Drummond Act, this created the Irish Constabulary to cover the entire country except the cities of Dublin and Londonderry and the town of Belfast. Both the Irish Constabulary and the Dublin Metropolitan Police had their headquarters in Dublin Castle; the latter was unarmed whereas the Constabulary carried weapons. The mind behind the new force was the Under Secretary, Thomas Drummond, who had learned much about Ireland during his time with Colonel Colby's Ordnance Survey. Command of the Constabulary was to rest with an Inspector General with two deputies; all three were required to live in Dublin. Each province had an Inspector and each county a County Inspector with eighteen chief constables, now called sub-inspectors. These were the officer ranks, below which were head constables, constables and sub-constables; the rank of constable was the equivalent of the modern sergeant while the sub-constable equated to the modern constable.

The appointment of the Irish Constabulary's first Inspector General was inspired; the choice fell on James Shaw-Kennedy, an Army officer who, in 1829, had rejected Peel's offer of a commissionership in the newly formed London force. Shaw-Kennedy had also served in northern England and had experience of the problems of using soldiers as police. He thus became a firm advocate of the need for an effective civilian police force. However, Shaw-Kennedy did not long remain with the Irish Constabulary, resigning after less than two years in post; his political overlords in Dublin Castle would not allow him to appoint and dismiss officers and nor was he allowed to organize the force as he wished. But he left a legacy that would influence and affect generations of Irish police officers in the form of his 1837 regulations. Those regulations emphasized to those joining the force that they were in an 'entirely new situation' as 'officers of peace', words that seem to have been aimed particularly at erstwhile soldiers. Policemen were to act 'with the utmost forbearance, mildness, urbanity and perfect civility towards all classes' and were never to allow their feelings to get the better of them and certainly never to express opinions of a sectarian or political nature. To ensure their political neutrality, policemen were not permitted to vote. The regulations also governed the day-to-day life of the policeman in a fashion that would remain familiar to RUC officers as late as the 1960s. Policemen were dispersed around the country in small numbers and based in posts known as barracks. Within those barracks, nothing was 'ever to be without its place appointed'; there were to be no pictures on the walls and the building was to be whitewashed on, at least, a six-monthly cycle.

Shaw-Kennedy's regulations specified the qualities of the various ranks, with the constable able to earn respect from his sub-constables but remaining detached from them while officers were to be friendly with both seniors and juniors while winning the respect of their men. Over the following decades the force would earn praise from many visitors to Ireland and its men became an essential part of Irish society. Dispersed in some 1,400 police posts, they carried out many tasks beyond the normal call of duty and could be found reading or writing letters for local people, completing forms and even doing accounts for shopkeepers. In villages and rural communities the constable, later sergeant, was one of the most important personages, ranking alongside the priest, rector and schoolmaster. Most important gatherings would see the man with the gold chevrons present. Their families were also important, although policemen were forbidden to marry until they had seven years' service, by which time they ought to have accumulated enough money to allow a reasonable standard of living as a married couple. Even then the bride had to be approved by the police authorities and the newly-weds could not live in the same county as the bride's family; this meant a transfer for a man who was already not allowed to serve in his own county.

By 1840 the Irish Constabulary numbered 8,500 men and rose to 12,358 ten years later before dropping to around 10,000. A Reserve Force was formed in 1839 and a depot established in Dublin's Phoenix Park in 1842. In that year also, a cadet training scheme was introduced, allowing suitable candidates to be appointed directly as sub-inspectors, the first such scheme in the United Kingdom. Before long the Irish Constabulary's organization provided the pattern for new forces throughout the Empire. Among those based on the Irish model were the British Columbia Provincial Police, in 1858, the New Zealand Constabulary, remodelled in 1871–73 and Canada's North West Mounted Police, later Royal Canadian Mounted Police. The first uniforms of the last-named force were also based on their Irish counterparts. Many Irish officers were appointed to senior positions in these and other forces across the Empire and in Britain itself. The London Metropolitan Police's first two commissioners were Irishmen, although neither had served in the police at home but were an Army officer and a barrister. In East Suffolk the local constabulary, established in 1839, had an Irish chief constable, John Haynes Hatton from County Wicklow, a former Irish policeman; Hatton later became Staffordshire's chief constable. In 1829 one of the London Metropolitan Police's first commissioners, Sir Richard Mayne, wrote an early definition of what today would be termed a mission statement for a police force.

> The primary object of an efficient police is the prevention of crime: the next that of detection and punishment of offenders if crime is committed. To these ends all the efforts of police must be directed. The protection of life and property, the preservation of public tranquillity, and the absence of crime, will alone prove whether those efforts have been successful and whether the objects for which the police were appointed have been attained.

Ireland was never free from tension much of which, in the Constabulary's early years, arose from the movement to repeal the Act of Union, led by Daniel O'Connell. Then came the Young Ireland movement and the 1848 rebellion, in which the sole action occurred between a group of rebels and Constabulary at Boolagh Commons near Ballingarry in County Tipperary. A few rebels were killed or wounded and the remainder captured. The leaders were dealt with leniently, their death sentences being commuted to transportation under a new Treason Felony Act introduced to prevent martyrs being created. One of the leaders, William Smith O'Brien, asked to be hanged, drawn and quartered but the judge refused his request. Instead the rebellion became known popularly as 'the battle of the Widow McCormack's cabbage patch' although it was to have far-reaching influences in later years.

The Young Ireland rebellion occurred in the aftermath of the famine as a result of which many Irish emigrated to the United States. There a hatred of England festered and Irish exiles created an organization styled the Irish Republican Brotherhood (IRB), better known as the Fenians. The Brotherhood was formed in 1858 and many Irishmen who fought in the American Civil War – 1861–65 – did so to learn the profession of arms so that they could fight for Ireland's freedom. Thus the aftermath of the war saw a two-pronged Fenian campaign with an attack into Canada involving the army of the IRB, which used the name Irish Republican Army (IRA), and a rebellion in Ireland.

However, the Irish Constabulary garnered excellent information on the Fenians and their plans and infiltrated the organization to such an extent that the 1867 rebellion was short lived, those outbreaks of violence that did occur being suppressed easily by police and military action. Many arrests were made, habeas corpus was suspended and the rebellion fizzled out, although there was an outbreak of violence in England in which a Manchester policeman was murdered. Three Fenians were executed to become instant martyrs, 'the noble hearted three' of popular myth in contrast to 'the vengeful tyrant' that took their lives. Although there was a revival of Irish political activity thereafter, the folk memories of 1867 would also play a malevolent part in future developments.

In the immediate aftermath of the Fenian rebellion tribute was paid to the Irish Constabulary for its part in quelling the rebellion. Now with some 1,600 stations throughout Ireland and 11,000 men, three-quarters of whom were Roman Catholic, the loyalty of the police was impressive. This was rewarded when Queen Victoria bestowed the prefix 'Royal' on the Constabulary, who were henceforth to be the Royal Irish Constabulary and to wear as their badge the harp and crown of the Order of Saint Patrick.

Although the Royal Irish Constabulary was now part of the fabric of Ireland it had been taken for granted by the authorities who starved it of funds and kept its men poorly paid. In addition, there were other grievances, including the long hours that policemen worked. There were no official off-duty hours, no rest days, no annual leave and no right to a pension while a constable was confined to barracks at night. Support for the RIC came from the press who pointed out the force's reliability and effectiveness; newspapers called for better pay and conditions.

9

Many officers had already resigned to join forces in England, where pay and conditions were better, or even farther afield. With threats of mass resignations – there were 1,388 vacancies in 1870 – government relented and appointed a commission in 1872 to enquire into pay and conditions for all ranks. Eventually improved pay and conditions were granted, together with a pension scheme. For all the grievances about pay and conditions, the Irish peeler was regarded as an honest man and corruption in the force was almost unknown; many officers were granted special testimonials from the areas they policed.

In the years since its formation many additional duties were given to the police. These included enforcing fishery laws, collating agricultural statistics, escorting explosives, acting as census enumerators, making enquiries on behalf of government departments, and enforcing both weights and measures and food and drug rules. The Constabulary also absorbed the Revenue Police in 1857; this body enforced the Illicit Distillation (Ireland) Act of 1831, and attempted to reduce the incidence of illicit distillation of poteen throughout Ireland. Both Belfast and Londonderry Borough Police forces were absorbed into the RIC, the former in 1864 and the latter in 1871. The rank structure changed in 1883 with sub-inspectors, constables, acting-constables and sub-constables becoming district inspectors, sergeants, acting-sergeants, and constables respectively. In spite of comments that the RIC was a military force this was the first time that a military rank, that of sergeant, was used. In 1883 the strength was 14,115, an increase of more than 2,000 in twelve years. However, force numbers dropped to 10,662 by 1900. Irish policemen in their distinctive rifle-green uniforms were also to be seen in London where a RIC detachment was deployed in 1883 to protect Whitehall following bomb attacks in London. This Republican activity also caused the creation of a Special Irish Branch in the London Metropolitan Police; in time this became Special Branch and was not confined to the capital's force. In 1884 Fenians struck at the Special Irish Branch and the Criminal Investigation Department in a bomb attack that damaged Scotland Yard and the nearby Rising Sun public house.

During the latter part of the nineteenth century the RIC was involved in the task of escorting and protecting bailiffs carrying out evictions, a particularly unpleasant duty for a force the majority of whose members came from rural areas. Although they performed their duties as required there were many instances of policemen sending money to their own families to ensure that they would not suffer eviction. As sectarian passions cooled in the latter years of the century and land reform made it possible for many tenant farmers to buy land, the lot of the policeman became easier. Already part of the community, the rural constable was able to patrol effectively and to learn all that there was to know about his area.

As the nineteenth century came to an end, however, opposition to the South African, or Boer, War indicated that all was not well in Ireland. Government had already attempted to introduce legislation granting Home Rule to Ireland but there had been considerable political opposition to this. Home rule remained the objective of the Irish Party at Westminster but was opposed by Irish Unionists, especially in Ulster. The ensuing political tension brought about the birth of yet another new political group, Sinn Fein, Gaelic for 'ourselves' but more often translated as 'ourselves alone', founded by Arthur Griffith in November 1905. Griffith and Sinn Fein did not consider home rule to be enough but wanted complete independence. In the years before the Great War, tension increased with the formation of rival private armies to resist (Ulster Volunteer Force) or support (Irish Volunteers) home rule. The passing of a Home Rule Act on the threshold of war threatened civil war in Ireland but the European war helped defuse tension as the legislation was suspended for the duration while tens of thousands of Irishmen, Nationalist and Unionist, joined the colours to fight for Britain. Those volunteers included many RIC men.

But the Nationalist Volunteer movement split with one group, John Redmond's National Volunteers forming the majority and encouraging its followers to support Britain, while the other, the Irish Volunteers, or Oglaigh na hÉireann, were prepared to take up arms against Britain. Both Ulster and Irish Volunteers had brought arms into Ireland, the latter aided by the IRB, revived by members of Sinn Fein. With the United Kingdom at war and Sinn Fein and the Irish Volunteers convinced that Germany would support them against Britain, the first steps towards rebellion were taken. This time, however, information on the rebels was lacking. A secret military council was created which began planning for rebellion and sought German aid through a former British diplomat, Sir Roger Casement, who tried, without success, to raise an Irish Brigade from prisoners of war in Germany. The council included another revolutionary group, the Irish Citizen Army, a socialist grouping led by James Connolly, an Edinburgh-born former British soldier. One of the most prominent prophets of violence was a teacher and Gaelic philosopher, Patrick Pearse, whose father was English.

Plans were laid for a rebellion across the country on 23 April 1916, Easter Day, but a series of events, including the capture of Casement and of a shipment of German arms, led to postponement and the rebels took to the streets on the Monday. Among their first victims were unarmed Dublin Metropolitan Police officers but these Irishmen tend to be forgotten in many accounts of the events of the week that followed during which a republic was proclaimed, buildings in and around Dublin city centre were taken over, some 500 people were killed and another 2,500 wounded. The rebels surrendered at the end of the week and were

11

treated with contempt by Dubliners. Nor had there been any national rising, the actions in Dublin being the major element of the rebellion. RIC casualties were fourteen men killed. But the rebellion was only the beginning. Public sympathy swung to the rebels when their leaders were sentenced to death by courts martial; sixteen, including Casement, were executed. Thereafter Sinn Fein's political star was in the ascendant and its position was further enhanced by the degree of work the party's members carried out at local level. It was not surprising that Sinn Fein overtook the Irish Party at the 1918 general election, although its success was not the landslide that Republican tradition would assert.

The newly-elected Sinn Fein MPs refused to sit at Westminster, setting up an Irish parliament in Dublin, Dáil Éireann, which claimed to be the rightful government of Ireland. Sinn Fein's armed supporters now called themselves the Irish Republican Army and declared war on the RIC at Soloheadbeg in County Tipperary on 21 January 1919 when two RIC constables, escorting dynamite to a quarry, were ambushed and murdered. Constables James McDonnell and Patrick O'Connell were the first victims of a campaign that aimed to destroy the RIC's effectiveness through attacks on members and barracks as well as a boycott in the communities the force served. As the year wore on there were more casualties and by 31 December twelve officers had died. Worse was to follow with 171 men falling to terrorists in 1920 and 230 in 1921. The following year, during which partition occurred, the death toll reduced to twenty-nine. In all, during what is variously called the War of Independence, the Anglo-Irish war or the Black and Tan war, 442 RIC members lost their lives; between 1916 and 1922 the toll was 457 dead. Another eighty-eight men died from a variety of causes, including suicide, in the same period.

Police stations had been attacked and destroyed, policemen murdered in their homes, as they patrolled by bicycle, or as they attended church on Sunday mornings. Nowhere was sacred to those who wished to destroy the RIC. Many stations had to be abandoned because they were indefensible; the term 'barrack' has led some to believe that these were fortified locations whereas many were rented terraced houses or small, relatively isolated buildings offering little protection. Some attacks were fought off, most famously at Kilmallock, County Limerick, where Sergeant Tobias O'Sullivan and ten constables fought off some 100 IRA men armed with guns and explosives. After more than five hours, with the station ablaze, and two policemen killed, Sergeant O'Sullivan ordered the survivors to fix bayonets. The RIC men charged out of the blazing station and the IRA fled.

Such was the strain on the RIC that the government decided to recruit policemen in England and Scotland. Ex-servicemen were sought and many answered the call. The first arrivals in Ireland found such a shortage of police uniforms that they were issued with a mixture of RIC rifle-green and military khaki and when the first party of such recruits was assigned to County Limerick they were dubbed 'Black and Tans' after a famous pack of local hounds. Although the uniform situation was soon regularized, and all officers wore the same uniform, the nickname stuck and is often applied both to these men, who were absorbed into the RIC, and to another body recruited from ex-officers. The latter was known as the Auxiliary Division and was highly mobile. Wearing a distinctive uniform of blue with a tam o'shanter, its men were both effective and ruthless. The future Field Marshal Montgomery, who served as a brigade major in Munster, summed up the war in his *Memoirs* when he described it as developing 'into a murder campaign'. And that is exactly what it had become with IRA attacks followed by reprisals, followed by more attacks. Although by 1921 the Army was beginning to gain the upper hand, the government no longer had any stomach for the fight and a traumatized Ireland was divided between those who wished to have a 'free state' and those who wished to remain within the United Kingdom. But, as with any such drawing of lines on maps, there were many who found themselves on what, for them, was the wrong side of that line.

On 11 July 1921 a truce was arranged and on 5 December representatives of Dáil Éireann agreed to partition, but this led to civil war in the new Irish Free State. In January Dáil Éireann set about forming a new police force, having rejected a British suggestion that the RIC be divided between both jurisdictions. But what was to happen about policing the part of Ireland remaining in the United Kingdom? As the campaign had developed it had spread into the north where there were outbreaks of sectarian violence. Unionist politicians feared that the IRA would wreak havoc in Ulster and appealed to government to establish a special constabulary to defend them. Those same politicians distrusted the RIC, which they saw as largely Catholic and, therefore, unreliable. Already there were Unionist vigilante groups, some of which it was hoped to bring within the ambit of an auxiliary force. Finally, in September 1920, the government agreed to raise a force of special constables for the northeastern counties only. This force would include about 2,000 full-time specials under RIC command; known as A Specials they would be paid almost £4 a week, considerably more than the fourteen shillings that was the reward of the private soldier and almost as good as the £1 per day of the Auxiliaries; their role was to support the RIC.

There were two other categories of Specials. B Specials, voluntary part-timers, were paid some expenses with a half-yearly allowance of £5 to defray wear and tear on clothing and travelling expenses. No uniform other than a cap and armband was provided and the idea was that B Specials would patrol with RIC men, except in Nationalist areas. The recruiting target was 30,000, which was never achieved. C Specials were to be an emergency reserve, to be called upon if necessary but with no regular duties, nor would they be issued with uniforms or receive allowances. The first B Specials went on patrol in Belfast, where some 4,000 were to be recruited for the city alone. Sinn Fein was quick to initiate a propaganda campaign against the Specials, claiming that the government was simply arming Protestants to intimidate Catholics. It was said that the Specials were Protestant to a man, which makes it difficult to explain the IRA's attempt to murder Special Constable McCullough, a Catholic, in Belfast on 4 December. Attempts had been made to enlist Catholics and it had been suggested that, with sufficient Catholic recruits, Catholic units might be formed to patrol Catholic areas. But the Nationalist Party followed Sinn Fein's line and the Ancient Order of Hibernians discouraged members from joining the Specials while the IRA targeted those Catholics who did join.

> The Irish Republican Army . . . announced their intention of treating any Catholics who joined as traitors and of dealing with them accordingly. Loyal Roman Catholics had to be brave men to volunteer as Special Constables and the majority preferred not to get involved.[5]

Some fifty years later they would do the same to Catholics who joined the Ulster Special Constabulary's successor, the Ulster Defence Regiment.

Sectarian bitterness in Belfast led to many incidents in which Specials were involved and when the men were B Specials without uniforms it was often difficult to decide whether they were trying to keep order or create disorder. Many reprisals taken by Protestants for IRA attacks were blamed on Specials but the policy of official reprisals was never extended to Ulster and discipline held in most cases. Nonetheless, the sectarian nature of the Belfast conflict touched the Specials and, in one instance, a raid on the Falls Road area led to fourteen deaths in a night of violence; of the dead ten were Catholics. An uneasy peace settled on Belfast with the truce, a peace broken in late summer and autumn by outbreaks of shooting and violence around York Street and Short Strand.

On 22 November 1921 the new government in Belfast assumed responsibility for Northern Ireland and the RIC in the province came under its control together with the Ulster Special Constabulary. Charles Wickham, the RIC divisional commissioner in Ulster, became, de facto, the province's senior policeman with about 2,300 RIC personnel under his command. Wickham was the right man in the right place at the right time. A former Army officer, he had fought in the Boer War with the Norfolk Regiment, earning the Distinguished Service Order. As a junior officer, commissioned in 1899, the award of the DSO indicated a display of gallantry close to that needed to earn the Victoria Cross. Wickham went on to serve on the Western Front during the Great War, where he was Mentioned in Dispatches, and in the post-war expedition to Russia. Leaving the Army, he joined the RIC in 1920. Of his personal courage there could be no doubt, but Wickham was also a man of high standards, dedicated to the law, and humane and tactful in his approach to all. Nor would he brook any interference with the discipline of his force. This was the man who would become the first Inspector General of the Royal Ulster Constabulary.

In November also, the RIC's Deputy Inspector General asked members if they would be willing to transfer to the service of the Northern Ireland government. This met with opposition within the force and a meeting of the Representative Body passed a resolution addressed to the Inspector General.

> We beg to inform you that we have directed our constituents not to fill in the Form issued under Circular dated November, 1921, relative to the transfer of powers to the Northern Parliament. All the men claim disbandment and refuse to serve any Government other than that of the British Parliament. In view of this we request the immediate withdrawal of the Circular.

In January 1922 the government agreed that the RIC would be disbanded and arrangements were made to begin the process. RIC equipment, including weapons and vehicles, would be handed over to the new government in Dublin, along with much military equipment. This move caused consternation in Northern Ireland where it was believed that the equipment might soon be turned against them. The disbandment of the RIC was a painful process. Many officers were threatened and forced into exile, some were abducted and murdered and others had to make their way north by sea. A formal disbandment parade took place at Phoenix Park on 4 April 1922 although the process was not complete until August. Men in the north were allowed to serve until 1 June so that transition arrangements for policing might be made.

On 31 January 1922 the Minister of Home Affairs for Northern Ireland, Sir Richard Dawson Bates, established a committee to examine the re-organization of policing. Wickham was included, as was the Chief Constable of Glasgow[6] together with MPs and JPs; a total of fourteen. The committee was to study ways in which the existing RIC organization might be adapted to suit Northern Ireland's needs; the recruitment and terms and conditions of service of officers; manpower of the new force and how it might include both RIC and Ulster Special Constabulary men; and the cost of the force. Chaired by Lloyd Campbell MP, the committee produced an interim report at the end of March. This proposed a force of 3,000 to cover the entire province; consideration had been given to creating local forces but this was rejected; the report recommended that 'There should be a single force under a single command for the whole of Northern Ireland'.[7]

The interim report also proposed that the new force should be composed of two-thirds Protestants and one-third Roman Catholics.[8] Some members dissented from this and their reservations were included in the report; this was not the only issue on which reservations were noted. This proposal was accepted by the Cabinet, but when it came before the House of Commons the following week there was opposition to the proposed number of Roman Catholics and the Constabulary Bill placed before Parliament in May had no clause on religious composition. R.D. Megaw, parliamentary secretary to the Ministry of Home Affairs, who had previously supported the proposal as indicating that 'we were playing "fair and square" ', now performed a volte-face and proclaimed that he did not think 'it would be a proper thing for the House to put anything in the Enactment about the religion of the Force'.

In view of the later stringent financial attitude of the Ministry of Home Affairs towards the force it is enlightening to note that the committee 'would have liked . . . to recommend a reduction in . . . pay'. Members transferring from the RIC and DMP were to retain their current pay rates and this would apply to all 'original members of the force'. After that, however, new entrants would be paid at lower rates. (An RIC constable received between £3 10s 0d and £4 15s 0d per week, depending on length of service; the report recommended a scale of between £2 15s 0d and £4 per week.)

The new force was to be called the Ulster Constabulary but it was recommended that permission be sought to incorporate the prefix 'Royal' in the title. On 29 April King George V gave formal approval for the prefix, which one newspaper described as a 'gratifying announcement'. The new force was to be established under the authority of the Constabulary Act (Northern Ireland) 1922 which was

An act to provide for the establishment, management, and control of the Royal Ulster Constabulary, and to amend the law with respect to the appointment of resident magistrates and special constables in Northern Ireland and for purposes connected therewith.

The Act stated that

There shall be established in Northern Ireland on and after the Appointed Day, a Police Force to be called, with the consent of His Majesty, The Royal Ulster Constabulary.

16

And so the Royal Ulster Constabulary came into being on 1 June 1922, the 'Appointed Day', with Wickham as Inspector General and headquarters in Atlantic Buildings, Waring Street, close to Belfast city centre. Recruits were to be trained at the Newtownards Training Camp that had been used by the Ulster Special Constabulary. This hutted establishment was not really suitable but more than a decade would pass before the RUC vacated it in favour of a redundant army barracks in Enniskillen.

The new force adopted the uniform of the Royal Irish Constabulary, the traditional rifle-green with black leather accoutrements. However, its badge was not to be that of its predecessor but a new emblem to indicate that this was an Ulster force. Out would go the harp and crown to be replaced by the Red Hand of Ulster on St George's Cross surrounded by a chain, all within a belt bearing the title Royal Ulster Constabulary; the crown remained surmounting the new design. Although the first RUC members continued using the RIC badge, the new emblem was introduced in 1923. It was a short-lived design that proved unpopular within the force and was withdrawn, to be replaced by the RIC badge, which was to survive for almost eighty years. Buttons with the new emblem were introduced but were also replaced by those they had been intended to replace.

There was little change in the organization of the new force, which continued the structure used by the RIC with Northern Ireland divided into eight major areas of command: the city of Belfast, with its commissioner, Londonderry City, and the six counties. By 1931, however, Londonderry was subsumed into the surrounding county with county headquarters in the city. However, those who policed the senior city had what outsiders might have considered a particular conceit of themselves as the 'Derry City Force', a term that survived for many years. Each county in turn was divided into districts, as was Belfast, under county or district inspectors. Belfast had the unique rank of commissioner; the man appointed to this post was the third highest ranking in the RUC. As with regional organization so too with the rank structure; the force retained that of the RIC with an Inspector General, Deputy Inspector General, Belfast City Commissioner, County and District Inspectors, Head Constables, Sergeants and Constables. Badges of rank remained as they had been. Little had changed from the RIC but in one respect the RUC was unique; it was the only British force with a land boundary with another state. The new force in that state, now called the Irish Free State, was initially called the Civic Guard but was later renamed An Garda Síochána. In 1925 it also absorbed the Dublin Metropolitan Police. (Incidentally, the Civic Guards also adopted the RIC-style sergeant's chevrons on the right forearm but not in gold; these were subsequently replaced with British police-style chevrons on the upper arm.)

Creating a structure on paper is easy but translating it into reality is entirely different. Three months after its official formation the RUC had only reached one third of its intended manpower and had no means of gathering intelligence, a grievous disadvantage in the unsettled state of the province. During 1922 there were almost 300 murders in Northern Ireland, the majority of which, 231, occurred in Belfast. Sectarian conflict led to families fleeing their homes and many Catholic workers in Belfast's shipyard were intimidated from their jobs. Nationalists laid the blame for much of the trouble, and many deaths, on the Specials who were classed as an entirely Protestant and Unionist force. The fact that efforts had been made to recruit Catholics, that there were some Catholic Specials and that these men had suffered intimidation and assault from their co-religionists, seemed to escape the attention of the critics. It was a characterization of the Specials that would persist even after the Ulster Special Constabulary was disbanded in 1970.

There were several incidents in which Specials may have been involved, including the murders of the McMahon family in Belfast on 24 March 1922 when five armed men smashed their way into Owen McMahon's home close to Crumlin Road gaol. McMahon's wife and a maid were tied up and McMahon, a publican, his sons and Edward McKinney, a barman who lived with the family, were ushered into another room and shot dead. Only the youngest of the six McMahon boys, John, survived by taking cover behind a sofa. John later said that the murderers had been in uniform. It was believed widely that the murders had been a reprisal by Specials for an IRA attack in Victoria Street on the 23rd in which William Chermside and Thomas Cunningham, two patrolling Specials, had been murdered.

Incidents of this nature led to a pact between Sir James Craig, Northern Ireland's Prime Minister, and Michael Collins, engineered largely by Winston Churchill. Agreed on 30 March, the pact aimed, among other things, to draw northern Nationalists into recognizing Northern Ireland and taking part in its institutions. Needless to say, one issue considered was policing and there were plans to establish an advisory committee that would try to ensure increased Catholic recruitment to the RUC. Among other policing aims was to secure a 50/50 representation of Catholic and Protestant policemen in mixed areas while parties searching for weapons and explosives should be similarly constituted. Collins was to undertake that IRA activity in Northern Ireland would cease and Craig was to ensure the investigation of controversial incidents by a committee comprised equally of Catholics and Protestants. Westminster was to provide a £500,000 fund for relief work schemes and to assist those left homeless by rioting. It was estimated that there were some 23,000 people in the latter category while about 10,000 Catholic workers had been forced out of their jobs. At the same time, Dublin was operating a boycott against anything made in Northern Ireland, or any services provided to the Free State from Northern Ireland. This led to the burning or destruction of a range of goods manufactured or produced in Northern Ireland, including whiskey from Belfast, bread from various bakeries and even coffins. Whether Collins ever intended to carry out his side of the pact is uncertain – he was arming the IRA in Northern Ireland while talking with Craig – but Unionists, especially Bates, the Minister of Home Affairs, wanted no truck with the Free State. And so the pact came to naught. While it is easy to speculate on this as a lost opportunity, a realistic assessment would suggest that it would not have succeeded in the long run since there was too much suspicion and pain for the necessary mutual trust to develop.

Craig's government made its own efforts to defeat the IRA and restore peace to Northern Ireland. They even made an attempt to establish and operate the police advisory committee, which held its first meeting on 16 May, although five of its twelve members were absent. The committee met on only two further occasions on which seven and then nine members were absent; its last meeting was on 7 June. Again it is easy to speculate that this committee might have ensured the independence of the Inspector General from the Ministry of Home Affairs but that would be to assume a willingness to cooperate that was not then present. Government enthusiasm for the committee was lukewarm while reaction among Nationalists was similar, allowing the IRA free rein to intimidate those Catholics appointed to it.

Among government measures to restore peace was the Civil Authorities (Special Powers) Act, which became law on 7 April and gave the Minister of Home Affairs wide-ranging powers, including arrest without warrant and internment without trial. He could also prohibit organizations, ban meetings, publications, marches or other gatherings, commandeer land and property for security purposes and dispense with coroners' inquests. There was almost no restriction on the measures he could take in an unforeseen crisis. Field Marshal Sir Henry Wilson, now a Unionist MP at Westminster, had been asked to act as military adviser to Craig's government but his advice was generally ignored. He had stressed to Bates the need to recruit Catholics into the Specials by issuing a proclamation that the force was open to everyone, irrespective of class or creed.

Wilson, who was murdered by the IRA in London on 22 June 1922, was succeeded as military adviser by one of his protégées, Major General Arthur Solly-Flood, another Irishman. Solly-Flood's role gave him authority over police and Ulster Special Constabulary and he aimed to strengthen the latter. His request for more arms for the force was approved in London but a parallel request for more funds was held in abeyance. Conflict continued with a campaign of arson against Unionist-owned businesses in Belfast and farther afield while the first political assassination in Northern Ireland was carried out on 23 May when W.J. Twaddell MP, a Unionist member of the Northern Ireland parliament, was murdered in Belfast city centre on his way to his draper's business in Lower North Street.

Following the Twaddell murder, Craig's cabinet outlawed the IRA and other Republican groups and authorized internment of suspects. That night the Ulster Special Constabulary and the Army rounded up some 300 suspects; these were later joined by about another 100 men who were eventually held on board a prison ship, *Argenta*, in Belfast Lough. Although violence continued – British troops drove the IRA out of the 'Belleek triangle' in County Fermanagh in June – the IRA soon turned its attention to the Free State where civil war had begun. Collins was killed in August and violence in Northern Ireland declined in the latter months of 1922. That decline was such that there were but four murders in 1923 and 1924, which allowed the curfew that had been imposed in Northern Ireland to be lifted while internees were released. Solly-Flood was also relieved of his post at the end of 1922, his plans for a Directorate of Public Security with 30,000 police officers appearing to smack of personal political ambition. Sir Charles Wickham was now firmly in control as Northern Ireland's chief police officer.

The Constabulary Act had set the RUC's maximum size at 3,000, a restriction that would remain for forty-one years. Even in 1922 this was very small and the force was only to manage its many tasks through asking more of its officers than did any other force in the United Kingdom. Recruiting had been difficult and it was 1924 before numbers were close to the establishment, at 2,990. The Northern Ireland Government had tried to recruit former RIC and DMP members as well as Special Constabulary men. A notice seeking recruits was issued in March 1922.

> Applications for Enrolment in the Ulster Police will now be received. Recruitment will, without distinction of creed, be open to all members of the Royal Irish Constabulary throughout Ireland, and of the Special Constabulary, and to a limited number of the D.M.P.

Since the DMP was to remain in being it was probably not considered diplomatic to suggest that anything other than a limited number of its personnel would be considered. It was also stated that RIC men who had not been born in Ireland and with less than two years' service on disbandment would only be considered 'in special cases'. This was a clear indication that Black and Tans or Auxiliaries would not be considered

With its numbers limited the RUC would have to rely on the support of the Special Constabulary but the latter was to be mainly a quasi-military organization whose members were given little training in ordinary police work and, although it performed a useful role in gathering intelligence, was never to be a true auxiliary police force. Compared with Specials in Great Britain there was a huge gap in their policing ability. Although British Specials have their own rank structure they are fully integrated with local forces and operate under local officers in carrying out routine police duties. The Ulster Special Constabulary not only had a separate rank structure but also existed largely apart from the RUC, only being used for ordinary police work in limited situations. Thus the burden that would be placed on the RUC was increased by this method of employing the Ulster Special Constabulary.

Fortunately, as the RUC got into its stride, emotions were beginning to ease in Northern Ireland and the level of conflict diminished considerably. The new force was soon able to turn its attention to routine tasks. As with the RIC these were many and varied, including normal district patrolling on foot or by bicycle, completion of annual tillage returns for the Ministry of Agriculture, prevention and detection of smuggling in border areas and the seizing of illicit stills. Added to these was concern about terrorist activity, especially the threat of cross-border incursions. The breakdown in relations between Dublin and Belfast had not been eased in any way by Collins's death and it would be over forty years before there was any formal relationship between the governments. In the meantime, although good working relationships were established between the police forces, suspicion and distrust festered at government level.

Who were the men who made up Northern Ireland's new police force? Some had come from the Royal Irish Constabulary and, for them, little had changed about their uniform or their stations. But there was one major change: no longer were the majority of those wearing rifle-green and harp and crown Roman Catholics. There were few Catholic recruits from Northern Ireland and with the desire to get the force established as quickly as possible the government relied on filling many vacancies with A Specials. Of those members of the RIC who transferred to the RUC, 434 were Catholic, including some senior officers; another 896 transferees were Protestant. These experienced officers formed the backbone of the new force. By January 1925, when there were 2,990 men in the force, 541 Catholic policemen were serving. Of eight county inspectors two were Catholics as were nine of thirty-eight district inspectors.

By 1930 the number of Catholics in the force had fallen slightly, to 514. They were represented as follows: three of nine county inspectors;

six of forty-three district inspectors; twenty-eight of seventy-one head constables; 144 of 468 sergeants and 333 of 2,268 constables. Five years later the overall Catholic figure had again decreased, to 489, with a similar representation across the ranks: three of nine county inspectors; six of forty-two district inspectors; twenty-five of seventy head con-stables; 134 of 462 sergeants and 321 of 2,248 constables. There had also been a slight decrease in the overall force strength, now almost 200 below establishment. Within the RUC there was no discrimination against Catholic personnel and their success in achieving promotion over many years proves this; in 1969 the Hunt Report would note that, although overall Catholic strength was about ten to 11 per cent, the percentage in senior ranks was almost 30 per cent. However, Ministry of Home Affairs' officials seemed to have an obsession with Catholic policemen and Wickham was asked to furnish a weekly return of Catholic personnel for Bates's attention. At the same time those officials pushed to have vacancies filled by Specials rather than by trying to recruit Catholics.

In spite of everything the RUC was carrying out its role throughout the province and providing a good level of policing. The 'peeler' on his beat was a reassuring figure whether on a bicycle or on foot. Serious crime was rare and the policeman of the 1920s was much more a community policeman than is generally realized. He knew the people on his beat, could name many of their children and was a power for good in the community. Children playing football in the streets would disperse quickly when told that the beat man was near. The practice of tying ropes to lampposts as makeshift swings was common at that time, and would remain so for many decades; this was another custom that was frowned upon, since there was a certain element of danger. It was not unusual for a policeman to be seen cutting the rope with his pocket knife and few parents would have objected to this. Nor would they have objected if told that their son had been dealt summary justice for some infraction of the law; it was considered acceptable for a policeman to give an offending youngster a 'clip around the ear' and send him home. It saved the policeman much paperwork and parents a lot of trouble.

There were, of course, more serious matters, one of which led to a gallantry award to a Belfast policeman. In March 1924 Constable Francis Austin Morteshed earned the Empire Gallantry Medal for arresting an armed robber. Three men tried to rob an office, in the course of which they shot and fatally wounded the office manager. All three fled the scene and were pursued by Constable Morteshed. One gang member turned and, at close range, tried to shoot the policeman but Morteshed, without drawing his own revolver, tackled the man and was able to arrest him. On 3 June the *London Gazette* carried the announce-ment that he had been awarded the Empire Gallantry Medal.[9] In 1941, on the institution of the George Cross, the Empire Gallantry Medal was withdrawn and all EGM holders were required to exchange their Medals for the George Cross, and the right to the post-nominal letters GC. Frank Morteshed, therefore, was the RUC's first George Cross holder. He later joined the Royal Air Force where he attained the rank of sergeant.

The RUC was also responsible for protecting the land boundary with the Irish Free State, although much of this work was carried out by Specials. Allied with border security was the need to protect against internal subversion; both were major concerns for Northern Ireland's government. The border established in 1922 had been a temporary measure and a Boundary Commission was appointed to set a definitive line. There was considerable nervousness that parts of Northern Ireland might be ceded to the Free State; it was felt that this could include Counties Tyrone and Fermanagh and the city of Londonderry. Until the Commission brought in its report, which was never implemented, that nervousness continued and saw the RUC's Intelligence Branch build up a remarkable picture of the strength and capabilities of the Irish Army, then almost 50,000 strong. But the Irish Army had problems of its own after the civil war, with plans to demobilize almost 30,000 personnel to reduce overall strength to some 20,000; in addition, it was only given full legal status in 1924. An attack by the Irish Army on Northern Ireland seemed unlikely, especially when elements of that army mutinied. One of their grievances was that former IRA men were being demobbed from the officer class while former British Army officers were being retained. It is interesting to note that the Civic Guards also suffered a similar crisis in its earliest days and were disarmed as a result.

Within Northern Ireland there was concern about the loyalty of Catholics, notwithstanding the large numbers of Catholics who had fought in the Great War. Even the loyalty of Catholic policemen and civil servants working in police stations was questioned and in January 1924 a deputation led by Sir Robert Kennedy KC alleged that chief clerks in the county inspectors' offices were mainly Catholics, many of whom were 'known' to be actively disloyal. The official response contained the information that, of ninety-six clerks, only twenty-seven were Catholic and the Inspector General was 'fully satisfied as to the loyalty and integrity of the Force under his command'. In March there was another complaint, this time about the number of Catholics in the clerical and detective staff. Wickham wrote to Spender, the head of the civil service, that it was

> obvious that the material for this [complaint], though not in all cases accurate, must have been supplied by a member of the Force in a moderately responsible position and probably a Protestant. . . . I am

forced to the conclusion that disloyalty . . . is not confined to RCs, even if this were substantiated.

Wickham was concerned that the Minister of Home Affairs seemed willing to entertain groundless complaints. Such an attitude can have done little for the morale of Catholic policemen, nor for the recruitment of Catholics.

There was another side to this coin. On 28 February 1924 Wickham dismissed District Inspector John Nixon, a Cavan man with twenty-five years' service, once the RIC's youngest-ever district inspector. Nixon was a founding member, and first Worshipful Master, of the Sir Robert Peel Memorial Orange Lodge, membership of which was confined to RUC members. He was also known to have very definite political views and was alleged to have been involved in the McMahon murders and another reprisal in Belfast. At a Lodge meeting in January 1924 Nixon made political comments that were reported to his senior officers and the government. At first Wickham attempted a damage limitation exercise by issuing a circular outlining the facts that RUC members could vote at elections and belong to certain approved secret societies, privileges neither of which had been granted to the RIC. He went on to advise members that they should not participate

> by speaking, or entering into discussions, at meetings where political or sectarian opinions are expressed, or by organizing or assisting in organizing meetings or gatherings at which political or sectarian speeches or discussions are likely to take place.

Nixon ignored this and continued making political statements, including one that played on fears about the Boundary Commission; he suggested that the Free State believed that they were to be given a large portion of Ulster and coined the phrase that they should receive 'not an inch'. Shortly afterwards Nixon was suspended from duty; at the end of February he was dismissed although with full pension rights. Nixon remained a bitter man until his death in 1949 and, as a councillor in Belfast and, later, a Stormont MP, took every opportunity to attack the police. He also sued successfully the *Derry Journal* and the publishing house Methuen for printing allegations that he had been involved in the McMahon murders.

Following the Boundary Commission report it was decided that the A Specials should be disbanded and the C1 Specials stood down. Dissatisfaction among Specials about financial arrangements for redundancy led to a mutiny that began in Londonderry and soon spread. A government ultimatum that disbandment would go ahead anyway and that the men would lose any right to discharge pay, brought the mutiny to an end. Strangely, the government blamed the trouble on ex-servicemen from outside Northern Ireland who had fomented agitation among their fellow Specials. There is no evidence that this was the case.

In line with the rundown of the Specials there were attempts to economize on the cost of the RUC. The force budget for 1926 was calculated at £840,000 and, to prune costs, the Ministry of Home Affairs decided that recruits' pay would reduce from £3 10s to £3 per week. Even at a time of austerity across the United Kingdom, this move cannot have been received with anything but dismay. It was a sign of the way in which the Ministry would treat the force over the coming decades.

The remaining years of the decade were mainly peaceful, in stark contrast to the way in which the 1920s had begun. In the latter years of the decade the most serious matter exercising the magistrate at Whiteabbey was the prevalence of courting couples in the suburbs parking their cars on the wrong side of the road.[10] However, that peace was not to last throughout the decade that followed.

Notes

1: Constable, from the Latin *Comes Stabulari*, or count of the stables, the guardian of law and order at the Emperor Charlemagne's court.
2: Belfast did not become a city until 1888.
3: www.btp.police.uk/policing_railway.htm
4: The fair at Donnybrook in County Dublin was the location of such bitter faction fighting that it gave the word 'Donnybrook' to the language as a synonym for a serious affray.
5: Hezlet, *The B Specials*, p. 23.
6: Another Chief Constable of Glasgow would sit on the Hunt Committee in 1969.
7: Interim Report, para 12, p. 5.
8: Ibid, para 7, p. 5.
9: The Empire Gallantry Medal was also awarded to Special Head Constable Samuel Orr MM, who later became a harbour policeman in Londonderry. *The Register of the George Cross* shows Orr wrongly as belonging to the RIC. He earned his EGM for two incidents – capturing an armed criminal early in 1922 and, later that year, trying to arrest two armed terrorists although unarmed himself; he grappled with one of the men but, while doing so, was wounded severely by the other. Orr's EGM was also gazetted on 3 June 1924.
10: www.policefed-ni.org.uk/history.htm

Chapter Two

Riots, Air Raids and the First Policewomen

The 1930s are remembered as years in which the world economy reached rock bottom and then began, slowly, to improve, aided by industrial preparations for a possible war that would become terrible reality in 1939. Poverty and disease were endemic and one of the enduring memories is of hunger; indeed the decade became known as the 'hungry thirties'. Added to this are images of tens of thousands of unemployed, of the Jarrow marchers, of the fall of Ramsay McDonald's Labour government and of clashes between police and hunger marchers. Farther afield, Franklin Delano Roosevelt was elected President of the USA and promised a 'new deal' to lift his country out of depression while in Europe Fascism was on the increase; before long Europe had three Fascist governments with Germany and Spain joining Italy. Even Britain had its Fascist party in Oswald Mosley's British Union of Fascists, while a similar body – the Blueshirts – existed in the Irish Free State. This was also the decade when the Free State ceased to bear that title and, under a new constitution drawn up by Eamon de Valera, became Ireland and claimed the entire island as the 'national territory'.

As usual Northern Ireland was different. The government still distrusted its next-door neighbour and de Valera's election, first in coalition and then in his own party's right, was not good news. De Valera represented the anti-treaty IRA, although he would soon turn on his former comrades, and his 1937 constitution laid claim to Northern Ireland. In other respects the province had much in common with the rest of the United Kingdom. Poverty was even more common, however, as was poor health; Northern Ireland's death rate from tuberculosis was 20 per cent higher than Britain's. Housing was particularly bad, there being little public investment in building houses in the province, thus leaving the majority of those who could not afford their own homes at the mercy of private landlords. Northern Ireland's government had declined to bring in legislation, similar to that in Great Britain, that

26

might have encouraged councils to build more houses. All the conditions existed for a strong socialist party in Northern Ireland, but this never occurred because of obsession with the constitutional issue. As we have seen, Unionists worried about the intentions of the government in Dublin and constantly made reference to the perceived danger, especially at election times. Moreover, the Unionist ruling classes, both the 'big house' Unionists and those of the business classes, were apt to point to Catholics as a source of some of the Protestant working class's problems. Thus when demobilized Protestant soldiers returned from the Great War they were told that disloyal Catholics, who had stayed at home far from danger, had taken their jobs. The truth was that many Catholics from Ulster had also fought. Any possibility of creating normal left/right politics in Northern Ireland was blocked by this attitude, which was mirrored in the Nationalist tradition. Northern Ireland's Catholics, most, but not all, of them Nationalists, had been told by their leaders that partition was temporary. They had been discouraged from taking part in the province's institutions and the politicians had taken the lead by not sitting in the local parliament until they realized that partition was permanent. The Catholic Church professed to be the one true faith and discouraged actively any form of fraternization with Protestants, usually referred to insultingly as 'non-Catholics'. Cardinal MacRory, leader of Ireland's Catholics, even declared publicly in December 1931 that

> The Protestant Church in Ireland – and the same is true of the Protestant Church anywhere else – is not only not the rightful representative of the early Irish Church, but it is not even a part of the Church of Christ.

Churchmen were also political and even after the Second World War members of the Catholic hierarchy would oppose many elements of the welfare state, a situation in which they found themselves in a rare meeting of minds with many Unionists.

Such attitudes meant that Northern Ireland became self-obsessive. The province seemed destined to remain in this state of sectarian introspection as sectarian riots flared in 1931 and early 1932. However, in autumn 1932 Belfast was shaken by riots that broke the traditional mould. These arose from demonstrations during a time of chronic unemployment, following the recession that caused huge reductions in the demand for ships and linen, Belfast's principal sources of employment. One shipyard, Workman Clark, closed completely in 1935 while Harland and Wolff launched no ships at all between December 1931 and May 1934; their workforce reduced from 10,248 in 1930 to 1,554 two years later. For those out of work in the 1930s there was a short period

27

of statutory benefits, paid for by national insurance contributions, before the unemployed had to rely on the Poor Law Guardians. The latter organized Outdoor Relief work schemes or provided vouchers for groceries and other necessities rather than money, which some of them thought would be spent in pubs. Since their powers were largely discretionary, Guardians could be biased towards some cases and dismissive of others. One Belfast Guardian achieved notoriety for telling Catholic fathers of large families that there was 'no poverty under the blankets'. Irrespective of such attitudes, Belfast's Guardians ensured that they paid the unemployed the bare minimum: a one-child Belfast family received 12s 0d (60p) a week whereas their counterparts in Liverpool received £1 3s 0d (£1.15p) and in Northampton £1 7s 0d (£1. 35p). With government seemingly unconcerned about the unemployed, it was left to the churches to express a voice of conscience. The Reverend John Spence, of Belfast's Methodist Central Mission, pointed out that the assistance given in Belfast was much less 'per head of population than any British city of comparable size' while the Presbyterian Church declared that grants to those 'entirely dependent on outdoor relief are inadequate to provide the barest necessities of life'.

The grievances of the unemployed gave birth to a protest movement, spearheaded by the Unemployed Workers' Committee, and a series of demonstrations during the summer of 1932. But the major effort came in the autumn. On 3 October about 60,000 workers marched in torch lit procession from Frederick Street labour exchange to Belfast's Custom House for a huge public meeting. For once Northern Ireland workers, Catholic and Protestant, had come together in common cause. That the demonstration was non-sectarian was indicated by the accompanying bands; normally these supported Orange or Hibernian marches but their usual repertoire was replaced by contemporary popular tunes, including what became the movement's anthem: 'We have no bananas today'.

Further demonstrations followed with a march to the Workhouse, later Belfast City Hospital, on 4 October, with 7,000 people accompanying a deputation to the Guardians. This almost brought the city to a standstill with traffic on Lisburn Road disrupted by men lying across the tramlines. Another march on 5 October drew an even larger crowd to accompany 300 men demanding admission to the Workhouse. For this demonstration the RUC had been ordered to put on a show of strength; armoured cars and personnel carriers, or tenders, were deployed along the route. In Bradbury Place rioting followed a police baton charge. Faced with this type of popular and large-scale demonstration of solidarity from the working class, the Cabinet agreed to increase by 50 per cent payments for outdoor relief and to abolish payments in kind. Northern Ireland had been almost untouched by the 1926 General Strike, although Westminster had been prepared for trouble in the province, but rumours of a general strike now circulated and the protest movement's leaders rejected the government's offer. A major demonstration, including a night of bonfires on the 10th, followed by another rally in Belfast the following day was called for; the rally would have five separate assembly points.

This situation was entirely new to Northern Ireland's government and caused such concern that the Cabinet invoked the Special Powers Act to ban any further demonstrations. It was probably the worst thing government could have done. The police were concerned about their ability to maintain order in the face of such demonstrations since there simply was not sufficient manpower; the ban meant that the RUC would have to confront demonstrators instead of overseeing marches.

The protesters' mood was such that fierce rioting broke out on the 11th and spread throughout Belfast. It seemed to begin at Templemore Avenue in east Belfast as marchers were assembling and a crowd began stoning an isolated party of policemen who drew their batons but 'things were looking very ugly when police reinforcements in a caged car appeared on the scene'. According to the *Belfast Telegraph* a baton charge followed and marchers 'went down like nine-pins, and the rest fled helter skelter'. Further baton charges followed as Catholics from Seaforde Street attacked police who were trying to drive away marchers, who were mainly Protestant, in police vehicles.

Officers in Crossley tenders and Lancia caged cars were deployed to keep main routes open but came under sustained attack from rioters whose favourite missile was the cobblestone pulled from the surfaces of side streets. In those same side streets trenches had been dug and barricades built to keep police out. Albert Street in the lower Falls seemed to be, according to the *Belfast Telegraph*, 'the cockpit' of the worst violence.

> Police reinforcements were summoned. Constables wearing bandoliers filled with bullets and with rifles at the ready were speedily jumping out of caged cars. Other constables with revolvers in hand peered cautiously round the street corner as the hail of stones came out of Albert Street. Batons were useless and the police were compelled to fire.

All day long the violence lasted and a curfew from 11.00 p.m. to 5.00 a.m. proved ineffective. Rioting continued throughout that night and into the next day. But Bates had issued orders to the police that played on fears of the IRA. In some areas officers were authorized to shoot to prevent the IRA using the disturbances to subvert the government but in other areas no firearms were to be employed, although batons could be used. Two men died in the disturbances and another thirty were injured.

Both dead men, Samuel Baxter and John Geegan, had been shot by police officers and fourteen of the injured had gunshot wounds. Baxter, a flower-seller, was a Protestant while Geegan was a Catholic. On the evening of the 12th there was a further outbreak of rioting in the York Street area and police opened fire on looters; one man, John Kennan, was killed by gunfire and many others wounded.

A severely frightened government had managed to divide the workers: traditional sectarian suspicions had been re-ignited by the government's actions and statements, and the rioting died down as solidarity evaporated in the autumn air. But the demonstrators had achieved one aim: weekly relief rates were doubled to £1 4s 0d (£1.20p). One relief scheme implemented in the wake of the violence was the resurfacing of side streets with reinforced concrete; the stone setts were removed.

Earlier that year there had been disturbances in the traditional sectarian pattern. Dublin was the host city for the Catholic Church's International Eucharistic Congress to which tens of thousands of Catholics from Northern Ireland travelled. The majority journeyed by train and were subjected to stone-throwing attacks by mobs that led to sectarian rioting in Belfast and Portadown; all trains from Northern Ireland to Dublin passed through the latter. Containing that rioting placed a great strain on the police with Wickham forced to bring officers into Belfast from all over the province, stripping many stations of all but the minimum needed to provide a service. Both those riots and the October disturbances had shown how under strength the RUC was but, although Spender could write in his diary that the cost of repairing damage in October could have been double the cost of increasing relief payments, there was no suggestion of increasing police manpower.

The following year brought further sectarian bitterness culminating in the murder of Daniel O'Boyle, a Catholic publican, in York Street, in November. There had been frequent clashes between Catholics and Protestants in Belfast during the year. This was also the year in which the RUC suffered its first fatal casualties. Although many RIC and Ulster Special Constabulary members had died between 1919 and 1922, the first RUC man to be killed in service was Constable John Ryan who was shot in Belfast's Grosvenor Road on 28 February 1933 during a strike. Ryan and another officer from Cullingtree Road station were on beat patrol when gunmen fired at lorries driving out of the LMS Railway goods yard. Constable Ryan and his colleague challenged the gunmen who fled but not before a gun battle in which Ryan was killed. Less than eight months later another policeman died from gunshot wounds. Constable Charles Anderson, also stationed at Cullingtree Road, was one of two officers on duty at a house in the Falls Road area when several gunmen shot at them on the evening of 8 October. Charles Anderson was hit and taken to hospital where he died early on the 9th. Sadly, the

Constabulary Gazette noted that he had no relatives in the country to attend his obsequies. The tensions of 1933 continued into 1934 with violence becoming more frequent; in one Loyalist attack an invalid was injured fatally by a kerbstone thrown through his window. But worse was to follow in 1935.

King George V celebrated his silver jubilee in 1935 and in Belfast, as in other towns and cities across the United Kingdom, there were festivities to mark the occasion. But it was marred in Belfast when Loyalists introduced a sectarian element into their celebrations and disturbances followed across the city with a Catholic man shot dead in his shop in Great George's Street and houses attacked. Such was the ferocity of the disturbances that the Ministry of Home Affairs decided to ban all marches from 18 June. The Grand Master of the Orange Order responded by proclaiming that Orangemen would be marching on 12 July. Since the Prime Minister was on extended holiday, Bates had to decide whether to defy the Orangemen and maintain the ban or give in and lift it. No one was surprised when Bates lifted the ban.

The demonstration in Belfast on 12th began peacefully and marchers made their way to the 'Field' for their traditional service and speeches. Sir Joseph Davison, the Grand Master, attacked the Anglican Bishop of Down, Dr John McNeice, who had appealed for people in Northern Ireland to forget the past. Davison asked if that meant forgetting the heroes of the past or that the new government in Dublin, under de Valera, wanted to establish an all-Ireland Catholic state. De Valera had become the bogeyman of Ulster Unionism and the economic war between Britain and the Free State exacerbated feelings in Northern Ireland. After the proceedings at the 'Field' were complete the march set off on its return journey. Once again all was quiet – until the marchers reached York Street. An *Irish News* reporter later wrote that a trivial incident led Orangemen to believe that a major attack had been launched on them and they rushed into Lancaster Street, smashing windows with poles and stones. A counter-attack by residents, also throwing stones, drove the marchers back into York Street. What one newspaper was to describe as the 'worst night of disorder since 1921–2' had begun. Policemen who tried to contain the Orangemen were pushed to one side. Soon a street battle was raging that saw police and gunmen firing on each other; from Donegall Street corner to halfway along York Street fighting continued for two hours.

That night two people were killed and thirty-eight injured; both fatalities and all but three of the injured were civilians; the others were policemen. Homes were set ablaze and many others damaged and pressure on police was such that the Army had to be called in. A curfew was imposed but violence continued next evening. Following the funeral of a Protestant victim, Loyalists attacked North Ann Street and, before police could stop them, smashed windows in Catholic-occupied houses. They continued their activities by attacking Earl Street and North Thomas Street where further damage was done. Rioting continued day after day and night after night, not ceasing until late August. Soldiers with fixed bayonets manned barriers to keep rival mobs apart while police patrolled the York Street area in large numbers on foot and in tenders; armoured cars stood by at various points across the city. Belfast's long hot summer cost the lives of eight Protestants and five Catholics while many more had been injured and over 2,000 people, mostly Catholics, had been forced from their homes. Although fifty-nine MPs at Westminster called for an enquiry, Prime Minister Stanley Baldwin refused the demand, saying that the matter was the responsibility of Northern Ireland's government. The Belfast coroner, at an inquest on riot victims, laid much of the blame on the province's political leaders, saying 'bigotry is the curse of peace and goodwill . . . there would be less public bigotry if there was less public speechmaking of a kind by so-called leaders of public opinion'.

Across the border de Valera was acting against his former IRA colleagues, as well as the Fascist Blueshirts. In May 1934 IRA leaders were jailed, their sentences including hard labour; those jailed included Tom Barry, an almost mythological Republican figure. The jailings continued and on 18 June 1936 the Irish government proclaimed the IRA an illegal organization. Although there was some hope of rapprochement between de Valera and the UK government following an easing of the economic war, this hope was dispelled with the introduction of the new constitution in the Free State, which now became Ireland, or Éire in Irish. De Valera's chimera of a Gaelic Irish republic with his vision of sturdy youths and comely maidens was anathema to Unionists and served only to heighten suspicion and fears; nor did it appeal to Northern Ireland's Nationalists who saw de Valera as the creator of a state that would further alienate Unionists from the idea of Irish unity.

Although many IRA men were in jail or had gone to Spain to fight in the civil war, there were signs of resurgence in the organization in Northern Ireland where it had been virtually dormant for more than a decade. In December 1935 Constable Ian Hay was shot and wounded seriously in an exchange of fire that began when RUC officers discovered an IRA attempt to steal weapons from Campbell College Officers' Training Corps. The raiders had tied up the caretaker and his wife in the gate lodge and Constable Hay had found them. No weapons were taken as they had been removed to Victoria Barracks for the Christmas holidays. (In June 1936 Hay, by then a sergeant, was awarded damages of £550; he still had 'metallic fragments . . . lodged in his body'.) Then, in April 1936, a beat policeman spotted some men whom he recognized as IRA members. Crime Special Branch was alerted and began surveillance which led to a raid that evening during which eleven IRA men were arrested. They had gathered to 'court martial' one of their number following the Campbell OTC raid. Three months later, police in Londonderry found two grenades, almost seventy sticks of gelignite and fuses as well as IRA documents in a house in the city. This followed raids by thirty officers under District Inspector Lynn and Head Constables Heuston, Dempsey and Kelly. Eight people were detained and two were later jailed.

Obviously, the IRA was planning a return to violence and it was not long before there were additional signs of activity; two IRA men were murdered by their fellows, one in December 1936 and the other the following month, having been accused of being informers. In July 1937 King George VI and Queen Elizabeth made their first visit to the province since the King's accession to the throne; the IRA reacted by bombing several customs posts, an activity to which they would return before long.

Across the United Kingdom there had been an increase in motor traffic on the roads since the Great War. The availability of cheap former military vehicles encouraged businesses to turn to the internal combustion engine. Private car ownership also increased and the results included many more collisions on the roads with a correspondingly high level of death and serious injury. In Britain some forces had created specialized traffic branches, known as 'courtesy cops', to deal with the increasing problems, encourage road users to adopt safer attitudes and improve traffic flow. The RUC followed suit in 1930 when Traffic Branch was established, initially to cover greater Belfast, where the highest traffic volume was to be found. Personnel were mounted on 498cc Triumph motorcycles fitted with sidecars, allowing officers to patrol in pairs. There were only twelve officers but it was soon apparent that traffic police were needed in other areas and the Branch gradually increased in strength and moved out to strategic stations across the province.

Cars were also bought and drivers sent to England for specialized training. The Metropolitan Police Driving School at Hendon had pioneered a technique developed by Lord Cottenham, a leading British racing driver, and police training thereafter centred on Cottenham's 'roadcraft' scheme. RUC Traffic drivers were trained to Grade 1 standard at Hendon or at Lancashire Constabulary's school at Hutton Hall near Preston, which was established in 1937.

Serious crime was rare in Northern Ireland but there were some problems to which police paid particular attention. One was the illegal distillation of poteen, which usually occurred in rural areas but was also known to happen in towns and cities; police involvement in tackling this offence was a result of the RIC's absorption of the Revenue Police. There were regular reports of seizures of stills throughout the period with some stations seeming to have more success than others. The first edition of the *Constabulary Gazette* reported that Sergeant O'Donnell and Constable Walmsley, 'whilst on revenue duty in south Derry' seized a still in the townland of Drumance Lower. The February 1934 *Gazette* noted that Sergeant Tom Carson of Dungiven with Constables Dunne and McCartney, also 'on revenue duty' made a similar seizure in the mountains between Dungiven and Garvagh. A year later Sergeant Tom Plunkett of Claudy was credited with 'the largest shebeen seizure ever made in the history of the RUC'; Sergeant John Brady of Feeny, partway between Claudy and Dungiven was also successful in tracking down poteen makers and seizing their equipment. (In late-1935 Brady also had the task of finding a coroner's jury when the 4,000 year-old remains of an 'unknown warrior' were found in his area.) Across the county boundary in Tyrone, Sergeant Blackstock of Plumbridge seized four stills in twelve months in 1936–7. Similar seizures were being made in other counties, illustrating the degree of the problem of illegal distillation at the time.

When a cock was heard crowing in a car passing a village patrol in County Tyrone, District Inspector Coulson, Head Constable Maguire and Sergeants Sullivan and Higginson from Dungannon set off in pursuit and discovered 500 cockfighters from surrounding counties at Derryloughan near Coalisland. Two dozen cocks were clipped, weighed and ready to fight when the police broke up the event; several names and car numbers were noted for prosecution. The suppression of cock-fighting events made frequent calls on police time. Police also dealt with cross-border smuggling and RUC Customs Patrols were based in border stations. Much money could be made from smuggling livestock, especially during the British–Irish economic war, and both RUC and Garda Síochána cooperated on this problem. During 1935 the Strabane Customs Patrol seized 650 cattle, 646 sheep and forty-six pigs while the Killeter patrol took 364 cattle and 189 sheep. In September 1933 the *Gazette* noted that Sergeant Sweeney and Constable Ferris, of Newry's Bridewell Station, attached to the Customs Patrol, arrested a sheep smuggler who was prosecuted and convicted. The Customs Patrols were permitted to cross the border in the course of their duties and a very high level of cooperation was achieved with the Garda.

In September 1931, Achmet Musa, a Turk, was found dead in a field near Carrickfergus. A murder investigation began, led by District Inspector F. W. Lewis who subsequently arrested an American called Eddie Cullens. The investigation had taken police to England in pursuit of their suspect. Cullens was convicted of the murder and executed in 1931. Sergeant O'Reilly from Bellarena Station arrested a Sinhalese seaman in late-1937 The sailor had carried out a series of burglaries in Limavady. At much the same time it was noted that the crime detection rate in County Londonderry had risen to 73 per cent while that in Londonderry City was 75 per cent. At this time there were no CID offices outside Belfast and Londonderry and local police were responsible for most crime detection work.

One of the major public events in Northern Ireland during the thirties was the opening of Londonderry's Craigavon Bridge. This replaced Carlisle Bridge, on virtually the same site, and was also a two-tier bridge, the lower deck being for railway traffic. The official opening took place in July 1933, on a scorching hot day. Such was the number of dignitaries invited to attend that there was a major call on police resources in the city and additional officers were dispatched to Londonderry for the occasion. These included recruits from the depot, one of whom was to spend much of his service in the city and to settle there after his retirement. Reggie Whitsitt, one of two brothers from a Monaghan family who joined the RUC, recalled that the day was so hot that sand had to be sprinkled on thoroughfares with tar surfaces. The sprinkling was done not by the staff of Londonderry Corporation but by policemen. Deploying senior recruits in such fashion was not unusual: they had also been deployed in Belfast during riots and the practice was still in use in August 1969 when recruits from Enniskillen were sent to Londonderry during the rioting there. Among other police drafted into the city for the occasion were parties from Dungiven under Sergeant Carson and Limavady under Head Constable Walker and Sergeant Sturgeon. Another major event in the Londonderry area in 1933 was the visit of Sir Alan Cobham's 'flying circus', which gave several officers from Limavady the opportunity to take to the air at Eglinton.

Among events planned for George V's jubilee was a review of the police forces of the British Isles and a large RUC party was to attend. With an average height of 6 foot 2 inches and with their rifles and bayonets the 250 strong party would have made an impressive sight but the Belfast riots caused a manpower crisis that forced cancellation of RUC participation. However, when George V died in January 1936 the RUC was represented at his funeral by the Inspector General, County Inspector H. Connor from headquarters, and a party of four head constables, eight sergeants and twelve constables.

As the 1930s began recruit training was still carried out at Newtownards but there was an urgent need for a new depot. When the Army gave up the Royal Barracks in Enniskillen – known locally as the Main Barracks – with the departure of a battalion of the Lincolnshire Regiment, the site seemed ideal to the Ministry of Home Affairs. Following an inspection, the Ministry decided that it was suitable and arrangements were made for the barracks to pass from the War Office to the Ministry. In early-1934 a contract was let for work on the barracks, which included building a gymnasium, and by August 1935 the new depot was being described as 'more like a modern hotel'.[1] Although Newtownards Urban Council fought a rearguard action to keep the depot in north Down, and other voices were raised in their support, it was announced in September 1936 that Enniskillen would definitely house the depot and the first recruits arrived in November. Even then the establishment was bleak, in spite of the work carried out since the Army's departure, and over the years it would improve but little so that the Hunt Report of 1969 would describe it as having been built for 'the soldiery of George III, and its amenities appear to have improved little since then'.[2] Although Hunt would recommend a new and modern police training centre, it would be 1986 before Enniskillen would be vacated and then only for another second-hand establishment at Garnerville in east Belfast.

Within the force discipline was strict and there were many instances of officers being penalized for relatively minor offences; some were transferred while others were fined and yet others were required to resign. The representative body – police officers were not permitted to belong to a union – had little power and many disciplinary cases of the period were instances of the exercise of arbitrary power by senior ranks. Among the penalties available to the authorities was that of demotion as happened to newly-promoted Head Constable John Blovis of Strabane who was reduced to the rank of constable and transferred for insubordination to District Inspector Parkinson-Cumine. The details of this offence, as outlined in the *Constabulary Gazette*, would today be more likely to see the senior officer appear in front of a tribunal; the entire affair seems to have been a result of a personality clash.

During 1935 a Belfast newspaper commented that the crest outside police stations was still that of the Royal Irish Constabulary. Before long this anomaly became the subject of a question in the House of Commons when the member for Willowfield, Mr A. Black, asked the Minister of Home Affairs why a new station at Woodstock Road bore an RIC station badge. Bates's answer demonstrated the parsimony of his department. The reason was financial: there was a stock of RIC crests and it had been decided to use these before introducing new ones. Black demanded that steps be taken to ensure that an RUC crest, and not that of any other force, be displayed on the front of every station. His comments offended the *Gazette* editor who asked:

> are not the Ulster Constabulary also 'Irish Constabulary'. We wonder
> Mr Black did not go further and demand the removal of the old RIC

badge from the frock collars of the police. Why not go on to demand a new colour and style of uniform altogether instead of that worn by the old RIC?[3]

However, it appeared that the Ministry had been embarrassed sufficiently to spend some money on producing new signs for stations. Lamps bearing the RUC crest, the only difference being that the word 'Ulster' replaced 'Irish', were manufactured and fitted to stations from 1937 at a cost of £1,000;[4] some were still in use until recently. The haste with which these and other RUC emblems were removed in 2001 stands in stark contrast to the length of time a Unionist administration allowed RIC badges to remain in place. Ever careful of its pennies, the Ministry of Home Affairs decided that the old RIC signs would not be sent to the scrapyard but would be sold to offset the cost of their replacement. The signs were then offered to serving policemen at 7s 6d each (37.5p), a princely sum to a young officer in 1937 according to Barney McGrath. Nonetheless, Constable McGrath was pleased to purchase a little piece of history.

The Ministry had spent some money on building or modernizing a number of police stations. Some of those inherited from the RIC had been in poor condition and were closed completely or replaced while others were renovated. This was the era in which the familiar white rural RUC station came into being. Such stations were built in Gortin, County Tyrone, and Feeny, County Londonderry; building costs varied from £3,524 for Swatragh through £3,774 for Gortin to £6,189 for Dunamore near Cookstown. The latter was a different pattern, however, and had more defensive features. Works at Draperstown cost £1,536 and at Dungiven £5,512 was spent. Most expensive of all was the new Clogher station at £6,706. In Londonderry the Ministry bought Gortfoyle House, on Spencer Road, to replace the Waterside station, which had been on Victoria Road adjacent to the County Donegal Railway station. At the new depot spending was in six figures.

Another illustration of civil service parsimony was the continued use of open Lancia cars. An unnamed officer wrote to the *Gazette* in September 1933 to complain about these vehicles, which provided no protection from the elements. This prompted the *Gazette* to ask why Lancias were still in service when light modern vans might have replaced them. At least one Lancia driver died as a result of the lack of protection from the elements: Constable Thomas Ayton received so many soakings while on driving duty in County Down that he succumbed to pulmonary tuberculosis on 21 January 1931.

The Second World War began in September 1939 when Germany invaded Poland. A joint British-French call for a German withdrawal was ignored and on Sunday, 3 September Prime Minister Neville Chamberlain broadcast to the nation telling them that the United Kingdom and Germany were at war. But an earlier declaration of war on Britain had been made by a familiar enemy. On 12 January 1939 the IRA had called on the British and Northern Irish governments to announce the immediate withdrawal of British forces from Northern Ireland.

> The Government of the Irish Republic believe that a period of four days is sufficient notice for your government to signify its intentions in the matter of military evacuation and for the issue of your Declaration of Abdication in respect of our country. Our Government reserve the right of appropriate action without further notice if upon the expiration of this period of grace, these conditions remain unfulfilled.

That this ultimatum was issued under the authority of the 'Government of the Irish Republic', a title the IRA claimed for itself, indicated that the organization considered itself on a par with the British government.

The IRA also addressed the ultimatum to Adolf Hitler and Benito Mussolini, the German and Italian dictators. By then it was certain that Germany would soon be at war with Britain, while Italy was Germany's ally. By sending their ultimatum to Hitler and Mussolini the IRA was indicating that the Fascist dictators were seen as allies. On 16 November 1940 the IRA's *War News* posed the question: 'with England in a struggle with Germany and Italy from what quarter should the government of the Irish Republic, i.e., the IRA, seek help?' The answer was that 'The lesson of history is plain. England's enemy is Ireland's ally'.

In April 1938 an IRA convention elected Sean Russell as its chief of staff. Russell was 'an ardent militarist, who advocated a bombing campaign against England' and the ultimatum was part of his strategy. This led, inevitably, to a campaign that began four days later, the IRA's threat having been ignored. The first devices damaged factories, telephone exchanges and electricity stations and were followed, on 19 January, by a bomb outside a Tralee hotel where Francis Chamberlain, son of Britain's Prime Minister, was holidaying.

Russell believed that bombing could be conducted without casualties but this soon proved to be woolly thinking, especially as the IRA was employing young recruits with little training and less technical knowledge and skill. However, they were causing problems for police and armed services in England and Northern Ireland as well as in Ireland. Scotland and Wales appeared to be exempt from the IRA's attentions since both were considered Celtic countries.

The problems had begun even before the first bombs exploded in

England. In November 1938, almost two months before the declaration of war, three IRA men, Jimmy Joe Reynolds, 'attached to GHQ', John James Kelly, from County Donegal and Charles McCafferty, from County Tyrone, were killed in the premature detonation of one of three explosive devices they were handling. The bombs had been brought from Sligo to Castlefin, near the Donegal–Tyrone border, to be used against customs posts at Strabane and Clady. The blast killed Reynolds and McCafferty immediately but Kelly survived for several days before succumbing. In his delirium he kept repeating what must have been the last words of one of his companions: 'Stand back John James, there's a wee mistake.' The 'wee mistake' was not to realize that one bomb was faulty. This information had been marked by an 'X' on one of the suit-cases in which the bombs were transported from Sligo. But the 'X' had been chalked on; it had disappeared by the time the suitcase reached Castlefin.

However, the customs posts were not spared but were destroyed over the next few nights. These incidents placed both the RUC and Garda on alert. RUC Special Branch intensified intelligence-gathering operations and, on 22 December, police arrested leading Republicans under the Special Powers Act; they were interned in Crumlin Road prison. But, since the arrests did not net all Northern Ireland's leading IRA men, the organization continued operating. IRA headquarters considered that its Belfast Brigade should act defensively 'to protect the Nationalist community in case the Orangemen ran amok' but the city could produce some men for the campaign in England, which was to be the main focus of activity. This did not prevent the Belfast IRA from making attacks. On the afternoon of 3 September a Supplementary Reserve soldier was stopped by six armed men in East Bridge Street and stripped of his uniform while another soldier was similarly treated in Kashmir Street following which his uniform was burned by the four armed men who had accosted him. The worst incident occurred in Upper Library Street where a member of 8 Anti-Aircraft Regiment[5] was shot and wounded in the stomach. Police patrols were stoned and bonfires lit in defiance of blackout regulations. Pro-Nazi slogans were shouted at police, the irony of the fact that the IRA was allied with the Nazis seemingly lost on the barrackers.

The small military presence in Northern Ireland was reinforced when war broke out, although Regular Army units were replaced by units of the Territorial Army; the regulars were dispatched to France or to Norway. This reinforcement was not a precaution against the IRA; in the early days of war, Northern Ireland was considered a training area. However, it was believed that there could be trouble from the IRA along the border and in the two cities. Headquarters, Northern Ireland District (NID) notified all units that:

Owing to unrest among certain sections of the population (both in Northern Ireland and across the border in Eire) troops stationed in Northern Ireland District must at all times be prepared to act in aid of the civil power. This, however, is only their secondary role – their primary role is to train for war against the enemy – GERMANY. This primary role must never be lost sight of.

To demonstrate the Army's presence, units were ordered to 'show the flag'. The battalion based in Ebrington Barracks in Londonderry when war began, 2nd South Wales Borderers, were to 'show the flag' in the area Londonderry–Claudy–Plumbridge–Newtownstewart–Strabane. This was extended in October to include Dungiven, Maghera, Castledawson and Cookstown; this area was handed over to 7th Royal Welch Fusiliers, the TA battalion that succeeded the Borderers in December.

In February 1940 the IRA stole a large quantity of rifles from Ballykinlar Infantry Training Centre. The raid had been assisted by IRA members inside Ballykinlar; at least one IRA man had been ordered to join the Army to obtain detailed information. An illegal radio station in Belfast announced the capture of 'a couple of hundred rifles'. However, the raid's aim had been to seize sub-machine guns but the raiders went to the wrong building. Thereafter, the Army began taking internal security more seriously and the General Officer Commanding, Northern Ireland, ordered the establishment of mobile columns across the province. On 20 May 1940 a GOC's directive stated:

In ULSTER there are only two areas of primary importance.
BELFAST
LONDONDERRY
Of the two BELFAST is the seat of government, and, on account of its docks, shipyards etc, is by far the most important.
    Furthermore, apart from its military garrison, Londonderry has a battalion (1,000 strong) of 'B' Specials, well organised and officered.
    Your defensive arrangements, therefore, should be *primarily* directed to the Defence of the Belfast area, against
A/ External aggression either by land, sea or air.
B/ Internal distraction caused either by the faction fight situation which always smoulders in the background, or armed sections of the IRA.
C/ Any combination of A and B.

Thus far the IRA does not appear to have been considered as an ally of the Germans by the British government, nor by the military authorities in Northern Ireland. IRA activities, even the Ballykinlar raid, were regarded as a nuisance more than anything else. The Irish government was adopting a harder attitude, however, especially after the IRA raided the Magazine Fort in Phoenix Park on 23 December 1939 and stole over a million rounds of ammunition. This caused the Irish government severe embarrassment. Although much of the haul was recovered in a major operation, that included the RUC, the embarrassment remained. As a result, the Dáil, in emergency session on 3 January 1940, voted additional powers to combat the IRA; the Minister of Justice could imprison, without trial, anyone suspected of IRA membership. An internment camp was established at the Curragh and hundreds were incarcerated.

In Northern Ireland IRA men were also interned. At first they were held in prisons in Belfast and Londonderry but were later transferred to a ship in Belfast Lough, the *Al Rawdah*, before being returned to conventional prisons as *Al Rawdah* was called into service to accommodate service personnel in the Clyde; an internment camp was also established at Ballykinlar. There were riots in Crumlin Road and Londonderry gaols and escapes from both in 1943, the most spectacular being when twenty-one IRA men broke out of the latter by digging a tunnel; most were recaptured. One early wartime prison riot in Londonderry was brought to a speedy conclusion when County Inspector J. K. Gorman MC called in the fire brigade to turn their hoses on the rioters, an early RUC use of water cannon. In the circumstances the alternative had been to open fire, a course of action County Inspector Gorman was unwilling to take.

The IRA remained active in Northern Ireland throughout most of the war although their activities were sporadic. Some incidents were staged as propaganda, including the prison breaks and the takeover on Easter Saturday afternoon 1943 of the Broadway cinema on Belfast's Falls Road by IRA men under Hugh McAteer. McAteer, who had escaped from Crumlin Road gaol in January, read out a statement of IRA policy before calling for a minute's silence for the dead of 1916.

But another earlier attempted propaganda event had fatal consequences, resulting in the death of a policeman and the subsequent execution of an IRA man. On Easter Sunday 1942 the IRA planned a 1916 commemoration in Belfast in defiance of a government ban. A distraction plan called for an ambush in which armed IRA members would hide behind an air-raid shelter at Kashmir Street and await a suitable target. That target presented itself in the form of a police patrol car on which the gunmen opened fire. One officer, Constable Patrick Murphy, jumped from the car to pursue the attackers into Cawnpore Street where they entered a house by the back door. By this stage the gunmen had dropped their weapons into a shopping bag, which was to be removed by two girls, but one man, Tom Williams, removed a gun from the bag and fired at Constable Murphy, fatally wounding him.

However, Murphy returned fire, wounding Williams who was unable to escape. When the other policemen reached the scene they found Patrick Murphy, a married man with nine children, dead on the scullery floor and nineteen-year-old Williams lying wounded upstairs. The IRA members surrendered and all eight, six men and two women, were taken into custody, although the women were released subsequently.

Constable Paddy Murphy, a Catholic, was a popular policeman who lived at Clowney Street and whose son Martin often played football with Paddy Devlin in Falls Park.

> The policeman was well known to the entire community in the Falls and it was unusual for him to be in a motor vehicle. More often he was out on foot around the area, where he was very popular with the kids, always joking with them or pulling their legs. He almost certainly knew the IRA group involved because they were all locals.[6]

For his courage Patrick Murphy was awarded the King's Police Medal posthumously. He was the second RUC man to die in as many days. On the Saturday Constable Thomas James Forbes died after being shot by the IRA in Dungannon. Constable Forbes was married with ten children. In less than twenty-four hours, therefore, the IRA had left nineteen children without fathers.

Those involved in the Cawnpore Street shooting were charged with murdering Patrick Murphy. All were found guilty and sentenced to death, the first such verdict in Northern Ireland. Subsequent appeals for clemency were made from a variety of sources. The case went to appeal but the Appeal Court upheld the earlier decision and the date of execution was set as 2 September 1942. However, at the end of August, five were reprieved. The exception was Williams, who had admitted in court that he had shot Constable Murphy. He was hanged on the morning of 2 September with rival crowds outside the prison.

Few incidents were reported, although there were some scuffles with police in central Belfast when two women made a Nazi salute to American servicemen. Stones were thrown at US servicemen travelling in a car while, near Crossmaglen in south Armagh, a police sergeant was wounded by gunfire. The IRA were forced to call off a planned attack on Crossmaglen RUC Station in which they intended to take a prisoner whom they would hang in direct reprisal for Williams' death. Over the next few days there was a spasm of IRA activity against the RUC with Constable James Laird and Special Constable Samuel Hamilton being fatally wounded in a gun attack at Clady near Strabane. In early October Special Constable James Lyons was wounded while pursuing men running away from Donegall Pass police station in Belfast after a bomb attack. His wounds proved fatal. Police activity against the IRA was increased and was largely successful, the prison escapes and the McAteer cinema incident notwithstanding. The IRA campaign fizzled out in 1944, but not before Constable Patrick McCarthy was shot and wounded whilst foiling an attempted IRA robbery on 1 October 1943. Patrick McCarthy tried to pursue the gunmen but collapsed and died from his wounds. The last wartime shooting incident involving the IRA in Northern Ireland occurred in February 1944 when James 'Rocky' Burns, an escapee from Londonderry gaol, was stopped by police in Belfast's Chapel Lane. The policemen, not satisfied with Burns' identity documents, decided to take him to Queen Street RUC Station for questioning. En route, Burns produced a handgun but was himself shot in the abdomen by a plainclothes officer of whose presence he had not been aware.

In England the IRA campaign had also been blunted by effective police action with many IRA members in prison as a result. The wartime IRA campaign, a series of attacks that served no strategic purpose but were only nuisance goads to the British, Irish and Northern Irish governments – and maintaining in the latter the extreme view that Catholics were untrustworthy in spite of the great number of Irish Catholics in Britain's forces – came to an end on 10 March 1945 when the IRA announced a ceasefire. Although strong action had been taken against them in Northern Ireland, and Williams was the only IRA man ever executed in Northern Ireland, measures taken across the border were even more severe. Jonathan Bardon summarizes de Valera's government's actions:

> De Valera consistently interned more IRA suspects than the Northern Ireland authorities: by hangings, street gunfights and incarceration in bleak camps, his government had shattered its former associates north and south. Gerry Boland, Éire's minister for justice, claimed with much truth that the IRA was dead. That Northern Ireland was entirely free of IRA activity by the end of the war was in large measure due to the unwavering repression administered by the Dublin government – a fact Stormont ministers certainly could not acknowledge in public.[7]

Four RUC officers and two Specials lost their lives to the IRA in the course of the Second World War; the terrorists who had aligned themselves with Adolf Hitler had also caused much damage and destruction in the province. It is, therefore, strange to find an academic study of policing in Northern Ireland asserting that 'the IRA was dormant during the years of the Second World War'. And this statement follows an earlier one – on the previous page of the same work – that there was an IRA campaign 'towards the end' of the Second World War.

*   *   *

The highest-ranking policeman to die during the war died not at the hands of the IRA but from a bullet fired by another policeman. Head Constable Thomas Dempsey was based at Londonderry's Victoria RUC Station where one of the station party was Constable Corr, against whom Dempsey appears to have been conducting a vendetta. Corr was assigned to a beat on the city's harbour, the Londonderry Harbour Police having come under RUC command with the outbreak of war. Constable Corr was a popular figure with the dockers, all of whom knew that Dempsey was victimizing him. As a result dockers would warn Corr if Dempsey were in the neighbourhood, especially if the former was having a chat or enjoying a cup of tea. On a pleasant Saturday evening in June 1940, however, while dockers were working late to unload a ship, Corr was surprised by Dempsey. The beat man had been talking to dockers when the Head Constable appeared. An angry Dempsey began to berate Corr for not performing his duty properly. Suddenly, the dockers were amazed to see the normally quiet, inoffensive Constable Corr draw his service revolver, aim it at Dempsey and shoot him dead. One man then realized that Corr was turning the revolver on himself and jumped at the policeman to try to stop him but was too late. Corr shot himself in the head and fell mortally wounded to the ground. Another witness, who was not as close, claimed that Corr chased Dempsey and shot him several times, including when he was already lying wounded, before killing himself.[8]

Londonderry became a vital naval base during the war as the Royal Navy's most important anchorage for escort ships in the Battle of the Atlantic, hosting ships from many Allied nations. The city's police worked with the Regulators, the Royal Navy's police, to ensure that this massive influx of servicemen did not cause too much disruption. One sergeant, stationed at Victoria, was assigned the task of liaising with the Regulators and became friendly with many naval personnel. This led to an invitation to visit a warship tied up in the Foyle, which the sergeant was glad to accept. What he did not expect was that the ship would be ordered to sea with him aboard. His efforts to be dropped came to naught and he carried out a patrol with an escort group. His return to Londonderry was a sad occasion for him; he had been away for several days and disciplinary action was taken. He was demoted to constable.

In early 1939 conscription had been introduced in Great Britain and the government contemplated extending the measure to Northern Ireland. Craigavon was enthusiastic about including the province. However, the idea met with considerable opposition; de Valera suggested that the conscription of any Irishman would be 'an act of aggression' while Cardinal MacRory stated that people would have a moral right to resist compulsory service and Irish-Americans lobbied Roosevelt to use his influence to stop the measure being extended to Northern Ireland. Against protests from Craigavon, the government abandoned the proposal. Perhaps they recalled the impetus to Sinn Fein propaganda of a similar proposal in 1918. However, British forces had a serious manpower problem throughout much of the Second World War and a review of manpower in 1941 led the government to again consider extending conscription to Northern Ireland. Once more there was strong opposition from many quarters, this time, surprisingly, including Protestant groups in the province. Among voices speaking against the suggestion were those of the Prime Ministers of Canada and Australia but the most important was that of Sir Charles Wickham who told the Cabinet that introducing conscription in Northern Ireland would create widespread disorder. Northern Ireland's new premier, John Andrews – Craigavon had died in November 1940 – managed a most diplomatic exit from the debate, writing to the Home Secretary that

> the strength of opposition would be more widespread than had been realised. While, speaking for themselves, the Government of Northern Ireland would like to see conscription applied, the real test, in their view, must be whether it would be for the good of the Empire.

Faced with this analysis the Westminster Cabinet decided that conscription in Northern Ireland 'would be more trouble than it was worth'.

But, while conscription was never applied in the province, the cruelty of war was brought home to its people when, in April and May 1941, German bombers targeted Belfast. On Easter Tuesday night the Luftwaffe inflicted on Belfast the highest single death toll for one night on any UK city outside London. More than a thousand died, many more were injured, large areas were devastated and thousands of homes destroyed. Further death and destruction followed on 5 May when the Luftwaffe returned. Although Northern Ireland had been unprepared for such an attack, much courage and initiative was shown by the civilian services, chief among whom were the men of the Royal Ulster Constabulary. Three officers earned the George Medal for their work in the bomb-ravaged city; a sergeant, six constables and two special constables were killed while another sergeant, eleven constables and eighteen special constables were injured and two police stations were destroyed. Killed in the bombing were Sergeant R. J. Wilson and Constables M. R. Armstrong, H. Campbell, W. J. Lemon, J. Meaklim, J. McKenna and R. Reid. The George Medals were awarded to Constables William Brett, Alexander McCusker and Robert Moore.

Constables Brett and McCusker were trying to extinguish incendiaries when a bomb landed nearby. The blast threw McCusker through a door into a house and both were buried under debris from collapsing houses. However, Alexander McCusker was able to extricate himself and rescue a boy who had been trapped by debris. Constable Brett then joined his colleague and they began rescue work, although both had been injured and were suffering from shock. They continued until help arrived.

> The two Constables displayed bravery and devotion to duty in face of great danger and disregarded their own injuries until they had done all in their power to rescue the casualties.

The award of the George Medal was announced in the *London Gazette* of 19 September 1941, which also included the news of a similar award to Constable Robert Moore. He had been involved in rescue work when a six-storey building was hit by bombs and collapsed onto nearby terraced houses, injuring and trapping many residents.

A squad of police officers rushed to the scene to assist in rescue operations. Constable Moore dug his way through debris and sawed through planks to rescue a family of three, including a child. Later he and Constable King went to another house where people were trapped.

> They saw a hole in the debris which had apparently been the stairway to the top of the house, but the stairway had collapsed and the walls on both sides, which were about three feet apart, were cracked and likely to cave in at any moment. Although warned of the danger, Constable King volunteered to descend and . . . succeeded in bringing the casualties to safety.

Robert Moore then went to another wrecked house and helped rescue a woman from under a beam. Digging down some six feet he found a little girl, aged about eleven, whose clothes were on fire. He got the child away from the flames and extinguished her burning clothing with his bare hands. In doing so he was badly burned.

Robert Moore 'showed outstanding gallantry and total disregard of personal safety'. He and his colleague, Constable King, were responsible for saving many lives on a night of mayhem and horror in Belfast. Not everyone could be decorated and nor did all the injured officers survive. Constable W. J. Bond, an Englishman who had joined the RUC on completion of his service in the Durham Light Infantry, and was a member of the RUC Band, suffered damage to his lungs from flames and smoke during a rescue attempt and later died from his injuries.

Extra pressure was placed on the RUC by the presence of large numbers of servicemen in the province. These included British personnel from all three services as well as US forces, Canadians, Free French, Norwegians, Belgians and even members of the Royal Indian Navy. In particular, the RUC was called on to play a significant role in the build-up of US forces in Northern Ireland – Operation Bolero – in preparation for the invasion of Europe. At all times, good relations were maintained with these many visitors and the cooperation of their service police helped to lighten the load that would otherwise have fallen on the RUC.

Female police officers are such a common sight today that it is difficult to credit that policewomen were introduced into the RUC only during the Second World War. Although the RIC had employed 'two semi-official policewomen in a civilian capacity' in both Belfast and Dublin from 1918 these 'were not given powers of arrest nor were they paid from Police funds, but were used to interview and take statements from females, to help with search and escort duties and to assist in enforcing curfew regulations arising from "The Troubles".' The two women based in Belfast were taken over by the RUC but, although described officially as policewomen, with no change in status or powers. (Although the *Interim Report on Police Re-organization* recommended pay increases for the women, it did not recommend any increase in numbers.) Both Mary Fallon and Jane Bell were attached to A District, based on Musgrave Street RUC Station, but operated from the Police Office at Townhall Street. They were supplied with uniforms and, in 1938, issued with warrant cards. Although officially employed by the Northern Ireland Civil Service Commission on behalf of the Ministry of Home Affairs, they were eventually assigned service numbers, Mary Fallon becoming PW 1 and Jane Bell PW 2. When Mary Fallon was discharged on medical grounds in 1940 her successor was appointed by the Civil Service Commission after the vacancy was advertised in Belfast papers as being for 'the Post of Policewoman (permanent and pensionable) in the Ministry of Home Affairs for Northern Ireland'. Mary Catherine Carton, daughter of a former RIC man, was appointed and assigned the number PW 3. In addition, there were female attendants in Belfast and Londonderry and female searchers in Belfast, Londonderry, Armagh, Omagh, Newry and Enniskillen.

The first-ever policewoman was Alice Stebbin Wells who was appointed to Los Angeles Police Department on 12 September 1903 while the London Metropolitan Police created a women's branch in 1918 but it took the Second World War and the influx of tens of thousands of servicemen to convince the Ministry of Home Affairs that the RUC also needed policewomen. Pressure from groups concerned about the moral welfare of girls and young women in Northern Ireland finally brought about the decision to recruit women. The Belfast Council of Social Welfare and the Church of Ireland Moral Welfare League were the main advocates of women police. On 30 March 1942 Belfast's City Commissioner, Mr R. D. W. Harrison, submitted a report to Wickham in which he suggested that additional policewomen might be deployed to deal with prostitution, take statements from women and children, especially in cases of sexual offences, deal with female prisoners, young children and travelling aliens, and political work. Harrison considered it important to get the right type of person for this job but that this, difficult at the best of times, would be more difficult in the existing circumstances. He did not

> see any advantage in translating Social Workers or Court Missionaries into Policewomen, they do the same work, probably at a higher rate of pay. I do not think we would get Policewomen ready made. If they are to be effective a full regular course of training is essential.

The historian of the RUC's policewomen believes that Harrison's report indicated that the idea of policewomen was not readily accepted and that there was probably a desire to shield women from some of the more unpleasant social aspects of a country at war.

Eventually, after further pressure, the Ministry agreed, in June 1942, to recruit an additional four policewomen but it took several months before the posts were advertised, thanks to civil service wrangling over finance. The new policewomen were to be full members of the RUC and the existing two women would be recruited to the force 'if found suitable and if satisfactory arrangements about pension etc can be made'. Not until 16 April 1943 did the Ministry of Home Affairs give approval in principle to the recruitment of four new female officers. The posts were advertised at the end of May with recruiting being dealt with by the RUC rather than the Ministry. Applicants were to be 'over 24 and under 35 years of age', it being felt that more mature females were needed. At the same time Wickham wrote to the Commissioner of the Metropolitan Police asking if he had a suitable woman sergeant to take charge of what was to become the Women's Branch. Within weeks Sergeant Marion Paterson Macmillan had volunteered; she transferred to the RUC on 6 September with the number PW 4; it was probably at this point that the existing women were allocated numbers.

The advertisement for policewomen drew 250 applicants, six of whom were selected to enter the Depot. Although it had been proposed that the existing two policewomen should become full members of the RUC this had not happened and thus the increase to six recruits. Sergeant Macmillan, who was involved in recruit selection, had also been busy preparing for their entry to the Depot. Since these were the RUC's first female officers it is worth recording their names: Rebecca (Ruby) Jones, PW 5; Florence May Brock, PW 6; Susan Sherrard, PW 7; Gertrude Drennan, PW 8; Annie May Bruce, PW 9; Gertrude McBrien,

PW 10. Ruby Jones was the widow of a police officer and served for seven years before resigning on remarriage. The six entered the Depot on 15 November 1943, the first of many girls who would pass through those gates in years to come.

In the Depot the six women were issued with navy-blue overalls and policemen's caps, there being no women's uniform. Drill was carried out alongside male recruits but classroom training was separate, generally from male instructors with occasional input from Woman Sergeant Macmillan on offences related to women and children. On completion of their five months' training, the six officers were posted to Belfast's F District and attached to the City Commissioner's Office. By now, of course, they had a proper uniform and one that proved to be the smartest policewomen's uniform in the British Isles with its unique cap and attractive bottle-green colour. The tunic was open necked, showing a white blouse with black tie and the skirt was worn to just below the knee. It was a comfortable and practical uniform, supplemented with a black greatcoat, raincoat and a bottle-green gaberdine for adverse conditions. A waterproof cover was also provided for the cap.

Policewomen's duties included patrols on the city's streets, usually carried out in pairs, as well as plainclothes work involving observation of brothels and street prostitution. There were also duties brought about by the war, including making enquiries about service families and 'frequent calls accompanied by Army personnel to Du Barry's, a well known pub in Prince's Street, Belfast, regarding "careless talk", which was an offence during the war years'. The deployment of policewomen proved a great success and Wickham's successor, Sir Richard Pim, a great believer in the value of female officers, decided to increase the number of policewomen in the force.

Notes
1: *Constabulary Gazette*, Aug 35
2: Hunt Report, para 116, p. 28
3: *Constabulary Gazette*, Jan 36
4: Ibid, Feb 36
5: From May 1940 this was 8th (Belfast) Heavy Anti-Aircraft Regiment.
6: Devlin, p. 33
7: Bardon, *A History of Ulster*, p.583
8: See Doherty, *Paddy Bogside*, pp 15–17, & *Constabulary* Gazette, Nov 40

Chapter Three

A New Era –
with Shades of the Past

The end of the war brought peace but did not usher in an era of prosperity. Rationing would continue until 1953, unemployment would rise and only the introduction of the 'welfare state' would cushion working class people from conditions similar in many ways to those of the thirties. While the war in Europe ended in May 1945, fighting continued in the Far East until August. Between these two momentous occasions Sir Charles Wickham retired as Inspector General and immediately set about organizing a group of RUC officers to establish a police force in Greece, which had been threatened by civil war in the wake of a sudden German withdrawal in late-1944; only rapid Allied intervention had prevented a descent into chaos. Fears of a communist takeover led to continued Allied involvement in Greece, including that RUC group. Among RUC officers to serve in Greece was Jamie Flanagan, who would later command the force. The Minister of Home Affairs, now Edward Warnock, announced that three RUC officers would also be seconded to the Allied Control Commission in Germany for policing duties while the Belfast City Commissioner, Mr R. D. W. Harrison, was being appointed Deputy Inspector General of the Public Safety Section of the British Element of the Commission; he also became Deputy Director of that organization.[1]

Wickham's successor was Sir Richard Pike Pim, who came of Quaker stock and had served in the Royal Navy during the Great War, afterwards choosing to become a policeman. He could have entered the family business – his father was a linen baron and Pim had been educated at Trinity College, Dublin where he received a degree in arts and law. However, he became an officer cadet in the RIC and served as a District Inspector in Dublin before moving to Ulster where he was stationed in Londonderry and Limavady. In 1922 he joined the Ministry of Home Affairs and was, for a time, Bates' private secretary. When the Second World War broke out Pim returned to the Royal Navy and, shortly afterwards, joined Winston Churchill's staff at the Admiralty. When Churchill became Prime Minister on 10 May 1940, Pim went with him and for the rest of the war was responsible for Churchill's map room. Pim accompanied the premier to the major Allied conferences and designed a travelling map display that so impressed President Roosevelt that he was asked to assist in producing a similar display for the White House.

Pim was knighted for his wartime service and, on his discharge, appointed as Inspector General of the RUC from 1 August 1945. He brought his wartime experience to policing; in his office at Waring Street he had a large map, on a scale of one-inch to one-mile, showing all Northern Ireland's police stations. A map of Belfast dominated the control room in the City Commissioner's office at Templemore Avenue; this was on a scale of eighteen-inches to one-mile. Pim took over at a time of great change and was more than able to meet the demands of the time. Identifying road traffic and the increase in collisions and deaths as a priority, he ordered the expansion of Traffic Branch. Twenty-six new cars were bought, although cars were difficult to obtain, and 100 additional officers were transferred to Traffic to man these cars, having first been sent to England for training. Pim later decided that Northern Ireland needed its own police driving school, which was established in Belfast in 1950. A school of instruction for 'Authorized Officers' was also started to train men to examine vehicles for mechanical defects, a task that has become ever more complex. Traffic Branch established a map room in which patterns in collisions could be identified and patrolling organized to cover areas of greatest priority.

Another branch that Pim felt needed strengthening was the small Women's Police Branch. The new Inspector General was impressed with the work done by policewomen and decided to seek approval for another twelve officers. When advertisements appeared in December 1945 the lower age limit had been reduced to twenty-two and rates of pay increased. Eight new recruits, including four former servicewomen, entered the Depot in May 1946; this expansion brought the Branch's first promotions with Marion Macmillan becoming the first woman head constable while Gertrude McBrien was promoted to woman sergeant.

Pim had also turned his attention to a large rise in crime in the late forties, one of the effects of increased unemployment in the wake of the war's end. A publicity campaign was mounted, probably Northern Ireland's first crime prevention campaign, in which the public was urged to dial 999 to report criminal, or suspicious, activity; this system was then relatively new, having been introduced in Britain in 1937 and in Northern Ireland in 1945. During 1948 fifty arrests were made as a direct result of 999 calls; in each case the offender was caught either in the act or with incriminating evidence on his person. Two years earlier a sharp-eyed Belfast policeman, Constable Lindsay, spotted some unusual items in a local gold dealer's window. He realized that they were part of a stolen collection – the Darmstadt–Hesse crown jewels, then worth some £400,000 – and began the process of recovery. The jewels, stolen by two US Army officers and a female accomplice, had been broken up for international distribution. Constable Lindsay's find made a major news story in Northern Ireland and was later exhibited at the trial of one of the original thieves.

During the war there had been many advances in technology and some wartime developments were transferred quickly to civilian applications, including the much-improved radiotelephony system used operationally by the forces. Pim introduced radiotelephones to police cars; these quickly proved their value with a series of arrests. The *Belfast Telegraph* took part in a successful publicity exercise when a reporter, who was allowed to study reports of some arrests in which radiotelephony had played the major part, penned a feature on this new form of policing. His article eulogized the system to such an extent that it must have been a deterrent to many would-be career criminals. The system was controlled from the Commissioner's office with its large-scale map of Belfast. Policing had come a long way in the first few years of Pim's appointment and there were to be many more innovative ideas in the years ahead, in spite of the Ministry of Home Affairs' continued frugality.

On 1 February 1946 the last officer cadets entered the Depot. Before the war the force had taken half its senior officers from direct-entry officer cadets, in much the same manner as the armed forces; other officers were promoted from the ranks. The five men of this final intake, all former servicemen, included David Corbett, from County Fermanagh, who had taken a patrol of Household Cavalry up the road to Arnhem, the only ground troops to reach the beleaguered airborne forces, Michael Magill, from County Down, who had served in the Royal Navy, Willy Moore and John Gorman, both of whom had served in the Irish Guards, each earning the Military Cross, and Nigel Spears, who had served in the Royal Air Force as a bomber pilot, surviving sixty missions. Three of the new cadets were sons of serving senior RUC officers. All five passed out and were appointed District Inspectors. At the passing out parade the guest of honour was Princess Elizabeth and the Depot Commandant, Anthony Peacocke, was keen that the cadets should lay on a demonstration for Her Royal Highness of something unique to Irish policing: seizing an illicit poteen still.

> We built a V-shaped hut and then used peat 'bricks' to make it look like a turf-stack. It even had a hidden door. Inside . . . was the still,

consisting of a barrel of 'wash', a mixture of molasses and other ingredients, a paraffin cooking stove and the 'worm' (a long coiled pipe) inserted in the 'cooler', which converted the steam from the 'wash' into liquid by cooling, resulting in a drip of highly alcoholic liquor into the final vessel. We had practised the operation and, when each of us had been presented to the future Queen and congratulated on being commissioned, wearing our Guards, Navy and Air Force uniforms, we hurried to our rooms, donned dirty dungarees and got the potheen still into operation. Princess Elizabeth was taken on a tour of the Depot, which ended with the novel exhibition of a working potheen still. She came into the 'turf-stack' with her Lady-in-Waiting to see these greasy rascals at their illegal work . . . [2]

But the demonstration had a rather unexpected side effect that was highly embarrassing for Peacocke. As Princess Elizabeth was being escorted to her car by the Prime Minister, Minister of Home Affairs and Inspector General, a 'rather eccentric but highly intelligent Head Constable Instructor' stepped forward to present her with a bottle, tied with a green ribbon, with the words 'Your Royal Highness, perhaps you would like a drop of the potheen'. The end result was a 'frightful row'; Peacocke accepted responsibility for the demonstration, the cadets for making it more realistic than necessary and the Head Constable was blamed by everyone. But the matter did not rest there for among the guests who had witnessed the presentation was a young fundamentalist minister, Ian Paisley, who brought the story to the attention of others who were able to raise it to the embarrassment of the government. Paisley's name would appear many more times in the history of Northern Ireland and the RUC.

During the early 1950s the force's founder members achieved thirty years' service and many chose to retire. Some had served for even longer, among them Constable Patrick Byrnes MM, who retired on 20 March 1956 after almost forty-three years. Patrick Byrnes, a policeman's son, had joined the RIC in 1913 and served first in Kanturk, County Cork. He volunteered for the Irish Guards during the Great War and earned the Military Medal for his gallantry in the Battle of Arras.[3] After the war he returned to the RIC and transferred to the RUC in 1922. All his RUC service was in County Londonderry, where he served in Limavady, Castledawson and Coleraine, spending twenty-six years in the latter. A popular policeman, he 'had an extensive local knowledge and was a real community policeman long before the title was used by Police. He was respected by all sections of the community' and was specially commended for good police work on three occasions. He died in 1972 at the age of seventy-eight and is buried in St Aidan's churchyard,

Magilligan. Patrick Byrnes was followed into the RUC by his son, Richard Patrick, while a daughter, Elizabeth Patricia, served in the City of Liverpool Police.[4]

The retirements of so many founder members created a manpower crisis that left the RUC some 200 personnel short of its establishment of 3,000. The fact that Canadian forces were recruiting in Northern Ireland at this time exacerbated the situation since Canadian salaries were much more attractive; Canadian policemen were already earning £1,000 each year, a figure that would not be reached by British forces, including the RUC, for several years. At this time the pay of an RUC constable was £500 per year. Thus the force had to initiate recruiting campaigns, the first time this had happened. A relatively unsophisticated campaign, owing much to contemporary recruiting for the Army's Irish regiments, was mounted with brightly coloured posters outside police stations. The posters showed RUC men in differing situations, riding a motorcycle, using a radio and taking part in sport, with the legend 'Join the RUC – it's a great career'. It did not allude to the unheated vehicles issued to the force. When Jack Truesdale left the Depot in 1954 he was posted to Keady where he found that the station had Land Rovers with fabric covers, a Dingo scout car with a perspex 'bubble' on top and a .30-inch machine gun fitted, as well as a half-track, which also mounted a Browning .30-inch machine gun. None had heaters, all of these having been removed to ensure that policemen did not park by the side of the road and sleep while on duty. Cold vehicles were also intended to ensure that officers would make regular stops in order to walk about and warm up. The lack of heaters meant that windscreens could freeze, or mist over, quickly which led to the practice of carrying a bottle of methylated spirit for use as a de-icer. (Windscreen washers were not fitted to any vehicles at this time and only became mandatory in the early 1970s.)

Nor did the recruiting posters mention the spartan conditions that new arrivals would meet in the Depot. Neil Falkingham, who joined in February 1953, remembers the freezing cold conditions and the inadequate clothing with which recruits were issued and in which they had to undergo drill on the parade ground. But the rigours of the Depot were good preparation for a recruit's arrival at his or her first station. The ghost of an RIC recruit from the 1870s would probably have remarked that the only significant change for his 1950s' successor was that the latter did not have to march to the new station. Indeed they were obliged to travel by train when possible. At the station the new officer would meet a routine that had also changed little over the years. Hours were long, personal freedom was restricted and food was variable. In smaller stations cooking was often done by a local woman. Some were excellent and treated the officers as family members; Alan McConnell was stationed in Pomeroy where the police party ate in a local house to which they had a key so that they could prepare food at unsociable hours. While this was a good arrangement, there were others where the cook's culinary talents were meagre; this led to much lamentation on the part of young officers, who always seemed to suffer hunger pangs, and to schemes to improve the diet. Most patrolling was done on foot or bicycle, there being few cars and only approved officers were allowed to drive those cars, for which they became personally responsible – although this did bring a small addition to pay. If the driver of a car was not available then that vehicle could not be taken out, even in an emergency. This situation prevailed well into the 1960s. Norman Lucy recalls that Donemana station was refused the use of the car at Strabane to respond to a fatal crash. The assigned driver was not on duty and officers from Donemana had to attend by bicycle. Rural patrolling was almost all done by bicycle and officers were given a small monthly allowance of 7s 6d (37.5p) to maintain their bicycles.

Bruce and Bruno joined the RUC in 1955. These were the first two civilian police dogs in the province but the Dog Section was to go from strength to strength as the trusty animals proved their value many times in a variety of situations. Although the main intention was to use dogs to guard government buildings, it was soon appreciated that they could perform a much wider range of duties. Bruno underlined this by making the first 'arrest' by an RUC dog a few weeks into his police career when he tackled a man who had just assaulted a female. At much the same time the Minister of Home Affairs announced that policemen would no longer be armed routinely, although firearms would continue to be available when necessary so that any criminal who chose to use a gun would have to consider that the police might also be armed. This effort to soften the image of the police was soon to come to naught following a series of incidents that led to the opening of a new campaign of terrorist violence.

In 1951 the Northern Ireland government enacted new legislation prohibiting all but traditional parades unless notice was given to the police. This, the Public Order Act, was followed in 1954 by the Flags and Emblems Act, which became law in spite of Pim's protests that it would be unenforceable. The Act made it an offence to interfere with the display of the Union flag while outlawing the display of any flag likely to cause a breach of the peace. Pim knew that the legislation was aimed at the Irish tricolour and that police would be expected to enforce it. In theory that meant that anyone complaining about a tricolour being flown anywhere in Northern Ireland could expect police to take action, even if the flag were being flown in an area where no resident was likely to take umbrage at its display. The Minister considered Pim to be unduly apprehensive about the legislation, which was pushed through Stormont with calamitous results for the police in the years ahead – and for the stability of Northern Ireland. Together these two pieces of legislation gave the impression that one section of the community was favoured above the other and the RUC, in having to enforce such laws, would, in the eyes of Nationalists and Republicans, appear to be favouring Unionists. Had the sound advice of Sir Richard Pim been heeded then Northern Ireland might have been spared much distress. Nor was this to be the last time that the advice of police officers was ignored to the detriment of society.

King George VI died in February 1952 and was succeeded by his daughter, Princess Elizabeth, who became Queen Elizabeth II. At the King's funeral the RUC was represented by a party of officers. The coronation of the new Queen took place in London in June 1953 and the RUC was represented at the subsequent review of British police forces in Hyde Park. In July Queen Elizabeth II and the Duke of Edinburgh visited Northern Ireland, which precipitated a major security operation. Venues to be visited by the royal couple and the routes along which they would travel were checked and rechecked by CID and Special Branch. The Queen and Duke visited Londonderry where they received a warm welcome as they drove in a limousine along a route lined by a crowd representative of the entire population of the city. A future Chief Constable was one of the officers on duty that day, posted on the roof of a building overlooking Shipquay Place; a Special Branch check that morning had found a trapdoor on which the padlock had been prised open and so Constable Jack Hermon was given a grandstand view of proceedings in the city centre.

The Road Traffic Act of 1955 authorized urban speed limits in Northern Ireland. These limits, generally 30 mph in built-up areas, were introduced the following year and their enforcement became a task for Traffic Branch. To enable officers to detect offenders, radar speed detectors that could be carried in cars were introduced; these were in use as soon as the new limits were in place. Although similar urban speed limits had been in operation for over twenty years in Great Britain, the RUC was the first force in the British Isles to use radar to enforce speed limits. It would not be the last time that the force would be in the forefront of innovation in traffic matters. Officers trained to use radar soon became so proficient that many could judge the speed of an approaching vehicle without looking at the read-out from the equipment.

That same Act also introduced 'zebra' pedestrian crossings. Although there had been designated pedestrian crossing points, marked by studs on the road surface, these new crossings were indicated by black and white stripes on the road with orange 'belisha' beacons mounted on black-and-white poles on either side. The first such crossing was laid under the watchful eye of the RUC on Londonderry's Strand Road outside Victoria RUC Station and remained until a new traffic system made it redundant in 1967. Zebra crossings were intended to help pedestrians cross without assistance. Elsewhere, due to busy traffic conditions, officers would be called upon to carry out 'points' duty at crossing places and it was at this time that policewomen first carried out such duty in Belfast, a practice that expanded as a means of placing female officers, still few in number, more firmly in the public consciousness.

On the night of 11–12 December 1956 there was a series of bomb and arson attacks across Northern Ireland. From Londonderry in the north-west to Newry in the south-east the IRA struck at targets that included the BBC relay transmitter at Londonderry's Park Avenue, which was bombed, to a B Specials' hut in Newry, which was set ablaze. Other targets included the new TA centre in Enniskillen, which was under construction, while bridges in Fermanagh were also damaged. However, attacks on a radar station at Torr Head and on the Royal Irish Fusiliers' Depot at Armagh were unsuccessful; in the former the raiders were intercepted by a police patrol and arrested after a brief exchange of gunfire while in the latter the Depot Commandant, Major Brian Clark MC, lifted an IRA bomb and drove it into the neighbouring countryside where it exploded harmlessly. The following night terrorists, using bombs and guns, attacked Lisnaskea and Derrylin RUC stations in County Fermanagh. No officers were hurt but, on 30th, the IRA attacked Derrylin again and Constable John Scally was killed, becoming the first RUC victim of the campaign. Another officer returned fire until a bomb at the front of the station exploded. Part of the building came down and he was buried in the rubble but the attackers then made off, possibly believing that they had killed him also.

It was a bad end to the year but the RUC reacted speedily to the threat. Stations throughout Northern Ireland soon had sandbags protecting windows. Dannert wire entanglements were thrown up around some stations and 'unapproved' roads across the border – those without customs' posts – were closed, either by cratering or by metal spikes. These steps represented passive protection against terrorist attack but more active measures were also introduced, including mobilization of some 200 Specials for full-time duty, checkpoints on roads, especially at night and in border areas, and armed guards, usually B Specials, on important installations.

Other measures implemented to counter the IRA included the introduction of internment, with known IRA members being taken into custody. The campaign had not begun out of the blue since there had been indications that the IRA was preparing for another outbreak of violence. These included a raid on the Royal Irish Fusiliers' Depot at Gough Barracks in Armagh in June 1954 when an IRA gang stole weapons from the armoury.[5] Another planned raid on a military armoury, at the Royal Inniskilling Fusiliers' St Lucia Barracks in Omagh, in October was foiled with eight IRA men arrested by police as they tried to escape. A new IRA campaign was, therefore, expected, especially when a breakaway Republican group, styling itself Saor Uladh, or Free Ulster, pre-empted their former comrades by attacking customs' posts and the border police station of Roslea. During the latter attack, a Saor Uladh member, Cornelius Green from Londonderry, was wounded mortally in an exchange of gunfire between the terrorists and the station party; Green died the following day. His background was surprising for a Republican terrorist; he had fought during the Second World War in North Africa, Italy and France.

However, intelligence had been built up on IRA members and shared with the Garda. Sir John Gorman, then District Inspector in Armagh, recalls that he showed his 'Crime Special' files to the Garda's Chief Superintendent in Monaghan who reciprocated. However, they did not discuss plans for internment.

> The day arrived, one Sunday, when we 'lifted' about thirty men in the Armagh area, about whom we had built up a prima facie case for believing that they were Republican activists, prepared for the 'armed struggle'. I was astonished to hear on the radio that across the Border precisely the same operation, on the same premise, was being carried out by the Gardai.[6]

Internment in the Republic did not begin until after the murder of Constable Cecil Gregg in an ambush at Forkhill in County Armagh on 4 July 1957. De Valera's reaction to that murder, the reintroduction of internment, would be a crucial factor in the eventual defeat of the IRA. Constable Gregg's wife, Carrie, was pregnant with their second child when her husband was murdered but subsequently joined the RUC herself and served for almost twenty years; she also chaired the RUC Ladies' Choir.

But a more immediate reaction to the IRA already existed in the form of the RUC's Reserve Force. Created in 1950

> its role was to provide back-up in civil commotion, to police sensitive areas at times of confrontation, and to 'show the flag' in a disciplined and impressive way to those who wished to break the peace. . . . Willy Moore MC . . . was chosen to command the new Force.[7]

The Reserve Force was 150 strong by 1956 and organized in platoons, of which there were five, each commanded by a head constable with four sergeants, one for each section. To ensure its effectiveness the Force was intended to be highly mobile and was provided with vehicles that included the then new Land Rover. About seventy military vehicles were on loan from the War Office, including half-tracks[8] as well as Ferret or Dingo scout cars and Humber armoured personnel carriers; the latter, based on the Humber one-ton truck, were known as Pigs. The half-tracks were ex-US Army open-topped troop carrying vehicles, so lightly-skinned that they would deflect only low-velocity rounds; US soldiers had dubbed them 'Purple Heart Boxes' for that reason. Reserve Force firepower included heavy automatic weapons while each section had a Bren gun, a light machine gun with a thirty-round magazine, as well as Sten guns, a cheap, wartime submachine gun,[9] and rifles. As the campaign developed, the Reserve Force was also supported by soldiers but most operations were undertaken by policemen. Cecil Gregg, murdered on 4 July 1957, was a Reserve Force member. He was sitting in the rear of an open-sided vehicle at Carrivegrove, some 200 yards from the border near Forkhill, in the early hours of the morning when IRA members opened fire after a landmine had failed to detonate beneath the vehicle. Constable Gregg was struck by gunfire and wounded fatally; another officer, Constable Robert Halligan, was wounded. The bomb was later found to include 100 sticks of gelignite.

Some six weeks later another policeman died in an IRA booby-trap attack. Sergeant Arthur Ovens was in charge of a party of police and soldiers who went to an empty house near Coalisland, County Tyrone, to investigate an anonymous report of suspicious activity. As they approached the house a candle was seen burning in the kitchen and Ovens ordered the dwelling to be surrounded. He then entered, followed by another policeman, and pushed open the kitchen door. However, the terrorists had booby-trapped the door and as soon as it swung open a bomb was triggered. The resulting explosion killed Arthur Ovens instantly but, as if by a miracle, the constable behind him survived.

By the time the IRA campaign was twelve months old it had claimed ten lives, those of John Scally, Cecil Gregg and Arthur Ovens of the RUC and seven IRA or Saor Uladh members. There had also been 366 incidents, which included gun attacks, explosions and arson attacks. Across the border, in the townland of Edentubber, County Louth, on 11 November, four IRA men were preparing a bomb in the home of a sympathizer when the device exploded, killing all four and their host. In traditional Republican fashion the dead became martyrs, in this case the 'Edentubber Martyrs', although the analogy is difficult to understand. The IRA was quick to protest that the bomb had not been intended for use against those attending a Remembrance Sunday parade near the border but the protest itself was almost an admission. Four years later this explosion would lead to another death with the murder of an RUC officer at Jonesborough.

One of the most remembered incidents of the campaign occurred in its early days when fourteen IRA men attacked Brookeborough RUC Station in Fermanagh on New Year's Eve 1956. The attackers, led by Dubliner Sean Garland, included men from several southern counties, among them two destined to become Republican 'martyrs', Sean South from Limerick and Fergal O'Hanlon from Monaghan. Garland's 'flying column' was one of at least two operating in Fermanagh; another column made the attack on Derrylin in which John Scally died. Garland's plan was foolishly ambitious. He intended to attack Brookeborough RUC Station as light was fading, using explosives, petrol bombs and machine guns, all carried, with his men, in a stolen lorry. Garland hoped to obtain a propaganda coup by forcing the police to surrender the station to the IRA. By now, however, the RUC in Fermanagh were on full alert and the station party in Brookeborough was no exception. Garland's group was behind schedule and arrived in Brookeborough, a town of which they had no real knowledge, at about 7.00 p.m. As the stolen lorry arrived outside the station, it was spotted by Sergeant Kenneth Cordner who sounded the alarm and raced for a Bren gun. In the meantime, the attackers attempted to place a large bomb outside the station and opened fire with a Bren at the front of the building; the weapon was, apparently, fired by South. Cordner, a former Irish Guardsman, was soon in action with his Bren from a first floor window and South found that the position of the lorry would not allow him to engage the police Bren. Several attackers were hit, with O'Hanlon grievously wounded. Cordner's fire had peppered the lorry, its cab was punched full of holes, the tipping gear had been punctured and the tipping body kept moving up while two tyres had been shot out. Garland ordered a withdrawal and the crippled lorry moved off, pausing only to pick up two lookouts who had been posted earlier. It was clear that South was dying and that O'Hanlon was seriously injured; both were abandoned in a byre, where their bodies were later recovered. Republican legend has it that local people were asked to fetch a doctor and a priest. In truth the pair were left to die.

Before long police vehicles were in pursuit of the lorry and its passengers had just abandoned it when two Land Rovers arrived at the scene. Some shots were fired by the police but the attackers melted off into bogland. Although they crossed into County Monaghan, they were arrested by the Garda and Irish Army and all received prison sentences. The dead men became the subject of Republican ballads while South's funeral was attended by thousands. The attack on Brookeborough had been a disaster for the IRA and was followed by a series of swoops by

60

Gardai on prominent Republicans. Garland had been a British soldier for a time but his military experience was limited and there is no sign of any careful planning in the Brookeborough attack. One principle to which soldiers will always adhere is that 'time spent in reconnaissance is seldom wasted'. Garland did not reconnoitre Brookeborough, relying instead on a map, which is no substitute for time spent on the ground, especially in an urban situation. In marked contrast to the IRA men, the RUC officers in Brookeborough showed a high standard of professionalism in their reaction to the attack and in the subsequent pursuit; Sergeant Cordner was awarded the BEM for gallantry, as was another officer who dealt with the IRA bomb. Garland was later arrested in Belfast as he boarded a train for Dublin, posing as a medical student; Woman Constable Madge Cubitt, working with Special Branch, noticed that his hair was dyed. He was jailed for four years.

At times IRA activities descended into farce. A plan to attack the Royal Navy's submarine depot ship, HMS *Stalker*, at Londonderry, was foiled when a patrolling B Special struck up a casual conversation with an IRA scout, whom he knew from civilian life. The latter was carrying a concealed revolver and kept reaching for it but could not remember whether he had the safety on or off and so was afraid that if he tried to pull it out he might cause himself serious injury. Close to HMS *Stalker* stood the city's electricity generating station on which several attacks were made but the city never lost its electricity although many windows were lost and one of the author's first experiences of the efficiency of the RUC was gained when he was woken from his sleep by police officers coming to fetch his father, the keyholder of the neighbouring Municipal Technical College. Having ensured the integrity of the 'Tech' the policemen then drove the author's father home to a rather excited son.

Nonetheless, some incidents during 1957 were much more successful from the terrorists' viewpoint. Perhaps their most successful attack in the campaign was that on the TA Centre at Dungannon on 18 January when six men placed two charges totalling some fifty pounds of explosive; these detonated causing extensive damage. What was probably the most spectacular incident occurred early on a Saturday morning in March when a goods train leaving Strabane for Londonderry was stopped by emergency detonators placed on the line by two men who then took over the train, threatened the crew never to carry police or soldiers and drove the train north towards the terminal at Foyle Road in Londonderry. Some miles outside the city – the line crossed the border on its journey from Strabane – the IRA men abandoned the train, having first overridden the 'dead man's handle' that would otherwise have stopped the locomotive. The train carried on and crashed into the buffers at Foyle Road station, causing considerable damage. However, the plan had been to blow locomotive and wagons into the Foyle thereby necessitating a breakdown crane being brought in to retrieve the first train. In turn, that train would also be blown up and its loss would cause temporary paralysis of Northern Ireland's railway network. But earlier IRA activity that night meant a considerable police presence close to the railway line near the city and they, who were to have planted the explosives to tip the train into the river, decided not to take the risk of being captured.

Attacks continued into 1958, in which year the RUC lost its next casualty to IRA violence. Even in border areas, policemen still patrolled on bicycles and Constable Henry Ross was carrying out such a patrol from Forkhill on 16 July 1958 when he was caught in the blast of a landmine buried at the roadside. Henry Ross died in hospital the following day. In Fermanagh the IRA continued to lose men with two members shot dead in clashes with police. Aloysius Hand was one of a group called upon to halt by a police patrol on the border in July. Hand opened fire with a Thompson sub-machine gun but died when police returned fire. The following month James Crossan died during an attack on a customs post; when police called on the IRA men to halt they fled for the border and Crossan was shot dead as the officers opened fire.

Even by the time of Constable Ross's murder, the IRA campaign had peaked. The number of incidents in 1958 was down on the figure for 1957; three IRA men, including their Fermanagh commander, Pat McManus, were killed, the latter with his own explosives on 15 July, and another Saor Uladh member was shot dead by police near Newtownbutler, also in Fermanagh. In 1959 the number of incidents reduced to twenty-seven, none of which caused death to a police officer. A number of RUC officers were decorated for courage during the campaign, including Woman Sergeant Maude Musselwhite, stationed at Victoria in Londonderry, who was awarded the British Empire Medal for her part in defusing an IRA bomb in the city. Sergeant Musselwhite, who joined the RUC in 1948, was the first policewoman in Northern Ireland to be decorated for gallantry. The male officer with Sergeant Musselwhite, Constable Alex Forsythe, who pulled the fuse from the bomb, was awarded the George Medal.

In 1958 the public image of the RUC was transformed when uniform changes were introduced. The tunic lost its high patrol collar, which would have been familiar to RIC men, in favour of an open neck that allowed officers to wear ties for the first time. From now on the officer's shirt was visible and an appropriate pale green colour was chosen; head constables and other senior ranks wore white. The tie was black and, for many years, was a standard item but was eventually replaced by a clip-on tie with a readymade knot, offering less chance of it being used in an

62

attempt to strangle an officer during a close-quarter altercation. Not all contemporary shirts had attached collars and the new RUC shirts followed the pattern of detached collars fastened with studs; it would be the early 1970s before these were phased out finally. Constables and sergeants in Belfast and Londonderry had worn numerals on their collars but these were now moved to their shoulder straps. Another distinction peculiar to the two cities was the issue of night helmets, similar to those worn by English forces although there was no bright silver badge-plate, a variation on the standard RUC badge being used. These helmets, worn until the late 1960s, were a legacy from the RIC and probably arose from the absorption of the two borough forces. The new uniform made the officer on the beat seem a less severe figure than heretofore and it was with this image that the force prepared to meet the 1960s. As the fifties drew to a close, however, the RUC remained on the alert with defensive measures still in place at stations across Northern Ireland.

Notes

1: Belfast Telegraph, 7 July 1945
2: Gorman, *The Times of My Life*, p.65
3: Constable Byrnes also held the 1914–15 Star, the British War Medal, the Victory Medal, the Defence Medal (1939–45), King George V Jubilee Medal and the Police Long Service and Good Conduct Medal. His medals were presented to the RUC Museum after his death.
4: Richard Byrnes to author
5: The Depot Commandant, Major Dermot Neill, was at his son's prize-giving at St Columba's College in Dublin but was held responsible for the success of the raid and his Army career was at an end; his son Sam has since become world famous as an actor. As a result of this raid the IRA acquired 670 Lee-Enfield rifles and thirty-six machine guns, of which nine were Bren light-machine guns and the remainder Sten sub-machine guns.
6: Gorman, op cit, p.87
7: Ibid, p.84
8: Most of these half-tracks had been built by the International Harvester Company but are better known by the White name.
9: The Sten was also unreliable and there were many accidental discharges as the safety catch could be released by a jolt, such as that experienced when jumping out of a vehicle.

Chapter Four

The Sixties

Newspapers love new years. They provide an excuse to run reviews of the previous twelve months, look forward to the next twelve, and, every ten years, an opportunity to cast a knowing eye back on another decade while trying to predict the trends of the new decade. And so as 1959 dissolved into 1960 newspapers, local, regional and national, indulged in this habit. Some looked for novelty: the *Belfast Telegraph* published photographs of cars bearing registrations with the numbers 1959 and 1960. Few, however, could have predicted how the 1960s would turn out. This was to be a decade of change, when the fruits of the welfare state legislation of the 1940s would finally be seen, when 'teenagers' became consumers, when pop music began to dominate culture. Before it was over the decade would see revolution in Czechoslovakia, riots on the streets of Paris, a huge anti-war demonstration in London and unrest in Northern Ireland. For the RUC there would also be much change while the unrest that would begin in the late sixties would alter the force forever. But, as 1960 opened, the RUC was still dealing with the terrorist campaign that had begun in 1956. Although soon to peter out, that campaign would claim more lives with two young officers becoming victims of the IRA.

During the final phase of the IRA campaign the RUC was led by Albert Kennedy who succeeded Sir Richard Pim at the end of 1960. With Pim's retirement imminent, approaches had been made to Major General Pat Scott, who had commanded the Irish Brigade in the Second World War, to become Inspector General but Scott declined and Kennedy was chosen.[1] He was the first Inspector General to have risen from the ranks. Born in Belfast in 1906, the son of an RIC sergeant, he had followed his father into the police. His rise was achieved through dedication and hard work. Kennedy had studied the workings of forces in Britain and North America and had a vast range of experience, heading Crime Branch and later becoming Pim's deputy. In his first year in post he had to deal with fifty terrorist incidents, including the murders of two policemen.

The first officer to die in 1961 was Constable Norman Anderson, based at the border station of Roslea, County Fermanagh. A single man from Ballyclare, County Antrim, Constable Anderson had met a girl who lived across the border in County Monaghan. They had been going out together for some time and the young policeman had visited her family home. Knowing that he was a policeman, the IRA laid an ambush on the night of 27 January. That evening the couple had been out together and were returning to the girl's home. With minor border roads closed off, it was Norman Anderson's practice to walk across the border with his girlfriend. This night was no different and, at 12.25 a.m., he left his van at Annaghmartin and returned some twenty minutes later. As he made for his vehicle the IRA gang opened fire with a machine gun and he was murdered, shot in the back. The crime was exacerbated by an IRA story that Norman Anderson had been spying in the Republic; this fallacious excuse was used to justify brutal murder. As Eunan O'Halpin writes, it also presaged the way in which specific officers would be targeted in a later campaign.

> The premeditated nature of the murder set it apart from the other five RUC and indeed the eight IRA deaths during the campaign. It was a harbinger of the tactics of the succeeding generation of IRA men.[2]

Throughout the year there were further incidents but normal policing continued. The summer marching season passed quietly but with its usual heavy call on police resources. Some soccer matches proved volatile, but there were no major incidents although there was some stoning at the end of a match on Saint Patrick's Day when Linfield beat Derry City at the latter's home ground. Since this was the first year of the decade it was a census year and RUC officers acted as enumerators, visiting homes to compile the necessary data on those in residence on census day. No one could have suspected that this would be the penultimate occasion on which police officers performed this task.

On 12 November, Republicans organized a commemoration at Edentubber where, in 1957, four IRA members and a sympathizer had been blown up while assembling a bomb. The IRA had decided to use the 1961 event to strike at police in the hope of reviving their waning campaign. In 1960 local police had established a checkpoint at Flurry Bridge outside Jonesborough, yards from the border, to check those crossing into the Republic to attend the commemoration. The IRA's intention was to fire at officers manning this checkpoint before escaping across the border.

Among the officers on duty that day was Constable Willie John Hunter, from Macosquin, County Londonderry, who was stationed at Forkhill. A pleasant and mild-mannered young man, Willie John was one of two members of his family in the RUC; his sister Agnes was stationed in Belfast. The day was cold and Constable Hunter remarked to a colleague that the crowd gathering at the Celtic cross where the so-called 'Edentubber martyrs' had died would not stay long. Several speakers were to address the crowd with the event due to begin at 2.30 p.m. However, before that happened, four terrorists moved into the grounds of Jonesborough Parish Church, taking up firing positions behind the wall. They were less than fifty yards from the checkpoint and overlooking the police position.

As five unsuspecting policemen watched the nearby crowd, shots from rifles and machine guns rang out from the church grounds. Four officers fell; Willie John Hunter was dead and three others were wounded, two of them seriously. Other policemen returned fire at the terrorists who made their escape under cover of the churchyard wall and the building itself. From there they had only to run about forty yards to cross the border where they abandoned their weapons before mingling with the commemoration crowd. Witnesses recalled that there were cheers as the men made their escape. A Catholic priest, Father Stephen Teggart, comforted the wounded officers and administered the last rites to one man, Special Constable Patrick Skehin, who was bleeding heavily. The injured were taken to Newry's Daisy Hill Hospital; they were later visited by the Inspector General and Brian Faulkner, the Minister of Home Affairs. As well as Patrick Skehin, son of a former RUC sergeant, who was stationed at Bessbrook, the wounded were Special Constable Hugh Gilmore, Bessbrook, and Constable Samuel Gault, Forkhill. (Constable Gault was murdered in the Remembrance Sunday bombing in Enniskillen in 1987.) The only uninjured officer was Sergeant Albert White, from Coleraine. Twelve years later, then an inspector in Newry, he was shot and wounded seriously near Jonesborough while visiting friends. On 18 June 1982, as a sixty-year-old civil servant managing the Newry CID office, Bertie White was murdered by the IRA.

A cross-border police operation was mounted to catch the murderers. County Inspector Wolseley led the RUC search, which unearthed a loaded Thompson sub-machine gun magazine. A search by Gardai from Dundalk was also carried out but with no result.

Willie John Hunter was laid to rest three days later after a service in Ringsend Presbyterian Church. Thousands paid their respects to a popular young man and extended their sympathy to his family. Colleagues from Forkhill carried the coffin draped with the Union flag and the Minister, the Reverend Dinsmore, told the congregation that Constable Hunter had been a happy young man, without malice against anyone but with a 'cheerful, helpful spirit which made him beloved by all'. His was the last RUC death of the IRA's 'Operation Harvest'

66

campaign. Reaction to Constable Hunter's murder was diametrically opposed to that expected by the IRA leadership. Instead of stimulating their campaign it brought further opprobrium. Newspapers were loud in their condemnation of the murder with the *Northern Whig* describing it as BORDER AMBUSH MURDER; the editorial of the *Irish Times* called the gunmen criminals and stated that no motives could 'be held good enough to justify the foul murder of a young Irishman'. The Irish premier, Sean Lemass, a former IRA member, condemned the killing without reservation and Garda officers from County Louth were said to have viewed with disgust the bloodstained ground where Willie John Hunter had fallen. Among many tokens of sympathy sent to the family from the Republic was a floral tribute from students of University College Dublin; the attached card read 'For a young Irishman who died in the execution of his duty'. Willie John Hunter's family was devastated by his death and his father never recovered from the loss of his son.

There was political reaction to the murder in the Republic. Lemass's government brought back a measure used by de Valera against the IRA in the 1940s – military tribunals. In the past these had proved most effective and were to do so again. There were no juries, senior Defence Forces' officers acted as judges and sentences were severe. Garda pressure on the IRA was also intensified.

Although its leadership realized that there was no support for the campaign, IRA activities did not end immediately. Three RUC officers were injured at Whitecross in County Armagh when a landmine detonated near their vehicle. But an IRA 'army convention' in January 1962 acknowledged that the campaign was going nowhere and decided to end it. Of course, someone else had to be blamed; it was the failure of the Irish people to support the IRA that brought their campaign to an end, according to the terrorists. Those Irish people were more interested in things material than in ending partition and so the IRA was dumping arms until such time as the final 'and victorious phase' of the 'struggle' could begin. The statement issued by the leadership noted that

> The leadership of the resistance movement has ordered the termination of the campaign of resistance to British Occupation launched on 12 December 1956. . . . All arms have been dumped and all full-time active service volunteers have been withdrawn.

Since December 1956 the IRA had killed six policemen. The campaign had cost the British and Irish treasuries about £10 million; this had been absorbed in providing resources to conduct the campaign, repairing damage and paying compensation. Eight IRA men had also died, as had four other individuals, two of them Republican supporters; the rest were members of Republican splinter groups.

In April 1962, the Queen Mother visited the Depot in Enniskillen and presented medals to two officers, of whom one, Sergeant Alexander Robinson, had been on the staff for twenty-five years. Queen Elizabeth then talked to members of the Guard of Honour and later to a number of policewomen, including Women Constables Carrie Gregg and Agnes Hunter, the former the widow of Constable Cecil Gregg and the latter the sister of Constable Willie John Hunter. Sympathizing with them, Her Majesty commented, 'What a tragedy for this sort of thing to happen'.

This was also the year in which Northern Ireland's first stretch of motorway, between Donegall Road and Stockman's Lane, was opened. Somehow the opening of the M1 captured the public imagination and seemed to point to a better future. For the RUC Traffic Branch, however, it meant another task, for which specialized patrol vehicles, capable of carrying the large numbers of traffic signs and cones needed to warn of an emergency, were needed. These new patrol vehicles were also distinctive, being painted white overall, a practice initiated by the Lancashire Constabulary who, in turn, had adopted it from American forces. The motorway patrol task was to increase in the years ahead as the network spread out, although the imaginative predictions of the early sixties never came to fruition.

As Northern Ireland settled down to the peace that followed the IRA campaign there was an air of change in the province. That the Catholic community had not supported the IRA led many Unionists to consider political change possible and some began to talk of drawing Catholics into the party. During this period also the Northern Ireland Labour Party drew support from all sections of the community and tried to break the mould of local politics. Then, in March 1963, Lord Brookeborough, who had been Prime Minister for twenty years, retired due to ill health and was succeeded by Captain Terence O'Neill who was determined to move away from traditional politics. O'Neill invited Sean Lemass to Stormont in January 1965, an unthinkable move some years earlier. Although this first such contact since the 1920s was welcomed by many, others saw it as a sign of weakness and betrayal. Opposition to the Lemass visit, led by Ian Paisley, presaged political developments later in the decade.

Within the RUC change was also taking place. The paraphernalia of security was removed from stations, many of the military vehicles were returned to the War Office and the Reserve Force was reduced with some ninety officers returning to normal duty. Spikes were lifted from border roads and flowers rather than sandbags decorated window ledges of police stations. Internment came to an end and a collective sense of relief was felt throughout the force.

*   *   *

In 1961 a national police pay award placed long-service constables in the £1,000 per year bracket. This increase applied to the RUC, although officers continued to work much longer hours than those in Great Britain and were denied overtime payments. The parsimonious Stormont administration would have preferred to keep the RUC on a lower rate of pay but accepted the new rates as it had accepted the need to replace the headquarters at Waring Street with more modern accommodation. The new headquarters, at Knock Road on the outskirts of Belfast, came into use in 1962, the Inspector General's office being housed in a fine nineteenth-century house called 'Brooklyn' which gave its name to the complex; a modern, low-rise office block had been added for the 200-strong administrative staff. Nor was Brooklyn the sole investment in new buildings; a new headquarters and control room had been established at Ladas Drive in Castlereagh from which to control operations in the Belfast area. New radio equipment was installed and, soon afterwards, police in the city began using personal radios, known as 'pocket-phones', which enabled them to stay in close contact with their stations.

More modern radio equipment was allowing a quiet revolution to take place in policing. Additional equipment was to be introduced for rural areas and more cars, equipped with radio, were to be brought into use. Over the next few years this would have significant influence in the development of policing across Northern Ireland. However, radios cost money and equipping officers and vehicles with radio meant a heavy investment. The Ministry of Home Affairs continued to be penny-wise and, although the Constabulary Act 1963 increased the force from the 3,000 set in 1922 to 3,200, there was no attempt to increase funding. Thus a modernized RUC was sought and County Inspector Tom Crozier was given the task of drafting modernization plans. Crozier was to make the force more efficient but without additional expenditure. For the first time the RUC was subjected to an analysis of its efficiency – a team of what were then known as Organization and Methods (O & M) experts was brought in to assess how the police did their job.

In March 1967 the Crozier Report was delivered. Crozier had cut his suit according to the cloth he had been given and that 'suit' was to be a radio-controlled model. Patrol cars fitted with radios would provide fast response to calls from the public although the man on the beat would continue to operate in urban areas; but there would be fewer such men. The trade for the money to buy radio equipment was the closing of twenty-four small stations, mostly in rural areas, but including the amalgamation of several Belfast stations. Some rural stations in towns and villages would become 'limited opening', manned only for a few hours each day; at other times callers would be advised to contact the nearest main station. The limited opening stations released for more useful duties, officers who previously might have spent up to eighty hours a week in those stations. However, the closure of so many small stations reduced contact with the public and was seen by many as a mistake. Crozier also introduced some much-needed reforms; the official working week was to reduce to forty-four hours while some personal restrictions would be abolished. There would be no more evening roll calls and less control of what an officer might do in his or her free time.

The pace of modernization seemed to accelerate in 1968, which saw the revamped RUC established. There were now only 146 stations, down from the 224 taken over from the RIC, and the strength of the force reached 3,031 officers; a further 180 Specials were mobilized for permanent duty. Recruiting efforts at this time included placing advertisements in the journals of Catholic schools; one appeared in the 1965 edition of *The Columban*, journal of St Columb's College, Londonderry, offering a career with a salary starting at some £700 per annum.

Although some new stations were built in the sixties these were usually replacements for outdated accommodation and areas that wanted new stations were denied them. One such area was Creggan in Londonderry, a large post-war housing estate of some 12,000 people, which was policed from Rosemount. Local people felt that they should have their own station but Nationalist councillors were reluctant to be seen supporting such a request and it fell to Luke Hasson, an independent councillor from Londonderry Rural District Council, to lead the deputation that sought a police station for Creggan. The request was turned down although it was believed that a possible site had been identified at Central Drive.

In October 1968 the RUC became the first force in the British Isles to introduce evidential breath-testing equipment with a Swiss machine that took an exact amount of breath to provide an accurate reading of a suspect's blood-alcohol level. The Ethanographe was issued to Traffic Branch whose officers were trained in its use and was normally deployed in adapted vans known as Accident Prevention Units. Since Crozier had also recommended that the force place an emphasis on public relations, the new equipment was publicized as part of the campaign to 'Help the Motorist'. Some may not have appreciated this particular form of help just as they may also not have appreciated another contemporary Traffic innovation, the use of unmarked high-performance patrol cars, which the press quickly dubbed Q-cars.

This concept came from County Inspector Harold Wolseley, who saw it as a means to detect cases of drunken, careless or dangerous driving, especially amongst young males, who had a tendency to drive as fast as possible without considering consequences. The Q-cars, including Mini-

Coopers, MGB GTs, Triumph TR6s and Lotus Cortinas, attracted both praise and criticism from the public, the former from those who believed that they would help reduce the number of road deaths and the latter from those who thought that they might become 'victims' of this 'ungentlemanly' conduct by police. However, Reggie Semple, who served on Q-cars from their introduction until they were disbanded in 1970, found that no one he ever stopped tried to excuse his bad driving: 'They all accepted that they had done something wrong and nobody ever said "I didn't do that". ' The deployment of Q-cars on all main routes was a strong deterrent to offenders which was reinforced in north Down by the knowledge that one resident magistrate handed down automatic three-month disqualifications for those detected speeding by Q-cars.

The scheme had a feature that may be unique in policing in the UK: civilians, known as 'courtesy drivers', could accompany police and even drive Q-cars under special insurance arrangements. These drivers were recruited from the Association of Northern Ireland Car Clubs (ANICC), whose cooperation was sought for the scheme. When Sir Arthur Young took command of the RUC in 1969 he decided that the scheme was 'not cricket', since the cars were not obviously police vehicles, and ordered that the team be disbanded. At a meeting to discuss this decision one supporter of the scheme asked Young if this meant that he would now put all CID officers in uniform. Young ignored the logic of that argument and went ahead with the disbandment plan.[3]

For much of the decade, however, police work was routine. Throughout Northern Ireland, officers walked their beats or rode bicycles. The latter was especially true in rural areas but some urban stations were still using bicycles; in Londonderry both Bishop Street and Pennyburn Stations carried out patrols on cycles. Only a small number of officers drove cars, including those of Traffic Branch; but cars remained unheated. There were also seizures of illicit stills, the making of poteen still being a regular occurrence throughout Northern Ireland. In January 1966 the *Constabulary Gazette* reported a seizure in County Tyrone.

> Sergt. Mervyn Rainey and Const. Ian Crawford of Pomeroy made the seizure while making an extensive search in a remote area of moorland at Altaglushan, Pomeroy.
>
> It is one of the largest to be made in the district for a considerable time.
>
> In addition to a still, cooler, worm and other equipment, the police found a large quantity of wash and poteen.

Those were the days when a search of moorland in high Tyrone was not associated with terrorism. Those were also the days when the *Gazette* would publish full details of promotions and transfers, information also available in newspapers. From time to time local newspapers, especially, carried photographs of police social functions, such as the annual Ballymena and District RUC ball, held in Leighinmohr House Hotel in 1965, or RUC Bessbrook's dinner dance in Newry where many guests came from around Crossmaglen in south Armagh. For the latter, held on a Friday, Catholic guests were able to obtain a dispensation from the requirement to abstain from meat on Fridays. Michael McAtamney recalls that the local bishop granted this dispensation regularly and that tickets were stamped 'Dispensation granted'. Other social functions included Christmas parties for officers' children at which a policeman would invariably play Santa Claus and catering was carried out by station civil servants and, in some cases, policewomen. At the 1965 Londonderry function some 200 children and parents attended; Head Constable McGowan's wife played the piano and Constable Calvin brought along his record player to provide additional music. Sergeant Gregg was Santa Claus and the catering committee included Sergeants Monaghan and Wallace, Constables McNeill, Coulter and Roddy and Woman Sergeant Vera Mair, who, one imagines, ensured that all went to plan. County Inspector and Mrs Kerr attended, as did District Inspector Montgomery.

Policewomen took a leading role in promoting Northern Ireland during the sixties. Under Terence O'Neill, Northern Ireland's government organized trade promotion ventures, or 'Ulster Weeks', in various centres in Great Britain at each of which three RUC women, a sergeant and two constables, would attend to perform duties in the host cities. The first such detachment was at Nottingham in 1964, followed by Bristol, Edinburgh, Newcastle-upon-Tyne, Leeds, Southampton, Manchester and Leicester. With two 'Ulster Weeks' each year the visits drew much praise for the smartly turned out RUC women in their distinctive bottle-green uniforms and caps. The final 'Ulster Week' was held in 1968.

But the fact that times were changing in the sixties was underlined by the departure of the last officers who had served in the Royal Irish Constabulary. The distinction of being the very last of these fell to Constable Ernest Moffett of The Birches RUC Station in County Armagh. Ernest Moffett had joined the RIC on 23 February 1921 and transferred to the RUC on its formation in 1922.[4] But the memory of the RIC would linger for as long as those who had served with former RIC men continued to police Northern Ireland.

While officers walked their beats, visited farmers to make the various returns that were still the responsibility of the police and tended the gardens of many police stations, the first waves of a new storm of unrest were beginning to lap Northern Ireland. In September 1964 Prime Minister Sir Alec Douglas Home called a general election and political parties in Northern Ireland prepared for the hustings. Among those to announce his candidature was Liam McMillan, who stood as a Republican in West Belfast. McMillan represented an attempt by IRA supporters to take a political path, but one that followed Karl Marx's teachings. However, the flag flown from his campaign headquarters in Divis Street was the Irish tricolour, claimed by the IRA as its own and a forbidden emblem in Northern Ireland. Nonetheless, local police were happy to ignore the tricolour, feeling that no one in the area would be offended whereas removing it might provoke disorder. But the flag was spotted by a supporter of Ian Paisley who reported it to the Free Presbyterian Moderator. At an Ulster Hall service on the evening of 27 September, Paisley announced that he would remove the flag himself if the authorities did not. By then the local police commander had advised that it would cause more trouble to attempt to remove the tricolour than to leave it in situ; his stand was supported by both the City Commissioner and Inspector General.

However, Paisley's threat frightened the Stormont authorities and the Minister of Home Affairs ordered Kennedy to have the flag removed. A squad of police officers was sent into Divis Street to seize it; this led to rioting by crowds that had gathered to prevent Paisley carrying out his threat. Some nights later the flag was replaced and another raid had to be launched. Steel-helmeted policemen removed the flag but were then faced with the worst rioting that Belfast had seen in three decades. The results of this ill-advised action showed the wisdom of listening to sound local advice from police officers, who knew the ground for which they were responsible, and the folly of political interference with policing. The Divis Street incident damaged police relations with the local Catholic community but, worse still, showed weakness in O'Neill's administration. Paisley, who was beginning an 'O'Neill must go' campaign, must have been encouraged by the reaction to his threat on this occasion. The West Belfast seat was won by the Unionist candidate and a tricolour was carried without incident at a Republican march on the Sunday after the election; there was no attempt to interfere by police and none by Paisley supporters. But many, including officers serving in the RUC at that time, believe that the embers of communal strife had been stoked once again.

Further life was breathed into those embers in 1966 with the commemoration of the 1916 rebellion. To Republicans this is the 'Easter Rising' and the fiftieth anniversary was to be an important landmark. The Republic's government held official commemorative events and Republicans in Northern Ireland, still small in number, announced that they would also commemorate the rebellion. Tension increased in

Belfast and the Ulster Special Constabulary was mobilized during April to assist in dealing with any disorder. Parades across Northern Ireland passed off peacefully although, in Belfast, officers had to form a barrier in Castle Street to keep apart Republican marchers and a counter-demonstration organized by Paisley. In Londonderry, District Inspector Montgomery ordered that a blind eye be turned to a tricolour being carried in a parade.

Reaction to the enthusiasm for commemorating 1916 was predictable. Northern Ireland has never been short of those who will either go out of their way to offend or be offended and so it proved on this occasion. A Loyalist organization calling itself the Ulster Volunteer Force (UVF), from the anti-Home Rule Unionist private army of fifty years before, was formed in the Shankill Road area and there were attacks on Catholic homes, schools and businesses with one elderly Protestant lady, Martha Gould, dying when the public house next door to her was set on fire; the pub was Catholic owned. In June Ian Paisley led a protest against the General Assembly of the Presbyterian Church, which was held in Belfast, marching his supporters through Cromac Square to do so. Catholics attempted to disrupt Paisley's march and clashed with police as they tried to shepherd the marchers through. The Governor of Northern Ireland, Lord Erskine, and Lady Erskine were among dignitaries subjected to jeering and heckling and Lady Erskine was taken ill. It was an acute embarrassment to O'Neill who lambasted the protestors' behaviour.

The tension had not bled off by any means. Belfast witnessed sectarian clashes and a beer bottle was thrown at the Queen when she visited the city in July to open the new Queen Elizabeth Bridge. Later on her journey a large block was dropped on the bonnet of her car from a building site in Victoria Street but the Queen was uninjured and un-flustered. A youth arrested by police was subsequently jailed for four years. But the worst incidents were perpetrated by the UVF, which declared war on the IRA and then shot and wounded a Catholic man whom they believed to be a prominent IRA member. But they had mistaken the wounded man for their intended victim; John Scullion died on 11 June. Then a Catholic barman, Peter Ward, was shot dead in Malvern Street in the Shankill area by the UVF, only days before the Queen's visit. O'Neill announced the proscription of the organization, making it an offence to be a member.

All this contributed to a volatile, tense situation. Across Northern Ireland people were trying to get on with their lives and thought that they had put the spectres of the past behind them. Now those spectres appeared to be returning. For police officers that summer of 1966 was a long and hot one with little respite from lengthy hours of duty. For Paisley part of it was spent in prison following his refusal to pay a fine

74

for disorderly behaviour at the General Assembly. For Terence O'Neill it was a summer of worry with an attempt to depose him from within his own ranks and a meeting with Prime Minister Harold Wilson that made it obvious that Westminster intended paying more attention to Northern Ireland affairs in the future.

O'Neill had attempted to build bridges between Catholics and Protestants but his cross-border links had raised antipathy from Paisley and his supporters while many Catholics, who had considered O'Neill a modernizer and reformer, began to lose faith in him. The vacuum that developed was filled partially by the creation of the Northern Ireland Civil Rights Association (NICRA) in 1967. NICRA embraced a wide political spectrum, including the IRA, which had by now adopted the tactics of political agitation. Others included campaigners for social justice, especially in relation to the allocation of council houses, and for political reform. One case of council house allocation made headlines in the summer of 1968 when a house in Caledon, County Tyrone, was allocated to a nineteen-year-old unmarried Protestant girl, Elizabeth Beattie. Dungannon Rural District Council controlled local housing allocation and this home was one of a new development of fifteen on the edge of Caledon. However, a local councillor and businessman appeared to decide who would be given houses and anyone wanting a home had a better chance of success if they patronized the councillor's business. That he did not do so meant that Constable Nugent of Caledon RUC Station had little chance of being given a house, even though his wife had recently given birth.

The Beattie case was a catalyst for NICRA. Although it was seen as unjust to deserving Catholics and Protestants alike that a young single woman should be so favoured, it was the Nationalist and Republican supporters of NICRA who took action and a family squatted in the house before Beattie could move in. When approached by Sergeant Ivan Duncan, the Halligan family refused to leave and the matter was referred to higher authority. Once again there was political intervention; police were ordered to remove the squatters, even though this was a civil matter.

> There was little legislation at the time against squatting, and we had to go back to the Government of Ireland Act (1846) to get the law to evict the Halligan family. The Act had been used against starving Irish peasants during the Great Famine, and I thought, 'The English landlords got away with it then, but will they now?'[5]

Media interest in the case mushroomed but the Halligans eventually came out willingly, gave a press conference and departed. However, they returned later and more protests ensued. One family member was arrested but subsequently released without charge. Later Austin Currie, a young Nationalist politician, and some friends took over the house but departed in haste when Miss Beattie's brother and several friends broke down the front door with a sledgehammer. The Beattie family then took possession. That ended the squatting but Sergeant Duncan was ordered to prepare a file for the prosecution of Currie, a move that the Sergeant regarded as being due to political pressure. Currie was convicted under the 1846 Act of 'unlawful entry and failing to vacate the premises on request'.[6] However, the publicity gained by NICRA was enormous.

NICRA had decided to follow the lead of American civil rights leader Martin Luther King by organizing street demonstrations and planned a march from Caledon to Dungannon on Sunday, 24 August. On the Friday evening, Currie was told by police that the march would not be allowed into Market Square where a rally was planned. This decision had been taken because Paisley had organized a counter-demonstration. Not for the last time police officers were placed in the middle of an unpleasant situation; while officers and tenders blocked off the approach to Market Square a large crowd of jeering Paisley supporters stood behind them. Fortunately the day ended relatively peacefully although there were some injuries.

The Caledon–Dungannon march provided the template for another demonstration planned for Londonderry on Saturday, 5 October over a route from Waterside railway station, along Duke Street to Craigavon Bridge and thence via Carlisle Road and Ferryquay Street to The Diamond. There was no intervention from Paisley on this occasion but the Apprentice Boys of Derry applied for permission to march over the same route at the same time. William Craig, the Minister of Home Affairs, then banned all marches in the city but NICRA was determined to go ahead and loudspeaker-equipped cars toured the city on the Saturday morning to drum up support for the march. Police reinforcements, including the Reserve Force, arrived in the city. Faced with Craig's blanket ban on marches in the city the police were obliged to try to enforce that ban when the most sensible tactic would have been to allow the march but to reroute it away from Carlisle Road to John Street and then via Foyle Street to Shipquay Place. In fact, County Inspector George Paul Kerr had written to Headquarters recommending that the march be allowed to go ahead. Once again politicians had ignored the informed opinion of a senior policeman.

Soon after moving off, the marchers met a police cordon and were advised that the march was illegal. Marchers were remonstrating with police when fighting began. Television pictures indicate that it may have started when one officer used his baton but before long a baton charge had begun. The German military expert von Moltke once said that no plan survives first contact between opposing troops and the same is true of attempting to police a demonstration once a baton charge takes place. Gerry Fitt, MP for West Belfast, was injured and arrested but others were more fleet of foot and left the scene rapidly. Water cannon were deployed and police also moved in at the rear of the marchers. Rioting ensued that lasted for several days although the Duke Street clash was short-lived.

The negative publicity of the Duke Street encounter was to plague the force well into the future. Although the sole TV cameras in Duke Street were from RTE, the Irish national broadcasting company, pictures were beamed across the world. Still pictures were added including those of a senior officer who was hitting a young man with his blackthorn stick. And the young man happened to be a journalist. In the aftermath of this day it was obvious that the police had to move into the age of instant news; that officers would have to be trained to deal with the media on a professional basis, presenting the police case in a logical fashion and as openly as possible. It was a lesson that many other forces throughout the British Isles were also learning as the sixties came to an end.

There had been many previous occasions when rioting had lasted over two or three days; it was almost a matter of course that such would be the case. But, although the situation in Londonderry was beginning to ease in the next week, agitation and street demonstrations continued. Another march was planned at which there was a confrontation at the city end of Craigavon Bridge but, after a token breaking of the police cordon, it carried on into the walled city. However, any hope of respite for police officers was short-lived as NICRA organized further demonstrations and Paisley countered them. Armagh was the venue on 30 November and Paisley, with some supporters, protested to the police. If it were not stopped they promised 'appropriate action', an attitude that the Cameron Report later described as 'aggressive and threatening'. The Armagh march was allowed to go ahead and Paisley announced a counter-demonstration. Although police intended to cordon off Armagh and allow the NICRA march to proceed unimpeded, this plan was pre-empted when Paisley and his supporters positioned themselves on the route an hour after midnight. During the morning there was the surreal spectacle of a religious service, complete with hymns, while supporters carried weapons that included baulks of timber and nail-studded sticks. Police seized over 200 weapons, including two revolvers, billhooks and improvised stabbing instruments but the Paisleyite crowd increased to some 1,000 people who were blocking the NICRA route. The counter-demonstrators refused to move when asked to do so by a senior officer after which it was decided to divert the NICRA march. This decision was accepted and NICRA organizers kept unruly elements on the march under control while police were able to keep both sides apart. There was one brief outbreak of trouble, although a cameraman was knocked unconscious by a Loyalist wielding a lead-filled sock.

That winter seemed to be one of march after march. Craig attempted to ban all marches in Londonderry but his ruling was broken regularly with local police unable to enforce it. Although O'Neill introduced a package of reforms that answered many NICRA demands, this was not enough for some. Those reforms included suspending Londonderry Corporation, a body considered responsible for many injustices (especially for ensuring that political control of the city was kept in Unionist hands), a points system for allocating houses, partial repeal of the Special Powers Act and a proposal to change electoral legislation to end the property qualification, thereby granting the demand for 'one man, one vote'. Eddie McAteer MP, leader of the Nationalist Party, now Stormont's official opposition, described the package in words that would haunt him, and lead to his political demise; 'half a loaf's better than no bread'. When O'Neill went on television on 9 December to appeal directly to the people of Northern Ireland in what became known as the 'Ulster at the crossroads' speech, NICRA leaders called off street protests and it looked as if peaceful resolution might be possible.

Among those not happy with O'Neill's package was a group of students at Queen's University, Belfast who had established an organization called People's Democracy (PD). These students were radical and, in keeping with the radical theme permeating Europe at the time, indifferent to religious affiliation and thus included both Catholics and Protestants. Against the advice of NICRA leaders and many politicians, the students' group planned to march from Belfast to Londonderry over four days beginning on 1 January 1969.

This march must rank as one of the most irresponsible ever in Northern Ireland. The route chosen seemed to be intended to inflame Unionists and it was not long before marchers were being attacked. Although there was a Reserve Force escort, there were scuffles between marchers and counter-demonstrators; the police escort was insufficient to ensure total security for the students. Some six miles outside Londonderry, marchers were ambushed at Burntollet on the last section of their trek. In the city, where demonstrators awaited their arrival, tension was high following a Paisleyite rally the previous evening. Stones were thrown at marchers who alleged that police failed to protect them. Indeed there were accusations of police assisting ambushers and that Specials were among the latter. Certainly the police present could do little to prevent the ambush; they were too few in number and the attackers had the advantage of higher ground while the policemen were tired after several days of duty without relief. Among the many stories from the Burntollet ambush, which became a Nationalist cause célèbre, is one alleging that a minister joined in the ambush. The unfortunate cleric was named by rumourmongers in the city, but the author can testify to the fact that the minister was a decent man who lived out his Christian beliefs, held no animosity for anyone and was not a stonethrower at Burntollet.

The tragedy of that January day was that it further eroded relations between police and Nationalists. Reports of the Burntollet incident, and of further attacks as the marchers neared the city, led to rioting in the city centre. That rioting continued into the night in the city centre and the Rossville Street/Lecky Road area, already becoming known as the Bogside. About 300 people were injured. The subsequent Cameron Report criticized the 'breakdown of discipline' that occurred; at one point some officers were said to have smashed windows in the Bogside area. But the police were faced with an almost impossible task and the manner in which they had been treated by the Ministry of Home Affairs over many years was now having its effect. There were too few officers to deal with the unrest. For too many years the members of a small force had effectively increased their numbers by working long hours – often nearly twice those of the average worker and always at least half as much again. This had acted as a form of 'force multiplier' but the policy could be effective only in a normal policing situation. It could not be so in an abnormal one, and such was already the case in Northern Ireland. Police officers were exhausted, often had no idea when they would get home – one Reserve Force platoon worked fifty-four consecutive hours covering the People's Democracy march – and human beings will make mistakes in such circumstances. Tempers are bound to be fraught and individuals more easily provoked.

The situation was exacerbated by the inadequate public order training given to police. Again the RUC was not the sole force in this predicament, although circumstances meant that it faced the problem in its worst manifestation before any in Britain. Protective equipment was pitiful with officers donning a steel helmet, of Second World War vintage, and carrying a short riot shield, of which there were not enough in store so that officers sometimes had to 'borrow' bin lids to use as shields. A hasty effort was made to rectify the situation with training courses based on Scotland Yard training films and new equipment was ordered. But the films dealt with a situation the RUC was unlikely to meet: where the numbers of police on duty were such that they could push good-humoured demonstrators into position. Thus the RUC was forced to develop its own tactics for public order duties. New helmets were issued but these were not full-face, being variants of motorcycle safety helmets, and riot shields continued to be short, leaving lower legs unprotected; many chose to wear footballers' shin pads.

Needless to say, many officers had been injured and significant numbers were on sick leave. The most common injuries had been inflicted by pieces of paving stone or by petrol bombs; the Northern Ireland street rioter had not taken long to discover the Molotov cocktail and there was certainly an element of IRA organization in the use of such weapons. Burns from petrol bombs caused serious injury and left scars whilst paving stones could cause massive bruising at best or broken limbs at worst, the penalty of the short shield. When disturbances broke out officers were called in to duty and men were moved from one part of the province to another, not knowing when they might return home. At times, some areas were left with no police cover while local police were driven off to deal with a sudden outbreak of rioting elsewhere. In spite of all the strain, however, morale remained high, the sense of camaraderie from shared danger compensating for the absence from home and loved ones. A few officers resigned but their numbers were insignificant and not enough to cause concern.

January 1969 had begun with the People's Democracy march and continued with a large NICRA demonstration in Newry during which there were signs that the more hotheaded civil rights demonstrators were in the ascendant. When the Newry marchers met a police cordon NICRA stewards were pushed aside by some marchers who then overturned seven police tenders; some were set on fire and others shoved into the canal. The Ministry of Home Affairs was now faced with a bill for new tenders; many policemen hoped that the new vehicles might have heaters.

The political situation had not settled and, on 3 February, O'Neill took the gamble of calling a general election. Sir Albert Kennedy resigned as Inspector General next day and was succeeded by his deputy, Anthony Peacocke. Highly educated, Peacocke had joined as a cadet in 1932 and was regarded as a good officer who spoke his mind honestly. But he would prove to be the wrong man to head the force at this crucial time since he believed that direct police action was the answer to the problems on Northern Ireland's streets. Nor did he endear himself to civil rights campaigners when he pointed to IRA involvement in the campaign, although he did not consider another IRA shooting war to be imminent since the civil rights campaign was achieving its aims. Some days later a mobile patrol in south Armagh was fired at and Peacocke announced that policemen on border duty would henceforth be armed and increased.

O'Neill's general election, held on 24 February, resulted in victory for the Prime Minister with a majority of the thirty-nine Unionists returned being his supporters. The radical People's Democracy had stood in nine constituencies, gaining 26.4 per cent of the vote but no seats. It was a different story for prominent civil rights campaigners with John Hume, Ivan Cooper and Paddy O'Hanlon returned as Independents and unseating Nationalists, including Eddie McAteer who lost his seat to Hume; his 'half a loaf' comment had been his political death warrant. No Paisleyite candidates had been elected although there were ten anti-O'Neill Unionists with another two unclear about their allegiance. Although no radical People's Democracy candidates were elected, one of their supporters, Bernadette Devlin, won a Westminster by-election for Mid-Ulster on 17 April, becoming the youngest woman ever to sit in the Commons. A few days later O'Neill announced that 'one man, one vote' was to become the standard for local council elections. But O'Neill's days in office were drawing to a close and his efforts to bring stability to Northern Ireland were doomed.

NICRA lost some of its founding members in March 1969 and it seemed that the militants, both Republicans and People's Democracy, were in control and eager to seek confrontation. Then came a series of terrorist attacks on utility targets – an electricity substation at Castlereagh on 30 March, a water pipeline in the Mournes and an electricity pylon in Armagh on 20 April, a pipeline from Lough Neagh on 24 April and yet another at Annalong on 25 April. At first, RUC Headquarters believed the attacks to have been carried out by the IRA but they were actually the work of the UVF. O'Neill announced the mobilization of 1,000 Specials and the arming of all police officers, except those on traffic duty. Soldiers were deployed to guard other possible targets; an additional infantry battalion was brought into the province to meet the new demands. However, officers continued to work at full stretch although, at long last, the Government had agreed to pay overtime, which provided a welcome boost to morale although hardly compensating for the hardship endured and the long hours of dealing with disorder.

Londonderry saw another outbreak of street violence on 19 April that lasted through the night and into the Sunday; over 200 policemen were injured. Civilian casualties included members of the Devenny family, injured when police pursued rioters who ran through their William Street home and escaped over the rear wall of the house. Samuel Devenny received head and internal injuries and was detained in hospital for some days. His death from a heart attack some months later was attributed by local politicians to his having been beaten by police officers. However, many people in the city were thoroughly disenchanted with what was happening on their streets and very angry with the rioters. One Catholic businessman told a sergeant that the police would do 'Derry a favour by machine-gunning some of them'. Doubtless, had police followed his intemperate advice he would have been one of the first to condemn them.

Violence became routine and the addition of the bombings made O'Neill's position untenable. He resigned, or as he put it himself, was blown out of office on 28 April. His successor – his cousin, Major James Chicester-Clark – tried to calm the situation by announcing an amnesty for everyone involved in violence, except those responsible for explosions. But whatever hopes he had of stabilizing Northern Ireland were smashed completely when the summer marching season began. To release RUC officers for public order duties some Specials were mobilized to provide cover in Protestant areas but, even with this additional manpower, the police were overstretched. The traditional marches on 12 July were very tense with outbreaks of violence in Belfast and Londonderry. When a Nationalist mob attacked an Orange hall in Dungiven, County Londonderry, police tried to stop them while Specials fired shots over a crowd leaving a dance hall. A man injured in the Dungiven clash died later and, once again, the death was blamed on police, which further increased tension.

Another increase in force establishment was announced but the immediate need for more manpower could only be met by mobilizing still more Specials, which led to further Nationalist criticism. One of their constant shibboleths was that the Ulster Special Constabulary was a sectarian organization that allowed no Catholics in its ranks. This was not true; although most Specials were Protestant there were some Catholics in the force, including some in Londonderry. At the end of July a group of Labour MPs travelled to Belfast to meet Peacocke and were vocal in criticizing RUC tactics, policies and the alleged misconduct of officers. They offered no positive suggestions for a force suffering from the greatest public disorder burden ever piled upon a police force in the British Isles and from the long-term effects of a government that had starved it of funds and kept manpower so low that the RUC was now threatened with being overwhelmed. The MPs' visit only added to the propaganda war being waged against the RUC, a war that the force was losing. And another round in that war was approaching with the Apprentice Boys' annual commemoration of the Relief of Derry due to be held on 12 August. A meeting between Chicester-Clark and the Home Secretary, James Callaghan, whose father was a Munster man, took place a few days before the Boys' march and it was made clear that no police from Great Britain would be lent to the RUC, even though such inter-force manpower loans are standard practice in England, Wales and Scotland. However, an under-strength company of soldiers was deployed from Palace Barracks to Castlereagh. In that deployment may be seen a suggestion that matters were moving out of RUC control.

The Minister of Home Affairs, Robert Porter, a Derryman, decided that the march could go ahead but some 700 police were to be deployed to Londonderry. Appeals were made for restraint in the city but others appeared intent on fomenting trouble. At a public meeting in St Mary's Girls' School in Creggan, the Derry Citizens Defence Committee outlined plans to deal with the 'Twelfth'. These included the use of 'the stone and the good old petrol bomb' while another platform speaker proclaimed that 'every policeman's a Paisleyite and every Paisleyite's a policeman'. The second speaker went on to say that the only difference between a policeman and the average Derryman was that the former was paid fifteen guineas a week and the latter fifteen pounds. Few in the audience seemed aware of the patronizing nature of such a comment.[7] One speaker from the floor claimed that 'over two hundred B-men go over Creggan Heights at four o'clock every morning'. Quite why such a number of Specials would want to carry out this exercise was not explained. Faced with what can only be described as bigotry, calls for restraint had little chance of being heeded. One such call, from John Hume, was made on the specious basis that if the march passed off without incident the government could never again justify banning a civil rights march.

The march's early stages were peaceful but, in the afternoon, as bands and Apprentice Boys marched through Waterloo Place, stones were thrown. It seemed as if some who had been determined to create trouble were about to succeed. Stewards tried, to no avail, to restore peace but stocks of stones, in wheelbarrow loads, had been prepared as had petrol bombs; many local people lost their milk bottles that morning as rioters built up their armoury. Before long, there were angry, and nakedly sectarian, clashes and police struggled to prevent them spreading. One Catholic man, identified because he was wearing a Pioneer pin, was attacked by a group of Loyalists; only the intervention of a Protestant friend of the victim and the appearance of a solitary policeman saved him from a beating.

Thus began what has become known as the 'Battle of the Bogside'. Even the early rioting was worse than anything seen before and it was soon obvious that this was no ordinary disturbance. That evening, the Deputy Inspector General, Graham Shillington, who had personal experience of the city, arrived to assess the situation. Following a meeting with County Inspector Gerry Mahon and District Inspector Michael McAtamney in Victoria RUC Station, Shillington went to the main trouble spot at the Sackville Street/Little James' Street junction. Buildings were blazing and exhausted policemen were struggling to keep rival mobs apart. But many officers were so tired that they could hardly move and had to sit or lie on the pavement. Others, with no weapons to use against the mob, had resorted to returning stones that had been hurled at them. And, of course, the story that swept through Nationalist areas was that police and Loyalist rioters were working together. Shillington decided that the police would have to use CS gas.

On his return to Victoria, Shillington received a phone call from the Minister of Home Affairs. Porter listened to Shillington's account and agreed that CS gas could be used, but that a loudspeaker warning should first be given. This was done, although whether many heard the warning is debatable, and, as Tuesday became Wednesday, the first canisters of gas were fired. Although it caused an initial dispersal of rioters, it also blew back on the police and those who did not have respirators suffered severe discomfort from the sharp gas. Those with respirators were almost worse off. They were choking and many had to remove their masks. It transpired that the soldier who had given them a hurried course in using respirators had neglected to point out that cardboard packing in the filter would have been removed.

Shillington remained in the city overnight to monitor the violence, which intensified throughout the hours of darkness. Reports came in of a catapult device on the roof of the Rossville flats, from which stones and petrol bombs were also being dropped. Barricades had been constructed to prevent a police 'invasion' of the Bogside. But there was no intention of entering the Bogside. Shillington's main concern was to confine rioting to that area and protect the city centre, which had already suffered considerable damage. Throughout the whole period of these disturbances, Shillington provided calm and courageous leadership to his embattled officers. As dawn broke he made a personal reconnaissance of the area. Any hopes that he might have entertained that fighting would diminish, or peter out, during the night were dashed. He walked part of the city walls, overlooking the Bogside, and then toured the edge of the barricaded area. Since the rioting showed no signs of abating he gave authority to several teams of police to use gas to prevent rioters from overwhelming their positions.

On his return to Victoria, Shillington contacted Peacocke to tell him that he believed it would be necessary to deploy the Army in Londonderry within twenty-four hours. Troops were already in HMS *Sea Eagle*, the former Ebrington Barracks, and, once the order was given, could move quickly on to the streets. Peacocke, however, continued to believe that the police could control the situation. He wanted to deploy the Ulster Special Constabulary but Shillington opposed this, since the Specials had not been trained for public order duties and would be an unknown quantity. Their use would also increase antipathy from Nationalists and provide propaganda for those with a more sinister agenda. And so Peacocke delayed asking for troops, allowing his officers to suffer more than another twenty-four hours of constant turmoil. Men were hit by bricks and paving stones, and suffered severe injuries; others were exhausted but found no opportunity for rest, while the city's few policewomen performed miracles in feeding their colleagues and acting as nurses. The worst injuries were sustained by those hit by petrol bombs. These deadly devices had the capacity to kill and Sergeant Ivan Duncan and Constable Charles Graham, both natives of the Republic, were fortunate to survive being set on fire. Ivan Duncan was the target of a petrol bomb thrown from the top of Rossville flats and a photograph of him as a human torch went around the world.

> I . . . started to run with this long trail of flames behind me. It may have actually saved me more than anything else, because my running drew the flames away from my face and I could breathe. My colleagues pulled me down to the ground, started to roll me over and threw their coats over me to blank out the flames. By this time, the rioters sensed blood and came in for the kill. The pictures clearly show missiles all around me and an armoured 'pig' in the background . . . I was pulled to my feet and someone shouted to me, 'Run!'[8]

Unfortunately, with face burned and eyelids almost sealed tight, he ran in the wrong direction, straight towards the mob. Then he was knocked unconscious by a missile that smashed in his helmet. At this stage his colleagues drew their revolvers to threaten the crowd, which pulled back, allowing him to be rescued. (Nearby, when another group of officers was later cornered by a mob, a sergeant drew his revolver and fired some shots to effect an escape; one rioter was wounded in this incident.) Ivan Duncan was driven to Altnagelvin Hospital for treatment; the officer driving the vehicle was Constable Victor Arbuckle who would be murdered in Belfast less than three months later.

Charles Graham, better known as Carol to family and friends,[9] was also saved by the actions of his comrades. He was hit as officers withdrew from a confrontation in William Street. As the last man in his section to fall back he was facing the rioters and using his shield to deflect missiles. One petrol bomb missed him completely as he ducked out of its path, another he was able to deflect and the bomb burst nearby but a third struck the shield and sprayed him with blazing petrol. Fortunately, his comrades rolled him on the ground and used a coat to extinguish the flames but he had suffered burns to his face. Next morning his daughter commented on what the 'bad men did to Daddy's face; they fried eggs on it'. It was some time before he was able to shave comfortably and even today he has to ensure that he uses plenty of water when shaving. These incidents were not unusual, and nor was the reaction of the officers; there was a fierce determination to protect colleagues and the camaraderie born of devotion to their role and honed by long hours of difficult duty over the past year was invaluable in sustaining those who served on the streets of Londonderry in those hot August days.

Finally, late in the afternoon of 14th, soldiers of 1st Battalion, The Prince of Wales's Own Regiment of Yorkshire marched into Waterloo Place, erected barbed-wire barriers and relieved the exhausted policemen. But the trouble was not over. In Belfast the situation was about to go out of control. Elsewhere, in response to the 'defence' organizers in Londonderry, rioting had erupted in Dungiven, Armagh, Newry and Dungannon. Belfast was worst since, with so much equipment and so many men committed in Derry, there were not enough vehicles to meet the demands placed on the force. So bad was the situation that attempts were even made to get forty-year-old vehicles into working order. Once again, the RUC was paying the price for penny-pinching by civil servants over the years.

Harold Wolseley, Belfast City Commissioner, and his deputy, Sam Bradley, had wanted troops placed at their disposal some two weeks before but had been unsuccessful. Now they considered the situation so serious that it required special measures. Believing the IRA was about to rise in arms in an effort to overthrow the government, they sought Peacocke's approval to fit heavy machine guns to the few available Shorland armoured cars. The Shorlands deployed, the machine guns were fired and by morning four Catholics had been shot dead while a Protestant had been shot and killed by a rioter; his was the first death from gunfire during this spasm of unrest. The machine guns had been counter-productive; the police were now unable to control the situation in Belfast. Wolseley, a quiet, almost shy man, was horrified, especially when he learned that among the dead was the nine-year-old son of a former soldier. Another death was that of a soldier home on leave. In Armagh a Catholic man was shot dead by a Special on Cathedral Road.

In the hours following there was a frenzy of looting; houses were burned and families intimidated from their homes. Police were unable to prevent any of this. By now, troops were being rushed to Belfast, flown in from bases in England. By early evening police had been relieved in west Belfast but disturbances continued in the north of the city and there was more burning, destruction and death; two people lost their lives to gunfire. Finally, there were enough soldiers on the ground to separate the rival mobs.

The Army erected temporary barriers to keep apart rioters in Belfast, little knowing that these would become part of the sectarian landscape, known as the 'peaceline'. As exhausted officers returned to their stations it was time to take stock of what had happened. But the RUC was to be pushed into second place behind the Army. On 19 August the GOC, Northern Ireland, Lieutenant General Sir Ian Freeland was appointed Director of Operations. Freeland was now the law and order supremo for Northern Ireland. Sam Bradley later commented that the Army simply took over; it would be eight years before the RUC resumed its position as the principal agent of the civil power.

The earliest phase of unrest had been investigated by Lord Cameron and Northern Ireland was now to be subject to further judicial examination.

This time the investigation was led by Lord Scarman whose report rejected categorically Nationalist accusations that the RUC was a partisan force whose officers had cooperated 'with Protestant mobs to attack Catholic people' although it noted that mistakes were made and that 'certain individual officers acted wrongly on occasions'.[10] While Scarman stated that policemen had 'struggled manfully to do their duty in a situation which they could not control' and that their courage 'was beyond praise' he concluded that the failure to maintain control was not due to any failing of the RUC, nor from any lack of professional skill but from the fact that there were not enough officers and too much was asked of exhausted policemen.[11] Acknowledging that there had been a 'fateful split between the Catholic community and the police'[12] it was Scarman's opinion that the public assertion of no confidence by Catholic and civil rights activists had affected the thinking and feelings 'of the young and irresponsible and induced the jeering and throwing of stones which were the small beginnings of most of the disturbances'.[13]

With the Army committed so deeply, Callaghan took a close interest in what was happening in Northern Ireland and decided that the RUC had to be expanded; but he also wanted reform of the force. Paradoxically, one aspect that he considered needed reform was the control that the Minister of Home Affairs had over policing but, as Home Secretary, he exercised similar control over London's Metropolitan Police. Callaghan chose to set up a committee to study policing in Northern Ireland and appointed Lord Hunt, conqueror of Everest in 1953, to chair that committee with the other members being Sir James Robertson CBE, Chief Constable of Glasgow, and Robert Mark QPM, the last Chief Constable of the City of Leicester and now a senior London officer who would later become Commissioner of the Metropolitan Police; there were two assessors, Alec Baker from the Home Office and Victor Morrison from the Ministry of Home Affairs while the secretary to the committee was Paddy Westhead, a senior Home Affairs civil servant.

Hunt worked quickly and took only six weeks to produce his report, which made forty-seven recommendations. These included disbanding the Ulster Special Constabulary, which was to be replaced by an RUC Reserve, fully integrated with the force, and the Ulster Defence Regiment, which was to take over those military-style duties that had so often fallen to the RUC and Specials. Hunt saw the Reserve as the equivalent of the Special Constabulary in Britain with its own rank structure paralleling that of the regular police. This was never implemented and the RUC Reserve was made up entirely of reserve constables; another difference was that Specials in Britain are unpaid whereas the RUC Reserve was to be paid. The force was to be disarmed – in practice it had operated unarmed in recent years anyway – and was to be expanded, with a central recruiting organization to bring in new officers. There would also be closer links with other British forces, training for RUC officers at Bramshill Police College, opportunities for interchange with other forces and the adoption of the rank structure used in Great Britain. Hunt also recommended adopting the traditional blue uniform of the British 'bobby', thereby abandoning the rifle-green inherited from the RIC. Although the Committee considered changing the force's name, they decided that this was unnecessary since

> There are objections to all the alternatives we have heard and there is no certainty that a change would succeed in creating additional support for the force. To make one would be a blow to the morale of many members of the force, and would be unpopular with many of its supporters.[14]

Some days before the Hunt Report was published Peacocke was summoned to Stormont where his resignation was requested. He complied immediately. His had been the shortest tenure of command in the force's history but the most tumultuous and he had not been up to the job. He had read the situation wrongly, made poor judgements and, according to Scarman, acted as if the police were strong enough to maintain peace. Senior officers of that era concur with Scarman's assessment and agree that had Peacocke called in the Army sooner then the tragedy of August 1969, especially in the two cities, could have been avoided. Wolseley and Bradley had recognized the situation in Belfast for what it was, as had Shillington and other senior officers in Londonderry, but Peacocke had never shown the vision needed to be a chief officer under such circumstances.

Peacocke retired in October and his successor appeared in the form of City of London Police Commissioner Sir Arthur Young. Callaghan brought Young to Northern Ireland, clad in a City of London uniform with RUC badge on his cap and took him to Londonderry. A policeman for forty-four years, since the age of eighteen, Young had served in Britain and overseas, with experience in the Gold Coast, the Malayan emergency and Kenya during the Mau Mau rebellion. In spite of Callaghan's Irish family background, Young's appointment contained more than a hint that Northern Ireland was being treated as another colonial liability rather than as part of the United Kingdom. Young soon proved to have no real understanding of the complexities of Northern Ireland's political situation but believed that he had and was apt to make contradictory promises to different groups. His attempts to introduce a new RUC uniform met with considerable opposition. In cavalier fashion he decided that blue uniforms should be worn and a stock of such garb was brought in for issue to serving officers. It soon became apparent that these were cast-offs from English forces and there was anger among officers who were used to good quality uniforms, tailor-made for each individual – one of the few things that had been positive about the Ministry of Home Affairs' treatment of the force.[15] A petition from officers who refused to wear the 'new' uniform was delivered to Brooklyn and Young experienced antipathy on the ground when he went out to stations to persuade officers to don blue. Michael McAtamney believes that he might have succeeded had he taken longer to introduce a blue uniform and ensured that the new clothing was of a quality equal to that which it replaced. Eventually a compromise was reached on the uniform. Senior officers, from the rank of District Inspector up, and policewomen wore a bottle-green uniform rather than rifle-green and it was decided to adopt this as the standard colour for all ranks; but it would be 1974 before the lighter coloured uniform was introduced. The new uniform would also see the demise of the RUC's black horn buttons – although these had been plastic for many years – to be replaced by an attractive black and silver design. A much better standard of cap badge would also be introduced, accompanied by similar collar badges.

One immediate problem that Young had to deal with was the existence of areas in Belfast and Londonderry where the RUC was not allowed to patrol. These 'no go' areas were controlled by defence committees, which even excluded civil servants from the Supplementary Benefits Commission from entering, an injunction that was soon lifted when it was realized that benefits might be affected. Barricades marked the boundaries of these areas, although the Army had persuaded defence committees to remove them in many places in favour of painted lines across which neither soldiers nor police could pass. In Londonderry the 'no go' area was known as 'Free Derry' and operated its own pirate radio station while the boundaries were 'policed' by vigilantes, some of whom used the opportunity to settle scores with neighbours. But the 'Free Derry' situation reached farcical heights when one defence committee representative asked that the Army respect 'Free Derry's air space'.

The Army was still enjoying what Freeland described as its 'honeymoon period' and arrangements were made for unarmed Royal Military Police (RMP) with their red forage caps to carry out some policing. In late-October agreement was reached that joint RUC/RMP patrols could enter the Creggan and Bogside areas of Londonderry and similar arrangements were made in Belfast. One of the best-known Catholic policemen in Londonderry, Constable Eddie Dolan, a native of County Fermanagh, was one of the first RUC officers to enter the former 'no go' areas and his photograph appeared in newspapers across the United Kingdom and further afield. Police posts and small Army camps were then set up within the former 'no go' areas but the defence committees still wanted restrictions on the RUC, demanding no plainclothes presence or police vehicles.

A fragile situation developed with beat patrols resuming but police being ever cautious. Political activists continued to try to make things difficult for the police and there were cries about previous RUC conduct, including the Devenny incident in Londonderry, which continued to be a matter of controversy. Relations with the Protestant community had also worsened and the announcement that the Ulster Special Constabulary was to be disbanded was received with dismay and anger. On 11 October, the night after the Hunt Report made that recommendation, there were protests on Belfast's Shankill Road that soon developed into riots. Police were unable to contain the rioters and the disturbances quickly developed into a gun battle between Loyalists and the Army. Spanning the period over midnight, hundreds of shots were fired and one found a policeman as its victim. Constable Victor Arbuckle, from Newtownstewart, County Tyrone, a member of the Reserve Force, was standing behind the Army lines when he was shot and killed by a UVF bullet. Soldiers of 3rd Battalion, The Light Infantry fired twenty-six rounds, killing two rioters.

Twenty-nine-year-old Arbuckle, married with two children, was the first RUC officer to be murdered on duty since Willie John Hunter almost eight years earlier. Tragically, he was not to be the last. And as with Willie John Hunter, Victor Arbuckle was accompanied by two officers who would also die at hands of terrorists: Sergeant Dermot Hurley, a former Royal Navy man from County Wicklow, would die two years later while Constable Paddy McNulty would perish in 1977.

And so the sixties ended as they had begun: with a pall of violence over Northern Ireland and the RUC in the forefront of the battle to contain that violence. But this time violence would last for decades rather than years and RUC deaths would be numbered in hundreds. As 1969 gave way to 1970, however, there was no intimation that the future would be quite so bleak and many young people across Northern Ireland, and some from the Republic, were deciding that they could make a contribution to peace and stability by joining the Royal Ulster Constabulary.

Notes
1: Information from Mrs Biddy Scott, widow of General Scott.
2: O'Halpin, *Defending Ireland*, p. 300
3: Information from Ronnie Trouton MBE FIRSO, a courtesy driver and Secretary of ANICC, who was a member of the delegation that met Young.
4: Ernest Moffett died on 16 May 1984.
5: Duncan, op. cit., p. 85

6: Ibid., p. 86
7: The first speaker was a former IRA man who had been interned in the 1956–62 campaign, while the second speaker had a son who would later be convicted of the murder of an RUC officer.
8: Duncan, op. cit., p. 95
9: The diminutive, bestowed by his family, was a tribute to King Carol of Romania.
10: *Scarman Report*, Ch 3.2, p. 15
11: Ibid., Ch 3.10, p. 17
12: Ibid., Ch 3.5, p. 15
13: Ibid., Ch 3.6, p. 15
14: *Hunt Report*, para. 141, p. 34
15: They did, however, scrimp on the cap and collar badges, issuing cheap plastic versions where once metal had been the norm. The supply of tailor-made uniforms was actually more economical in a small force than maintaining a stock of many different sizes of uniform.

Chapter Five

Bombs and Bullets;
Death and Destruction

During the winter of 1969–70 Sir Arthur Young mounted a public relations campaign with the community and with the force itself. However, his habit of making often contradictory promises to various groups soon earned him the doubtful soubriquet of Sir 'Artful Tongue'. Behind the scenes, planning was underway to implement the changes recommended by Hunt. Although much has been said and written about the more recent *Patten Report*, this was not as far reaching as Hunt's work. The changes wrought by Hunt were dramatic, although they stopped short of a name change. For the officer on the ground the effects of Hunt were seen in the new structures introduced at the beginning of June 1970. Many Hunt recommendations were enshrined in new legislation, the Police Act (Northern Ireland) 1970, which came into effect on 1 June. Out went the traditional ranks of Head Constable, District and County Inspectors, City Commissioner, Deputy Inspector General and Inspector General. Out, too, went the old counties and districts, also inherited from the RIC.

From June 1970 those who had been Head Constables removed their forearm badges and replaced them with two or three stars – or 'pips' – on their shoulders; Senior Head Constables now wore three pips as Chief Inspectors while all others wore two as Inspectors. District and County Inspectors became Superintendents and Chief Superintendents; henceforth the abbreviation DI in Northern Ireland would denote a detective inspector. Belfast's City Commissioner became an Assistant Chief Constable (ACC) while the Deputy Inspector General and Inspector General became the Deputy Chief Constable and Chief Constable. Although several sources suggest that Young took the rank of Chief Constable when he became the RUC's chief officer this is not so; he served his first eight months as Inspector General, the last person to hold that rank.

From June 1970 the principal unit of command became the territorial division, of which there were sixteen, denoted A to K – the letters I and Q were not used – plus Traffic Division; six divisions – A to F – were in greater Belfast while Headquarters was S Division. Each division was divided into subdivisions although L Division, in Fermanagh, had but one. Subdivisions were known by territorial designations or the name of the principal station. Across the province officers on patrol were no longer routinely armed in yet another attempt to make the RUC an unarmed force.

Hunt's recommendations had provided the starting point for a number of senior police officers from Great Britain seconded to assist in their implementation: Deputy Chief Constable Robert Boyes, Mid-Anglia Constabulary, Commander Jack Remnant, from London's Metropolitan Police, and former RUC man, Chief Superintendent Wilson Hill, then serving with Kent Constabulary. In January 1970 Boyes produced a report – *Establishment and Redevelopment of the RUC* – that outlined changes to be embodied in the Police Bill. These encompassed the rank and divisional structures, training and recruitment, and the aim of having 4,490 officers by 1975; the Depot would also be renamed the Training Centre. A new training organization would be created to deal with the great increase in numbers; Chief Superintendent John Hermon was appointed Training Officer to oversee that expansion.

The Ulster Special Constabulary ceased to exist on 31 March 1970 to be replaced by the Ulster Defence Regiment, which was to take over those military duties previously performed by the Ulster Special Constabulary. To support the RUC in its policing role a new force of special constabulary was created but the name 'specials' could not be used and so was born the RUC Reserve. Hunt had recommended that this be organized in the same manner as special constabularies in Britain with its own rank structure but it was decided that, to allow better integration with the regular force, there should be only one rank, that of reserve constable. The title RUC Reserve might have created confusion with the Reserve Force had this not also undergone a name change, becoming Special Patrol Group (SPG). It was planned that the Reserve would number some 1,500 and, with the regular force expanding to almost 4,500 officers, provide much more operational flexibility. Given the difficulties suffered in the recent past, even this number of regular officers was small, although it was intended that reservists could relieve regular officers in the event of disorder that required deploying a large number of police to a particular area.

However, the most dramatic change of all was the final breaking of the shackles of the Ministry of Home Affairs. Hunt had recommended the establishment of a police authority, as was the case with forces in

Great Britain, with the notable exception of London; membership should reflect the different groups in the province in proportion to their size. PANI, the Police Authority of Northern Ireland, was created under the Police Act and held its first formal meeting on 29 June. It was 'responsible . . . for the establishment and maintenance of an adequate and efficient police force'. The first Chairman was one of Northern Ireland's most distinguished surgeons, Sir Ian Frazer, a man regarded highly by all who knew him and with an impeccable record as a doctor in peace and war.

The first summer of the new-look RUC was a period of cautious optimism. But there were already signs that some did not want normality. After the summer 1969 violence in Belfast, graffiti accusing the IRA of cowardice appeared on walls in the city: the initials IRA were said to mean 'I Ran Away'. The organization had become more than a joke among Nationalists; it was now an object of mockery. But Republicans were determined to change that and saw the Army's presence as an opportunity to swing Nationalist opinion in their favour: the Army represented the 'old enemy' and could be portrayed as an occupation force more easily than the RUC. Towards the end of 1969 a split occurred in the IRA with the traditional wing claiming the title 'Official' and the breakaways styling themselves 'Provisional' IRA. The latter provoked violence on a low scale on a regular basis in Belfast and Londonderry from early March and created a confrontation with soldiers in Belfast over Easter 1970, drawing the Army into using stronger tactics that gave rise to cries of brutality. Freeland called for reinforcements in April and announced that petrol bombers might be shot.

At the end of June there was widespread rioting in Londonderry when Bernadette Devlin gave herself up for arrest, following conviction for her part in the previous summer's disturbances. That rioting rocked the city for a weekend. Soldiers confronted mobs and the usual hotspots in and near the city centre again suffered. During that weekend, on 26 June, three men and two children died in a house in Creggan's Dunree Gardens as a result of the men trying to make a bomb in the kitchen.[1] The resulting explosion caused devastation and also created the Provisional IRA's first 'martyrs'; the human sacrifice of innocent children was overlooked. Carol McCool was only four years old while her sister Bernadette was nine; their father was one of the three IRA men who perished. Military policemen had tried, unsuccessfully, to enter the blazing building in a rescue bid. The Londonderry violence was mirrored by another outbreak in Belfast following an Orange Order march that passed close to Catholic homes. Five men were shot dead and another died of wounds two days later. Three of the dead were shot in a gun battle around St

94

Matthew's Catholic Church in East Belfast. All but one of the dead were Protestant.

As we have seen there had been earlier confrontations between soldiers and rioters in Londonderry, Belfast and elsewhere. Even the 1970 Eurovision Song Contest victory of Londonderry's Dana was marred by rioting with youths attacking soldiers of 1st Battalion, The Gloucestershire Regiment. That the Glosters wore steel helmets painted oxford blue – which, like rifle-green, appears black – with their drab-coloured combat uniforms led to local Republicans dubbing the regiment 'the Black and Tans'. Every effort was made to stoke up hatred and create turmoil on the streets. And yet, by day, RUC officers were patrolling throughout Northern Ireland, although there were some restrictions on night-time foot patrolling.

The Provisional IRA made its first bomb attack on 31 January 1970 when a hole was blown in a wall of Brown Square RUC Station in Belfast. Further attacks did not materialize until the summer with the first being a device that exploded without warning at a bank in Belfast's High Street; thirty were injured, two of them seriously. On a night of torrential rain a bomb exploded at the Royal Navy recruiting office in Belfast and two policemen were left to secure the shattered remnants of the building from looters. One was a recruit recently posted to Queen Street RUC Station who would become the RUC's last Chief Constable.

Inevitably, one of these attacks was going to cause death and that is what happened when the next bomb exploded. This was intended to take lives, specifically those of RUC officers. In August a car stolen in Newry was abandoned about a mile from Crossmaglen, County Armagh. The theft was reported to police who then learned that the stolen car had been spotted on the Lisseraw Road. On 11 August Constables Samuel Donaldson and Robert Millar from Crossmaglen RUC Station drove out to investigate. One of them opened a front door, thereby switching on the interior light which immediately detonated the bomb, about twenty pounds of explosive. Both officers were blown over a hedge into a field. The blast was heard by their colleagues in Crossmaglen. A local priest and a district nurse arrived and tried to comfort the men until an ambulance came to take them to hospital in Newry. However, both died within hours of each other the following day. The Provisional IRA had claimed its first RUC victims but the atrocity caused only revulsion in Crossmaglen. At that time the village was not a hotbed of Republicanism and local police were well known and respected; both dead constables would have been known by name to many of the population. Wreaths were sent from Crossmaglen to the funerals and the village paid its own tribute a month later when a memorial Mass was celebrated for the dead officers. In the Catholic tradition many churches have what is known as a month's mind Mass and this is what was organized for Samuel Donaldson and Robert Millar. Chief Superintendent Michael McAtamney, commanding H Division, which included Crossmaglen, attended the service. Constable Donaldson had joined the RUC in 1966 while Constable Millar had only recently been posted from the Depot. In February 1985 Samuel Donaldson's brother, Chief Inspector Alex Donaldson, was one of nine officers murdered in an attack on Newry RUC Station.

Relations between Nationalists and the Army were deteriorating in spite of an active 'hearts and minds' campaign by the latter. As the Provisional IRA grew stronger it was better able to manipulate events to suit its own propaganda purposes and stories about brutality from soldiers were increasing. At the beginning of July, soldiers of the Royal Scots searched a house in Belfast's Lower Falls area and found some weapons and ammunition. A riot followed which led Freeland to order the sealing-off of the area and a curfew on its inhabitants. For three days violence convulsed the area and soldiers from three battalions were deployed. Thirteen soldiers suffered gunshot wounds, another five were injured by bomb or grenade splinters and many more were hurt by bricks and other missiles. Three civilians died from gunshot wounds sustained in battles between the Army and members of both IRA factions; a fourth man was killed after being struck by an armoured personnel carrier. Many more weapons had been found but the overall effect had been to increase Nationalist antipathy towards the Army and further the IRA's aims.

There were fewer street disturbances over the summer but the IRA remained active, with the High Street bomb and the double murder near Crossmaglen clear indicators of their intentions. On 4 September an IRA member was killed by his own bomb while attempting to destroy an electricity transformer in Belfast. Petrol bomb and bomb attacks on police officers' homes underlined the dangers, as did the murder of a man due to give evidence in court in a hijacking case. That murder prompted the move from jury trials to single-judge courts in terrorist cases. There were also incidents at police stations, the Brown Square bombing being the worst, and officers began to feel particularly vulnerable. When plain-clothes patrols were deployed in Belfast to look for bombers the officers were unarmed and, therefore, an unlikely deterrent to any terrorist. In August the Chief Constable established a working group to examine the problem of arms and produce recommendations. This was followed by a ballot within the force that returned a narrow majority against re-arming. However, with government approval, a limited issue of arms was made to stations for their protection; the principal weapon provided was the Browning automatic shotgun, a five-round weapon that could be devastating in spite of its age. Supplied from military stocks these were probably the oldest weapons in the Army's inventory.

Sir Arthur Young retired in November 1970, having served just over a year. His successor was Graham Shillington, his Deputy, who had great experience in policing Northern Ireland and would have been a much more suitable man in command in 1969 than the unfortunate Peacocke. Shillington was an intelligent, highly educated Cambridge graduate with a passion for policing. But his appointment was unpopular in Nationalist circles since he was the son of a former Unionist MP; some Nationalists seemed to believe that it was impossible for him to be impartial. In his memoirs, the late Field Marshal Lord Carver described Shillington as 'respected, pleasant but ineffectual'.[2] Carver was being unfair to a man who did much for the force at a very difficult time. Michael McAtamney recalls that Shillington was a 'decent man, a good organizer' who was not an egotist and was 'always prepared to listen' to others. In fact, Shillington proved an excellent chief officer in one of the most trying periods of the RUC's history. His own statement when he took command was an extremely accurate forecast of his tenure.

> My job is to consolidate the considerable achievements which have already taken place and to see to it that the Force which I command is one which constantly becomes more effective and efficient in its work and one which its members and the population at large can respect and admire.

Shillington could not have taken over in more trying circumstances. Both IRA factions were intensifying moves towards an all-out campaign of violence. RUC/Army relations were not good and there was considerable distrust; the Army continued to hold the view that the force was unreliable. Sharing of information was rare and each organization tended to guard jealously its own sources. One dispute was over guarding police stations and with more responsibility for this role handed to the police, the level of arms available to the RUC was increased. The threat to officers also meant that flak jackets were provided; these were Second World War vintage and of limited use against the high-velocity weapons that would soon appear in the terrorist armoury.

As the New Year of 1971 dawned the Republican campaign of violence was increasing. Riots were a regular occurrence with gunmen making frequent appearances from the cover of mobs. In such circumstances on 6 February the Army suffered its first fatality from violence when Gunner Bobby Curtis was killed by a fluke shot during riots in Belfast; another soldier later died from wounds. Almost three weeks later, on 20 February, two policemen were shot dead in similar circumstances. Detective Inspector Cecil Patterson, of Special Branch, died with

Constable Robert Buckley when terrorists opened fire with sub-machine guns from the cover of a rioting mob at Alliance Avenue in Belfast. Cecil Patterson, a native of County Cavan, had over twenty years' service and had seven commendations. Robert Buckley was a Special Patrol Group member with thirteen years' service; he was married with two young daughters. SDLP leader Gerry Fitt described Cecil Patterson as an officer who had always acted impartially. His funeral was attended by members of the Gardai and London Metropolitan Police. As a result of these deaths Graham Shillington telephoned Brian Faulkner to say that

> he was withdrawing all unarmed patrols in Belfast and was issuing revolvers to any RUC men going out on duty. It was the effective end of hopes that the RUC could operate as an unarmed 'English Bobby' style police force.[3]

Intense rioting was now a feature of both Nationalist and Unionist areas and was becoming almost a nightly occurrence. Once again, Freeland warned that petrol bombers faced being shot but there was no easing of the pressure. Belfast was subjected to bomb and arson attacks and then, on 10 March, occurred the worst act of cold-blooded violence yet perpetrated when three young Scottish soldiers, two of them teenage brothers, were abducted and murdered by the IRA. Such was the outrage felt at this triple killing that detectives from Scotland Yard were brought to Northern Ireland to assist the investigation. No one was made amenable for the crime and the Scotland Yard team departed with much less publicity than had greeted their arrival.

By the end of March, Northern Ireland had a new Prime Minister, Brian Faulkner succeeding James Chicester-Clark who resigned on the 20th. By then, also, almost three-dozen incidents of shooting at police officers had been recorded across the province. The argument for re-arming police was unassailable. Such was the level of terrorist violence that a campaign to introduce internment was launched. Police vehicles began to be fitted with basic protection against bullets and blast. With shots having been fired at marked police cars it was also decided to remove roof signs from patrol cars. Another telltale sign of a police car, the single black-hooded spotlight above the front bumper, was also to be removed over time while new cars were to be ordered in colours other than the standard blue. Soon the only conspicuous police cars on Northern Ireland's roads would be those of Traffic Division.

Tension mounted as the days grew longer. Each clear evening offered opportunities for more violence and gun attacks. On 25 May a suitcase bomb was thrown into Belfast's Springfield Road police station. Not having made a reconnaissance the terrorists did not know, or did not care, that there were civilians in the reception area. Patrick Gray, his daughter Colette and neighbour Elizabeth Cummings, with her four-year-old son Carl, were seated there when the bomb was thrown. One account of what happened next suggests that Sergeant Michael Willetts, of 3rd Battalion, The Parachute Regiment, pushed both children into a corner, shielding them from the blast, which killed him instantly. As a result, Willetts was awarded the George Cross posthumously. Inspector Ted Nurse, who received the George Medal, believed that Willetts actually tried to escape from the reception area and was killed by a cabinet.[4] Brian Faulkner wrote that Nurse 'was seriously injured while shielding some children from the blast'.[5] The subsequent behaviour of a crowd of youths outside the station was an indication of how far people can be blinded by hatred. These young people jeered and shouted obscenities as Willetts' body and stretchers bearing the wounded were carried from the station. Twenty-two people were injured, among them a two-year-old whose skull was fractured.

Further terrorist incidents led to more clashes between soldiers and rioters, especially in Nationalist areas where IRA efforts to provoke confrontation were having ever more effect. During one such confrontation in Londonderry on 8 July a civilian, Seamus Cusack, was shot and wounded after dashing into the line of fire of a soldier who was about to shoot at a gunman; the wounded man was trying to retrieve a helmet as a souvenir. Cusack's injury might not have proved fatal had his companions not taken him for treatment to Letterkenny, over twenty miles away and, then, by a poor road, stopping en route to get him a drink. Further rioting the next afternoon, partly in protest at Cusack's death, led to the death of another man, Desmond Beattie, who was also shot by the Army. Because the government would not grant an independent inquiry into these deaths the SDLP withdrew from Stormont. The Irish government backed the SDLP claim that both men had been shot in situations that involved only stonethrowing, which does not explain the explosions heard on the afternoon of Beattie's death. At this time there were many shootings at police or soldiers from the cover of mobs and soldiers were always on the alert for possible gunmen. In another incident in Londonderry in the same week, gunmen fired several shots from Butcher Gate along Butcher Street at policemen in the Diamond. When firing broke out no policemen were in the line of fire but a fifty-six-year-old widow was walking along the street and was fortunate not to be shot. She ran towards the Diamond where a policeman dashed into the firing line and dragged her to safety, placing himself between her and the gunmen. The policeman's action was witnessed by the author; the woman was his mother.

By now any hope of restoring normality had all but died. There was certainly no possibility that the RUC could become a force of unarmed 'Bobbies' in the English mould – and that image owed more to television than to real life since many English forces had serious image problems and were unwelcome in many inner city areas. But Northern Ireland's situation was about to worsen. Already few days passed without incident somewhere in the province as the IRA campaign 'reached an unprecedented level of ferocity'.[6] July saw 'more explosions, more shooting incidents, more injuries to civilians, policemen and soldiers than in any previous month of the crisis.'[7] Although the traditional parades on 12 July passed off relatively peacefully, in spite of ten explosions over the route of the Belfast parade that injured nine and damaged many buildings, by the end of the month there had been over 300 explosions and some 320 shooting incidents across Northern Ireland since the beginning of the year. Those first seven months of 1971 saw fifty-five violent deaths and over 600 injuries. There was much anger in the community and especially amongst Unionists who demanded that the government take firmer action against the terrorists. Brian Faulkner, the GOC – now Lieutenant General Sir Harry Tuzo – and Graham Shillington held long meetings to see if any tactical improvements could be applied. 'But the message was beginning to come through that there was only one major unused weapon in the government's anti-terrorist arsenal – internment.'[8]

Faulkner was reluctant to implement internment and had argued against its use when Chicester-Clark was Prime Minister. His chief concerns were that it was a last resort in any democratic society and that the 'no go' period might have 'undermined the RUC intelligence on which any successful internment operation' would be based.[9] In March thousands of shipyard workers had demanded that all known IRA leaders be interned while some senior Army officers had also argued for the measure in April. Chicester-Clark had asked that Special Branch and Army Intelligence draw up a list of potential internees. By July Faulkner had even received representations from prominent Catholics to intern those who were holding Nationalist areas to ransom; he had had letters in similar vein from housewives in places such as Andersonstown.[10] Neither Faulkner, Shillington nor Tuzo wanted internment but were faced with the impossibility of getting witnesses prepared to go into open court to give evidence against terrorists, such was the level of intimidation. By mid-July the die had been cast and the decision made to intern Official and Provisional IRA suspects. Home Secretary Reginald Maudling urged Faulkner to 'lift some Protestants' if this was possible but there was little to suggest that Loyalists were organized terrorists at this time. Over 500 suspects were to be detained to 'strike a crippling blow' to both IRA wings. On reflection, Faulkner considered that a more selective operation, akin to that mounted on previous occasions, might have been more effective.

In the early hours of 9 August police and soldiers carried out

100

Operation Demetrius, taking into custody 337 men, ninety-seven of whom were soon released. But, although a successful operation, the results and reaction had the opposite effect to that planned. Riots broke out in Nationalist areas, Nationalist politicians issued statements condemning the move, barricades were erected and gun battles broke out. Even an evacuation of 'refugee' women and children was organized. The world's media seized on the Republican version of events and internment was portrayed as another piece of Unionist anti-Catholic bigotry. In short, the introduction of internment was a failure in political terms. Matters were not helped when it was alleged that some internees were treated to in-depth interrogation that amounted to torture. A subsequent official inquiry described the interrogation as 'ill-treatment' rather than torture, but the propaganda damage had already been done. It is worth noting that the 'ill-treatment' was something that was an integral part of training in escape and evasion for aircrew and other service personnel. The propaganda battle had already been lost, however, within days of the arrests when several prominent IRA leaders held a secret press conference in Belfast to proclaim that their organization was unaffected by internment.

Events on the streets seemed to support that particular claim as incidents increased in the later months of 1971. So, too, did the quantities of arms and explosives seized. Nationalist politicians, especially the SDLP, abrogated leadership in favour of going with the Republican tide and rushed off to Dublin to meet Jack Lynch, the Republic's Prime Minister. A campaign of civil disobedience was planned, with Lynch's support, and an alternative parliament, at Dungiven, was cobbled together. Catholics were urged to quit public life and most Catholic politicians began boycotting local authorities and public bodies, even where there was little or no political content in their work. Once again Nationalist areas of Belfast and Londonderry became virtual 'no go' areas for police and Army, with only limited military patrols under cover of darkness. Barricades were manned by armed IRA members; that organization imposed its own rule inside barricaded areas.

Since the GOC was still Director of Operations, the major role in internment had been taken by the Army, supported by the RUC. Much of the blame, however, was laid at the door of the police, especially Special Branch, by Republicans and Nationalists and, sadly, the scene was set for some of the worst months in Northern Ireland's history. Attacks on police increased and on 18 September two officers were shot in Strabane. Twenty-year-old Constable Roy Leslie was wounded fatally while Constable Reg Waterson survived the attack, although wounded. They had left the RUC Station at Bowling Green just after midnight and were shot almost as soon as they reached Abercorn Square. One of the first officers on the scene, Constable W. Browne, told the subsequent inquest that there was no heartbeat from Constable Leslie.[11] Although officers continued to patrol in pairs, they were ordered not to stay too close together so that it would be more difficult for terrorists to kill or injure both members of a patrol. Roy Leslie was the sixth RUC man to die since 1969, equalling the number murdered in the 1956–62 campaign.

Less than a month later, on 15 October, Constables Cecil Cunningham and John Haslett were carrying out security surveillance from a car when they were fired upon by the occupants of another car. Both men were killed. Cecil Cunningham was forty-five years old while John Haslett was only twenty-one. Twelve days afterwards, a call to a fire at a farm near Toome was responded to by police. The call was a false alarm, designed to lure police into an ambush in which Sergeant Ronald Dodd was shot dead. Another attack followed only two days later when Chichester Road RUC Station was demolished in a no-warning bomb attack. Inspector Alfred Devlin was sitting at his desk when the bomb went off; he died as the building came down around him. A burglary at a boutique in Andersonstown on 1 November brought two detectives to the scene. Both men, Detective Constables Stanley Corry and William Russell, were then shot dead. Only ten days later another two officers died in similar circumstances in an off-licence at Oldpark Road in Belfast. Sergeant Dermot Hurley and Constable Thomas Moore died instantly when terrorists fired on them. Fifty-year-old Dermot Hurley was a native of County Wicklow and had been on duty with Victor Arbuckle on the night the latter was murdered by Loyalists on the Shankill Road. A Royal Navy veteran of the Second World War, Sergeant Hurley had met and married a Londonderry woman and decided on a career in the RUC.

Eleven policemen had died in 1971, the worst year in the history of the RUC, bringing the death toll since 1969 to fourteen. A review of the unarmed force policy was prompted and Shillington advised the Police Authority of the need to arm officers, a move to which the government gave its consent. Walther pistols were to be issued for personal protection with automatic weapons being supplied to protect police stations. That these were personal protection weapons was emphasized by the fact that no holsters or belts were issued; officers had to provide their own. In principle the force remained unarmed. As an interim measure, Webley .38 revolvers were issued to officers; some were still carrying these in 1974. Recent recruits had received no firearms training but still found themselves issued with weapons. Norman Hamill arrived at Strabane to be told that he would have to carry a revolver and was given only the most rudimentary instruction in its use.

Protests against internment ushered in another new year but there was little optimism as 1972 dawned. Twelve days into the year, Reserve

Constable Raymond Denham, at work in his civilian employment at Waterford Street in Belfast, was murdered by two gunmen. He was the Reserve's first fatal casualty. In the wake of his death many reservists were given firearms certificates for personal protection weapons.

Less than two weeks later, on the morning of 27 January, Sergeant Peter Gilgunn and his section left Victoria RUC Station in Londonderry to relieve the section in Rosemount RUC Station, which had been under virtual siege since August. The five officers were travelling in a blue Cortina which, although unsigned, was clearly a police car. As the car climbed Creggan Road, known locally as Rosemount Hill, on the final stage of its short journey, it had to pass a mews lane and then Helen Street, both blind entries. From the lane appeared a gunman who fired at the car. Then, from the mouth of Helen Street, appeared two more gunmen, one with a Thompson sub-machine gun, who opened fire. Seventeen bullets struck the Cortina with many penetrating it. Sergeant Gilgunn was mortally wounded while Constable David Montgomery was killed; Constable Charlie Maloney was wounded. The death toll might have been worse had the driver not accelerated coolly out of the killing zone towards Rosemount RUC Station. A soldier on duty in a watchtower at the station fired four rounds at the attackers but was too late in doing so. Peter Gilgunn, a twenty-seven-year-old Cavan man and fluent Gaelic speaker, survived until the car reached the station where he died. Peter Gilgunn and David Montgomery were the first RUC officers murdered by the IRA in Londonderry and the first policemen to die at the hands of terrorists in the city for over fifty years.

Local reaction to the double murder was enlightening. Although people were shocked and disgusted, there was little public show of sympathy for the dead men. Nationalist Party leader Eddie McAteer, who lived close to the murder scene, issued a statement that the killings were 'a direct result of involving the police force in para-military activities'. The local Stormont MP, the SDLP's John Hume, remained silent although his colleague Ivan Cooper described the murders as 'dastardly'.[12] Peter Gilgunn was a Catholic and his requiem Mass took place in his parish church, St Patrick's at Pennyburn, two days later. The church was far from crowded, the majority of the congregation being police officers, and the Catholic Bishop of Derry, Dr Neil Farren, was noticeable by his absence; a representative was sent in his place. Hume was also absent. Following the Mass, Peter Gilgunn was buried in Kilkeel, his wife's home village. (This first murder of police officers in Londonderry is often overlooked by Nationalists who prefer to remember the events of the following Sunday when soldiers of 1st Battalion, The Parachute Regiment shot dead thirteen people in the city following an anti-internment march. Bishop Farren led the obsequies for the dead of that day.) David Montgomery had been engaged to a local girl and had asked to remain in Londonderry until after their marriage. He was only nineteen.

The events of the following Sunday have created much controversy in the years since, as well as two official inquiries, many books, documentaries and even two films. It also undoubtedly caused many young men to join the IRA, as had the introduction of internment, and drove even deeper the wedge between Nationalists and the RUC. However, it is important to remember that the handling of the march was principally an Army responsibility and that the advice of Chief Superintendent Frank Lagan, commander of N Division, was to allow the marchers to reach Shipquay Place but to note the names of the organizers for prosecution. Had his advice been heeded, the tragedy of what was instantly dubbed 'Bloody Sunday' by Hume would never have occurred. (The march had been banned under a blanket government order.)

One effect of the Bloody Sunday shootings was the prorogation of the Stormont parliament on 24 March after Brian Faulkner's government refused to hand security responsibility to London. Thereafter, Westminster took full control of Northern Ireland and Prime Minister Edward Heath appointed William Whitelaw as Northern Ireland's first Secretary of State. 'Direct rule' had begun.

The day after the murders on Creggan Road, Constable Raymond Carroll, a twenty-two-year-old car enthusiast, was working on his car in a friend's garage on Belfast's Oldpark Road when he was gunned down. Accomplices of the murderer were jailed for conspiracy but the gunman fled to the Republic. It was obvious that police officers were targets at any time, whether on duty or off; personal security was becoming a major issue. This had not been so in the previous IRA campaign, except for the murder of Norman Anderson in 1961, which, as Eunan O'Halpin notes, presaged IRA tactics in this new campaign. The murders of Raymond Denham and Raymond Carroll indicated a clear policy of targeting specific officers and attacking when they were most vulnerable and off guard.

Sergeant Thomas Morrow was shot and seriously wounded at a Camlough factory on 29 February. He died on 2 March. Less than two weeks later, on 14 March, the IRA ambushed a joint police/military patrol and wounded Constable Billy Logan, a twenty-three-year-old Londonderry man, who succumbed the following day. He was buried from his family home in the Fountain area of his native city on St Patrick's Day. Billy Logan's family was to suffer further tragedy less than a year later when his sister's husband was murdered. Three days after Billy Logan's funeral, an IRA bomber abandoned his car with a primed bomb on board, in Belfast city centre. At the time a bomb alert was already holding up traffic and the car exploded without warning, killing eight people and injuring 146. Among the dead were Constables Ernest McAllister and Bernard O'Neill, who were trying to clear members of the public from the area around the *Newsletter* offices.

In the midst of this litany of death and destruction, police officers continued to provide a service to the public. 'Ordinary' crime had not disappeared, nor had Northern Ireland's road users learned to be any better. But pressures on the force were tremendous and there were still insufficient officers. To ease the manpower situation, members of the Corps of Royal Military Police were deployed to reinforce the RUC and the Corps' Special Investigation Branch (SIB) was assigned to assist CID. Although in many cases soldiers worked in harmony with police there were tensions, while Republicans claimed that the RMP presence was intended to oversee the police. But reinforcement of the RUC did not come solely from the RMP. Officers from Great Britain were offered attachments to the RUC and a number served in various stations, including some who had begun their police careers in the RUC but had transferred to obtain better working conditions. A further increment in manpower had been achieved by the virtual disbandment of Traffic Division, with all but motorway patrolling ceasing in the aftermath of internment. This proved a short-sighted decision as 1972 witnessed the rate of death and injury on Northern Ireland's roads soar to un-precedented levels.

At this most difficult of times, the role of policewomen was increasing. Since the creation of the Women's Branch, the RUC's women had always been a most important element of the force with a reputation out of all proportion to their numbers. Women officers dealt with a wide variety of duties, specializing in cases that involved women and children. While policewomen would perform points duty, court duty and deal with shoplifters, they also had to concern themselves with crimes of a sexual nature – prostitution, rape and indecent assault. A young girl walking home from work and being subjected to indecent exposure by a male could speak to a policewoman, which was a much less traumatic experience than having to discuss her ordeal with a man. The RUC's women dealt with their cases with great sensitivity and earned praise from all sections of the community, including clergy, probation officers, solicitors, fellow police officers, teachers, youth workers and distraught mothers and fathers.

In April 1971 there had been only about 100 women officers stationed in the major cities and towns of the province. As Branch numbers increased it became possible to extend the presence of female officers to other stations. Expansion also led to promotions as the Branch sought to attain the establishment recommended in the Boyes Report of 7 January 1970. Boyes had noted that

The proportionate strength of policewomen, some 2%, is well below that which is normal in England and Wales and is also below that which is considered . . . realistic for the effective policing of the Province by women officers. A very substantial increase is therefore recommended.

Boyes recommended that there should be 174 women officers, from constable to chief superintendent, by 1975. By the end of 1971 the force was well on its way to that target with 144 female officers; women served in all sixteen divisional headquarters. Expansion was being implemented and, for the first time, policewomen in a rank senior to sergeant were based outside Belfast. Maureen Boylan was posted to N Division as a Woman Inspector based at Victoria, Londonderry while Woman Sergeant Vera Mair and Woman Constable Hazel Hunter moved across the river to Waterside RUC Station to become the first policewomen based there in spring 1972. That the old days had not yet entirely gone was shown when the two officers had to clean the disused accommodation that was to be their new office. Shortly afterwards they were joined by a third officer, Woman Constable Joy Lindsay.

During this time also, Woman Constable Agnes Adair was becoming well known to schoolchildren throughout the Londonderry area as a result of her visits to schools to talk about road safety. Woman Constable Adair was a familiar and welcome visitor to local primary schools and her work with children played a part in her later award of the British Empire Medal.

Equality legislation meant that policewomen were to be paid the same salaries as their male counterparts from 1975. Although they were already on a par – being paid 9/10ths of the male salary for working the equivalent of 9/10ths of the male officers' hours – the new legislation meant equal value and equal hours. The RUC implemented the legislation in advance of schedule from late 1974.

1972 was the worst year in Northern Ireland's history, eclipsing the horrors of 1971. It had begun badly and would end with 483 people dead in the province as a result of terrorism and another thirteen in Britain or the Republic; the latter included a Garda inspector killed by a bomb on the Fermanagh border. However, there was an attempt to bring the conflict to an end that led to an IRA ceasefire in the summer. On 26 June, the day before that ceasefire began, Constable Samuel Houston, a twenty-two year-old who had been married for a year, was shot dead in Newry when he interrupted terrorists who were planting a bomb in a bar in Water Street. Spotting a car with registration plates obscured by tape and paper Constable Houston challenged the driver. As he tried to arrest the man he was shot three times by the other terrorists. Constable Houston was posthumously awarded the Queen's Police Medal for 'courage and devotion to duty in the highest traditions of the police service'.

The ceasefire broke down following a sectarian clash engineered by the IRA in Belfast. Soon the IRA was again targeting police officers and eighteen-year-old Constable Robert Laverty was killed on 16 July when his police vehicle was ambushed on the Antrim Road in Belfast. Robert Laverty, a native of Ballycastle, had been in the force for only eight months. Five days later a series of IRA bombs rocked Belfast on what came to be known as Bloody Friday. In about an hour some twenty bombs exploded and nine people were killed with another 130 injured. Among the dead were four Ulsterbus employees who died at Oxford Street bus station; one of them, fifty-seven-year-old Robert Gibson, was also a Reserve Constable.

Bloody Friday caused widespread revulsion and was a considerable tactical setback to the IRA, although the organization claimed that it did not intend to cause casualties but only widespread disruption. An attempt was made to blame the authorities for failing to pass on warnings but warnings had been passed on and police had tried desperately to shepherd people to safety. The fact that there were many hoaxes made matters more difficult for officers on the ground who, at one point, were dealing with twenty-one bomb warnings, of which twenty were genuine. A police spokesman described the situation as 'a nightmare in the true sense of the word'.

In the aftermath of Bloody Friday, William Whitelaw took the decision to retake the 'no go' areas of Belfast and Londonderry. On 31 July the Army launched Operation Motorman – Operation Carcan in Londonderry – in the largest military operation since Suez in 1956. Resistance was almost non-existent but was followed by one of the worst atrocities of the conflict when the IRA left car bombs in the quiet village of Claudy, County Londonderry, killing six people, including a nine-year-old girl, and injuring many others, three of whom later died. The bombers had tried to phone a warning from Dungiven but IRA bomb damage to Dungiven and Claudy telephone exchanges had prevented them from doing so. By the time police in Londonderry received a warning the first bomb had already exploded. Although the IRA subsequently denied the attack, few in Northern Ireland doubt that they were responsible. It is now believed that a Catholic priest, the Reverend James Chesney, was involved with the IRA unit that bombed Claudy and was probably its leader.

As the terror war continued Northern Ireland was sinking ever deeper. A Loyalist vigilante group, the Ulster Defence Association (UDA), had been formed and the UVF remained active. Although the Army was able to deal with the UDA's overt vigilante presence, that organization continued in being and began to develop as the Loyalist parallel to the IRA, organizing its own network of control, complete with kangaroo courts; both groups would spawn protection rackets and organized crime. Sectarian tension was higher than ever and the year was marked by many sectarian murders. Of the 483 deaths in Northern Ireland that year, 106 were sectarian with seventy Catholic and thirty-six Protestant victims. This could have been even worse had speculation that a Catholic priest played a major part in the Claudy bombing come to light; the consequences for innocent Catholics might have been horrendous, especially when one considers the particularly brutal nature of some Loyalist killers. At the time of the thirtieth anniversary of the Claudy bombing, it was suggested that police had suspected Chesney of involvement in the atrocity but that there had been a cover-up between the force and Cardinal Conway, then head of the Catholic Church in Ireland. This must remain as speculation until files covering the case are made public, which may not be until the centenary of the event.

Gathering intelligence to blunt the operations of sectarian murder gangs was especially difficult because of witness intimidation. To counter the killers a special task force was established in late 1972, which included joint patrolling by RUC and RMP personnel as well as a dedicated detective group from CID and SIB. The creation of the new 'murder squad' was announced by Whitelaw on 6 December. Another initiative introduced during the year was the confidential telephone that allowed individuals to pass information to the police without compromising their identities or personal safety. While much useful intelligence was garnered through this system it was also open to abuse for malicious purposes, or use by terrorists to draw police or soldiers into traps.

It was October before another policeman lost his life. The circumstances of the death of Detective Constable Robert Nicholl were especially tragic. He was shot after failing to stop at an Army checkpoint at Castle Street, Belfast on 13 October. At the time he was off-duty and accompanied by an Army staff sergeant. The Ministry of Defence later paid an undisclosed sum in damages to the dead policeman's family; his father was also a policeman. Only four days later a Traffic motorway patrol stopped a stolen car on the M2 near Belfast. As the occupants were being searched one drew a gun and shot Constable Gordon Harron, wounding him seriously. Constable Harron died on 21 October; he was awarded a posthumous Queen's Police Medal. Gordon Harron's killers were Loyalist terrorists, from the Ulster Freedom Fighters, a cover name for the UDA, possibly intent on murdering Catholics, and the man who fired the shots was later sentenced to death; his sentence was commuted to life imprisonment by William Whitelaw. This decision caused considerable anger in the RUC.

Reserve Constable Joseph Calvin became the Reserve's third fatal casualty when he was killed by a bomb under his car on 17 November. Constable Calvin, who died instantly, had just come off duty in Enniskillen; his car had been in a public car park close to the town's police station. Fermanagh was also the scene of the next IRA murder of a police officer when Constable Robert Keys, aged fifty-five, was killed in Belleek RUC Station when the warhead of an RPG7 rocket, fired from across the border, penetrated the wall of the building and struck him in the chest. This was one of the first occasions on which terrorists had used this shoulder-launched Soviet anti-armour missile. Two more RUC officers would die before the end of the year, together with a member of the Police Authority.

James Nixon was only five months away from retirement after thirty years' service when he was murdered in Belfast on 13 December. Constable Nixon had been attending a social function at the Chester Park Hotel on the Antrim Road. As he left an IRA gunman, hidden behind a hedge, fired up to thirty shots at him, hitting him in the back and killing him instantly. His twelve-year-old daughter had a nervous breakdown while a son who had followed his father into the RUC suffered stress and collapsed on duty; he subsequently resigned. James Nixon's widow later worked in a cross-community scheme for deprived children. On 15 December Constable George Chambers, a father of six, was shot dead by the Official IRA in Lurgan's Kilwilkie estate. With two other officers he had been delivering Christmas presents to an eight-year-old Catholic schoolgirl who had been injured in a collision involving a police vehicle; the presents had been bought with the proceeds of a collection at Lurgan RUC Station. As the four policemen drove out of the estate they noticed a stolen car and, fearing that it might contain a bomb, began evacuating nearby homes. As they did so, at least six gunmen opened fire, hitting three officers. As the injured fell to the ground one IRA man came out of cover to stand over a policeman and shoot him at close range but ran away when the sole unwounded officer returned fire. The mother of the child to whom the policemen had taken the presents expressed her grief that their kindness had led to such a tragedy. She said that she believed the officers knew the risk they were taking and added that she would have preferred them to have sent the presents than to have 'such a terrible thing happen'. A local man was jailed for life in 1974 for murdering George Chambers. During the court case it was revealed that the shooting was opportunistic; the men had been given guns to rob a local factory and their attack on the police had been against Official IRA policy, that organization having ceased such attacks earlier in the year.

On 18 December William Johnston, a Police Authority member, a councillor in Armagh and a store owner was helping one of his staff measure a house in the Drumarg area for new carpet when both were kidnapped by the IRA and taken across the border to Monaghan. They were later brought back to Middleton in County Armagh where the employee was released and Councillor Johnston was murdered. He had been a member of PANI since its creation more than two years earlier.

This year of death and destruction had also seen the RUC celebrate its fiftieth anniversary in June while the Chief Constable was knighted in the Queen's Birthday Honours. In spite of all that was happening in Northern Ireland it was decided to mark the anniversary and Deputy Chief Constable Jamie Flanagan gave responsibility for the golden jubilee event to Chief Superintendent Jack Hermon, the Training Officer. Hermon considered the initial plans 'totally unrealistic and impractical' and told Flanagan so and was then told to make his own arrangements. Thus, on 12 June, the RUC celebrated its golden jubilee with a parade at which the salute was taken by Lord Grey of Naunton, the last Governor of Northern Ireland. The parade included officers from each division and unit within the force as well as the Reserve and Cadets; in all 176 officers marched past with Chief Superintendent Hermon commanding. Neither the Secretary of State, Whitelaw, nor the Chief Constable, Sir Graham Shillington, was present, the former because of 'pressure of business', the latter because he had suffered a heart attack.

Scarcely two weeks into 1973 the RUC suffered three deaths on one Sunday. On 14 January, Sergeant David Dorsett, a native of Wolverhampton who had served in the Royal Navy, met and married a local girl, and Constable Mervyn Wilson, whose wife was the sister of Constable Billy Logan, murdered at Coalisland in March 1972, died after a bomb exploded beneath Mervyn Wilson's car at Londonderry's Harbour Square. With two other officers, Cecil Davies and David Gray, all from Traffic Division but attached to N Division on ordinary duty, they were going home for a meal break. Such was the overcrowding in Victoria RUC Station that there was no room for private cars and many officers parked in Harbour Square under the eye of soldiers manning a nearby sangar. However, that afternoon, soldiers in the sangar were distracted by female IRA members while the bomb was planted under Mervyn Wilson's Ford Escort. The car had moved only a matter of feet when the device exploded beneath David Dorsett, killing him instantly. That day was David Dorsett's son's eighth birthday. Mervyn Wilson was so badly injured that he died in Altnagelvin Hospital as surgeons fought to save his life. Cecil Davies's injuries were believed to be so critical that he would not survive and David Gray had also suffered serious injuries, especially to one of his feet. However, both men did survive and returned to duty. David Gray later recalled that all his clothes except his underpants had been blown off in the blast but that his watch had not stopped.[13] Later that evening Reserve Constable Henry Sandford was killed when his Land Rover was blown up by a landmine on a mountain road between Pomeroy and Cappagh in County Tyrone. Another officer was seriously injured. With the deaths of three officers, that day was the worst in the RUC's history. The pain felt by officers in Londonderry at the loss of two respected colleagues was exacerbated by the behaviour of some local women outside the city's courthouse next morning. These women jeered, shouted abuse and generally celebrated the double murder, even singing their own grotesque parody of the 1960s' hit song 'Bits and Pieces', a reference to the fact that David Dorsett's body had been shattered by the explosion.

Two incidents cost the lives of officers in February. Both illustrated how simply doing his job put a policeman at risk. Constable Charles Morrison had gone to a traffic collision in Dungannon and was comforting an injured woman when he was hit in the back by a burst of machine-gun fire. He died almost immediately; a sub-machine gun was found nearby. A native of Ballycastle, Charles Morrison had joined the London Metropolitan Police before transferring to the RUC and was engaged to be married. Three Dungannon ministers issued a statement condemning the murder, which they described as 'the devil's work', and asked how humanity could sink so low as to murder a man carrying out an errand of mercy. On the 27th Constables Raymond Wylie and Ronald Macauley were shot while investigating a suspect car at Aghagallon near Lurgan. The gunmen were inside the car and Raymond Wylie was hit in the thigh as the policemen approached the vehicle but returned fire before being shot again and killed. Although hit in the chest Ronald Macauley engaged the IRA men for some fifteen minutes until they withdrew. He was taken to hospital but died on 25 March. Both were posthumously awarded the Queen's Police Medal. Some weeks later an Army patrol arrested one of the gunmen as he and another IRA man tried to cross the border with an elderly couple whom they had kidnapped and forced to drive them.

Although there continued to be many murders and terrorist incidents it was June before another police officer lost his life. Once again it was an officer carrying out routine duty. Constable David Purvis and a colleague were patrolling in Enniskillen on 5 June when two gunmen fired at them with Thompson sub-machine guns. At least twenty-five rounds were fired and David Purvis was wounded seriously, although his colleague had a miraculous escape. Constable Purvis, aged twenty-two and engaged to be married, died in a helicopter while being flown to Belfast for surgery. Before the summer was out another officer had been murdered, this time in Armagh. Reserve Constable William McElveen was shot dead at his civilian workplace, a factory on Cathedral Road where he was a security guard. He was approaching a car that had just pulled up beside the factory when the occupants opened fire, hitting him in the stomach. Witnesses later said that there had been four men in the car. Two months later, on 16 October, another Reservist, William Campbell, was murdered when gunmen fired on him and a second policeman on the Antrim Road in Belfast. The officers were checking the outside of the Capitol cinema when the killers struck. A twelve-year-old girl playing nearby was also hit in the leg. On the 28th Detective Constable John Doherty, a native of County Donegal, was shot dead while visiting his family at Ballindrait near Lifford. His girl-friend, who was in his car with him, was uninjured. Stationed in Omagh, John Doherty had been in the London Metropolitan Police but had transferred to the RUC in 1970 to be nearer home. At his requiem Mass at St Patrick's Church, Murlog, the Reverend Michael Flanagan said that John had left London for love of his home and his mother and that it was that 'same love which made him overcome the risks he knew he was taking when he crossed the border'.

Detective Constable Doherty's funeral was attended by a number of senior RUC officers, including Sir Graham Shillington who was about to stand down as Chief Constable, as well as representatives of the Garda. He was the first RUC officer to be murdered in the Republic. Two men, one a former UDR soldier, were later arrested for his murder but acquitted for lack of evidence. The murder of John Doherty illustrated the risk that citizens of the Republic took in joining the RUC. For many it meant exile as the IRA kept their homes under observation in the hope of mounting an attack. Whether the officers were male or female the risk was the same and it was best not to cross the border. The same applied to many Catholic officers who could not visit their families in Nationalist areas.

On 31 October 1973 Sir Graham Shillington left RUC Headquarters for the last time as Chief Constable. His successor was his deputy, Jamie Flanagan, who made his own piece of history on 1 November by becoming the first Roman Catholic to head the force. There were to be two deputies; the senior was Kenneth Newman, appointed from the Metropolitan Police; the other was Harry Baillie, a serving Assistant Chief Constable. Flanagan was a popular officer, the son of a policeman who had risen through the ranks and had been involved in RUC sporting circles. He may have been intended as a caretaker chief and a signal to Catholics that there was change in the RUC – although the fact that Flanagan had already risen so high suggested to anyone unblinded by

112

prejudice that Catholic officers had not suffered discrimination – but he soon established his independence, which did not enhance his popularity with either Police Authority or government. This would be especially marked during the IRA ceasefire that began at the end of 1974. Nor was he popular with the IRA who made several unsuccessful attempts to murder him.

In Flanagan's first two months as Chief Constable three RUC officers and a former officer were murdered. Constable Robert Megaw lost his life when his mobile patrol came under fire at the junction of Lurgan's Edward and Sloan Streets on 1 December. Twenty rounds were fired at the Land Rover from a vacant house. Robert Megaw was hit twice and died in hospital. Detective Constable Maurice Rolston of Special Branch was killed on the 12th when a bomb exploded under his car outside his Newcastle home. It was believed that the bomb had been placed while he was having dinner with his wife and three children. That same night two similar devices were planted elsewhere in County Down; one was spotted by its intended victim, a policeman, but the other exploded; its victim, also a policeman, lost a leg. Three days later the IRA claimed to have murdered another Special Branch officer but Ivan Johnston, who was kidnapped and tortured before being shot twice in the head, had left the RUC in October and was working as a lorry driver.

On 1 January 1974 the new bottle-green uniform came into use for constables and sergeants. Its introduction was not effected immediately and it was allowed to replace the old uniform on a gradual basis. Tragically, the first occasion on which one young officer wore his new uniform was for his own funeral. Constable Michael Logue was murdered by Loyalist terrorists in Belfast on 29 December 1973. As the twenty-one-year-old officer lay dying, terrorists stole his pistol. A Catholic from the Waterside area of Londonderry, Michael Logue was buried after requiem Mass in his parish church, St Columb's on Chapel Road. The church was packed but, once again, the Catholic bishop of Derry, Neil Farren, did not attend.[14] However, the president of Constable Logue's old school, St Columb's College, the Reverend James Coulter, was in the congregation, even giving up his seat to a policeman. Father, later Monsignor, Coulter, had a high regard for the RUC and was a friend of the local divisional commander, Chief Superintendent Frank Lagan, who had been a classmate of his at St Columb's in the 1930s.

As Northern Ireland looked back on 1973 there was little with which to be satisfied and no sign of an end to terrorism. However, there had been fewer deaths and explosions and never again would the province suffer a year as traumatic as 1972. Deaths dropped to 250 in 1973, of whom fifteen were either policemen or former policemen, as against the RUC death toll of seventeen in 1972. While the overall picture may have changed, the situation for the police was not very much better. One of their greatest difficulties was the widespread degree of intimidation; 3,656 cases had been reported in 1972 with 3,096 in 1973 while 1974 would bring another 2,453. Some stability had been achieved but there was much more to do and the RUC was still operating in a secondary role to the Army. A major police priority now became that of achieving primacy for the force in the security role, placing the Army in its correct position, that of aiding the civil power.

Another fifteen officers died in 1974, among them a much-valued Special Branch veteran, Inspector Peter Flanagan, who was murdered in an Omagh pub on 23 August. Sean O'Callaghan, from County Kerry, who later became a security forces' agent, was one of the gang that shot the forty-seven-year-old head of Omagh Special Branch. Another inspector died in 1974: William Elliott challenged armed robbers at Rathcoole in County Antrim on 6 September but was shot dead by them. He was posthumously awarded the Queen's Police Medal. Inspector Elliott's killers were members of the Official IRA.

The year had started badly with two reservists murdered in Glengormley and Londonderry. John Rodgers was on foot patrol with a colleague when a single shot was fired at them near a public house. Reserve Constable Rodgers, who had four children, was killed by that shot. Three days later, Reserve Constable William Baggley, a former Royal Navy man from Surrey and father of three, died when he and his colleague were ambushed on Londonderry's Dungiven Road as they neared the end of their patrol. Bill Baggley was hit and wounded and one gunman fired at him as he lay on the ground. This was the third successive year in which the IRA had murdered police officers in Londonderry during January. Four years later a local man walked into Strand Road RUC Station and confessed to involvement in a series of terrorist crimes, including having been a lookout during the murder of Bill Baggley. By then, Bill Baggley's daughter Linda, also an RUC Reservist, had been murdered by the IRA. This murder was condemned by local MP John Hume, then Minister of Commerce in the Northern Ireland executive.

Constable Thomas McClinton was shot five times in the head and back outside a Catholic church while on beat duty in Upper Donegall Street, Belfast on 2 March. He died instantly. One killer was only fourteen, an indication of how the culture of violence and hatred was corrupting young people. On 16 March Constable Cyril Wilson was shot and wounded while driving a Land Rover responding to a genuine emergency call near Craigavon. He died the following day. Among the mourners at Cyril Wilson's funeral was Sergeant Frederick Robinson. On the night of the 19th, at about 10 o'clock, he got into his Mini, which had been parked in his driveway at Glenkeen Avenue, Greenisland, to garage the car for the night. As he drove forward, a bomb exploded under the car and Sergeant Robinson was killed. His wife and three children were in the family home at the time. Less than a month later, on 16 April, Constable Thomas McCall was shot dead at a security barrier in Newtownhamilton, County Armagh. He was talking to a fellow officer who was driving through the barrier when he was hit. In a subsequent statement claiming responsibility for the murder, the IRA proclaimed its intention of intensifying its campaign 'against members of the occupation forces until there was a declaration of intent by Britain to withdraw from the North'. Thomas McCall was the fiftieth RUC officer to die since the conflict began; he left a wife and two baby daughters. Constables John Ross and Brian Bell were patrolling their beat at Finaghy on the outskirts of Belfast on 10 May when they were shot dead by IRA gunmen who had just got out of a car. Noticing one of the wounded officers moving, one of the gunmen walked back and shot him in the head at point-blank range. For John Ross's family it was the second such tragedy; his brother, Constable Henry Ross, had been murdered at Forkhill in July 1958.

On 18 June police in Lurgan were called to the scene of a possible bomb, having received a telephone warning that a device had been left at Market Street. A bomb was found in an entry off High Street but, while police searched for other devices, a second bomb exploded, killing Constable John Forsythe. This murder was followed by another IRA statement threatening further intensification of their campaign 'in a bid to force acceptance of the Provisional IRA demands for a just peace'. Further evidence of that intensification was provided on the 22nd when IRA gunmen opened fire on two police officers as they walked down Crumlin Road an hour before an Orange march was due to pass. Sergeant Daniel O'Connor was shot and killed when the gunmen fired from a passing car. His colleague and a civilian were also struck and wounded. Daniel O'Connor, a Catholic from Ballycastle, had joined the RUC in 1958; he was married with three children.

Peter Flanagan and William Elliott were the next officers to die, followed on 8 October by Reserve Constable Arthur Henderson who was killed when police were called to a booby-trapped car at Stewartstown, County Tyrone. Reserve Constable Henderson died instantly as he opened the car door. A colleague was slightly injured and a man standing nearby suffered severe injuries to head, eyes and ears. Another terrorist booby-trap, on 20 November, took the life of Constable Robert Forde at Rathmore, Craigavon. This bomb was planted between houses and exploded as Constable Forde was examining dwellings to assess damage from controlled explosions intended to destroy unstable explosives abandoned by the IRA. It was believed that the bomb was detonated by remote control and that earlier warnings about unstable explosives in the area had been intended to lure police or soldiers into a trap. Robert Forde, who had also served in the Royal Navy, left a wife and two children. The last policeman to die in 1974 was nineteen-year-old Constable David McNeice, who was killed en route to investigate a burglary at Killeavey in County Antrim. David McNeice was travelling in plain clothes accompanied by a soldier, Rifleman Michael Gibson of 1st Battalion, The Royal Green Jackets, when they were ambushed by the IRA. Nine rounds hit the policeman who died almost instantly from a chest wound. Rifleman Gibson, also in plain clothes, was wounded and died fifteen days later.

Another year had come to an end and Northern Ireland was weary of conflict. There had been times when it seemed as if civil war might not be far away and it is possible to consider the violence of this period as a low-level civil war. However, the brutal nature of 1972 had caused Northern Ireland's politicians to try to reach some form of accommodation that might allow the province to settle and bring an end to violence. Accommodation came following discussions involving the major parties in the province and representatives of the British and Irish governments at the Civil Service College at Sunningdale in Berkshire. The outcome was a new form of government for Northern Ireland in which Unionists and Nationalists could share power. Elections to a new Assembly had been held in June, as had a referendum on the border, the latter boycotted by the SDLP. The Assembly elections showed considerable support for both the Faulkner Unionists and the SDLP, these being the largest parties with twenty-two and nineteen seats respectively but Unionists had won thirty-two seats; the other ten had not pledged their support to Faulkner. There was also a strong Loyalist Coalition, led by Ian Paisley and Bill Craig, with eighteen seats; the Alliance Party took eight seats and Northern Ireland Labour one. From this result it was clear that the executive would be composed mainly of Faulkner Unionists and SDLP. In the end the Executive included six Unionists, led by Brian Faulkner, four SDLP, led by Gerry Fitt, and one Alliance member, Oliver Napier. Faulkner was chief executive with Fitt his deputy. Negotiations came close to breaking down, however, over policing. Paddy Devlin, one of the SDLP team at Sunningdale and a socialist, recorded that there was an impasse within the policing sub-committee at the talks. 'Our side of the policing sub-committee were proving intractable, especially when Hume had joined them.'[15] It was Devlin, a former member of the IRA, who asked Faulkner what he needed from the SDLP and was told that 'he needed the SDLP, his partners in government, to recognise and publicly support the RUC';[16] and it was Devlin who persuaded his colleagues to adopt a more accommodating stance. However, with the subsequent departure of both Fitt and Devlin from the SDLP the party followed the Hume line on policing.

The power-sharing Executive came into being on 1 January 1974 and many hoped that it would achieve a peaceful resolution to Northern Ireland's problems. But this was not to be. The SDLP had insisted on a Council of Ireland being part of the overall deal which allowed Loyalists to attack the agreement as leading to a united Ireland. In May a body called the Ulster Workers' Council (UWC) called a strike that caused massive disruption throughout the province and led to the Executive's downfall. Throughout the strike, the RUC was at full stretch trying to keep some semblance of normality but the new Labour government seemed unprepared to use the Army to confront Loyalists and unwilling to take over the power stations which were the key to the strike's success. Police protection was provided to power station employees who continued to work but there were not enough of them and it was the threatened collapse of the grid that brought matters to a head. Once again, opinion was polarized with Nationalists claiming that police had not done enough to confront Loyalists and remove roadblocks but Flanagan's assessment was more phlegmatic; he believed that the RUC had behaved well in the circumstances. Since there had not been a single example of a police officer supporting the strikers the force had held firm. Had any officers joined the strike, the consequences for the force could have been dire.

In the wake of the UWC strike and the fall of the Executive, Northern Ireland returned to direct rule under a Labour government with Merlyn Rees as Secretary of State. Rees had appeared to dither during the strike and his performance, combined with that of Harold Wilson, had done much to create support for the strike and convince Nationalists that their traditional view of Northern Ireland was right.

By this stage in the conflict the IRA had begun a practice of announcing a Christmas truce but there had been much speculation that a longer ceasefire might occur. Towards the end of 1974 this speculation began to harden, especially following talks between senior IRA figures and a group of prominent Protestants, including clergymen. True enough, a ceasefire was announced that would last for eleven days from 22 December. This was later extended, twice, and the government reciprocated by recognizing 'incident centres' set up by Sinn Fein, the IRA's political wing, through which government officials could maintain contact with the IRA to monitor the ceasefire. Civil servants were asked to volunteer as liaison officers with the incident centres and it was believed that office equipment for these was supplied from public funds. Jamie Flanagan was not convinced that the ceasefire was genuine and warned that the IRA was using it as an opportunity to reorganize while

117

the incident centres were only helping to strengthen the IRA grip on local communities.

Although the government would have preferred the police to take a 'softly, softly' line during the ceasefire, Flanagan felt that this was wrong and exercised his operational independence by ensuring that patrols were not cut back. In various areas patrolling was increased and particular attention was paid to unlicensed vehicles. Officers continued to visit schools to deliver road safety talks and Community Relations Branch maintained a high level of contact with local community groups and schools in Nationalist areas. The latter Branch had been created in 1970 and its members were to carry out excellent work throughout the years but not without loss since a number of Community Relations Officers were targeted and murdered by the IRA. One example of the type of work the Branch did involved a Catholic family who moved house on Christmas Eve 1973 and found themselves without gas in their new home – and therefore likely to be without a Christmas dinner. The family contacted the police to see if they could influence the gas company and, when a police request to the undertaking failed, a Community Relations Sergeant took a bottle-gas cooker to the family from his own home.

It soon became clear that the IRA's definition of the word 'ceasefire' differed from that of anyone else. For one thing, it appeared not to include RUC members as was evidenced by the murder of Sergeant George Coulter who was shot from ambush near Dungannon on 25 January; he died on the 31st. On 10 May, a beautiful Saturday afternoon, Londonderry was thronged with shoppers and the local railway society was running an open day at the old County Donegal Railway station on Victoria Road. Police officers were patrolling the city centre and two had been sent to the city walls overlooking Shipquay Place. The latter were leaning over the wall looking down at the crowds when a gunman opened fire from the back window of a nearby building overlooking the walls. Constable Paul Gray was hit in the back and died of his injuries. He was only nineteen and had not long been stationed in the city. As his body was carried to an ambulance a group of bystanders, including women and young girls, laughed, jeered and spat at him. The IRA claimed responsibility and made it clear that their ceasefire did not apply to the RUC. On 7 July police were called to a school in Lurgan where there had been a burglary. The crime had been carried out to lure police into a trap. When Detective Constable Andrew Johnston lifted the top of a desk he set off a booby-trap that killed him instantly.

However, the Provisional IRA were not the only Republican terrorists operating in Northern Ireland. In the latter part of 1974 the Official IRA's political wing Sinn Fein, The Workers Party, had fractured with a breakaway group styling itself the Irish Republican Socialist Party

118

1. The first Depot was at Newtownards in an old military training camp. The huts in the background had been temporary accommodation for soldiers in the Great War.
   (RUC GC Historical Society)

2. At Newtownards the RIC practice of training officers for colonial police forces continued. This group, pictured in November 1929, includes officers from Tanganyika, Fiji, Nigeria and Palestine. Scrabo tower is visible in the background.
   (RUC GC Historical Society)

3. In 1932 Amelia Earhart, the American aviatrix, became the first woman to fly solo across the Atlantic. She landed her Lockheed Vega in a field near Londonderry. Here her machine is under the watchful eye of three members of the 'Derry City Force'. *(RUC GC Historical Society)*

4. A constable whitewashing the police station under the careful eye of the sergeant. The crest of the RIC may be seen above the door. *(RUC GC Historical Society)*

5. The first traffic police took to the roads around Belfast in 1930, patrolling in motorcycle-sidecar combinations. Those first officers and their machines are seen in this picture. *(RUC GC Historical Society)*

6. Many officers of the 1930s were familiar with the illicit distillation of poteen and many stills were seized by the RUC. A sergeant and his section display their capture to a DI in this photograph. *(RUC GC Historical Society)*

7. The 1930s saw the closure of many former RIC stations while a building programme provided a number of new stations. It was during this decade that the familiar white rural RUC station, designed by English architect, T. F. O. Rippingham, came into being. This is Markethill RUC Station photographed in the late-1950s or early-1960s. A recruiting poster may be seen on the station noticeboard. *(RUC GC Historical Society)*

8. As well as providing accommodation for single men, stations also had married quarters which were usually occupied by the sergeant and his family. Sergeant Tom Carson, seen here with his wife, Rose, and their children, was the station sergeant in Dungiven. He retired in 1944 due to ill health and died in May 1945. Rose survived him for almost sixty years, dying in December 2003 at the age of ninety-nine. *(Mrs E. McDonald)*

9. During the 1930s the RUC had to deal with a number of outbreaks of rioting, usually of a sectarian nature. In this photograph a police Lancia caged car is seen in a Loyalist area of Belfast during a lull in the violence. *(RUC GC Historical Society)*

10. Sport was an important feature of police life and there was a special enthusiasm for tug-of-war, which had also been popular in the RIC. This is A District's catchweight team which won the British Police Championship in 1933, '34 and '35, as well as the AAA Championship in 1934 and '35. *(RUC GC Historical Society)*

11. The outbreak of war brought a change of pace to the force. By now the Depot had moved to Enniskillen but the familiar white façade had been stripped from the main building to make it less obvious from the air. This is a wartime recruit squad drilling with rifles. *(RUC GC Historical Society)*

12. Wartime also brought the introduction of policewomen to the force. This is the first group of female recruits pictured at the Depot with Head Constable Major James Cherry. The policewomen are: Standing, L to R: Gertrude Drennan, Susan Sherrard, Florence May Brock and Gertrude McBrien; Seated, L to R: Rebecca Jones, W/Sgt Marion Macmillan and Annie May Bruce. No uniforms had been issued at this stage, hence the fatigue dress and male forage caps. *(RUC GC Historical Society)*

13. Recruits at the Depot in Enniskillen learn about court routine through role play. Recruits may be seen in the witness box (left) and dock (right) while members of the Depot staff take the parts of the petty sessions clerk, magistrate and police prosecutor.
(RUC GC Historical Society)

14. A new generation of police officers was 'growing up' in the 1950s and this led to younger sergeants. This is Sergeant Robin Sinclair (later C/Supt R. J. K. Sinclair MBE, and first curator of the RUC Museum) on beat patrol.
(RUC GC Historical Society)

15. On 14 July 1954 a review of the UK police forces was held in Hyde Park before Her Majesty Queen Elizabeth II. This is the RUC group marching past the dais. Probably the smartest officers on parade that day, the group includes at least two policewomen. *(RUC GC Historical Society)*

16. Another IRA campaign began in December 1956 and forced the RUC to adopt defensive measures for buildings and personnel. Some armoured vehicles were borrowed from the War Office, including Humber armoured personnel carriers, known as 'Pigs'. Not fully armoured, this 'Pig' has a fabric cover to the rear compartment. The photograph was taken after 1958 as the officers are wearing the 1958-pattern uniform with open-neck tunics. They are also wearing cross-belts to support their revolvers. *(RUC GC Historical Society)*

17. Air support was provided by the Royal Air Force with Bristol Sycamore helicopters. Two RUC officers are travelling in this machine; the rear doors have been removed, which was a common practice as it allowed easy access and exit and also allowed the carriage of a stretcher across the helicopter. Royal Navy helicopters from Eglinton, near Londonderry, were also used to support the RUC. *(RUC GC Historical Society)*

18. Brookeborough RUC Station, the target of an IRA attack on New Year's eve night, 1956, in which two IRA men were killed in an exchange of fire with the station party. *(RUC GC Historical Society)*

19. The financial stringency of the Ministry of Home Affairs is shown in this photograph taken outside Omagh courthouse in (about) 1956. Two of the vehicles already look antique. The centre and right vehicles are Reserve Force Fordson tenders, used from 1950 to 1957, and were converted from National Fire Service tenders. They were open-sided and the sole protection that officers had from the elements were roll-down curtains. *(RUC GC Historical Society)*

20. This picture was also taken in Omagh on the occasion of County Inspector Hamilton's last inspection before his retirement in 1958. CI Hamilton is seated in the centre of the front row, flanked by H/Con McQuaid and DI Briggs. *(Mr Alan McConnell)*

21. Queen Elizabeth The Queen Mother visited the RUC Depot in Enniskillen in April 1962. She is seen speaking to two officers who had been bereaved in the recent IRA campaign. On the right is W/Con Carrie Gregg, whose husband Cecil had been murdered in 1957 at Forkhill and W/Con Agnes Hunter, sister of Willie John Hunter. *(Mrs Agnes Adair BEM)*

22. The 1956-1962 IRA campaign cost the lives of six RUC officers. The last to die was Constable Willie John Hunter, seen here at Forkhill, who was murdered at Jonesborough in November 1961. *(Mrs Agnes Adair BEM)*

23. Constable Reggie Semple of Traffic Branch demonstrates one of the Branch's Q-cars to the Mayor of Lurgan, Cllr William Gordon. The photograph was taken in 1966 and the car is a Lotus Cortina Mark II. Reggie Semple retired from the force as a Chief Inspector. *(Mr Reggie Semple QPM)*

24. During 'Ulster Weeks' in the 1960s groups of RUC women carried out duty in the host cities in England. This photograph was taken in Leeds in 1967 and shows Brian Faulkner, then Minister of Commerce, with Inspector George Holly of the Leeds police and RUC officers W/Head Constable J. G. Gallagher, W/Constable Agnes Hunter and W/Constable A. Aukinson. *(Mrs Agnes Adair BEM)*

25. A typical station party at Claudy, Co. Londonderry in the 1960s. Constable Paddy McNulty (right) later became a Detective Constable in Special Branch and was murdered by IRA terrorists in Londonderry in January 1977. *(Mr D. & Mrs F. Walker)*

26. Armagh's new police station, a typical 1960s structure which might have been seen anywhere in the UK.
(RUC GC Historical Society)

27. A Humber 'Pig' crashes into a barricade during rioting in William Street, Londonderry in 1968/9.
(RUC GC Historical Society)

28. Lurgan RUC Station became a target for the IRA and was demolished by a terrorist bomb in November 1973. As may be seen from this photograph, the station was part of a row of buildings and was not a fortified 'barracks'.
(RUC GC Historical Society)

29. Personnel were also attacked. This Land Rover was destroyed in 1975 in an explosion in which one officer lost his life. *(RUC GC Historical Society)*

30. Secretary of State Merlyn Rees talking to three women officers at Victoria RUC Station in Londonderry during a visit to the city. The officers are Linda Craig, Joy Lindsay and Agnes Adair. They are wearing the revised women's uniform that was introduced in 1969. This uniform retained the distinctive French-style cap but introduced a velvet top to the cap which was matched by the shoulder straps. These proved impracticable in wet weather and were later abandoned. *(Mrs Agnes Adair BEM)*

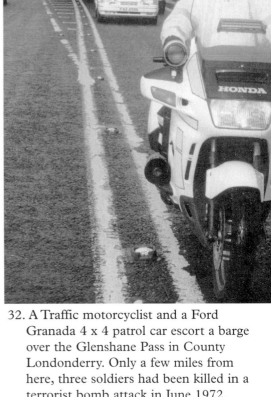

31. In spite of the terrorist campaign, officers continued to perform normal duties. Sergeant Neil Falkingham (later Chief Inspector) is seen carrying out a cycling proficiency test at a school in Londonderry in 1975.

(J. J. McCauley)

32. A Traffic motorcyclist and a Ford Granada 4 x 4 patrol car escort a barge over the Glenshane Pass in County Londonderry. Only a few miles from here, three soldiers had been killed in a terrorist bomb attack in June 1972.

(RUC GC Historical Society)

33. An Air Support Unit was formed within the RUC in the 1990s and was based at RAF Aldergrove. Operating a Britten Norman Islander, the unit is used on a wide range of duties, including surveillance of marches and support in search operations.

(RUC GC Historical Society)

34. RUC officers were included in the United Nations international police force that was sent to Kosovo. This blue-bereted RUC constable, presenting armbands to schoolchildren, is the son of Sir Ronnie Flanagan, the last Chief Constable of the RUC. *(RUC GC Historical Society)*

35. An armoured Land Rover patrols a Republican area of Belfast. A soldier can be seen in the background close to a wall that bears Republican graffiti, including an attack on the SDLP. *(RUC GC Historical Society)*

36. This woman officer, armed with a Ruger sidearm and a Heckler & Koch SMG shows the change in the face of policing that was forced on the RUC by the constant threat of terrorist attack. The RUC's first women officers could never have imagined that their successors would operate in such a fashion.

(RUC GC Historical Society)

37. An improvised mortar, such as the one that killed nine officers at Newry in 1985. This weapon is of the type known to the RUC and Army as the Mark 10/11.

(RUC GC Historical Society)

(IRSP). Inevitably the IRSP spawned an armed wing, the Irish National Liberation Army (INLA). Following a bloody feud with the Official IRA, INLA turned its attention to other targets. Their first police victim was Constable Noel Davis, Special Patrol Group, who was killed on 24 May as he made to drive away a stolen vehicle that had just been recovered in south County Londonderry. The twenty-two-year-old was recently married and had already survived a car crash involving a police vehicle when he had been stationed in N Division. On 26 July the INLA struck again in County Londonderry, killing Constable Robert McPherson in Dungiven. The policeman had just challenged men who had aroused his suspicions at the town's post office when they fired at him. Constable McPherson was awarded posthumously the Queen's Commendation for Bravery. The IRA ceasefire came to an end in September, the Provisionals believing that they could extract no concessions from the government. Within the Republican movement the leaders who had negotiated were seen as having been duped by the British and a younger, more hard-line leadership began to emerge.

In early October an armed robbery was carried out at a rural pub outside Limavady in County Londonderry. Police responded and Detective Constable David Love died when a bomb left by the IRA exploded. Little over a month later, on 15 November, police in Tyrone were called to the scene of a blaze in a hayshed near Sixmilecross. However, the fire had been started deliberately by the IRA who had prepared an ambush. As a Land Rover approached, a landmine was detonated, injuring seriously Reserve Constable Joseph Clements who died the following day.

The IRA were using every form of ruse they could imagine to draw police into traps but few were worse than the circumstances surrounding the next double murder. For many years the RUC had willingly taken messages of family bereavements and other major domestic crises to homes that did not have telephones. This had been just one of a number of ways in which police had served the community outside the normal demands of police work. Everyone in Northern Ireland was aware that such a service was performed but few expected it to be used to set up the murder of officers. But that is what happened on the night of 25 November when Gardai in Monaghan contacted Dungannon RUC Station to ask them to pass a message of a family death to an address at Clonavaddy near Pomeroy. The request had been made by a woman who remained in the Garda station as it was passed to the RUC. Sergeant Patrick Maxwell, aged thirty-six, was in charge of the officers who drove out to deliver the message. As their unmarked Cortina made its way down a laneway, terrorists in ambush opened fire, killing Patrick Maxwell and Reserve Constable Samuel Clarke, who was driving. Another officer was injured but the fourth policeman was unhurt and radioed for help. Patrick Maxwell was killed by a bullet in his chest but he had been hit by six or seven other rounds, all from a Soviet AK47 assault rifle. Samuel Clarke, aged thirty-five, died from head and chest wounds. All the entry wounds were in the dead men's backs. Following this double murder the RUC ceased the practice of delivering such messages.

Reaction to this incident was considerable. The IRA claimed it had been carried out in retaliation for 'police harassment' in east Tyrone but the Church of Ireland Archbishop of Armagh, Dr George Simms, said that 'The tactics of a bogus mercy mission used by the murderers in this latest attack are sickening, and must surely be despised by all people'. The Chief Constable pointed out that police carried many such messages and that 'the community relied on them to do this'. Tom Donnelly, a Belfast SDLP councillor, called on his party to support the RUC, claiming that senior SDLP members shared his views and that he would leave the party if it refused to change its stance. No such change was forthcoming and Donnelly duly resigned; in 1999 he was appointed to the Northern Ireland Human Rights Commission.

During 1975 another low point had been passed with the province's first murder of a policewoman. Reserve Constable Mildred Harrison, aged twenty-six and married with two children, was killed when a bomb exploded as she passed a bar in Bangor's High Street on 16 March; it was her older daughter's sixth birthday. The explosives had been left on a windowsill by the UVF; the bar was Catholic-owned and had been attacked once before, in September 1973. Mildred Harrison had been in the Reserve for only two months and had, according to her sister, always wanted to do something for her town. Her funeral took place at St Comgall's Church and was attended by a large congregation from the town. The cortege was led by the RUC band. A man was later jailed for her manslaughter; he said that the bomb had only been intended to 'scare Republicans'. Until then only one female member of the security forces had been killed; Private Eva Martin of the UDR had died in an IRA attack on Clogher UDR base in 1974. Loyalists now had the dubious distinction of having killed both the first policeman and the first police-woman of the conflict.

In spite of the IRA ceasefire the RUC had lost eleven officers to terrorism in 1975, of whom eight had been killed by the IRA, two by the INLA and one by the UVF. The force had lost another female officer when Reserve Constable Cherry Campbell died in Altnagelvin Hospital in November. She had been in a police team carrying out routine vehicle checks at Maydown, near Londonderry. Officers had asked a young man to step out of his car and were talking to him when another car drove into them at speed. Cherry Campbell was seriously injured and the Sergeant in charge of the patrol, John Mullan, was also hurt badly, so much so that he never resumed duty. The young driver to whom the officers had been talking was struck by the second car and thrown into a field where he was later found dead. Cherry Campbell survived for some days in intensive care before succumbing to her injuries.

In the course of the year Jamie Flanagan had been knighted in the Birthday Honours' List in June. He had devoted much time to developing good relations with the Garda Síochána and had welcomed the Garda Commissioner, Patrick Malone, to Belfast early in his tenure as chief constable. Building on that meeting Flanagan visited Dublin and further meetings were held between high-ranking officers in both forces in an effort to improve cross-border security, especially in the areas of shared intelligence and border patrolling. Loyalist car bombs, which killed over thirty people, in Dublin and Monaghan during the UWC strike added further emphasis to the need for better cooperation.

Flanagan had also carried out some restructuring within the force. The expansion of the early seventies meant that the Hunt/Boyes structure was no longer as effective as it had been. To improve matters, two operational regions outside greater Belfast were created; North Region included N, O and P Divisions while South Region included all other divisions. At the helm of each was to be an Assistant Chief Constable. On 1 April 1974 the new structure came into being; Frank Lagan was promoted to command North Region while Charlie Rodgers later took command of South Region. Jack Hermon was also promoted to ACC responsible for a new Personnel and Training Department overseeing recruiting, training, manpower planning, career development, welfare and internal communication.

The winter of 1975–76 was marked by brutal sectarian murders in north and west Belfast carried out by a UVF gang that became known as the 'Shankill butchers' because of their practice of mutilating victims. These murders were often spontaneous affairs, decided on after a night's drinking. Victims were chosen at random; the gang looked for a Catholic who was abducted, subjected to a severe beating and bludgeoned, shot or hacked to death; the victim's throat was usually cut with a sharp knife. Their first victim was murdered on 25 November 1975 and several more followed. In one case the group claimed that their victim, Thomas Quinn, had been killed in retaliation for the IRA murder of Sergeant James Blakely.

Tracking down the murderers was a task assigned to one of the RUC's best detectives, Chief Inspector Jimmy Nesbitt, whose team in C Division had probably the best record for solving murders in the province; they had cleared up 101 of 132 murders in the Division since 1974. They also had excellent insight into Loyalist hardliners. Even with this background it was proving very difficult to obtain leads. As so often with police work a breakthrough came with the help of information from the public. Following an attack on two Catholic women in a car, an Army patrol pursued the gunmen's car. Although they lost contact with the vehicle, police were certain that a burning car found shortly afterwards was that used by the gang. This was followed by a 999 call the following day – 12 March – from a Shankill woman who reported a man behaving suspiciously. Police reaction was quick and the man, who was searching hedges, was arrested; a gun was recovered in a follow-up operation. The man was Lennie Murphy, a well-known UVF member, and he had been involved in the previous night's attack; he had thrown the gun in a hedge as he fled after abandoning the car. Although the 'butcher' killings continued – Murphy had sent a message to his henchmen to that effect – the police knew that they had one of the main men but it was 1977 before the murderous reign of the gang was finally brought to an end. Eleven men eventually appeared in court and received no fewer than forty-two life sentences and prison terms totalling 2,000 years; two were sentenced to spend the rest of their natural lives in prison for crimes that the judge, Mr Justice O'Donnell, described as 'a memorial to blind sectarian bigotry'. Murphy was already in prison for possessing a gun and did not stand trial with the others, none of whom would give evidence against him. Released in August 1981 after earning full remission, Murphy returned to his crimes but was himself murdered by the IRA on 16 November 1981.

Sir Jamie Flanagan was due to stand down on 30 April 1976 but his final months in post were marked by a series of incidents that rank among the worst in Northern Ireland's recent history. The old year ended with an INLA bomb attack on the Central Bar in Gilford, County Armagh that prompted UVF reprisal attacks in the first days of the new year. Six men were killed in two attacks on Catholic families in south Armagh which led the IRA, using the cover name of Republican Action Force, to murder ten Protestant workers at Kingsmills. The men were in a minibus on their way home from work at Glenanne when the bus was stopped. Each occupant was asked his religion and the sole Catholic was told to 'get out of the way'. The Protestants were then lined up and shot; one man survived although wounded eighteen times.

The Kingsmills murders occurred on 5 January, the same day on which Reserve Constable Clifford Evans lost his life. Constable Evans was in a car with two other officers when it was ambushed by the IRA near Toome. The vehicle was struck as it stopped at a junction with all three occupants being hit by bullets. Clifford Evans, thirty years old and married, died en route to the Mid-Ulster Hospital in Magherafelt; his colleagues were not wounded seriously. At his funeral in Bellaghy Presbyterian Church, the Minister warned against any retaliation 'by unauthorized individuals or groups [which] only perpetuates the carnage and misery we want to overcome'. One immediate reaction to these killings came from Harold Wilson who announced that the SAS would be deployed to Northern Ireland. As usual, Wilson was being less than honest; less than a squadron of the regiment arrived in the province.

Before the month was out two more officers had been murdered. Inspector George Bell, fifty-four years old and with twenty-eight years' service, died along with thirty-seven year-old Detective Constable Neville Cummings when a booby-trapped shotgun exploded while being examined in Donegall Pass RUC Station. Both were married with three children. Another four policemen were injured, two of them seriously. A telephone caller had told police of armed men at a house in Benburb Street, off Donegall Road, and a search had uncovered the shotgun, swathed in a quilt, in a coal shed behind the building, which was bricked up. While the gun, which had been stolen about six months earlier, was being dismantled the booby-trap device was triggered. It contained about four ounces of gelignite and a detonator, materials usually associated with Republicans. However, there was no claim of responsibility for the incident which has never been attributed to a specific group.

February saw three deaths in less than a week with the murders of Sergeant James Blakely, Inspector William Murtagh and Reserve Constable Victor Hamer. Both Sergeant Blakely and Inspector Murtagh were shot at Cliftonville Circus in Belfast on the 7th. James Blakely was hit five times and died almost immediately while William Murtagh, hit three times in the back, died next day without regaining consciousness. Both were married and Sergeant Blakely had three children. William Murtagh's wife was a policewoman, and he had followed his father into the force; William Murtagh senior had been a Sergeant Instructor at the Depot in Enniskillen for many years. Reserve Constable Victor Hamer was on patrol in the village of Claudy with Constable Bob Crozier on 12 February when both were shot from behind by the IRA. Victor Hamer, a thirty-one year-old farmer, died instantly while his colleague survived but with injuries that caused his right leg to be amputated below the knee. In later life, Bob Crozier was unable to have heart by-pass surgery because of his injury; he died in 2000. A former member of the Irish Guards, Bob had been awarded the Queen's Commendation for Brave Conduct following the 1972 Claudy bombing.

The last policeman to die during Sir Jamie Flanagan's tenure as Chief Constable was Reserve Constable William Crooks who died in South Tyrone Hospital on 23 April, having been shot by the IRA the previous evening. He was in a mobile patrol intended to prevent sectarian murders or bombings near Coalisland when IRA gunmen opened fire from behind a wall as the police car turned a corner. One tyre was blown out and the car crashed into a hedge. Two other officers were injured.

William Crooks was buried after a service at Tullanisken Church attended by some 2,000 people. The twenty-nine year-old father of two was given full police honours with the RUC band playing as his coffin was carried into the church.

As Sir Jamie Flanagan left office at the end of March he could reflect on a period of command that, while it had seen further suffering within the force, offered some hope for the future through the background work that had been carried out in recent years. On the ground Northern Ireland was heading for its second worst year of violence but the RUC was now much better equipped to deal with that violence and had much more manpower.

In the aftermath of the UWC strike, Rees had asked Flanagan to study some proposals he (Rees) had outlined on 'suggestions for a community-corps type of organisation to be loosely under the RUC's control, and capable of working without threats or obstruction from the IRA and other paramilitary groups'. The Secretary of State was concerned by the political chaos in Northern Ireland and by the various demands from the Unionist community that some new force was needed to deal with terrorism. At the same time, some SDLP politicians were again trailing their ideas for a separate force for Nationalist areas. Rees had asked that a working party from the RUC chaired by Assistant Chief Constable Jack Hermon should study his ideas and produce a viable scheme within two weeks.

Hermon was asked to select a group of officers for the working party, which convened on 2 August 1974 with a deadline of 6 August to present a report to Flanagan.

> The brainstorming began and ideas, queries, criticisms and every conceivable thought on the matter poured out of the group. These were recorded on flip-chart sheets which, when full, were taped to the walls until most of that space, in a generously proportioned office, was covered. It was a volatile and demanding, indeed exhausting, experience. Rank was ignored, except when I occasionally had to call for order! Our hours were 9 a.m. until late evening, with short breaks for sustenance.[17]

The report drawn up by Hermon's working group rejected any ideas of a 'Third Force' as suggested by Rees and was the subject of debate throughout August that included the Northern Ireland Office, Army Headquarters, the Police Authority and the Chief Constable. Some urgency was injected into proceedings by an announcement on 1 September by the Catholic Ex-Servicemen's Association (CESA) that it was making plans for the possible mobilization of 10,000 men on a parish basis throughout the province. Rees, therefore, decided to adopt the report from the RUC and announced that there would be a

> gradual extension of normal policing services into all areas of Northern Ireland . . . to harness the widely expressed desire of men and women in Northern Ireland to play a part in ensuring the security of their own areas.

This statement made the RUC the focus of improved local security and led to a further increase in the strength of the force, this time by a further 1,500 personnel to 6,500. The Women's Branch was to increase to 750 while the Reserve was also to be strengthened. Indeed, the Reserve was to be an important element in the new initiative, which established local police centres to be staffed by Reservists who would thus police their own areas while being linked to main police stations and other emergency services. To this end the Reserve was doubled from 2,000 part-time male officers to 4,000, with the number of part-time females increased by 1,250; the number of full-time male officers was to be increased to 1,000, from 350, and full-time female reservists were to be recruited for the first time; the number sought was 400.

In January 1976 Rees made a statement to the Commons in which he said that plans for maintaining law and order in Northern Ireland would include investigating how best to achieve 'the primacy of the police . . . and the progressive reduction of the Army'. This led to yet another working party to be chaired by John Bourn, a Northern Ireland Office civil servant, and including an Army brigadier with John Hermon representing the RUC. The result of that group's deliberations, the Bourn Report, entitled *The Way Ahead*, was presented to parliament by Rees on 2 July. It was to set the tenor of the years to come.

Notes

1: One of the men, Thomas Carlin, died in hospital on 7 July. He was a veteran Republican, having been jailed in 1957, and was believed to be one of the founders of the Provisional IRA.
2: Carver, *Out of Step*, p. 430
3: Faulkner, op. cit., p. 74
4: Information from Paul Clark.
5: Faulkner, op. cit., p. 101
6: Ibid., p. 113
7: Ibid., p. 115
8: Ibid., p. 116
9: Ibid., p. 117
10: Ibid., p. 118
11: *Derry Journal*, 14 April 1972
12: *Derry Journal*, 28 January 1972

13: In 1981, Colin Dean, then Chairman of the Institute of Road Safety
Officers and a former Bristol City Police sergeant, who had been David
Dorsett's sergeant and manager of the divisional soccer team in which
David played, visited Londonderry and met the surviving officers as well
as David Dorsett's widow. During the course of the visit, David Gray,
then a sergeant in Traffic Division, provided these details of the incident.

14: Bishop Farren had retired as Bishop of Derry in 1973 but, in the absence
of a successor, remained as Apostolic Administrator of the diocese until
March 1974 when Bishop Edward Daly succeeded to the post.

15: Devlin, op. cit., p. 209

16: Ibid.

17: Hermon, op. cit., p. 94

Chapter Six

The 'Wee Man' –
the Newman years

Kenneth Newman took over as Chief Constable on 1 May 1976, having already served almost three years as Senior Deputy Chief Constable. In London, he had been a commander at New Scotland Yard and had been responsible for community relations. Earlier he had planned the policing of the October 1968 anti-Vietnam War demonstration at the US Embassy, where over 4,000 officers were deployed on crowd control and the London police were held up as an example to all on how to handle demonstrations. It was a series of films made by the Met that had been provided to the RUC as a training aid in crowd control when the situation in Northern Ireland had gone far beyond crowd control; and nor did the RUC ever have the numbers to deal with such situations in the fashion extolled in those films. There is a certain irony in the fact that when violent demonstrations erupted in London in 1981 the tactics used were those that the Metropolitan Police had learned from the RUC. And the principal conduit had been Newman, who by then was the Met's Commissioner.

Newman already had a reputation across the RUC when he was appointed Chief Constable. His diminutive stature had earned him the soubriquet 'the Wee Man' but he had also gained respect from many officers, not least those of Community Relations Branch for which he had obtained an increase in personnel and resources. Although he was known as a good organizer and planner, many were curious to see how he would fare in his new role where the main priority was continuing terrorist violence. Under Shillington and Flanagan much had been done to strengthen morale and *The Way Ahead* report would provide Newman with a template for his incumbency; he would serve for just over three and a half years before returning to London as Metropolitan Police Commissioner.

In the early years of the terrorist campaign the initiative had lain generally with the terrorists. The Army lacked experience in dealing with this type of situation and events since 1969 had brought a new breed of recruit to the IRA, on whom Special Branch and Army Intelligence had little information. But that was beginning to change; there was a feeling that the Army and RUC were working much better together – although suspicion had not evaporated entirely – and that intelligence on terrorists was much better. Using *The Way Ahead* as his foundation, Newman hoped to steer the RUC into the lead role. This, he knew, would be a lengthy task, one that might take decades rather than years and, while the principle of unarmed policing was still the core of his thinking, it would be necessary for the RUC to adopt a much higher profile, with the 'harder' image that came from bearing arms and using lightly-armoured vehicles. Already there had been controversy about issuing rifles to the force with the SDLP spokesman on policing, Michael Canavan, criticizing a proposal to purchase assault rifles from the United States. In fact, there was probably a misunderstanding here, since the SDLP appeared unaware that an assault rifle was designed for use at much shorter ranges than traditional infantry rifles. But the word 'assault' had connotations that spurred the SDLP to their criticism. The American rifles were not bought then, but the force received a number of Army rifles, the modern SLR, or self-loading rifle, with its NATO-standard 7.62mm round, a much more deadly weapon than that criticized by the SDLP.

Relations between the force and the SDLP, the main Nationalist party, were strained and comments such as that made during a television interview by Hume that some policemen were 'scoundrels' did not help matters. However, Gerry Fitt and Paddy Devlin, who represented the socialist wing of the SDLP, had a more positive attitude. Devlin recorded in his memoirs that

> I was persuaded that the force had changed irrevocably since 1969.
> Jamie Flanagan, the first Catholic to head the force, had responded
> thoroughly to everything we asked of him, yet in turn the SDLP
> refused to give the police the wholehearted support they needed.
> Gerry Fitt and I regularly stood alone from the party on this issue and
> made our views clear. A new breed of officers like Jack Hermon, who
> later became a mould-breaking chief constable, had transformed atti
> tudes and promoted professionalism within the force.[1]

Devlin was convinced that the SDLP was now being run 'autocratically from Derry by John Hume and his cronies' and that Hume was 'pursuing his own initiatives and making policy on the hoof', policy that did not include supporting the police.[2] Although opposed to violence, Hume, who would become leader of the SDLP, could not bring himself to support the police, relying instead on the sterile policy of criticism. Had there been SDLP support for the RUC at this stage there was a chance that the increasing power of the IRA, soon to be converted into political power, might have been broken. There might even have been some moderate Unionist support for the party, something that Gerry Fitt had been keen to promote since the formation of the SDLP in 1970. Against this background Ken Newman intended to implement a policy of police primacy, or what became known as 'Ulsterization'.

Newman's new Deputy was Harry Baillie with John Hermon promoted to Deputy in charge of operational matters. Hermon was then only forty-seven and his appointment was seen as heralding a new era, as Paddy Devlin indicated. It was not well received by some; Sam Bradley, ACC for Belfast, resigned in protest after almost forty years' service. The new Chief's first public engagement was, appropriately, a passing-out parade on 5 May where he made a speech in which he looked forward to a time when every soldier was returned to barracks. Only a day earlier, Rees had announced the reduction of the Northern Ireland garrison by 500 soldiers. Eight days after his Enniskillen speech, Newman made the same points to a seminar for senior officers at Hillsborough, telling them that only through the RUC taking the lead in the fight against terrorism would there ever be any chance of removing the Army from the streets. His declaration of policy was issued as a poster and as a full-page advertisement in the major newspapers. No one could be in any doubt that Newman meant business by bringing to an end as quickly and as professionally as possible the criminal reign of terror of the various terrorist bodies, Republican and Loyalist, and that he wanted the force to be identified with the Northern Ireland community through sensitivity to the needs of people and their feelings. Stripped of the inevitable jargon that came from his Met days, Newman was saying that he wanted full support for the RUC from across the community and that the force would do its best to rid the community of the scourge of terrorism.

There was no 'honeymoon' period. No fewer than eight officers lost their lives to terrorism in Newman's first month in post with one incident causing three deaths. This followed an overnight attack on the police station at Belcoo, County Fermanagh, on the border with County Cavan. Shots were fired at UDR soldiers leaving the station at about 3.30 a.m. At about 6.30 in the morning of 15 May, during a follow-up operation, Sergeant Henry Keys and Reserve Constables Francis Kettles and Thomas Evans were examining what was believed to have been the gunmen's firing point on the disued Sligo–Leitrim railway line about 200 yards from the police station when a bomb exploded and killed all three; a fourth officer was injured seriously. A local Catholic priest described the scene of the murders as 'a horrible sight and I felt quite sick'. All three were natives of Fermanagh; each was married, Sergeant Keys with two children and Reserve Constable Kettles with two. Only two days earlier, as Newman was addressing the Hillsborough seminar, *Republican News* had carried an IRA warning of 'a long hot summer' for the RUC. And this day seemed to support that threat for, with another officer murdered across the province in Warrenpoint, it now became the worst in the RUC's history. The officer who died at Warrenpoint was Sergeant James Hunter, who was based at Newry. He was travelling in a police car on the Newry Road near Warrenpoint when gunmen opened fire. James Hunter, a thirty-three year-old married man, was killed and two other officers wounded.

Within twenty-four hours another policeman had been murdered. Reserve Constable Kenneth Nelson had come off duty at Benburb RUC Station and was about to lock up his dog at his home at Terryscallop, some three miles away, when IRA gunmen opened fire from a nearby field. Although hit by rounds believed to have come from an Armalite rifle, Kenneth Nelson managed to stagger to his home where he collapsed and died while his killers ran across fields to a waiting car. At Reserve Constable Nelson's funeral service a minister made an impassioned plea for more support for the RUC and added

> Bullets can rebound. Retaliation is a dead-end thing and, wherever you are hiding today, one day there will be no escape from your conscience.

Five days later, Constable John McCambridge was returning to his lodgings at Bush, near Dungannon, to prepare for night duty when he was shot from behind a hedge by two IRA gunmen. John McCambridge died from a high-velocity bullet wound to the chest. Two rifles used in the attack were later found by the UDR. A native of Ballycastle, Constable McCambridge was twenty-two and engaged to be married later that year.

On the evening of 23 May two RUC officers were on patrol in the Dungiven Road area of Londonderry, not far from Waterside RUC Station and only yards from where Reserve Constable Bill Baggley had been murdered in January 1974. One of the officers was Bill Baggley's daughter, Reserve Constable Linda Baggley, aged nineteen. Near the junction with Chapel Road they were approached by a number of individuals who opened fire from close range. Linda Baggley was hit and seriously wounded. She died on 2 June, the first policewoman to be shot dead by the IRA. One IRA member who was jailed for her murder later escaped from the Maze Prison in the 1983 mass breakout but was subsequently involved in a border gun battle with SAS soldiers and drowned. Three young men and a girl were convicted of Reserve Constable Baggley's murder.

On the day that Linda Baggley died in Altnagelvin Hospital, Detective Constable Ronald McAdam drove his girlfriend to Belfast's Royal Victoria Hospital for an appointment, returning an hour later to collect her. As he was getting into his car he was shot three times in the back. Thus, in his first month as Chief Constable, Newman had to attend eight police funerals. There seemed no end to the murderous onslaught on the men and women in green. And across the province there were areas that were under the control of terrorist organizations, whether Republican or Loyalist. The overall security situation was, as Rees told the Commons shortly before he vacated Hillsborough Castle, at its worst since 1972. A pall of fear hung over Northern Ireland and many who collected money on a regular basis, such as bread salesmen, milkmen and insurance agents, were all too frequently targets for armed robbers, while public houses were also a favoured source of income for terrorists. By now, respect for law and order was disappearing rapidly and the ambivalent attitude to the RUC of politicians such as Hume was not helping matters. Investigating such crimes became more and more difficult and there was a tremendous backlog of fingerprints for processing, so much so that Newman arranged for experts to be lent from other forces; their work assisted in putting a number of terrorists in prison.

On 30 June Oliver Eaton, a prominent businessman and member of PANI was shot by the IRA as he arrived at his place of business on Belfast's Springfield Road. Hit in the head and chest the forty-two year-old father of four died some thirty minutes later. Although he was a colonel in the Territorial Army, Oliver Eaton was targeted because of his membership of the Police Authority. He was buried in his native Londonderry.

There was much discussion about the relationship between the RUC and the Army at high level with many senior Army officers keen to maintain their leading role in security but Newman held firm and by the time Lieutenant General Timothy Creasey took over as GOC in late 1976 he had won his argument. On 1 January 1977 Newman and Creasey signed a joint directive that acknowledged the primacy of the RUC. Newman was now Director of Operations; after almost eight years the RUC was the lead element in the province's security.

But the police were still suffering on the ground and the terrorist campaign had lost none of its viciousness. On 31 July 1976 fifty-two year-old Constable Thomas Cush was on duty at a security barrier in Lurgan with a female colleague when he was shot by an IRA gunman in a nearby building. Thomas Cush, who had served in Lurgan for fifteen years, was dead on arrival at Craigavon Area Hospital. His funeral took place from Shankill Parish Church, close to where he had been murdered. An appeal was made by his minister for no retaliation, which, he said, would only be 'evil against evil, crime against crime' and no solution to Northern Ireland's problems.

Twenty year-old Constable James Heaney was stationed at Waterside in Londonderry and had served in the RUC for almost two years. He had been an RUC Cadet when the cadets were attached to the Metropolitan Police and was a Catholic from Andersonstown in Belfast. On 25 August he went home to Belfast to visit his widowed mother and the following morning, at 9.00 a.m., as he was checking his car outside his mother's house, he was shot in the back five times by the IRA. James Heaney died shortly after being taken to the Royal Victoria Hospital. The Chief Constable attended the requiem Mass in St Theresa's Church, Glen Road, and the funeral to Milltown Cemetery.

This was the summer and autumn of the Peace People, an organization formed after the deaths of three children of the Maguire family, Joanne, aged eight, John, two, and Andrew, six weeks, who were killed after a car driven by an IRA member went out of control, mounted the pavement and struck them. The IRA man, Danny Lennon, had been shot by soldiers while driving a getaway car. In the aftermath of this incident there were peace demonstrations across Northern Ireland. It seemed that the community was heartily sick of the killing and destruction, which, in the three months up to August, had seen thirteen police or soldiers murdered with another 111 injured, a total of 230 attacks on the RUC and Army and almost 200 explosions. In a newspaper advertisement the Northern Ireland Office also pointed out that police officers and soldiers were routinely working up to sixteen hours each day, had been searching for the murderers of sixty-nine civilians, made safe eighty-one bombs, recovered almost 5,000 pounds of explosives and charged 264 suspected terrorists.

In spite of the demonstrations the killings continued. On 18 September Sergeant Albert Craig, an Enniskillen man with fifteen years' service, was controlling traffic at Portadown's Brownstown Road; a stockcar racing event was taking place at nearby Shamrock Park. Sergeant Craig was accompanied by a reserve constable. A Triumph 2000 driven by a woman pulled up behind Albert Craig who was shot four times in the back by two IRA gunmen in the car. The vehicle had been stolen earlier in Lurgan and the owner warned not to report the theft. Sergeant Craig was married with one child. Less than three weeks later, on 8 October, Reserve Constable Arthur McKay was involved in the recovery of a stolen car near Kilrea. He was steering the vehicle as it was being towed to Kilrea RUC Station when a device exploded underneath it and he was killed. Five soldiers were also injured. The car had been declared safe after an examination by the Army, who had carried out a controlled explosion. As the vehicle moved off, a pressure switch under a wheel triggered the booby trap that killed Arthur McKay. An SDLP spokesman, Hugh Logue, criticized the Army for its negligence but pointed out that this 'in no way absolves those responsible for this hideous murder'.

Only a few weeks after this murder Detective Constable Noel McCabe was shot and fatally injured on Falls Road in Belfast. As the policeman stopped at the junction with Clonard Street, gunmen approached his car and fired through the window, hitting him in the head and chest. Noel McCabe was dead before he reached hospital. A married man, he had already been awarded the Queen's Gallantry Medal and was a member of the RUC rugby team; he had four years' service.

Before the year was out three other officers were murdered, all of them in December. The first was one of the softest of targets, a reservist engaged in his daily job. Reserve Constable Joseph Scott was also a traffic warden in Dungannon and, on 3 December, a foggy morning, was assisting a school crossing patrol in seeing children across the busy Chapel Corner. A witness later said that he saw a youth run up behind Joseph Scott and shoot him three times. The schoolchildren, some of whom were about to sit their eleven-plus, scattered in panic. Joseph Scott was himself the father of five children. Another reservist died on 22 December at Maghera in County Londonderry. Samuel Armour, a sales representative for a Coleraine timber firm, had just got into his car to drive to work when a booby-trap device killed him instantly. He was the father of three children whom he usually drove to school each morning before travelling to work but the children were on holiday from school and still in their beds when their father was murdered. At the family's request Reserve Constable Armour was not given a formal police funeral.

A week earlier Constable Norman Campbell and a reserve constable had been on duty at a security barrier in High Street, Portadown. Gunmen in a Ford Cortina drove up and fired more than thirty rounds from an automatic weapon. Norman Campbell died instantly when he was hit in the head. His colleague was uninjured. The nineteen-year-old, who was due to be married, was a promising athlete and a member of the RUC hockey team. He was buried from his Kilkeel home in a funeral led by the RUC band.

Not surprisingly, police stations were now better protected than ever and officers had much more effective body armour, the Second World War-vintage flak jackets giving way to modern Bristol body armour, capable of stopping low-velocity rounds at short range and offering some protection against high-velocity fire. More armoured Land Rovers were on the road, with a version known as Hotspur developed for RUC use. This gave some protection against gunfire and shrapnel, as well as against the missiles that were typical of a riot situation. Patrol cars were also armoured to protect against blast and gunfire and their effectiveness would be demonstrated on many occasions. Added to these were rifles, Sterling sub-machine guns, riot guns to fire baton rounds, and handguns, all a far cry from the unarmed force of a few years earlier while the protective equipment now being issued for riot situations was light years away from that of 1969.

That the RUC was now preparing to meet riot situations was a direct result of the new primacy policy. Since its deployment on the streets of Northern Ireland the Army had had to learn new methods of crowd control and dealing with riotous mobs. The tactics used in 1969 soon proved of limited value when bricks and petrol bombs started flying and of even less value when gunmen began using the cover of rioters. Thereafter, considerable thought had gone into developing new ways of containing riots. Better equipment had also been developed; when the Army first deployed its riot gear was no better than that issued to the RUC and would have been familiar to an earlier generation of soldiers. But new materials, such as makrolon, a tough, clear plastic, allowed the creation of better equipment. Makrolon was used to provide shatterproof windows in vehicles and to cover windows in buildings to remove the danger of flying shards of glass. New, larger, clear riot shields were issued and Federal or Webley-Schermuly riot guns became available to fire baton rounds; at first these were rubber but were later changed to the less lethal plastic version. Grenade launchers could be fitted to rifles to fire CS canisters and some water cannon were also deployed but, by the mid-seventies, these were no longer in use. Much of this equipment was also available to the RUC who received training in riot control, or public order duties, from the Army. The first policemen so trained were those of Special Patrol Group but, gradually, training was extended to a much wider range of officers. In order to provide more officers trained in public order duties, Special Patrol Group was later supplemented by Divisional Mobile Support Units, which eventually superseded SPG.

In 1977 the RUC lost another fourteen officers to terrorist activity. First to die was Reserve Constable William Greer, killed instantly by an under-car booby trap as he left home at Portglenone on 14 January to drive to his work in a bacon factory at Ahoghill. William Greer was only twenty-seven and had been married for four months; his wife had earlier left to travel to her work in Ballymena. Claiming responsibility for the murder, the IRA warned that they were stepping up their campaign against the security forces.

William Greer was an easy target, a reservist at his own home at the beginning of a new day who was obviously unsuspecting. The IRA's next victim was not unsuspecting. Detective Constable Paddy McNulty was a member of Special Branch based at Strand Road RUC Station in Londonderry; this was the new headquarters of N Division that had replaced the antiquated Victoria in November 1975. Paddy McNulty had recently bought a new car and had arranged to have the vehicle serviced at a nearby garage on 27 January, the fifth anniversary of the first IRA murders of police officers in Londonderry. Unfortunately, Paddy McNulty had been recognized by an employee who was involved with the IRA when he went to the garage to arrange the service. That employee told the terrorists that a policeman would be leaving his car at the garage on the Thursday morning and when Detective Constable McNulty arrived that day terrorists were waiting across the road in a stolen car. As the detective waited for the garage entrance to be opened the gunmen walked over, opened fire and Paddy McNulty was wounded mortally, dying within minutes of being shot.[3]

Paddy McNulty was buried in St Mary's cemetery at Ardmore after requiem Mass in St Columb's Church in the Waterside, the same church from which Michael Logue had been buried three years before; the two men lie only yards apart in the graveyard. Unlike Michael Logue's funeral, however, the Catholic Bishop of Derry was present at Paddy McNulty's requiem Mass. Bishop Edward Daly made a trenchant condemnation of the murder and told the congregation: 'We must all take a share in the murder of Paddy McNulty. There is no such thing as a legitimate target.' The IRA had tried to justify this murder, which had left two young boys without a father, on the grounds that police officers were 'legitimate targets', a justification they used for many of their deeds. Bishop Daly's comments, and his presence at the funeral, represented a clear message to the IRA that they did not have the support of Catholics in their campaign against the RUC.

A week after Paddy McNulty's funeral, on 5 February, police received a report of an incendiary device in a shop in Gilford. Two officers went to the scene but the call was a hoax. As the policemen left the shop at about 8.30 p.m. gunmen in a car drew up alongside their vehicle and opened fire as the officers were getting in. Reserve Constable Robert Harrison was killed and the other officer injured so severely that he later had his left forearm amputated. Robert Harrison was very well known around Gilford. Not only had he worked as an assistant nurse in the Special Care Hospital at Bannvale but had also been involved in community work of every kind. He had played the accordion and was a member of Gilford Flute Band, which later changed its name to the Robert Harrison Memorial Band. Reserve Constable Harrison, aged fifty, was married with two children.

Exactly a week later Reserve Constable Samuel McKane, a factory manager, was turning into the driveway of his home at Cloughmills having come off duty at the local police station. As he did so he was shot by IRA men waiting in ambush. Samuel McKane was hit in the head and chest and died almost immediately. The killers made their getaway in two vehicles, a red minivan and green minicar. A local farmer was later given a two-year suspended sentence for withholding information about the killers who had come to his farm and hidden their weapons in his cowshed. The farmer had also made a meal for the four IRA men and then bought them drinks at a nearby pub as well as providing information about local police.

Towards the end of the month there occurred two murders of policemen, one of which is still the subject of speculation and controversy. Sergeant Joe Campbell, a forty-nine-year-old married man with eight children, was a popular local policeman in Cushendall. Originally from County Donegal, Sergeant Campbell was closing the gates of Cushendall RUC Station after a colleague had driven out on the night of the 25th when he was shot dead by a single rifle shot. Another policeman, Charles McCormick, was later acquitted of the murder and the Campbell family continue to seek an answer to the question: who murdered Joe Campbell?

The day before Joe Campbell lost his life, an attack was made on a party of officers preparing to open a security barrier at Lurgan's Church Place. Inspector Harold Cobb was shot dead and two reserve constables wounded; a fourth officer escaped injury. Harold Cobb, married with three children, had been transferred to Lurgan from Banbridge in July 1975. He lived at Hillsborough and was thirty-eight.

On 13 March Constable William Brown became the youngest policeman to be murdered when he was killed by a single bullet in the ambush of a mobile patrol at Ballagh Cross near Lisnaskea, County Fermanagh. Constable Brown was driving the car, which went out of control, slewed off the road and overturned into a ditch. The terrorists continued to fire but Constable Lyn Luney

> scrambled out through the shattered windscreen and courageously took over the dead Constable's firearm and returned fire defending herself and the patrol car. While not physically injured herself she suffered mental and emotional trauma afterwards.[4]

Lyn Luney's quick thinking and gallant reaction to this frightening situation undoubtedly saved her own life as well as that of the third officer in the car. She was 'barely out of training as a probationer'. The dead officer was a native of County Tyrone and was two months short of his nineteenth birthday. Constable Luney was later awarded the Queen's Commendation for Brave Conduct.

John McCracken and Kenneth Sheehan were both Special Patrol Group constables and were on duty on the Magherafelt–Moneymore road in County Londonderry on 8 April. They tried to stop a Volkswagen car at Gortagilly but the occupants opened fire and both officers were killed; a third was shot in the legs. Constable Sheehan, aged nineteen, was from Enniskillen and had just returned to duty having recovered from serious injuries sustained in an ambush the previous year. Constable McCracken, aged twenty-two, was from Ballymoney.

Police chased the Volkswagen which later crashed. The occupants opened fire with automatic weapons and tried to escape across country. They also fired on a Special Patrol Group Land Rover as it approached the scene. As the three terrorists made their way across fields they provided covering fire for each other in a disciplined fashion. One of the three was believed to be Francis Hughes, one of the most dangerous of IRA men, who later died on hunger strike in the Maze Prison; Hughes was responsible for at least twelve murders with most of his victims being security forces' members. Another member of the gang that murdered Constables McCracken and Sheehan was Dominic 'Mad Dog' McGlinchey who subsequently joined the INLA and was murdered in Drogheda in 1994.

This incident may have been a chance encounter between the IRA gang and the Special Patrol Group patrol but the death of Reserve Constable Robert North in Benburb, County Tyrone on 20 May was a carefully planned affair. Robert North, whose wife had died from cancer two years before, was a former Royal Marine and a school bus driver, employed by the Southern Education and Library Board. The father of four children, he was a popular but quiet man who had earned the respect of his neighbours. At 8.45 a.m. on the morning of 20 May, Robert North was driving his bus along Drumlee Road to collect children for school when he was ambushed by gunmen who fired at the bus, hitting it fifteen times. Although hit in the chest he drove some 600 yards to his sister-in-law's home where he lost control and crashed into a hedge. His sister-in-law ran out to find him slumped over the wheel, still alive; he died soon afterwards. In protest at the murder, drivers from both Southern and Western boards staged a twenty-four hour stoppage.

Three officers died together in another ambush at Ardboe, near Lough Neagh, on 2 June. They were travelling in a Ford Escort when three IRA gunmen armed with Armalite rifles fired on them from behind a hedge. All three were probably hit at this stage as the car crashed out of control. The gunmen then approached the Escort and fired another twenty shots into it. A passing motorist found the dying policemen. A local man who arrived at the scene said that he found Hugh Martin dying in the middle of the road while two young officers lay in the car, each barely alive. A search of the area uncovered a bottle of orange squash and sandwiches where the gunmen had lain in wait. Hugh Martin was fifty-eight, the father of seven children and a local man, having been brought up a quarter of a mile from the spot where he died. He was a part-time reservist. Constables Samuel Davison and Norman Lynch were twenty-four and twenty-two respectively; the former was married. Samuel Davison was a native of County Donegal while Constable Lynch was from Donemana in County Tyrone.

Aughnacloy in County Tyrone is known to those travelling between Dungannon and the west or Dublin and the north-west as the town with the very wide main street. That main street is also the scene of a weekly market and on 6 July three policemen were preparing to place traffic cones in readiness for the market. The three were about to get out of their Ford Cortina outside the Catholic church when gunmen jumped from a stolen van and began firing, hitting all three. Reserve Constable David Morrow was dead in the back seat while both men in the front had been injured; the driver was able to radio to his station. The murder took place while Mass was being celebrated in the church and members of the congregation threw themselves to the floor when they heard the gunfire. The killers escaped across the border. David Morrow was thirty-five and had two children, one aged three and the other just a year-old. He was the last RUC officer to be murdered in 1977.

The RUC had faced a major crisis in the spring of 1977 with an attempted repeat of the UWC strike of 1974. Once again the planned strike had a political objective; Ian Paisley and the Ulster Unionist Action Council promoted it as a protest against the perceived inadequacy of the government's security policy and as a demand to return devolved government, with majority rule, to the province. Jack Hermon, the Deputy Chief Constable, played a leading role in police reaction to the strike, which began at midnight on 2 May. It was known that the majority of people in the province did not support the action but there were elements that 'would attempt to compensate for that lack of support by using all forms of violence'.[5]

Pressure was brought to bear on workers at Ballylumford power station to join the strike and Hermon was asked if he could do anything to help. His response was to provide additional uniformed police at the power station and to assign plainclothes teams to patrol the areas of the workers' homes. As he prepared to go to Ballylumford to brief officers, he was telephoned with news that the situation had worsened and that workers, concerned for their own safety, were about to walk out. Hermon's immediate reaction was to promise that each of the sixty workers on duty would be given a police escort home. In spite of the presence of Paisley and Ernest Baird at the power station, Hermon's resolute action succeeded and there was no walkout.

On the morning of Monday, 9 May more than 50 per cent of the work-force reported for work, and the extra police deployment remained in position until the strike ended. There was no further threat of a stoppage at Ballylumford.[6]

Another major confrontation, with the potential to stretch police and Army resources to the limit, occurred in Ballymena where the town centre had been taken over by strikers with shops and other businesses forced to close. Once again Hermon went to the scene and, as he entered the police station, was jeered by strikers. A plan was conceived to deal with the barricades but it required Army support in the form of equipment to drag vehicles in the barricades to the sides of the road; it would be twenty-four hours before that equipment could be assembled. Newman was adamant that the barricades would have to be broken although Hermon was concerned that any use of force could lead to violence across Northern Ireland. A further meeting was held with the strikers' committee, led by Paisley, in Ballymena at which Hermon made it clear that police would use whatever force was necessary to clear the town and that anyone who resisted would be arrested and charged.

When the police operation began about three hours later, two groups of officers, each commanded by a superintendent, advanced in a pincer movement on the strikers. One group was confronted by Paisley and eight supporters who stood across the road. The superintendent asked Paisley and his supporters to move off the road or face arrest for obstructing the police. They refused to move and were arrested. Paisley then turned to those manning the barricades to say that he and the others were under arrest 'that they would be martyrs, taken prisoner for their cause, and that thereby they had achieved their goal'.[7] He also called on the strikers to disperse, which they did.

This was a turning point in the strike and, although matters remained tense for several more days with many cases of intimidation and an attempt to murder a petrol tanker driver, the strike was finally called off on Friday, 13 May. Roy Mason, the Secretary of State, the RUC and Army had stood firm and defeated an attempt to bring Northern Ireland to its knees.

> detailed planning and determination had won the day, but during the eleven days of strike action, three people had been murdered . . . , and forty-five RUC officers injured. One hundred and twenty-four people were also charged with offences, ranging from murder and attempted murder to hijacking, intimidation and rioting. A clear signal – if one were needed – had gone out from the RUC that, even though its members were predominantly Protestant, it would not kowtow to Protestant extremists and their paramilitary allies.[8]

Although terrorist activity and street violence continued throughout that summer, levels were much lower than in previous years. Even so, there was no respite for the RUC. This was the year of Queen Elizabeth's Silver Jubilee and a Royal visit had been planned for 10 and 11 August. Less auspicious dates it would have been hard to imagine. The anniversary of Internment, usually marked by violence and demonstrations, occurred on the 9th while the 12th was a major date in the 'marching season', the day when the Apprentice Boys of Derry celebrate the relief of that city in 1689. Thus these three events would place enormous strain on the security forces, involving around 30,000 personnel. Some idea of the strain can be gleaned from the fact that civil servants were drafted in as part of the Queen's protection team; men over six feet tall were used, not for any skill in protection work, but for the simple fact that their height might obscure a gunman's view of the monarch or, failing that, they might stop a bullet meant for the Queen.

In spite of protests from Republicans and boycott by the SDLP, the Royal visit went off well. There was one minor incident when a bomb exploded at the New University of Ulster in Coleraine; there were no injuries and little damage. The Apprentice Boys' parade presented another problem, as there was a prohibition on members marching across Craigavon bridge into the walled city, a traditional part of their activities on the day. Hermon did not believe that the ban could be enforced without causing violence and sought Newman's permission to use his discretion in negotiations with the marchers. As a result of sensitive negotiation between senior officers, led by Hermon, and Apprentice Boys' leaders, a compromise was reached and the march was allowed across the bridge. There were no serious incidents. What might have been a very difficult week in the history of Northern Ireland had passed with little to mark it, thanks very largely to the work of the RUC.

That seven months were to pass without a policeman being murdered was due in part to the improved professionalism of the force, a greater awareness amongst members of the dangers of booby-traps, especially under-car devices, or UCBTs, the availability of more armoured patrol cars and the fact that the IRA was going through a period of internal struggle. The Provisionals had been split over the 1975 ceasefire with many younger northern members criticizing the older leaders for 'selling out' to the British. They saw no benefits for the IRA but rather an opportunity for the Army and RUC to consolidate their positions, re-organize their structures and press on with efforts to break the terrorist groups. Out of this internal debate emerged a new Provisional IRA with a 'northern command' to oversee activities in Northern Ireland and run by the younger men from Northern Ireland. If anything, the Maze Prison, formerly Long Kesh internment camp, had proved to be a university for terror strategy and tactics. It also provided yet another battlefield on which to fight the government as Republicans of various hues began campaigning for political status for their prisoners, a campaign that would culminate in the hunger strike of 1981 and the greatest boost for the IRA since Bloody Sunday in 1972. More emphasis was to be given to the political wing of Republicanism, with Sinn Fein setting out to become a political party that would challenge the SDLP. Any idea of a quick victory for the IRA had now been abandoned as Republicans began preparing for the 'long war'. Thus Republicanism saw the future as themselves with 'an Armalite in one hand and the ballot paper in the other'.

In 1971 and 1972 the IRA had perfected the car bomb with which they had devastated large areas of Northern Ireland's cities, towns and villages. Countermeasures included the sealing off of vulnerable areas, spot checks on vehicles close to town centres and a permanent Army presence in those areas together with searches of pedestrians; a Civilian Search Unit had been established to relieve soldiers of the routine task of searching. In addition, it had become much more difficult to obtain the quantities of explosives needed for bombs, although one alternative was the 'co-op mix' homemade explosive based on fertiliser. All these measures had combined to make it more difficult for terrorists to bring car bombs into town centres and so the IRA looked for a new way to wreak havoc. It found it in a very simple weapon: the incendiary. Although these had been used earlier in the campaign they assumed a greater importance in the IRA's arsenal in the mid-seventies. An incendiary could be made from very basic materials: a cover from a tape cassette, a chemical mix of inflammable materials – some robberies were carried out on schools to steal phosphorous but incendiaries made from this were rare – with a detonator, battery and some means of timing. Smuggling these into shopping areas was not difficult; much use was made of female couriers to carry the devices and even to plant them. Targets could include clothing shops, bookstores, paint and furniture shops, in any of which it was easy to conceal an incendiary and difficult to find one. In such targets the effects of an incendiary were horrific, creating a fire that spread rapidly and was often out of control before firefighters arrived. The north coast resort of Portrush was firebombed in the summer of 1976 while the commercial centres of Belfast and Londonderry also suffered heavily, as did many other town centres. Damage from incendiaries across the province was estimated at £50 million in 1976.

A more fiendish refinement of the incendiary device was the case charge or blast incendiary in which a small quantity of explosive, a timer and detonator were fixed to a can of petrol. The resulting explosion spread flaming petrol over a wide area; these devices could be used against all types of commercial property and those where owners had fitted security grills at the behest of their insurers found such measures defeated by the simple addition of a wire hook to suspend the bomb from the grille. So that bomb disposal teams would have least chance of disarming these devices the time delay was usually only sufficient for the bomber to make his or her escape.

The first policeman to die in 1978 was the victim of a blast incendiary. Reserve Constable Gordon Crothers was enjoying a night out at La Mon House in the Castlereagh hills. It was 17 February and there were two large functions taking place at La Mon; both the Northern Ireland Collie Club and the Northern Ireland Junior Motorcycle Club were holding prize presentations and, with other social gatherings in the complex that night, over 300 people were present. This was the night the IRA chose to target La Mon with two blast incendiaries. The evening was still young – it was not quite 9 o'clock – when the bombs, hooked onto security grilles on the function room windows, exploded. There was no warning as a fireball shot into the crowded building, almost vaporizing those closest to the windows, cremating others and burning clothes, skin and hair from yet more victims. Panic spread almost as quickly as the fireball as guests and staff tried to dash to safety but, with lights failing and acrid smoke surrounding them, the sense of despair deepened.

The Chief Constable was on the scene quickly and later described what he saw as the 'ultimate in inhumanity'. At that stage he was not aware that one of his officers was a victim. Twelve people died and another twenty-three were injured seriously. It was one of the worst terrorist incidents until that date. Reserve Constable Crothers and his wife Joan were among the dead. They had been married for five years and had a daughter aged two-and-a-half.

During the previous winter there had been a blitz of incendiaries, both the small cassette and case charge, across Northern Ireland. Some 600 devices had been used and shops, hotels, cinemas and offices were targets, as was a bus station. On one night sixteen incendiaries exploded in nine towns; nine more were made safe. However, the effect of the La Mon atrocity was such that the IRA was condemned widely at home and abroad and sympathy for the organization reduced. A more noticeable effect was the reduction in the use of incendiaries with only twelve such attacks in the ten weeks following La Mon whereas there had been eighty between the New Year and the La Mon attack.

While Gordon Crothers was an incidental victim of an attack that was not targeted specifically at him, Charles Simpson was clearly a target for the IRA. A member of the RUC Reserve in his native Coleraine, he had become a regular officer a year earlier and was stationed in Londonderry. On the night of 28 February he was in the back of a Land Rover as it turned into Clarendon Street when gunmen fired from the

142

grounds of Foyle Special Care School. Charles Simpson was hit in the head and died about an hour after admission to Altnagelvin Hospital. A civilian was hit in the foot and children in the street scattered in panic as gunmen fired their automatic rifles. Constable Simpson was married with three sons, the youngest only ten months old.

Reserve Constable John Moore was fifty-seven and a bachelor who farmed at Armoy. In 1977 he had fought off IRA gunmen who had tried to force their way into his house and he would have been acutely aware of the danger he faced. On the morning of 15 April he left his home just before 7 o'clock to drive to another farm about two miles away to tend sheep. In his car were his dog, Jip, and a lamb that had been rejected by its mother. As he drove down the laneway from his farmhouse he triggered an IRA booby-trap bomb that killed him instantly; the two animals were also killed. The device had been set up overnight and was detonated by the breaking of a length of fishing line stretched across the laneway. A fiendish device, it was obviously the terrorists' answer to the courage of a man who had already fought them off once. They were not going to allow him a second chance. A year after his death his colleagues at Ballymoney RUC Station provided a memorial plaque for John Moore's church, First Kilraughts Presbyterian, while the congregation created a memorial fund to provide for the Christian education of children in the congregation and for the planting of thirty trees to commemorate their murdered friend.

A week later Constable Millar McAllister, a photographer based in Lisburn, was at home when one of his two sons called him to the front door where two men waited to speak to him. The callers expressed an interest in Millar McAllister's pigeons and the policeman invited them around the back of his house to see his pigeon loft. At that point one of them shot the thirty-six year-old at point-blank range. Although wounded four times in the head and stomach, Constable McAllister staggered back to his kitchen where he died. The killers had found the policeman's photograph, name and address in a pigeon fanciers' magazine. Three men were convicted of the murder in 1979 and sentenced to life.

Nineteen-year-old Robert Struthers was an apprentice electrician and member of the Reserve stationed at Strand Road in Londonderry. He lived in the still predominantly Protestant Cloughglass estate, off Northland Road. The young man, who wanted to make his career in the RUC, had received threats at home and at work but continued to serve in the Reserve. On 16 June he was murdered by IRA gunmen who walked into the electrical business where he worked, close to the city centre, and shot him several times before running off. Reserve Constable Struthers was dead on arrival at Altnagelvin Hospital.

The next afternoon the IRA ambushed a patrol car at a crossroads at

Sturgan's Brae near Camlough lake in County Armagh. Constable Hugh McConnell was killed instantly but Constable William Turbitt was abducted. The IRA later claimed that he was being interrogated but it is unlikely that he survived very long, having received a head wound from a high-velocity round. His body was recovered from a derelict house on 9 July but it had been concealed in bog or marsh for some time before being moved to the house. Both murdered officers were married; Hugh McConnell had two children and William Turbitt four.

In the wake of the abduction of Constable Turbitt a Catholic priest, the Reverend Hugh Murphy OBE, was kidnapped at gunpoint from his parochial house at Ahoghill. The kidnappers claimed to be from the UFF and said that Father Murphy, a former Royal Navy chaplain, would be released in return for Constable Turbitt. In spite of her own suffering, Mrs Margaret Turbitt appealed for Father Murphy's release, as did the Reverend Ian Paisley. Eventually the kidnappers acceded to the pleas and Father Murphy was released near a parishioner's home that evening, over thirteen hours after his abduction. At first the police believed that the UFF was responsible for kidnapping the priest but an anonymous telephone call led them to the real kidnappers, a group of police officers. Constable William McCaughey led the group that included two sergeants, John Weir and Gary Armstrong; the latter had been decorated for rescuing a soldier in a terrorist ambush.[9] The gang had already murdered a Catholic shopkeeper, William Strathearn, and carried out a gun and bomb attack on a bar near Keady. All were arrested and brought to trial. Lord Lowry, the Lord Chief Justice, commended the RUC and especially those detectives who had brought their former colleagues to trial. McCaughey was jailed for life for offences including murder, kidnapping, armed robbery and bombing the Keady pub; he pleaded guilty to all charges. Armstrong also pleaded guilty to kidnapping and other offences and received a two-year suspended sentence. Weir was given life for the murder of William Strathearn while Ian Mitchell and Laurence McClure received suspended sentences for their parts in the pub bombing. David Wilson was given a one-year suspended sentence for withholding information. McCaughey's father received a similar sentence for withholding information and obstructing police; Hugh Murphy had been held in his outhouse.

The RUC was praised widely for its handling of this case, which was seen as fair and even-handed. Senior officers considered that the case would demonstrate the force's impartiality. A similar case in 1979 also saw three police officers jailed for carrying out shootings, in one of which a youth was wounded. Derek Gilliland received an eight-year sentence, Wilfred Kelly six years, John Elliott three years and William Arnold, a recent recruit, was given a two-year suspended sentence.

*   *   *

Three more RUC officers died at the hands of terrorists in 1978. On 4 July Reserve Constable Jacob Rankin was leaving Castlederg RUC Station when he was shot and seriously wounded by three gunmen in a car. A full-time reservist, Jacob Rankin died soon after being admitted to Tyrone County Hospital in Omagh. Married with three children, he was known as a quiet, unassuming man. Another reservist, John Lamont, was shot in George Street in Ballymena on 2 August. He was alone at the time, having just escorted a policewoman back to the station. Shortly before midnight a car pulled up behind Reserve Constable Lamont and he was shot four times. Although given first-aid by customers from a nearby bar, he was dead on arrival at the Waveney Hospital. John Lamont was the first member of the security forces to be murdered in Ballymena. The tenth and last police death of the year was that of another reservist, Howard Donaghy, who was building a house near Loughmacrory in County Tyrone. The twenty-four year-old was planning to marry in June 1979 and was working on the bungalow with his brother and his brother's girlfriend on 11 September when IRA gunmen appeared, held his brother at gunpoint and began shooting at Reserve Constable Donaghy. His brother raised the alarm and contacted their mother, a nurse, who rushed to the scene with a first-aid bag. She was unable to help her son who died in her arms. Howard Donaghy had served in the Reserve for four years.

Although 1979 began with a period during which there were no police deaths, this came to an end with the worst single incident to date for the RUC in which four policemen lost their lives. A Transit van belonging to a business in Dunleer, County Louth, was taking a load of cheese from Dundalk to Castleblayney when it was hijacked close to the border at 8.45 a.m. on 17 April. The driver was held while his vehicle was filled with explosives and parked on Millvale Road near Camlough in County Armagh. At about 11.30 a.m. a two-vehicle police patrol, that had just left Bessbrook RUC/Army base, spotted the van and was immediately suspicious of it. But, as the policemen prepared to check the Transit, the explosives were detonated by remote control. The first vehicle, a Land Rover, was blown to pieces and its occupants were killed instantly.

Four men died. The senior man was twenty-eight year-old Constable Richard Baird, a father of two with three years' service. Also killed were Constable Noel Webb, aged thirty, who had been in the force for only thirteen months, Constable Paul Gray, aged twenty-five, who had less than a year's service, and Reserve Constable Robert Lockhart, aged forty-four, who had joined the previous November. Both Noel Webb and Paul Gray were single men, although the latter was to have married in June, while Robert Lockhart had three children. Eleven other people were injured in the blast. The Transit's driver was released when the bomb exploded. A Crossmaglen man was later jailed for the murders. In 1981 five soldiers were also killed in a massive explosion in the same area.

This quadruple murder had been planned carefully as was the next attack on the RUC. On Sunday, 6 May Detective Constable Norman Prue, of Special Branch, and Sergeant Robert Maughan, of 9th/12th Royal Lancers, stopped outside Holy Cross Catholic Church in Lisnaskea, County Fermanagh, to buy a copy of *Republican News*, something that police officers did every Sunday. Mass was being celebrated as the IRA shot Norman Prue from behind a wall. Other gunmen in a van shot Sergeant Maughan as he sat in an unmarked green Lada. The attackers escaped in the van but struck a car which they then stole at gunpoint to make their getaway. There was pandemonium inside the church and a doctor rushed out to help but both men were already dead. Although Sergeant Maughan was involved in intelligence work, he was not in the SAS as the IRA later claimed.

That a church or its precincts were in no way sacred to terrorists was proved yet again in Londonderry two weeks later when Reserve Constable Stanley Wray arrived at the city's Claremont Presbyterian Church on Northland Road for morning service. Stanley Wray was leaving his car when he was shot from behind and killed. His teenage son and daughter were with him and thus witnessed the murder of their father. The car used by the IRA had been taken from its driver only minutes earlier; the owner had been held hostage in a nearby Catholic church and was released when his car was returned to him. Stanley Wray was fifty and had survived a murder attempt in 1976 when he was shot in the chest. His murder was seen not only as an attack on the RUC but also on the Protestant population of the city; Claremont Church has since closed due to a diminishing congregation. Reserve Constable Wray's funeral took place from Glendermott Presbyterian Church, on the other side of the Foyle, where he had been married.

The vulnerability of police officers, especially reservists, was emphasized by the murder of another two reservists in June. On the 2nd, Alan Dunne, a father of five, was chatting to a friend outside his home at Ballinahone Crescent in Armagh at about 2.00 p.m. when a car drove by and INLA gunmen opened fire, killing both men. The other victim was David Stinson. Both Alan Dunne's wife and his son saw the gunmen's car and heard the shots that killed the two friends. Less than three weeks later, Reserve Constable Jack Scott, from Cookstown, was shot dead by the IRA near Ardboe while driving a milk tanker on his regular route. Reserve Constable Scott was hit in the head and body by rounds from an Armalite and crashed his lorry into a hedge. He had been in the Reserve since 1974. His nine children were planning a silver wedding celebration for their parents in July. The rifle used to kill Jack

Scott was recovered when two IRA men were shot dead by the SAS; it had been used in three other murders as well as numerous additional incidents.

On the day after Alan Dunne's murder in Armagh, police and soldiers were carrying out a search about two miles from the border in County Armagh. A Queen's Own Highlanders' officer saw two policemen walking down a lane and called on them not to go any farther; when one waved to him he turned away. Unfortunately, the policemen did not turn back and were killed seconds later when a bomb in a milk churn was detonated by radio control. One of the pair was forty-eight year-old Superintendent Stanley Hanna, subdivisional commander in Bessbrook, who came from Carryduff and had almost thirty years' service. The other was Constable Kevin Thompson, a twenty-two year-old from Portrush, who was to be married in September; he had been in the RUC for eighteen months.

The INLA struck again in Armagh on 31 July when gunmen fired at a police car parked outside the courthouse. Constable George Walsh, a fifty-one year-old father of one, was killed. Three days later two soldiers who had been inspecting the burnt-out remains of the car used by Constable Walsh's killers were blown up by a landmine close to the border.

On 2 August, also, the IRA shot and killed Constable Derek Davidson in a carefully staged ambush in Belfast. A hoax call about a burglary in Clondara Street, off Falls Road, was received at Springfield Road RUC Station but when police checked back on the call it seemed to be genuine and so it was decided to investigate. The practice for such calls was that uniformed officers would protect detectives as they made their investigations and one of those who went to Clondara Street was Derek Davidson, a native of Edinburgh who had been in the RUC since January; he was married with a daughter aged four. As Constable Davidson climbed out of a Land Rover he was shot by gunmen who were holding hostage the occupants of a house across the street; he died instantly. A CID officer later told an inquest that he dived for cover but that five bullets tore his clothing although the only injury he received was a graze to his hip.

Springfield Road RUC Station lost another officer to the IRA in November and, by coincidence, he was also called Davidson. Constable Gerry Davidson was getting into a Land Rover that was leaving the station on 28 October when he was shot in the head and back by gunmen who had taken over a house facing the police station. An Army warrant officer, David Bellamy, was also killed, another soldier was hit seven times but survived and a second policeman was injured. Gerry Davidson was taken to hospital and placed on life-support after surgery but died on 18 November. He left a wife and two children.

147

Reserve Constable Stanley Hazelton was stationed at Moy RUC Station in County Tyrone and owned a garage in Dungannon. On 22 December he crossed the border to County Monaghan to collect the family Christmas turkey but was ambushed by the IRA. His car was hit by more than twenty rounds on an isolated road. Stanley Hazelton had survived a previous murder attempt when his business had been bombed three years earlier. Aged forty-eight, he had one child and was described by Dungannon priest, the Reverend Denis Faul, as 'a good neighbour'. He was the last RUC officer to be murdered in 1979 and the last during Sir Kenneth Newman's time in office; the Chief Constable had been knighted in 1977.

On 2 January 1980 John Hermon was sworn in as Chief Constable with Michael McAtamney as Deputy. Hermon was to remain in office longer than any other Chief Constable; only the first two Inspectors General, Wickham and Pim, held the office for longer. The policy of primacy of the police still held good although Newman had had a difficult period in August 1979 when the IRA murdered Lord Mountbatten off the coast of County Sligo. That same day, the 27th, IRA terrorists, operating from across the border, killed six Parachute Regiment soldiers with a bomb planted in a trailer at the roadside at Narrow Water Castle. Soldiers of the Queen's Own Highlanders and more paras were flown in and casualties evacuated by helicopter. As the helicopter lifted off there was a second large explosion that threatened to pull the aircraft out of the air but the pilot maintained control and flew away. However, another twelve men had been killed, some mutilated so badly that they could be identified only by their boots and socks. Lieutenant Colonel David Blair, Queen's Own Highlanders, was vaporized and his remains have never been found, although an epaulette, allegedly from his combat jacket, was shown to Prime Minister Margaret Thatcher who visited the province in the wake of the murders. At a briefing and lunch from which police were excluded, attempts were made by senior Army officers to persuade Thatcher to return to a situation in which the Army had primacy. When the Prime Minister subsequently met Newman and expressed her concerns, and those of the Army, he had his arguments ready and pointed out that the Army plan would be a backward step. Thatcher decided on a compromise, appointing Sir Maurice Oldfield as Security Coordinator in October but his reign was cut short when he was compromised by an incident in a public house and lost his positive vetting. His successor was sidelined by both Hermon and the GOC.

Margaret Thatcher also backed the policy of police primacy by authorizing an additional 1,000 recruits for the RUC, as Newman had requested. Thus when the 'Wee Man' left office he left a force that was much stronger than on his arrival in 1973, deployed better equipment

148

and had developed highly professional strategy and tactics. Some of these Newman would take back with him to London and they became part of the standard operational procedures of the Metropolitan Police and were first seen in action during the 1981 riots in London.

As Newman departed, how was the RUC perceived in Northern Ireland? The force had achieved a high reputation for professionalism and had demonstrated its impartiality with its effective handling of the 1977 Loyalist strike. Its success in tracking down and bringing to justice the 'Shankill butchers' was also proof positive of its professionalism and effectiveness. Indeed, the RUC was having more success against Loyalist terrorists than against Republicans. (One reason for this, in the view of many officers, was that Loyalists were nowhere near as well organized as the IRA and were inclined to boast in pubs about their crimes.) But still they were criticized by Nationalist and Republican politicians. The latter indulged in a litany of complaints against the force, making allegations that prisoners were tortured to obtain confessions and that the RUC was biased against Republicans, Nationalists and Catholics. In some cases, Republican prisoners were injuring themselves in order to make allegations of ill treatment.

However, the principle Nationalist party, the SDLP, still withheld support for the force. Both Paddy Devlin and Gerry Fitt had left the party and John Hume had become leader. Hume's attitude to the RUC was not encouraging and under his hand the SDLP was to become an ever greater critic of the force, developing an ambivalent policy that claimed to support the RUC when carrying out normal police duties but withholding support when the force was involved in security duties. The hypocrisy of this stance is difficult to comprehend but probably owed much to Hume's old-fashioned nationalism, although he would deny being a Nationalist. A parallel might be a party in Great Britain, say Labour, withdrawing support for the Metropolitan Police when that force was engaged in anti-terrorist operations, which, of course, include the policing of London's Heathrow airport, or of Kent Constabulary in a similar situation; that force's Special Branch is responsible for security at some of Britain's main cross-channel ports. In 1973 this author was engaged in a discussion with an SDLP member who criticized the RUC on the grounds that all its personnel were 'farmer's sons', ill-educated and 'nearly all Protestants'. Exactly what is wrong with being a farmer's son he could not explain; but he was probably exhibiting a town-dweller's patronizing attitude to those from rural areas. Nor would he be swayed by the counter-argument that his own comments were bigoted, nor by the fact that the force had attracted many Catholics and that these members had been promoted out of all proportion to their overall numbers. He also refused to believe that there were police officers who had earned degrees before joining the force, or who were working for such qualifications. The loss of more open-minded men such as Devlin and Fitt ensured that the SDLP would never attract real support from Protestants.

However, Amnesty International had taken an interest in the allegations of ill treatment of suspects and produced a report in May 1977 outlining seventy-eight such cases. Secretary of State Roy Mason asked for details which Amnesty refused to provide. Most complaints centred on Castlereagh interrogation centre. Newman asked Mason to establish an independent inquiry to review 'present practices and procedures in relation to the interrogation of suspected terrorists'. The inquiry was chaired by Judge Harry Bennett QC and included John Marshall, Professor of Clinical Neurology at the University of London, and retired Home Office Chief Inspector of Constabulary, Sir James Haughton.

The subsequent Bennett Report concluded that a small number of officers had used force to extract statements from terrorists and recommended a number of changes to interrogation procedures, including closed-circuit television to monitor proceedings, a code of conduct for interviewing officers, more supervision by uniformed and senior officers and access to a lawyer after forty-eight hours, as well as medical examinations after each individual interview. Bennett had identified a number of cases where the injuries to suspects had been 'inflicted by someone other than the prisoner himself'. This was only a fifth of the Amnesty total and, if anything, proved that many prisoners were harming themselves in order to bring police officers into disrepute.

The Bennett recommendations angered many detectives who predicted that the previous one-in-ten conviction rate would not be sustained if these were put into place, but within months thirty-five of the recommendations were in place. In July 1980 one IRA man, Edward Brophy, was acquitted on forty-eight of forty-nine charges, which included the La Mon murders, because the judge refused to admit statements made in Castlereagh in September 1978; Brophy was sentenced to five years for IRA membership. He was later released on appeal when the conviction was quashed.

In an ideal world police officers should not harm anyone in their custody. However, in that same ideal world, no one should be murdering police officers or committing outrages against the community in which they live. The frustrations of detectives involved in the interrogation of terrorist suspects can only be imagined; quite often they knew that those before them had been involved in the most horrendous crimes, including the murders of police officers, but had no proof that could be used in court unless the suspect were to provide a confession. That some officers resorted to 'thumping a prisoner around the ear' might be understandable and prove that the officers were only human; but that so few officers did so was a sign of the RUC's high degree of professionalism.

Sadly, the Bennett Report was used to pillory the police, especially by Republicans. It could be argued that had Newman moved sooner to deal with the complaints coming from Castlereagh, then controversy would never have reached the scale that it did. But would that have made any difference to the criticisms from Republicans and the SDLP? It is highly doubtful in the case of the latter and would have made no difference at all to the former. The simple comment of one police officer to the author sums up the dilemma: 'I never went to work in the morning to kill a Catholic but others got out of bed to kill a policeman. That's the difference between me and an IRA man.'

Notes
1: Devlin, op. cit., p. 279
2: Ibid.
3: Paddy McNulty's car was booked in for its service under the name Murphy leading many to assume that he was trying to conceal his true identity. The truth is that the car had been bought through a maternal uncle on Merseyside who worked for the manufacturer and was entitled to buy a car at reduced price each year. This uncle had offered Paddy the chance to buy this car but, in order to keep the warranty, the uncle's name remained on the vehicle registration papers and was used when booking the car in for its service.
4: Cameron, *The Women in Green*, p. 170
5: Hermon, op. cit., p. 104
6: Ibid., p. 106
7: Ibid., p. 107
8: Ibid., p. 108
9: McCaughey had been a member of a Loyalist terrorist group before he joined the RUC.

Chapter Seven

Hermon takes Control

When John Hermon was sworn in as Chief Constable on 2 January 1980 he took command of a force that had changed almost beyond recognition from the one he had joined thirty years earlier. But while the RUC had burgeoned in numbers the circumstances in which it had to operate were also very different, as Hermon pointed out at a passing-out parade a month after becoming Chief Constable.

> I have been fortunate enough during my career to know what it is like to walk down a street on my own, meeting and talking with people, without a flak jacket, without a gun. I want to see the day when you too can do the same. It will be a good day for you and it will be a good day for Northern Ireland.

As a statement of what he hoped to achieve in his time in command it was idealistic and optimistic but Hermon knew that no policeman really wants to carry a gun or wear a flak jacket and that the concept of a force with no need for such equipment would have an appeal, especially to young recruits. By the time he made that speech, however, four officers had been murdered in three incidents since he had taken office.

Those victims were two reservists and two regular constables and the first to die was Reserve Constable Robert Crilly. Once again the murder took place while the policeman was engaged in his everyday occupation. Robert Crilly, sixty and single, owned a garage in Newtownbutler, County Fermanagh, in which he was working at lunchtime on 3 January when a car drew up outside. Two men got out and shot Robert Crilly, who was dead before an ambulance arrived. The murdered man had run a business in the town for forty years and was well known and popular. In December a communion table was dedicated in his memory in Galloon Parish Church. Reserve Constable William Purse was on duty at a football match on Belfast's Shore Road on 12 January when he was killed. Players, officials and spectators dived for cover but the referee restarted the match when the shooting ended. However, when it was realized that Reserve Constable Purse was dead, the match, between Crusaders and Portadown, was abandoned.

Between those two murders, the IRA also killed three members of the UDR in a landmine explosion near Castlewellan in County Down. With those murders the total of dead in Northern Ireland since 1969 passed the 2,000 mark; with deaths in the Republic, Britain and elsewhere included, it had touched that figure with the murder of Reserve Constable Gordon Crothers in February 1978.

On 11 February, two days before Hermon's speech at Enniskillen, an IRA landmine was detonated in a culvert under the Roslea-Lisnaskea road near the border in Fermanagh as a two-vehicle patrol passed. The bomb, some 800 pounds of explosives, was controlled from nearby high ground. The second Land Rover took the full force of the blast and Constables Winston Howe and Joseph Rose died instantly. Winston Howe, thirty-five with two children, was a local man who attended St Mark's Church, Aghadrumsee. At his funeral service the minister recalled the number of terrorist incidents in the area in recent years; the parish had seen four violent deaths in six months. Constable Rose was twenty-one, single and came from Dundonald, outside Belfast.

It was a bad start to the year for the RUC but the force's death toll for the whole year remained in single figures with nine officers murdered. This was also a year in which the province's overall death toll dropped to eighty-six, the lowest since 1970. However, this could be no consolation to those who lost loved ones that year.

Of the nine policemen who died during 1980, only three were regular officers; the others were reservists and, except for William Purse, off duty when they were murdered. On 4 April Bernard Montgomery was working part-time in his brother's business at Glenbank Industrial Estate in Ligoniel when two IRA men walked into the office and shot him; they also wounded a sixty-three year-old colleague. Bernard Montgomery had served in the Reserve for just over a year and was waiting to join the full-time Reserve; he was thirty-four and had one child. Frederick Wilson worked for the Northern Ireland Housing Executive and was walking to work on 11 April when an IRA gunman shot him from the pillion of a stolen motorcycle. Aged forty-three with two children, Reserve Constable Wilson was actually believed by the IRA to be a UDR soldier. Following this murder, priests of St Malachy's Catholic Church, some 200 yards from the scene, read a statement at all services saying that those who approved of murder could be just as guilty as those who pulled the trigger.

However, the murderers paid little heed to such admonitions, nor to the pain they caused to families. That was especially true in the case of

Reserve Constable Wallace Allen who was abducted on 31 August. The father of two did a milk delivery run every third Sunday and was doing so when he was abducted. In spite of appeals from Seamus Mallon, SDLP deputy leader and a neighbour of the Allen family, and many others for his safe return, there was no response from the IRA until 4 September when they said Wallace Allen had died from injuries received during his abduction, which they described as an 'arrest'. They had also booby-trapped a churn on the lorry but the device had exploded without causing injury. A widespread search finally uncovered Wallace Allen's body on 12 September; he had been murdered at the time of his abduction, dying from a single head wound. The removal of the murdered officer's body was simply an additional piece of cruelty with which to afflict his wife, family and friends.

On 23 September Reserve Constable Thomas Johnston finished duty at Roslea RUC Station and drove home to Lisrace, near Magheraveely. As he was preparing to put his car in the garage he was shot by IRA gunmen from behind a hedge and suffered multiple wounds. Neighbours took him to Enniskillen's Erne Hospital but he was dead on arrival. Thomas Johnston, thirty-four and a father of two, had been injured in the blast that killed Constables Howe and Rose in February.

Constable Stephen Magill was in a patrol investigating an apparent burglary at Suffolk Library on Stewartstown Road on the outskirts of Belfast. However, terrorists had taken over a nearby house, holding the family hostage. As police arrived they opened fire with an M60 heavy machine gun. Over 100 rounds were fired and Stephen Magill was killed as he climbed from the Land Rover. Three other officers, one a woman, were injured. A pensioner, Michael Madden, was later murdered by the IRA, who claimed that he had given police information about the attack. Stephen Magill, a native of Larne based at Woodburn RUC Station, was married but had no children. At his funeral service in Woodlands Presbyterian Church he was described as an outstanding young man of strong character and a committed Christian.

At the end of 1980 there was some cause for believing that the RUC and Army were winning since the province had had its least violent year for a decade. Certainly RUC/Army relations were better than ever; Hermon and the GOC, Sir Richard Lawson, had established a harmonious working partnership. Cross-border relations with the Garda had also improved, especially at top level. Police intelligence on the various terrorist groups was also much better and it looked as if an end to the violence might be in sight; but those in command were cautious. And rightly so, for festering in the Maze Prison was a dispute over the status of convicted terrorists. Merlyn Rees had removed their 'political status' but, ever since, prisoners and supporters had campaigned for its return.

Paddy Devlin had supported the original granting of special status in 1972 but had changed his stance on the question.

> The unprecedented barbarity of the Provos' campaign and their wanton disregard for human life had long removed from me all vestiges of sympathy for them and I was no longer in favour of them having these privileges.[1]

The IRA men in the Maze had embarked on a protest in 1976 by refusing to don prison uniform and wearing only a blanket. This was ratcheted up two years later when some 300 prisoners began a 'dirty protest' with prisoners urinating and defecating on cell floors and then spreading their excrement on the walls. However, it looked as if the IRA leadership might not support this protest until an ally appeared in the form of the newly appointed Cardinal Tomas O'Fiaich. A man of Republican views, O'Fiaich visited the 'dirty protestors' and described their conditions as akin to Calcutta's slums. Whatever his familiarity with the slums of that Indian city, the Cardinal missed one vital point: Calcutta's poor were forced to live in such conditions; those in the Maze had chosen them.

However, the government agreed to a suggestion from O'Fiaich that he act as a mediator, for which the Cardinal enlisted the support of Bishop Edward Daly. But there was no real progress and the European Human Rights Commission ruled that there was no justification for political status. Although eighteen prison officers were murdered by the IRA, the government was determined not to give in. Finally, the IRA leadership decided on a hunger strike. The churchmen met Humphrey Atkins, the Secretary of State, and secured an agreement that prisoners could wear their own clothes rather than prison uniforms but this was not accepted; the hunger strike began on 27 October.

Tension increased throughout Northern Ireland with demonstrations in support of the hunger strikers while the Republican publicity machine moved into top gear across the globe. The RUC were stretched to contain the demonstrations; a twelve-hour shift pattern was introduced and Traffic Division personnel were redeployed to public order duties, with a planned Christmas anti-drink-driving campaign sidelined. During November and December the number of prisoners on hunger strike increased to thirty and Hermon was

> not happy about our ability to deal with widespread violence should a hunger-striker die. On 17 December, the condition of one of the first seven prisoners deteriorated so much that local news bulletins reported that he was likely to die at any time. A dreadful sense of foreboding enveloped the community and the security forces alike, all anxiously awaiting what seemed the inevitable fatal outcome.[2]

155

Fortunately, last-minute mediation brought the strike to an end on 18 December. Northern Ireland had been spared a bloody Christmas; but it was a temporary reprieve.

Following what, in Northern Ireland terms, had been a relatively quiet year, 1981 did not get off to a propitious start. In the first month, another two reservists were murdered, one while on duty and the other at home. Reserve Constable Lindsay McDougall was the first victim, shot in the back of the head while checking a suspicious car in Great Victoria Street, Belfast. The murder was carried out by an INLA gang who failed to shoot another policeman because the gunman ejected the magazine from his Browning pistol. Lindsay McDougall, a father of three, was taken to hospital but died on the 14th. One of his killers had been cleared of charges in court only two days earlier.

The second murder of a reservist was in retaliation for a murder attempt on Bernadette McAliskey, the former Bernadette Devlin, who, with her husband, was shot several times by a Loyalist gang in their home near Coalisland. The gunfire was heard by nearby patrolling soldiers whose prompt arrival ensured the survival of the couple, who had been shot in front of their children. On the 21st, five days later, an IRA gang hijacked two cars from families in Tynan, County Tyrone and, leaving some of their number holding the families, drove to Tynan Abbey, home of Sir Norman Stronge, erstwhile Speaker of the Stormont House of Commons, and his son James, a former Grenadier Guards officer and serving part-time RUC reservist. Smashing into the house with an explosive device, the gang murdered both men and set the house ablaze. As they drove away a police car from the local station arrived and the officers stopped the vehicle across the gateway to prevent a getaway.

Two gunmen ran to the armoured Cortina and began firing with high-velocity weapons. When they realized that their bullets were not penetrating either the body of the car or its windows they tried firing into the gaps around the doors. They sustained fire for about ten minutes, leaving only as police reinforcements arrived. The armour on the car had more than proved its value although subsequent analysis showed some weakness; a priority rectification programme was begun. At eighty-six, Sir Norman was the oldest person to be deliberately murdered by terrorists. His son had also been a Stormont MP and later Assembly member who had then joined the Reserve. The IRA claimed that their deaths were in retaliation for a series of Loyalist attacks on Nationalists. It was a direct assault on the Unionist tradition; eight generations of Stronges had lived at Tynan and an ancestor had been speaker of the old Irish Parliament in Dublin. A Monaghan man was later extradited from the Republic to stand trial for the murders but was acquitted.

The Stronge murders re-opened the issue of cross-border cooperation, especially as they came at a time when the UK and Irish premiers, Margaret Thatcher and Charles Haughey, had been involved in negotiations that heightened Unionist fears of a sell-out to the Republic. One reaction to this was a stunt organized by Ian Paisley who arranged for journalists to be taken to an Antrim hillside under cover of darkness to witness a body of men, paraded in ranks and wearing pseudo-uniforms, wave in the air what Paisley claimed were firearms certificates. This was Paisley's so-called 'Third Force', an organization that, he claimed, would help defend Ulster against terrorists and any attempt to hand it over to Dublin rule. The show of strength was an embarrassment to the police, especially as Paisley claimed that members of the Reserve and UDR were involved in the 'Third Force'.

As Paisley was preparing his hillside demonstration, the IRA and INLA were planning the murders of two more reservists. On 6 February, Reserve Constable Charles Lewis was gunned down and killed while leaving a newspaper shop. He and another officer were en route to take up duty at the RUC facility at Newforge Lane in the Malone area of Belfast. Although seriously wounded, the second officer survived. Charles Lewis had two children. Two days later, also in Belfast, Reserve Constable Alex Scott was shot dead by the INLA as he locked up the family shop in the Ravenhill Road area. His only child, a daughter, witnessed the killing. INLA man Gerard Steenson was later convicted of the murder but acquitted on appeal. Steenson, who was subsequently killed in a Republican feud, had been stopped by a police patrol in the Ravenhill area two days before the murder of Alex Scott; it was later believed that he had been reconnoitring for the murder.

Constable Kenneth Acheson was the father of an eleven-month-old child, had been married for three years and was based at Bessbrook. On the night of 2 April, as he drove home along Derrywilligan Road, a device exploded under his car, killing him instantly. The bomb had been placed while the car was parked close to the police station. Kenneth Acheson was described as 'conscientious about his duties and popular with his mates'. Less than three weeks later, on 27 April, Constable Gary Martin was killed by the INLA on Shaw's Road in Belfast. Police officers had gone to check a lorry that had been stolen earlier in west Belfast. The cab and back of the lorry had been checked by an inspector who found nothing and Constable Martin then volunteered to drive the vehicle away but, as he put his hand on the driver's seat, an explosion killed him instantly and injured two other officers. A coroner described the father of two as having shown 'awesome bravery' and commented that the public did not appreciate how often police officers in their daily routine risked their lives to safeguard society.

*   *   *

Eight days later Northern Ireland exploded. Republican prisoners in the Maze had decided that the government had fooled them in December and recommended their campaign for political status in January with a threat to resume the hunger strike. Their leader, Bobby Sands, chose to be the first of a new wave of hunger strikers, beginning his fast on 1 March after the government stood firm. Once again tension mounted and there was an alliance between IRA and INLA prisoners with both joining the strike. Matters were exacerbated when Frank Maguire, MP for Fermanagh/South Tyrone, died suddenly and Sinn Fein nominated Sands for the by-election, which he duly won. Legislation was rushed through Parliament to prevent any other prisoners following Sands' lead although others won seats in Dáil Éireann.

In spite of intervention on an international level, with the Pope sending a representative to try to stop the suicidal protest, Sands died on 5 May. News of his death was immediately relayed through Republican areas by loudspeaker. It was also passed to all police stations and the new Divisional Mobile Support Units (DMSUs) deployed to pre-arranged positions ready to meet whatever the reaction to Sands' death might be. Tension was already high in many areas; in Londonderry the IRA had murdered Joanne Mathers, a census enumerator, on 7 April – in the first census in which enumerators were not police officers – while two youths in a rioting crowd had been killed by an out-of-control Army Land Rover on the 20th, Easter Day. Paisley had also been active with a series of rallies styled the 'Carson Trail' – from Sir Edward Carson's anti-Home Rule rallies – that began in Omagh. A Special Branch study of the original event allowed police to anticipate and counter Paisley's effort, which was not the success he had sought. Loyalists had attacked police near Omagh during one 'Third Force' demonstration and frustrations had built up everywhere.

It was not long before violence broke out. The first victims included a teenager, Desmond Guiney, and his milkman father, Eric, stoned to death on their delivery run in Belfast's New Lodge area; the teenager died at the scene, his father on the 13th. Constable Phillip Ellis was shot dead by a gunman close to a peaceline barrier at Duncairn Gardens, between Catholic New Lodge and Protestant Tiger's Bay. The former soldier had been a policeman for less than a year; his wife was expecting their first child. On the 14th Constable Samuel Vallely, whose wife was also pregnant, was travelling through New Barnsley in a Land Rover when the vehicle was hit by an RPG7 round; he was killed instantly. Constable Vallely and his wife, who already had one child, had been planning to move to Canada following the birth of their second child.

The deaths of Constables Ellis and Vallely had followed that of the second hunger striker, Francis Hughes, on 12 May. Although there had been a reduction in violence at the time of Sands' funeral, this had been followed by an upsurge, which worsened when Hughes died. The brunt of the violence was taken by the RUC, although the Army remained in the background and the Spearhead battalion[3], had arrived in Northern Ireland on 4 May. The Divisional Mobile Support Units were the pivotal element of police strategy for dealing with rioters. Based on their existing experience, and that of the Army, the RUC had rewritten the handbook on public order, creating a tactical manual that would provide the model for every British force. One of the main lessons gleaned from past experience was not to allow rioters to get too close, thereby reducing the degree of injury that their missiles, whether rocks, petrol bombs, acid bombs or explosive devices, might cause.

The first stage in ensuring that distance was maintained was to use Divisional Mobile Support Unit Land Rovers to break a rioting mob into smaller groups. Those groups could then be dispersed further by use of baton rounds and, when they had been well reduced in size, arrests could be made. It was vital not to become involved in anything akin to the street battles of 1969 and so emphasis was placed on officers remaining in their vehicles as much as possible with still and video cameras being used to identify rioters. Infrared cameras were provided for night-time use. The hunger strikers' funerals presented the RUC with a major problem, as these were highly charged with emotion while the IRA invested them with considerable propaganda value. There was little doubt that Republicans intended using the funerals to irk Unionists and thus the police had a very careful balancing act to consider.

The overall strategy adopted by Hermon and his senior officers was one of containment, trying to keep Republican parades and other demonstrations within Republican areas to prevent retaliation from Loyalists. Appeals would also be made to the community not to become involved in confrontations with the security forces. To execute this policy the RUC would deploy in strength at interfaces between Catholic and Protestant areas; the force would also try to keep all main roads open.

As each hunger striker died, arrangements were made for the body to be taken into police care with officers supervising formal identification and post mortems while also preventing any attempts to stage processions through mixed areas where disturbances might break out. Hermon was concerned about the government's attitude, as was the GOC, Sir Richard Lawson. Both felt that 'there had to be room for some recognition of the feelings of the Catholic community, which could not accept that rejection of the prisoners' demands for "special status" justified them being allowed to die'. Following a meeting with Humphrey Atkins, the Chief Constable and GOC flew to London to meet the Prime Minister. Four men had already died at this stage and Hermon emphasized to Thatcher that the others were determined to continue the protest.

I repeatedly made the point that, while totally supporting the principle behind the British Government's stance, I thought it necessary to recognise the human tragedy behind the deaths of people by starvation, and in street disturbances; the Government had to be seen to care about this aspect of the strike. I also emphasised my view that there was a hardening of attitudes, and a resolve growing amongst Catholics in Northern Ireland against the British Government, even though the majority of them did not support the prisoners' terrorist activities.[4]

Thatcher decided to visit Belfast and, in a press conference at Stormont, expressed sympathy for the families of the dead strikers and for those whose sons might yet die. It seemed to mark a turning point in the strike, although there were many weeks and more deaths to come. Two more policemen had died in May and a further two in June, to add to the sad litany of death. One of them, Neal Quinn, was the 100th RUC officer to die since October 1969.

Constable Mervyn Robinson was off duty and leaving a public house at Whitecross, County Armagh, only 200 yards from his home, when he was shot dead by the IRA on 27 May. Stationed in Newry and with twelve years' service, he left three children. At his funeral a Church of Ireland rector said

Human rights and human dignity have figured prominently in the flood of propaganda in which we have been immersed during the past weeks, but the sad thing is that more often than not these have been the alleged rights of those who have deliberately and directly set themselves to oppose much of that which our society holds dear.

Reserve Constable Colin Dunlop was shot dead while on guard duty at the intensive care ward of Belfast's Royal Victoria Hospital on 31 May. The thirty year-old father of four was shot by an IRA gang that included two men and a woman. He had been a full-time reservist for only four months, having previously served as a part-timer. Colin Dunlop was the first Mormon to die in Northern Ireland and, at his funeral in Holywood Road Mormon Chapel, a message of sympathy was read from the Church's leader, President Spencer W. Kimball. On 17 June Reserve Constable Christopher Kyle was shot and fatally injured by IRA gunmen close to his home at Mullaghslin, near Omagh. His father found him slumped over the wheel of his car. The twenty-five year-old mechanic died a few hours later in Tyrone County Hospital. Constable Neal Quinn, a native of Coalisland, was one day short of thirty years' service when he was shot dead by the IRA while having a lunchtime drink in a Newry bar. Aged fifty-three, he had three children and was buried on the day that he would have retired from the force.

The hunger strike continued but there were now divisions among the strikers' families about its future with some demanding that the IRA order an end to it. On 31 July, when Paddy Quinn lapsed into a coma after forty-seven days, his mother immediately intervened to allow medical treatment that saved his life. But others persisted and the deaths continued with two strikers, Kevin Lynch and Kieran Doherty, dying within days of each other. Doherty had been elected to Dáil Éireann. On the day that he died, 2 August, two RUC officers were murdered near Loughmacrory in County Tyrone. Constables John Smyth and Andrew Woods died when an IRA landmine, estimated at some 600 pounds of explosives, was detonated under their car, the second of a two-vehicle patrol. The officers in the first car fired at men running away, but claimed no hits. A ten-foot deep hole was left by the blast. John Smyth had three children and had been in the RUC since 1968. Andrew Woods had six children and had joined in 1970.

The Loughmacrory attack was repeated at Cappagh, County Tyrone, on 7 September. This was almost a carbon copy with a land-mine destroying the second of a two-car patrol that was investigating a report of a forest fire and killing Constables Mark Evans and Stuart Montgomery, stationed at Pomeroy. The blast blew the wreckage of the armoured Cortina some seventy yards and the victims had to be identified by their fingerprints. A crater fifteen feet deep and fifty wide was left by the explosion which took place about two miles from the home of a dead hunger striker. Both men were single and new to Pomeroy. Mark Evans, twenty, had arrived a week earlier after spending his first six weeks in the force at Armagh while Stuart Montgomery, nineteen, was on his first patrol, having arrived at Pomeroy only an hour before. Stuart Montgomery was the third gener-ation of his family to serve with the RUC and RIC. Two men were later charged with the murders but the charges were withdrawn when two witnesses withdrew their statements.

Before the strike ended, James Prior succeeded Atkins as Secretary of State. Prior was faced almost immediately with the murder of an MP, the Reverend Robert Bradford. At the MP's funeral RUC officers had to restrain Loyalist mourners who were abusive to Prior. Prior's appoint-ment was seen as facilitating moves towards an end to the hunger strike although the government continued to say that there would be no concessions. Efforts by Catholic clergy, especially Father Denis Faul of Dungannon, to end the strike increased and Faul worked closely with families. Eventually the strike was called off on 3 October but not before another four policemen had been murdered.

John Proctor was visiting his wife and newborn baby in Magherafelt's

Mid-Ulster Hospital. As he walked back to his car he was gunned down and killed. The twenty-five-year-old reservist had another child. Earlier that day Reserve Constable Proctor had been a pallbearer at the funeral of friend and neighbour Alan Clarke, a full-time UDR soldier also murdered by the IRA. Silas Lyttle owned a drapery shop in the Tyrone village of Ballygawley and was also a member of the Reserve. On 18 September he had closed his shop and was walking home when he was shot at the gate of his own house. He was taken to hospital but, after several operations, died from a bowel infection seven weeks later on 17 November. Two men were subsequently found not guilty of the murder of the fifty-nine year-old father but one was jailed for manslaughter and another for IRA membership and possession of firearms. They were said to be mentally defective; one had shown remorse and had tried to commit suicide.

George Stewart, known as Sandy, was shot dead by two hooded IRA gunmen while off duty in a public house at Killough in County Down on 26 September. Stationed in Lisburn, he was with his fiancée when he was murdered. Constable Stewart, thirty-four, who had escaped death twice before, loved poetry and had written a poem entitled 'A Breath of Hope for Ulster' that had been published in a book, *Contemporary Poets' Collection*, in 1975. On 28 September, Constable Alexander Beck was driving a Land Rover on Suffolk Road, Belfast when the vehicle was struck by an RPG7 round. Alexander Beck, a father of two, was killed instantly while another officer was seriously injured. Less than two years later, Alexander Beck's father was discovered dead in the grounds of his Kilkeel home. A legally held weapon was also found; no crime was suspected.

When the hunger strike ended it had left seventy-seven people dead. Ten hunger strikers had died while fifteen RUC officers, fifteen soldiers and thirty-seven civilians were killed. Over 700 were injured and the force had dealt with over 1,200 Republican demonstrations at which there had been some 355,000 people. The bill for about 2 million hours of overtime came to £9 million. But the long-term effects of the hunger strike were to be felt in the years ahead as Sinn Fein's political profile increased and Republicans pursued actively their ballot and Armalite strategy. For the RUC there was to be no respite as the IRA continued its murderous campaign.

Even before the year was out the IRA had claimed another policeman with the death of Constable William Coulter in an explosion at Unity Flats in Belfast. Following the murder a crowd jeered at police and threw stones and bottles. There had been a disturbance in the area to which police had been called but this was a ruse. No one in the immediate area was injured, which led police to conclude that residents had been warned about the bomb; the Catholic Bishop of Down and Connor, Dr William Philbin, proclaimed that those residents shared the murderers' guilt. There was controversy over the death with suggestions from the Police Federation that Constable Coulter should have been warned about a possible bomb attack and, in 1984, his widow, who had alleged negligence, was awarded undisclosed damages in the High Court. Three weeks after her husband's death, Mrs Coulter gave birth to a son, whom she named for his father.

The hunger strike had not been the RUC's sole problem in 1981. Paisley's 'Third Force' and 'Carson Trail' provided considerable irritants. At any other time these displays might have been regarded as some form of comic opera but, against the background of the hunger strike, they could only exacerbate matters for the police. They might also increase support for the hunger strikers within the Nationalist population as Sinn Fein could point to Paisley's demonstrations as being anti-Catholic and anti-Nationalist. Paisley appeared to be pursuing a personal crusade against Hermon, who had gone toe-to-toe with him in Ballymena in 1977 and forced a climbdown; the Chief Constable was described as an 'enemy of Ulster', thereby placing him in company with Thatcher, Atkins, the IRA and various other individuals and organizations, a puppet and a 'Führer'. Had Paisley bothered to translate the last epithet into English he would have realized that he was describing Hermon as a 'leader', which hardly squared with his being a 'puppet'. At this stage, Hermon's leadership was vital to the RUC and to peace and stability in Northern Ireland.

The presence at one of Paisley's 'Third Force' rallies of the father of a murdered Reservist and Paisley's claim that many Reserve and UDR members were members of his 'home guard' were worrying, especially to Hermon. But the Chief Constable had already put in place an internal counter-intelligence organization to uncover anyone who might be supporting Paisley's illegal force or who might be providing information to it. By the end of November the 'Third Force' had come to the end of the road with a public declaration by Hermon that no private force acting outside the law would be allowed to usurp the RUC's authority. The threat of prosecutions also took the steam out of the organization.

Another problem besetting the force in 1981 came with a series of murders that had begun in November 1980 when the body of Peter Valente was found in Belfast's Highfield Estate, an apparent victim of Loyalists. However, things were not as they appeared; Valente was a police informant and the RUC were certain that he had been murdered by the IRA and his body dumped in Highfield to create the appearance of a sectarian murder. On 1 January 1981 Eugene Simons disappeared.

His body was not found until May 1984. He, too, was a police informant. But the IRA had made no statement about his death and when Valente was murdered the organization claimed that the UDA had been responsible. Then two more informants were murdered, Maurice Gilvary on 21 January and Patrick Trainor on 24 February. In both cases the IRA admitted responsibility and claimed that the men were 'informers'.

A police investigation had already uncovered a policeman who had been providing information to the IRA. The officer was neither a Nationalist nor a Catholic, but a 'Walter Mitty' type full-time reservist attached to a DMSU in Belfast. He wanted to be a Special Branch officer but reservists could not serve in the Branch and the man therefore tried to create a reputation by cultivating Republican contacts. He only managed to bring himself to the attention of Special Branch; he was arrested and admitted passing sensitive intelligence to the IRA but his case never came to trial since this would have involved disclosing too much operational information. The officer was dismissed and told to leave the province. Such treachery was unusual, if not unique, and it is to the great credit of the RUC that the overwhelming majority of officers held true to their calling and the oaths they took on joining the force.

The New Year Honours' List of 1982 carried the announcement of a knighthood for the Chief Constable. But he had little time to celebrate; Paisley was again making trouble for him, this time by using information from the Police Federation and threatening to call a 'day of action'. The whole affair created a crisis for the Federation but, fortunately, matters were resolved after some tough talking, although the aftertaste would linger for some years. And there was another issue that was soon to dominate the headlines, that of the 'supergrass'. This had begun in 1981 with the defection of an IRA activist in Londonderry but had developed in recent months. In late November the police had arrested three men seen acting suspiciously in the Ardoyne area of north Belfast. One of the trio, Christopher Black, recently released from prison and now facing another sentence to which would be added the balance of his earlier sentence, decided to make a deal with detectives. He offered to turn Queen's evidence if given his own freedom.

Following a high-level discussion about the implications of the case, it was decided to accept Black's offer. This was not a unique decision; an accused turning Queen's evidence is a long-established principle in law and had been used previously by the RUC against terrorists, both Loyalist and Republican. Other forces, including the Garda, also used it and the Metropolitan Police found it more than useful in tackling gangland crime. The Black case, therefore, followed precedent. In a speedy operation, Black's family were moved from their home and into secure accommodation inside a military camp. On the basis of Black's information, some forty arrests were made by the RUC while Gardai uncovered an IRA training camp. IRA leaders could not fail to realize that the raids were based on inside information, especially as police had arrested men who were on the run and did not normally sleep in their own beds. These individuals had been arrested in mid-morning, at a time when they would have judged it safe to visit their own homes; some were even said to be enjoying leisurely breakfasts when the police arrived.

No one could have appreciated then that this case would lead to a flood of what the media dubbed 'supergrasses' as a series of Republican and Loyalist terrorists followed Black's example. In all, over the next year and a half, some twenty Republican and ten Loyalist terrorists turned Queen's evidence with their confessions leading to some of the most damaging strikes inflicted on terrorist groups. About 500 arrests were made for about three times that number of offences, including murder, using firearms and causing explosions. Hermon saw the development as suggesting that the community was tired of the terrorists' depredations and the intimidation and organized crime that were part and parcel of terrorist control of many areas. The Chief Constable termed those who turned Queen's evidence as 'converted terrorists', an apt description although the sincerity of most 'conversions' was doubted by many police officers. But it was the media term 'supergrass' that stuck; the Provisional IRA referred to them as 'supertouts' or 'paid perjurers' but none of the alternative terms had quite the snappiness of the media's own invention.

The first 'converted terrorist' to give evidence in court was a Loyalist, Clifford McKeown, who implicated another twenty-nine men. McKeown was sentenced to death by the UVF, according to his testimony in a preliminary hearing, but after five days in the witness box he refused to give any further evidence and withdrew evidence he had already given. McKeown was later jailed for ten years, a sentence upheld on appeal. Christopher Black went to court some five months later and spent sixteen days in the witness box in a 120-day trial that involved 550 witnesses. Thirty-five of the thirty-eight people implicated by Black were given sentences that included four life terms for murder. Black, his wife and children were taken out of Northern Ireland for their own protection and given new identities.

Needless to say, the terrorist groups were concerned at these developments and began their own counter-attack that went beyond accusing the witnesses of being paid perjurers or supertouts. The IRA offered an amnesty to those who confessed to the organization before moving on to legal manoeuvres that included relatives seeking court orders requiring the Chief Constable to produce either the witness or his wife. Christopher Black's wife's family tried this approach but it failed in court. With that legal path closed to them, and the amnesty offer not flushing out those they wanted, the IRA went back to what they knew best: the threat of violence. The wife of one witness and the father of another were kidnapped but neither gave in to the threat and the hostages were released. Other witnesses did succumb to pressure and made the mandatory appearance at IRA press conferences.

One 'converted terrorist' case caused police to consider that the system had been used as a propaganda tool by the IRA. Robert Lean was arrested in September 1983 and his family were taken into protective custody. Several high-ranking Belfast IRA members were arrested on the strength of Lean's statements but, in early October, Lean's wife and family returned home and his wife made a public plea that Lean should withdraw his statements against the 'innocent men' he had implicated. On 20 October Lean left the barracks where he had been staying and returned home before appearing at a Sinn Fein press conference to withdraw his evidence. Those arrested on that evidence were then released. Lean had earlier claimed that police had offered him £80,000 for his help in breaking the IRA in Belfast. Similar claims about money paid to those who turned Queen's evidence and those who were informing on their terrorist comrades were exaggerated highly; the sums involved were not great but the attraction was a new start with a new identity, safe from reprisals. Lean's about-turn was a severe blow to the system but it was to receive many more with the reliability of some witnesses being questioned by the judges to whom they gave their evidence until, finally, in 1986, twenty-four INLA members were released by the appeal court, having been convicted on the evidence of Harry Kirkpatrick. Many of those convicted were released on appeal and those who remained in prison were there because there had been other evidence against them, sometimes confessions they had made when arrested.

While the 'converted terrorist' system was in place there was a noticeable reduction in the level of violence. In every year from 1983 to 1986 the death toll was less than 100, with 1985 having the lowest figure, at fifty-eight. These include not only deaths in Northern Ireland but also those linked to the Northern Ireland conflict elsewhere, including the bombing of the Conservative Party conference in 1984. However, there was considerable political pressure brought to bear on Thatcher's government by the Irish government, especially after the Anglo-Irish Agreement of 1985 which, Sir John Hermon noted, saw British support for the system wane dramatically. There was also political opposition within Northern Ireland with SDLP members failing, yet again, to provide any support for the police.

The people who died in those years 1982 to 1986 included many police officers with 1985 being the worst year for the force; twenty-three

RUC officers died that year, nine of them in a single incident when terrorists mortared Newry RUC Station. But 1982 saw a dozen officers die, the first of whom perished in March in an attack that once again indicated the IRA's total disregard for the sanctity of religious worship.

Norman Duddy was an inspector in Londonderry where he had served for over twenty years. He had been the last serving police officer to live on the west bank of the Foyle, only leaving his Belmont Park home for a new house close to the golf club at Prehen, shortly before his death. Afterwards it became clear that Inspector Duddy had been targeted by the IRA, which initially believed him to be a Catholic. IRA members carried out reconnaissance at Catholic churches in the city and surrounding area before discovering that Norman Duddy was a Presbyterian and a member of the congregation of Strand (Second Derry) Church. He remained a regular attender at Sunday worship and had gone to church with his two teenage sons on the morning of his death, 28 March. When the service had finished, Norman and his sons returned to his car, which was parked nearby in Patrick Street. As usual the popular policeman stopped to talk to some of his fellow congregation members and, as he was chatting, a motorcycle drew up alongside and two masked gunmen opened fire. Norman Duddy was dead on arrival at Altnagelvin Hospital. The murder was condemned by the city's SDLP Mayor, Joe Fegan, who spoke about Inspector Duddy's popularity and qualities as a policeman. A massive crowd attended the funeral and there were tributes from many in the city who had known him throughout his long service, during which he became involved deeply in Londonderry's cultural fabric.

For police officers there was one aspect of the local response to this murder that rankled when a local newspaper, published on Tuesdays, consigned the news of the murder to an inside page. A Catholic officer telephoned the paper to complain and was told by the acting editor that it was his decision not to carry the murder on the front page since, by Tuesday, the news was two days old. Some months later the same officer phoned the paper again when news of the death of an IRA member, killed on a Wednesday morning, was carried as the paper's main story in its Friday edition; the same acting editor was in the chair. This was a man who told this author in 1973 that there were no Catholics in the RUC Reserve in N Division; the author decided not to tell him that he knew at least two.

Norman Duddy's murder was the first of four in Londonderry that year. Constable Alan Caskey was on beat patrol with a female colleague in Ferryquay Street, near the Diamond, on the morning of 4 May when a van drew up alongside them. Thinking that the driver was seeking directions the policewoman approached the van only to see a side door opening to reveal a masked man crouching inside. She tried to shout a warning to Constable Caskey but was herself shot and wounded while Alan Caskey fell dead. The twenty-one year-old had joined the force eight months before and had been in Londonderry for three months. He was a native of Desertmartin, County Londonderry. His colleague was treated in Altnagelvin Hospital's Intensive Care Unit where her condition, although serious, gradually improved.

On 11 June soldiers searching a house at Shantallow, to the north of the city, came across a hoard of radios and televisions in a garden shed. After a sniffer dog had checked for explosives without result, the search was handed over to the police and CID officers arrived to remove the goods. One of those officers was Detective Constable Reggie Reeves, a single man from Portstewart, who died instantly when a television exploded as he examined it; two other officers were injured. An IRA member, later shot dead by the Army, was responsible for Reggie Reeves's murder.

The fourth policeman to die in Londonderry that year was Charlie Crothers, a reservist, who was murdered at his workplace. Reserve Constable Crothers was a security guard at the Water Service's western division headquarters at Altnagelvin and was shot by two men who drew up in a Cortina outside the gate as he opened it for another car. As Charlie Crothers lay wounded, one gunman walked over and fired three more rounds into his body. The father of four lived in nearby Irish Street.

Sergeant David Brown died in hospital on 16 April having been wounded in the chest and arms on 30 March as he drove to collect a cleaner in New Barnsley RUC Station from her home. As he turned into the woman's street he was shot from ambush by the IRA. The woman heard three loud bangs but thought at first that David Brown had had a puncture. A Coldstream Guard applied dressings to the policeman's wounds before an ambulance arrived. David Brown was a father of two who had joined the force in 1976, after full-time reserve service. He had passed the sergeant's examination and was promoted to that rank only days before he died.

John Eagleson was riding his motorcycle from his Cookstown home to his work at a nearby cement plant when he was ambushed and shot just before 7.00 a.m. on 1 October. Three shotgun cartridges were found at the scene of the ambush, which was carried out by the IRA. A lorry driver, he was the father of two grown-up daughters and a teenage son. At his funeral service Canon Thomas McGonigle told his murderers that 'No cause, however sincerely held, could possibly justify what you did to John Eagleson'.

Sergeant Sean Quinn and Constables Alan McCloy and Paul Hamilton were in an armoured Cortina that was blown up by a 1,000lb landmine at Kinnego embankment near Lurgan on 27 October. The explosion was heard by Sir John Hermon who, with Lady Hermon, was travelling to Lurgan College where the Chief Constable was the main speaker at Speech Day with Lady Hermon presenting the prizes. Kinnego Embankment had been placed out of bounds to police and military patrols but permission had been given for Sergeant Quinn's patrol to visit the scene of a reported theft; a police surveillance unit had carried out a check. Sean Quinn, a Catholic, was a Newry man with three children. Alan McCloy had two children and was from Lurgan. Paul Hamilton, a Belfastman, had married a month earlier. There were to be long-term repercussions from this triple murder for it would have an influence on subsequent investigations by Greater Manchester Police's Deputy Chief Constable, John Stalker, into the shooting of six unarmed individuals by the RUC.

Detective Constable Garry Ewing was stationed in Enniskillen. His hobby was archery in which he conducted classes in Enniskillen's Lakeland Forum. On the night of 9 November he had finished a class and was about to drive home when an IRA bomb exploded beneath his car, killing him and seriously injuring his passenger, Helen Woodhouse. As Miss Woodhouse was being taken to the Erne Hospital she died in the ambulance. She was a family friend who baby sat for the Ewings, played squash with Mrs Ewing and attended Garry's archery class at the Forum where she worked as a recreation officer. At Garry Ewing's funeral in Seskinore the minister described his killers as a 'faceless gang of freedom murderers' and added: 'All evil is self-destroying and it will one day destroy you.'

A week after the murder of Garry Ewing and Helen Woodhouse, the INLA claimed two victims in Markethill, County Armagh. The dead were both full-time reservists, Ronnie Irwin and Snowden Corkey. They were standing at security gates in the village at about 5.30 p.m. when almost fifty rounds from automatic weapons were fired at them by gunmen who had got out of a car. One of the killers was believed to be a woman, Mary McGlinchey, wife of Dominic 'Mad Dog' McGlinchey; she was later shot dead herself. One of the first on the scene was local SDLP councillor, and later MP, Seamus Mallon, who had known Reserve Constable Corkey all his life. Ronnie Irwin had one child and his wife was pregnant; Snowden Corkey was the father of three. A man, described in court as the INLA commander in Armagh, received three life sentences for these murders and that of Constable John Wasson.

At this period in late-1982 the security situation had worsened, especially in the Armagh area. There appeared to be a competition between the IRA and INLA, the latter under McGlinchey, to cause the greater degree of havoc and murder. In many cases good police intelligence thwarted terrorist operations but in others terrorists were able to make attacks that resulted in many lives being lost, including those of the police officers at Kinnego and Markethill. Then, on 11 November, the RUC's Headquarters Mobile Support Unit shot dead three IRA men in the Lurgan area; Sean Burns, Eugene Toman and Gervaise McKerr died when HMSU members opened fire on the car in which they were travelling. Members of the IRA men's families disputed the police account of what had happened and claimed that security forces were operating a 'shoot-to-kill' policy. Burns and Toman were suspected of involvement in the Kinnego embankment murders two weeks earlier. On 24 November HMSU shot dead Michael Tighe and seriously wounded Martin McCauley in a hayshed near Lurgan. Then, on 12 December, the Unit also shot dead Seamus Grew and Roderick Carroll in Armagh city, after the pair had apparently failed to stop at a checkpoint.

All these deaths became the subject of investigations, and allegations of conspiracy were made against the RUC – and consideration was given to charging some officers with conspiring to pervert the course of justice – as well as the 'shoot-to-kill' claims. It was grist to the Republican propaganda mill. However, it is difficult to see how there could have been a conspiracy within HMSU. There were some thirty officers in the Unit and no single officer was involved in more than one of the three incidents. Sir John Hermon commented that

> No conspiracy to kill, or to pervert the course of justice, would or could have been contrived or, if contrived, have been concealed by so many for so long.[5]

Similarly, the allegation that security forces were operating a 'shoot-to-kill' policy falls down on at least two points. The first is that the primary aim of police operations against terrorists is to bring them to justice, by putting them in the dock with sufficient evidence to ensure a conviction. Using firearms in an arrest operation is always a last resort for police officers. In the first shooting, where Burns, Toman and McKerr died, exhaustive forensic tests indicated that HMSU officers had reason to believe that they were under fire. When the car broke through the check-point, shots were fired at it and officers believed that these were returned, which led to more firing from the police. The Forensic Science Laboratory simulated the conditions and discovered that strikes from the first shots fired by the police would have caused flashes from the rear window and other metal parts of the car that 'could readily be mistaken for muzzle flashes from guns fired from the back of the car'. Three officers appeared in court charged with murder but Lord Justice Maurice Gibson acquitted them, saying that he regarded each 'as absolutely blameless' and commending their courage and determination. Subsequently the judge and his wife were targeted by the IRA and murdered as they crossed the border at Killeen on their way home from holiday; the couple died when a 500lb landmine exploded as they drove by. In a statement justifying the double murder the IRA cited Lord Gibson's comments when acquitting the police officers.

The second argument against the 'shoot-to-kill' allegations is that these are based on a popular myth that stems from generations of Hollywood 'western' movies in which the 'hero' shoots a weapon out of the hand of an adversary. Such things happen only in movies; in real life such a shot could only be a fluke since few people firing a handgun can achieve accuracy of this degree. Similarly, the argument is made that a speeding car can be stopped by shooting out its tyres. Notwithstanding the fact that this could be every bit as dangerous as shooting into the car, it again requires a degree of marksmanship that is extremely rare and, in adverse conditions such as at Lurgan, non-existent. Firearms training emphasizes firing in such a way as to have the best possible chance of hitting a target – and that means firing at the largest part of the target, which, in a human being, means the torso rather than limbs. For police officers, it is also emphasized that using a firearm is a last resort; in many cases it signifies failure of some degree.

In the wake of these deaths Greater Manchester's Deputy Chief Constable was brought in to conduct an inquiry. Much has been said and written about the Stalker affair, not least by Stalker himself, and Hermon was the subject of, often, adverse comment. The latter includes an allegation that he wrote down part of Stalker's family pedigree on a cigarette packet as a subtle form of intimidation. There is no truth in this story at all and Hermon's notes from the time make it clear that he thought the Greater Manchester officer's name was 'Stocker', which would have made it difficult to produce the genealogical information Hermon is supposed to have done. The fact that the Chief Constable was also a non-smoker, and not a member of organizations he is alleged to have been in, further erodes any credibility in this and other stories.

Mistakes were made in the handling of these incidents but not as the result of malice. Rather they were made to protect lives, especially those of police informants. Thus the officers involved originally covered up their role as members of HMSU, as this would have been a clear signal to terrorists that there had been information about their planned activities. Instead the officers said that they were on routine preventive patrolling. This was a cover story often used at headquarters level when providing information about incidents but never for inclusion in statements or other evidential documents. That it was on this occasion led to consideration being given to conspiracy charges being laid against some officers.

Procedures had gone wrong and Hermon was quick to order closer liaison between the branches involved, Special Branch, which provided intelligence, HMSU, which was under Special Branch control, and CID, which was responsible for investigating such incidents. The real tragedy was that these incidents gave ammunition to the enemies of the RUC and were used by Republicans in an effort to demean the force.

The RUC's Diamond Jubilee was celebrated in 1982 with a series of functions including an inter-denominational thanksgiving service in St Anne's Cathedral in Belfast in June and concluding with concerts at the Ulster Hall in October. A new standard was presented by PANI and it was announced that there was to be an RUC Service Medal to recognize the extraordinary conditions under which officers had worked. A hundred surviving original members of the force were entertained by senior officers at Brooklyn and a special souvenir book, appropriately entitled *Arresting Memories*, was published. At the October concerts the RUC bands and choirs were included on the bill as was a choir from An Garda Síochána. Following the concert the Garda representatives were guests at a reception at Brooklyn, in the course of which one Garda officer, known as the Bard, presented Sir John Hermon with a poem that he had written in tribute to the RUC.

> We salute you, gallant comrades,
> on your Diamond Jubilee.
> You've won yourselves an honoured place
> in Ireland's history.
> Your bravery in times of trial
> is recognised by all.
> You have not failed whate'er the cost
> to answer duty's call.
> Some have paid the highest price
> Their deaths caused grief and pain.
> Together we will show the world
> They did not die in vain.

The poem was a striking tribute from professional police officers who recognized the professionalism of their comrades. It was also a symbol of good relations between the two forces, both born of the Royal Irish Constabulary in 1922.

Although relations may have been good between the RUC and the Garda in October 1982, there was a distinct change the following year as a result of the 'Dowra affair' in which accusations were made of collusion between the RUC and individuals in the Republic to pervert the course of justice in that jurisdiction. This was said to have been behind the RUC arrest of James McGovern on the morning he was due to appear in court in Dowra in the Republic. Although the arrest was a routine matter it was made to appear as if it had been organized to prevent McGovern appearing in court and was blown out of all proportion by the media. For a time it strained relations between the two forces at chief officer level but this, in Sir John Hermon's view, was largely due to political pressure being brought on his counterpart; there being no police authority in the Republic, the Garda came under the control of the Department of Justice.

There were many other, more pressing, problems as 1982 drew to an end. Terrorism had increased and one of the worst incidents of the conflict occurred at Ballykelly, County Londonderry, on 7 December; seventeen people, including eleven soldiers from nearby Shackleton Barracks, died when an INLA bomb exploded in the crowded Droppin' Well bar in the village. Although the bomb contained no more than five pounds of explosive it was placed in such a way that it wreaked major damage to the building; falling masonry caused the majority of deaths and injuries.

On a more positive note for the force, the year had also seen the conviction of senior IRA man Bobby Storey, who had been acquitted on several previous occasions. Some acquittals had been the result of witnesses withdrawing statements, others because there was only witness identification with no additional evidence. Storey was finally arrested in possession of firearms and sentenced to eighteen years' imprisonment. Once again, however, he was acquitted on another charge, that of attempted murder. Securing convictions required firm evidence to link the accused with specific crimes and, with increasingly sophisticated terrorist operations, especially on the part of the IRA, this was not always easy. In spite of Republican propaganda to the contrary, the courts operated without bias and were apt to acquit when a judge was not satisfied that there was sufficient evidence to convict. Of course, this left many police officers frustrated, especially when they knew that the accused was guilty. But knowledge and evidence are not synonymous.

The death toll in 1983 was eighty-seven, of whom eighteen were RUC officers, the first of whom died when the new year was less than a week old. Sergeant Eric Brown and Reserve Constable Brian Quinn were members of a Mobile Support Unit guarding a post office in Rostrevor, County Down, on 6 January. About an hour before noon, DMSU members went to check a suspicious Ford Escort parked outside the post office. Gunmen in the car opened fire, hitting three officers, all of whom were rushed to hospital in Newry but Sergeant Brown and Reserve Constable Quinn were dead on arrival. Eric Brown, a father of three, was buried with full police honours after a service at Moira Church of Ireland parish church; Brian Quinn, a single man, was buried after requiem Mass at the Church of the Holy Redeemer in Ballyholme. It appeared that the policemen had surprised an IRA gang waiting to rob the post office since the incident did not have the trademarks of a planned ambush.

Ten days later the IRA murdered a senior member of the judiciary, Judge William Doyle, as he left Sunday Mass at St Brigid's Church on Derryvolgie Avenue in Belfast. A year later another Catholic member of the judiciary, Tom Travers, a magistrate, was shot outside the same church in an attack in which his daughter, Mary, was murdered. Earlier IRA plans to murder Sir Jamie Flanagan at another Belfast church, St Bernadette's at Rosetta, had been foiled by vigilant police officers. The murder of Judge Doyle emphasized, yet again, that the terrorists held nothing in respect.

Two days after the murder of Judge Doyle, death struck again at a reservist in Londonderry. Reserve Constable John Olphert, a father of two, was gunned down in his shop at Nelson Drive on the outskirts of the city. John Olphert spotted the gunmen coming and ran for cover behind a door but the IRA men fired through the door, wounding him, before pushing it open and shooting their victim again. He died in his wife's arms. Reserve Constable Olphert had already resigned from the Reserve to concentrate on his shop, which he had just opened but his resignation had not taken effect. The murder was widely condemned with the Bishop of Derry and Raphoe, Doctor James Mehaffey, commenting at the funeral service that if people such as those who had murdered John Olphert were 'the liberators of Ireland, then God help Ireland'. Condemnation also came from a group of Catholic priests who warned of the deception perpetrated by the IRA of portraying their victims as 'enemies of some noble cause' to justify murder.

But the murders continued. On 20 and 21 February two officers died in separate incidents. In the first Reserve Constable Edward Magill died in a hail of IRA bullets as he left Warrenpoint RUC Station at lunchtime to walk to a grocery shop. He was hit by thirteen rounds as a number of gunmen fired either at him or the police station; a grenade was also thrown during the attack. Twenty year-old Reserve Constable Magill had joined the force in June 1981; he came from Glencairn Crescent in west Belfast. Sergeant Gordon Wilson was killed by an IRA bomb in Armagh the following evening. A DMSU member, Sergeant Wilson was in charge of an armoured patrol car that stopped at a chip shop. While the driver went in to buy food for the patrol, Gordon Wilson and another policeman provided cover, the Sergeant going to the nearby corner outside the Albert Bar in Lower English Street. As the driver left the shop, a 50lb bomb was exploded by remote control and Gordon Wilson was killed instantly, his body flung across the road. Gordon Wilson was one day short of his thirtieth birthday and, with his wife and six-week old daughter, had just moved into a new house in Armagh. His funeral was held in his native Warrenpoint.

On 2 March Constable Lindsay McCormack, a fifty year-old community policeman, was shot dead by the IRA outside a primary school on the Serpentine Road in north Belfast. Constable McCormack, a community policeman for eleven years, was approached by two gunmen who shot him five times in the head; according to a witness the killers may have been teenagers. As the policeman lay on the ground one gunman fired further rounds from a .38 revolver into his head. Considerable revulsion was expressed locally at this murder since Lindsay McCormack was popular with all sections of the community. An added dimension of callousness came from the nature of the murder and the fact that it happened outside a primary school at 2.45 p.m. Constable McCormack had a nineteen year-old son.

Frederick Morton was a breadman with Rank Hovis McDougall and a part-time reservist. His usual morning delivery round took him to Lisdrumgullion, a mile from Newry on the Tandragee Road, and it was there that he met his death on the morning of 15 March. He was shot by two gunmen from a stolen Datsun car that drove alongside his Mother's Pride van; he was struck in the chest and head by at least ten high-velocity bullets. Reserve Constable Morton died instantly and his vehicle left the road, dropping down a steep embankment to lodge in a ditch on the bank of the Clanrye river. From Drumbanagher, near Poyntzpass, he was well known and popular in his local community and had joined the Reserve on its formation in 1970. His son captained Newry Town soccer team and his daughter was a nurse who had been Nurse of the Year.

Two months later, on 16 May, Constable Gerry Cathcart, a member of the technical branch responsible for radio equipment at RUC Headquarters, was shot dead by an IRA gunman as he arrived home. His eighteen year-old daughter had been with him in the car but had left her father to collect a bag from the car; she was at the back door of their home when she heard the shots. The gunman made his getaway on a motorcycle, driven by an accomplice, that at first refused to start. Gerry Cathcart was a very popular man, described by neighbours as being loved by everyone. His older daughter was pregnant with the family's first grandchild. Gerry Cathcart had survived an earlier murder attempt when he spotted a bomb attached to his car.

Ten days after Gerry Cathcart's murder, Reserve Constable Colin Carson died in an INLA attack in Cookstown. Reserve Constable Carson was manning security gates in the town centre when an INLA gang drove up in a Toyota Hiace van. Colin Carson approached the van but, as he did so, the side door slid open and he died in a burst of automatic fire. A further burst, estimated at twenty seconds long, was directed at the nearby sangar and when police returned fire at the van there was another burst of automatic fire. A gunman also sprayed the police station with bullets after running past the gates. Police pursued the van and another exchange of fire followed before the gang escaped across country. Both Dominic McGlinchey, whose finger and palm prints were found in a car used in the attack, and his wife Mary were believed to be involved in the murder for which a man from Toome received a life sentence while another was jailed for ten years. Colin Carson left a wife and two young children.

John Wasson was sixty-one, the second-longest serving member of the RUC, with forty-two years' service, and had served in Armagh city for thirty-six years. He never carried a firearm and worked in the communications room at Armagh RUC Station; he was due to retire in October and, with his wife, was planning a holiday in Spain in mid-September. His plans were never to be realized for the INLA murdered him in his own driveway as he got out of his car after driving home from work on 7 September. He was shot six times in the head and chest. Nearly twenty years earlier Constable Wasson had helped rescue children and nuns from a burning convent at Windmill Hill and was described by one colleague as 'the hero of the night'. The car used in his murder was found abandoned not far from the spot where he had shown such heroism two decades before. A native of Newry and father of five, John Wasson was also a Catholic and was buried after requiem Mass in St Patrick's Cathedral in Armagh. The service was attended by over 1,000 people, including police officers, priests, nuns and schoolchildren. One of the lessons was read by an RUC superintendent who was related to Constable Wasson.

The Meadowlands estate in Downpatrick was a mainly Catholic area but there were Protestant families living there and complaints had been made of intimidation against them. As a result police patrols were increased and on 6 October Reserve Constables William Finlay and James Ferguson were patrolling the estate on foot. They had just left a confectioner's, where they had been talking to some local people, and were walking along a footpath, separated by about fifteen yards, when they were shot by IRA gunmen who had been in hiding behind trees beside the road. About nine shots were fired and the policemen were hit in the necks and shoulders before the gunmen ran off. William Finlay died almost immediately with a local woman holding his hand and praying for him while James Ferguson died shortly after being admitted to the Downe Hospital, where he worked as head gardener. Both were married and each had three children. Reserve Constable Ferguson's two daughters and son sang in the choir of Downe Cathedral where their father's funeral service was held. William Finlay was a full-time reservist and held the Queen's Commendation for Brave Conduct following an

176

incident in Ardglass in 1978 when he had persuaded a man with a shotgun to surrender his weapon. A man given a life sentence for the murders showed no remorse in court and, while being led from the dock, made a clenched-fist salute.

The RUC Community Relations Branch did sterling work throughout Northern Ireland and strove to provide a service to all areas. Branch members would often visit community leaders in their homes, thereby taking many risks. When Constable John Hallawell left Strand Road RUC Station in Londonderry on 28 October to visit a house in Ballymagroarty on the northern outskirts of the city he also chose not to take a firearm. John Hallawell was making arrangements for a young people's disco with a local community worker but, when he left the house, four gunmen were waiting for him. As Constable Hallawell got into his car, the gunmen opened fire and he was hit as he drove off. The car swerved, crashing on to a footpath and came to a halt. One gunman ran over and shot his victim in the head before making off with his accomplices in a nearby car. Ironically, John Hallawell was a first-class shot and might have been able to save himself had he been armed. A policeman for fourteen years he had been a neighbourhood constable in Strathfoyle, outside the city, before joining Community Relations. A father of three, he was a native of Ballinamallard, County Fermanagh.

Within the next two weeks the IRA struck at further soft targets, taking the lives of four RUC officers and seriously injuring another officer who died in August 1984. On 4 November a bomb exploded behind a ceiling panel in a lecture room of the Ulster Polytechnic at Jordanstown, outside Belfast. The room was being used for a police Higher National Certificate course and the intended targets were officers attending the lectures. One man was killed instantly, Inspector John Martin, a father of two, while Sergeant Stephen Fyfe, who had one child, died later that day. Sergeant William McDonald was seriously injured and never recovered consciousness; he died in the Royal Victoria Hospital on 12 August 1984. William McDonald, who had eleven years' service, had two children, aged four and six. Another injured officer was still unconscious when Sergeant McDonald died.

On the day after the explosion at the Polytechnic, Reserve Constable John McFadden was on duty in Ballymoney. He finished shortly after midnight and drove home to Rasharkin. As he parked in his driveway, IRA gunmen who had been lying in wait shot him. John McFadden died as neighbours tried to help him. (Four months later, following a gun battle between soldiers and IRA men in which a soldier and two IRA men were killed, an Armalite rifle was recovered by the Army and was shown to have been used in the murder.) Five days later, Reserve Constable William Fitzpatrick was working on a house he had bought near Annalong when he was shot and killed by IRA gunmen. William

Fitzpatrick was single and a security man at the Silent Valley reservoir. He was a Catholic and felt safe enough in his own area not to carry a gun; he had joined the Reserve in 1976 and was stationed at Newcastle, County Down. Then, on 12 November, came the final RUC death of the year when Constable Paul Clarke died in a mortar attack on Carrickmore RUC Station in County Tyrone.[6] Six other officers were wounded in the attack. Constable Clarke had joined the Reserve in 1978 and became a regular policeman in 1981; he had three children. Although he was a Catholic he was buried following a Church of Ireland service at his own request. Two men were later sentenced to eighteen years in prison for this and other murders. As sentence was passed they shouted 'Up the IRA'.

On 1 October 1983 a reorganization saw the RUC's territorial divisions reduce from sixteen to twelve. This was designed to reflect changes in the distribution of Northern Ireland's population, particularly around greater Belfast. In the west it saw the demise of M Division, based on Omagh, most of which was absorbed by L Division. There was some criticism of Hermon for carrying out this reorganization without consulting MPs, Assembly members and other elected members. The other divisions that disappeared were R, based on Larne, C and F in Belfast which reduced Belfast Region to A, B, D and E Divisions; North Region continued with N, O and P and South with G, H, J, K and L.

The Chief Constable was used to criticism by this stage but Paisley continued to castigate him and accused him of snubbing the Assembly. This was yet another attempt to return power to local politicians but had been doomed from the start by SDLP refusal to participate. The party was shocked at the support that Sinn Fein and the IRA had garnered from the hunger strike and seemed determined to claw this back by adopting a 'greener' stance than before. Matters were not helped by the fact that Paddy Devlin and Gerry Fitt had gone and Hume had become the party leader. A man with little or no empathy for Protestants or Unionism, the breadth of his vision was summed up in his mantra 'our divided people' which he recited without realizing how much he himself had contributed to division in Northern Ireland. Instead of participating in Prior's experiment of rolling devolution, the SDLP took themselves off to Dublin and sought the support of the Republic's government to create a 'New Ireland Forum'. Once again, Hume, the architect of this move, failed to see that he was creating yet more division; Unionists could only see this as another attempt by the SDLP leader to drag them down the road to Dublin. Needless to say, Unionist support for the Forum was not forthcoming.

Against this background the Chief Constable was avoiding meetings with politicians. Whenever he received an invitation to speak to

178

Assembly members he usually delegated the task to an assistant chief constable. Prior attempted to arrange a meeting between Hermon, the GOC and leaders of the main political parties in the aftermath of the INLA murders at Darkley when three elders of Mountain Lodge Pentecostal Church were shot dead during a service on the evening of Sunday, 20 November. The congregation was singing the first hymn, 'Are You Washed in the Blood of the Lamb', as the terrorists burst in and murdered William Brown, John Cunningham and David Wilson; several others were wounded. The leaders of the four main churches described this as an 'act of sectarian slaughter on a worshipping community which goes far beyond any previous deed of violence' but Prior was concerned that there might be retaliation against a Catholic congregation and hence his effort to bring political leaders and security chiefs together. He was disappointed that only the Alliance Party accepted the invitation, the others choosing to play politics even in such circumstances.

In the aftermath of the Darkley murders, Ian Paisley called for a midnight session of the Assembly, which had the positive effect of allowing Unionist representatives to express their own and their constituents' anger and revulsion at the INLA. Early in the new year the Police Authority arranged meetings with political parties at which the Chief Constable was present. Not surprisingly, Paisley emerged from one meeting with the comment that he had no confidence in Hermon. It is unlikely that the Chief Constable was inspired to any confidence in Paisley or any other political leader by these meetings. Certainly none of the parties showed any real interest in moving the debate on security to a more mature level. Their idea of a policy on security seemed to be either to criticize the RUC and Army for what they were doing or to claim that they were not doing enough. Paisley wanted the government to go on the offensive against terrorism and root out terrorists while SDLP politicians would condemn acts of terrorist violence, often in quite trenchant terms, but then demonstrate their ambivalence by condemning some aspect of security policy. It appeared as if the SDLP wanted the police to bring an end to terrorism by being nice to terrorists. The naiveté of such a policy would be shown in the full course of time.

Hermon's attitude was that the RUC was trying to create a situation in which all politicians could sit down together and work at resolving Northern Ireland's problems. However, the increasing strength of Sinn Fein ensured that the SDLP, in its quest for votes and support, became ever more critical of the force. No serious attempt was made by the party to extend its support across the sectarian divide, which might have been possible had Hume shown even the slightest support for the police. But it was the intransigent nature of the SDLP and its leader that ensured that Unionist suspicions of the party's intentions not only remained but also intensified. That nature was demonstrated all too clearly when the party refused to allow elected members to accept awards in the Queen's New Year or Birthday Honours' Lists and ostracized those who defied the leadership's diktat and accepted such honours. There could be little doubt that the face of the party was turned resolutely against the RUC.

Notes

1: Devlin, op. cit., p. 284
2: Hermon, op. cit., p. 120
3: The Spearhead battalion is the title given to an infantry battalion kept on immediate readiness to move anywhere in the world where it might be needed. It is not a reserve maintained specifically for Northern Ireland.
4: Hermon, op. cit., p. 124
5: Ibid., p. 153
6: Carrickmore RUC Station had been closed in the 1960s but it was reopened following political protests after the BBC filmed an IRA checkpoint operating in the village.

Chapter Eight

The Hermon Era Continues

Sir John Hermon's problems were not restricted to politicians' attitudes to the force, although the treating of the RUC 'as a bargaining counter' was a major distraction. There were other problems, including the Stalker inquiry, Dowra and Kincora. The first two have been considered in preceding pages but Kincora involved neither accusations of a 'shoot-to-kill' policy nor of politicians meddling in policing; instead it centred on allegations of sexual misconduct at a Belfast boys' home.

What became known as the 'Kincora affair' first emerged in January 1980, shortly after Hermon became Chief Constable. An article in the *Irish Independent* on 24 January dealt with allegations of an official cover-up of the recruitment for homosexual prostitution of boys at Kincora boys' home on Upper Newtownards Road. Under the headline 'Sex Racket at Children's Home', the article also alleged that a member of the home's staff was involved with a Loyalist terrorist group called 'Tara'. It was further suggested that staff of the social services department were aware that there had been serious sexual abuse of boys at the home but that relevant files had been destroyed on the orders of a senior departmental official.[1] Sir John Hermon notes that no victim of alleged abuse at the home had ever complained to the RUC.[2]

As a result of the article a team of detectives, under Detective Chief Inspector George Caskey, was formed to investigate the allegations. Caskey's team found sufficient evidence initially to have three Kincora staff members suspended. William McGrath, the housefather, Raymond Semple, assistant warden, and Joseph Mains, were later convicted of offences including indecent assault, gross indecency and buggery and received prison terms of four, five and six years respectively. The investigation also led detectives to four other men in two homes in Belfast and Newtownabbey; they were convicted in May and December 1981.

These convictions did not end the matter, however. Speculation continued and further allegations emerged suggesting a police cover-up to protect senior government officials who had been involved for some

181

years in a vice ring focused on Kincora. Additional speculation centred on McGrath when it was revealed that he had been involved in 'Tara'; this provided grounds for claiming that McGrath had been blackmailed by MI5 which, allegedly, had known about the vice ring but used that knowledge as a blackmail tool against prominent politicians and others who might have been implicated. Such rumours and allegations surfaced regularly in the local media and Hermon decided that Caskey's team should carry out a thorough investigation.

At the same time, mindful of the damage that these rumours could do to the RUC's reputation, the Chief Constable decided to ask Her Majesty's Inspectorate of Constabulary to investigate the cover-up allegations. Sir George Terry, Chief Constable of Sussex, was appointed as the investigating officer while Jim Prior told the Commons that he would appoint a committee of inquiry to investigate the management of children's homes and make recommendations for their future adminis-tration. When the Terry Report was published in May 1983 it found that the allegations were not substantiated: there was no vice ring and nor was there any terrorist organization connected with the homosexual misconduct in boys' homes. The report also made clear that there had been no cover-up, concealment of evidence or disciplinary breaches by RUC personnel.[3]

In 1986 the committee of inquiry established by Prior produced its report and made fifty-six recommendations on the running of children's homes, ranging from staff selection to the rights of children and parents to complain to outside bodies, including the police, and the establish-ment of a formal complaints procedure about which children would be told in easily-understood leaflets.

Ten RUC officers died in 1984, including one as a result of his injuries in the Polytechnic bomb of November 1983. This was a year in which seventy-two people died, including members of the Conservative Party attending their annual conference in Brighton, the New Ireland Forum produced its report, which was rejected by Thatcher, and John Stalker himself came under investigation.

Reserve Constable William Fullerton, a father of two, was shot dead by the IRA as he drove home from Warrenpoint RUC Station at 4.30 p.m. on 10 January. He was approaching a roundabout near Green Bank Industrial Estate when he was ambushed. His wife collapsed on hearing the news and was taken to Banbridge Hospital by cardiac ambulance. William Fullerton had been a reservist since 1976 and was well known and respected in the Warrenpoint area. His divisional commander commented that this was one of the reasons why 'he, and others like him, can be soft targets. Because they are so close to the community they are at risk.' Jim McCart, SDLP chairman of Newry and Mourne Council, described Reserve Constable Fullerton as a 'fair-minded community policeman'.

Sergeant William Savage and Constable Thomas Bingham died on 31 January when their patrol car was blown up by a 1,000lb IRA landmine as they drove from Forkhill to Newry at lunchtime. Both were based at Forkhill. Although both were single, Thomas Bingham was to have been married on 18 February and the minister who was to officiate at that ceremony instead took part in his funeral. He had served in the RUC since 1980 and was from Dundonald while Sergeant Savage had almost six years' service and had been a sergeant since 1982; he came from Newtownards.

At 2 o'clock in the morning of 12 April, Peggy Whyte, a Catholic mother of eight, arrived home from her part-time taxiing job to find a sports bag on the windowsill of her University Street home in Belfast. She called the police and Constable Michael Dawson was walking to her door when a bomb in the bag exploded, killing both of them. The Whyte family had suffered a campaign of terror for some seven years but had refused to move. Police believed that the UVF was responsible for this double murder. The minister who conducted Michael Dawson's funeral service said that the bombers had brought shame on Protestantism. At Peggy Whyte's funeral, the priest, an uncle of the dead woman, extended sympathy to Michael Dawson's family. He commented that Constable Dawson had attempted bravely to 'protect Peggy's life and home' and asked that God would give his young widow 'the courage He has given us and give to his parents and family the strength and fortitude to bear their sorrow and grief'.

Yet another 1,000lb IRA landmine took the lives of Reserve Constable Trevor Elliott and Constable Neville Gray on 18 April. Trevor Elliott, a father of two, died at the scene while Neville Grey died in hospital on 19 May. They had been driving along the Camlough–Crossmaglen road when the device exploded, blowing their car off the road. Reserve Constable Elliott lived in Tandragee but was a native of Castlederg, County Tyrone; Constable Grey was from Dromara, County Down.

Michael Todd, from Lambeg, County Down, died in a planned search-and-arrest operation in Belfast's Lenadoon Avenue. Constable Todd and a sergeant kicked open the door of a flat at 3.00 a.m. but, as they did so, shots were fired at them and three rounds hit Constable Todd. Two other officers were wounded seriously. The police had stumbled upon an INLA hideout in which four men were hiding. One INLA man, Paul McCann, also died in the incident although police did not return fire. It was believed that McCann may have committed suicide or been hit by a ricocheting round from the AK47 with which he had murdered Constable Todd. That rifle had the words 'Black Widow' burnt into the butt. The sergeant who accompanied Michael Todd into the flat escaped injury. Three INLA men, including McCann's brother, were arrested and later convicted.

The IRA continued to use their landmine tactic and on 11 August detonated another device aimed at a police car, this time in County Tyrone on the road between Gortin and Greencastle. Although the car was blown into a field, one of its two occupants survived, with serious injuries, but Sergeant Malcolm Young died next day. A lorry travelling in the opposite direction was also caught in the blast and the driver and a passenger were injured. As other RUC officers arrived at the scene, the IRA detonated a second device but, fortunately, this failed to cause further casualties. Malcolm Young had just been promoted. His brother-in-law, David McBride, died in a similar incident in 1986.

At Sergeant Young's funeral the Bishop of Clogher, the Right Reverend Gordon McMullan, spoke of the difficulties faced by the RUC.

> The RUC is a police service called to fulfil its duty in a setting where every telephone call for help may also be an elaborate plot to lure members of the service to their death. It's a police service where the most routine journey may be the last a person may ever take, as violent and lawless men and women from safe distances trigger remote control. It's a police service where even as members attend places of learning, there's the possibility of being the victim of the bomber or the gunman.

On the day that Malcolm Young died, so too did Sergeant William McDonald, injured in the bomb at the Ulster Polytechnic on 4 November 1983.

Half of 1985's fifty-eight murder victims were RUC officers or soldiers. Although this was the lowest overall death toll since 1970, it was a black year for the RUC with twenty-three officers losing their lives, nine of them in a single incident when the IRA launched a mortar attack on Newry RUC Station on 28 February; four officers from the same station died in a landmine attack in May. This was also the year that Loyalists attacked police officers' homes, the Anglo-Irish Agreement was signed and Sinn Fein won fifty-nine council seats across Northern Ireland.

The first police officer to die in 1985 was a member of the Community Relations Branch. Sergeant Frank Murphy took fifteen children and two teachers to an inter-schools' quiz in Armagh Royal School on 21 February. He drove the children and teachers back to Drumsallen Primary School after the event and, as he left the school, was shot by three IRA gunmen. Over thirty rounds were fired from three automatic weapons and at least two bullets struck a classroom where some children, who had travelled in the minibus, were watching Sergeant Murphy depart. The terrorists had stolen a van from a local man who was held captive until after the murder. Frank Murphy had three children, the youngest a year-old baby daughter, and was a Belfastman. He had been injured in an attack on Keady RUC Station in 1973, a year after he joined the RUC. A Catholic, he had been in Community Relations Branch for a year.

A week later the worst single terrorist incident in the RUC's history happened in Newry. At about 6.35 p.m., officers were at their evening meal or relaxing in the games room adjacent to the canteen of Newry Station. The canteen, a temporary prefabricated building inside the station grounds, had no protection against blast. Outside, in Monaghan Street, the IRA had parked a stolen lorry fitted with nine mortar tubes, of the type known to the RUC and Army as the Mark 10. A salvo was fired over the roofs of houses, using the warning light on the station's radio mast as an aiming reference. One mortar, estimated at 40lb, struck the canteen, killing or fatally injuring nine officers; many others were injured. It was the only bomb to clear the station boundary wall; six exploded outside with some civilian casualties, and two failed to detonate.

The dead were Chief Inspector Alex Donaldson, a father of three, who was attached to Complaints and Discipline and was in Newry to interview a priest about allegations of police misconduct; Sergeant John Dowd, who had joined the RUC from Thames Valley Police in 1974 and was married to a policewoman; Constable David Topping; Constable Ivy Kelly, married to a policeman and a member of the RUC Ladies hockey team; Reserve Constable Geoffrey Campbell, who had joined only a month earlier; Reserve Constable Denis Price, who had joined in 1983 and who had had an uncle, Joseph Blaney, murdered by Loyalists in 1972; Reserve Constable Sean McHenry, aged nineteen and with less than five months' service and Reserve Constable Paul McFerran, who had joined in October 1983. Constable Rosemary McGookin was pulled from the wreckage of the canteen but died shortly afterwards.

Sir John and Lady Hermon were in the United States when they learned of the multiple murders in Newry and made immediate arrangements to return. They arrived in Northern Ireland in time to attend the first funeral and Sir John visited the stricken station where he saw the extent of the damage, the grief of the officers and their 'intense resolve to carry on as normal'. He was also impressed by the attitude of local people in the wake of the attack. In spite of attempts by Republicans to intimidate those wishing to pay their respects, a large crowd had gathered outside the station about ninety minutes after the attack. Learning that the crowd was led by nuns from a nearby convent, the

Chief Constable arranged to visit the convent where he was introduced individually to the sisters.

> I have a lasting memory of us all sitting in a large circle, talking and reminiscing about the past days in Newry and about police officers mutually known to us. The oldest resident, who was well over eighty, was the daughter of a Royal Irish Constabulary constable, who had later joined the Royal Ulster Constabulary and had been stationed for many years in Springfield Road police barracks in Belfast. Several others also had relatives in the RUC. I felt a oneness between us as we sat there together.[4]

The killings brought out both the best and the worst in people across Northern Ireland with many condemning what had happened in Newry and expressing sympathy to the force and the bereaved families. But there were those who rejoiced in the murders. Graffiti appeared in Republican areas celebrating what the terrorists had done; one wall in Strabane carried the graffito 'Newry cooked ham'.

Sergeant Hugh McCormac, a father of three, had twenty years' service in the RUC, which he had joined at the age of twenty, and was an instructor at the Training Centre. On the morning of Sunday, 3 March he arrived with his family for Mass in St Gabriel's Monastery at the Graan, near Enniskillen but, as he locked his car, he was shot and collapsed. A gunman then ran up and fired from point-blank range. Hugh McCormac died, clutching his missal, with his family around him. A few days later there was a passing-out parade and Sergeant McCormac's widow was invited to address the recruits. She told them to

> Keep your heads high and remember everything he told you. He regarded you as very special. Don't harbour any bitterness. Be proud of your job and your uniform, and be careful.

Two reservists were murdered in five days at the end of March and beginning of April. Reserve Constable John Bell, who had two children, was shot dead at his petrol station in Rathfriland on 29 March. He had earlier telephoned the police about a car that had been at his garage, the two occupants of which had enquired about tyres. A check on the car disclosed that it belonged to a family who lived two miles away and had not been reported stolen. However, a patrol was told to look for the car but before they left the station John Bell had already been murdered. The car had been taken from the family who had been held hostage overnight by the IRA. John Bell's wife whispered prayers in her dying husband's ear as they waited for an ambulance. At his funeral in Rathfriland First Presbyterian Church, his minister spoke of his frequent worries about

John's safety, 'knowing he was a specially soft target for such a cowardly attack. But, undeterred, he went about his business despite the risks.'

On 3 April Reserve Constable Michael Kay, a father of one, died in an IRA car bomb attack on Newry courthouse. As a police Land Rover reversed towards the building's entrance, the 20lb bomb, in a Toyota car, was detonated by remote control. Michael Kay, from Blackburn, Lancashire, and a former soldier in the Royal Tank Regiment who had married a local girl in the 1970s, died immediately. The courthouse care-taker, also from England, died later in hospital. Ten others were injured. The bombers had taken over a house overlooking the courthouse the previous evening, holding hostage the seventy-year-old occupant; when his home help arrived in the morning she was also held. Both victims were Catholic.

Tragedy struck Newry RUC Station again on 20 May when two cars from the station, each carrying four officers, drove to the Killeen border crossing point to escort an armoured bullion van travelling from the Republic. One car was to precede the van while the second would follow but, as the police vehicles moved into position, there was a huge explosion that destroyed the first car and killed all four occupants. The IRA had placed a 1000lb device at the side of the road, detonating it by remote control from a firing point inside the Republic. No suspicion had fallen on the trailer in which the explosives had been placed since it was common to see commercial vehicles parked on the roadside close to the border. The trailer with the bomb had been stolen at gunpoint near Newtownhamilton the previous night and driven into place by a tractor unit that morning. Those in the bullion van and the officers in the second police car escaped uninjured.

The dead were Inspector William Wilson and Constables David Baird, Tracy Doak and Steven Rodgers. Inspector Wilson was the oldest at twenty-eight, David Baird was twenty-two, Tracy Doak twenty-one and Steven Rodgers nineteen. William Wilson was married with two young children. Tracy Doak, whose father and brother were also in the RUC, was engaged to be married. She had spoken to her father on the phone shortly being leaving on that last fateful journey. That afternoon Sir John Hermon joined officers searching the area around the scene to recover the victims' remains and any clues that might yield forensic information. In a statement made after discussions with officers in Newry, the Chief Constable thanked the Irish government for its offer of assistance in apprehending the perpetrators of this multiple murder and made it clear that the RUC was satisfied that the terrorists involved had come from the Republic, as had their explosives. This caused an immediate reaction from Garda Headquarters, the Irish government and the SDLP. Hermon was surprised by the ferocity of the SDLP's attack but, in hindsight, considered that it had been due to fear that discussions between the UK and Irish governments might have been compromised by discussing the origin of the explosives. Both the Irish government and the Garda denied that there was any evidence to support Hermon's claim. However, the offer of help from FitzGerald, the Taoiseach, suggests that the Irish government were aware of the true picture.

Once again, the SDLP were playing politics with the RUC and this time with the lives of four young police officers. Only days before the party had taken a dusting in the local council elections from Sinn Fein. In this, their first participation in such elections, Sinn Fein came away with fifty-nine seats. This was a setback to the SDLP and, typically, the party's reaction was to criticize the police in order to establish further its 'green' credentials. With sectarian feelings running high, the SDLP stance was no help at all either to improving relations across Northern Ireland, or to policing demonstrations during the summer. The Chief Constable and his senior officers had decided that a firmer hand had to be taken with loyal order parades, or, more especially, some of the bandsmen and followers of those parades. Some parades would also be rerouted by police to avoid causing provocation and disorder in Nationalist areas.

Before those demonstrations took place, another two RUC officers lost their lives. Reserve Constable Willis Agnew died when an IRA gunman shot him as he sat in his car outside his fiancée's home at Kilrea on 16 June. The widower had been in the Reserve for ten years and was well known and respected by the people of Kilrea. Ten years earlier he had helped clear the area around a 750lb bomb in the village. He had also refused to leave Kilrea although he knew that his life was at risk. Two days later a police car travelling between Kinawley and Florencecourt in County Fermanagh was caught in the blast from a 1,000lb landmine about a mile from Kinawley. Both men in the car were seriously injured and had to be cut free. Constable William Gilliland, a father of two, died in hospital as surgeons tried to save his life.

RUC Headquarters had prepared a strategy, based on its Civil Emergency Plan, for policing Loyalist parades in the summer of 1985. Divisional Mobile Service Units would play a critical part and DMSU personnel underwent refresher training in public order duties, as did officers from stations throughout the province. The local knowledge of the latter would be vital in providing intelligence on demonstrators. Since many of those who created problems came from bands, each travelling band would be accompanied by a local police officer. Standard operational procedures would apply when dealing with any outbreak of disorder: police would avoid direct confrontation, unless attacked, while photographs and video recordings would be made for use in later criminal proceedings. The principal focus of RUC effort was to be on

188

Portadown, the heartland of the Orange Order and a town with the strongest Orange tradition in Northern Ireland.

For many years part of the route for Orange parades in Portadown had been the Tunnel/Obins Street area. This had caused tension because the local population had changed from being predominantly Protestant to being predominantly Catholic and matters had been exacerbated on St Patrick's Day when the police had decided, at the last minute, to reroute a Catholic band parade in the town. Hermon believed that Orange parades would have to be dealt with in similar manner and so made himself familiar with the route for the Orange Order's parade by both driving and walking it several times before making his decision to reroute the traditional 'Twelfth' parade away from the Tunnel.

Talks were held between representatives of the various churches and of Nationalist and Loyalist groups to discuss the situation. Most were positive in their reactions to the Chief Constable's proposal but he encountered scepticism from the Catholic primate, Cardinal O'Fiaich, who doubted the 'will or the ability' of the RUC to close the Tunnel/Obins Street area to the Orange Order. Having outlined his plans for deploying police officers, Hermon then added that a battalion of soldiers would provide support by occupying the Tunnel and Obins Street so that no marchers could proceed there. This seemed to convince the Cardinal but left Hermon with an urgent need to ask the GOC for a battalion of soldiers, such a degree of support not having been part of the original plan. Soldiers of 1st Queen's Own Highlanders were deployed, although they were only some 250 in number; there was no space to deploy more.

On the first Sunday of July each year, Portadown's Orangemen hold a church parade to commemorate the 1916 Battle of the Somme. This takes the Orangemen to Drumcree Parish Church where a service is held before they return to Portadown along Garvaghy Road. This had been a quiet byroad but, more recently, had been built up to become part of the town and had a large Nationalist housing estate close by. That year's Somme parade and service were held on 7 July and made heavy calls on police officers in the town; but there was only minor disorder. There was also a fear that Loyalist terrorist elements might seek to exploit the Portadown parade on the 'Twelfth' itself and arrangements were made to counter any such attempts.

In spite of all the preparations and talks, however, the Portadown 'Twelfth' parade did not pass peacefully and there were attacks on police by Loyalists. Officers had to fire baton rounds from the cover of Land Rovers to keep rioters at bay but, even so, fifty-two RUC officers were injured over the 12th and 13th; 1,000 officers had been deployed to Portadown. But the march did not enter the Tunnel/Obins Street area and the Army was not called upon to confront rioters, although violence spread elsewhere in Portadown. Forty-three rioters were arrested and many others were later identified for prosecution from photographs or video film. There were further disturbances arising from parades before the end of August, some of which were Loyal order parades and others Republican parades commemorating the introduction of internment and the deaths of hunger strikers. In all, the RUC arrested 468 Loyalists and 427 Republicans for public order offences. And for the first time, Sinn Fein was notifying local police commanders of their parades and accepting police directions on routing. For their part, the Orange and other Loyal orders were moving to deal with rogue bandsmen and talking with police about future demonstrations.

In spite of all the RUC's efforts that summer the force received little praise from Nationalist quarters, with many Nationalist politicians adopting a cynical attitude towards the force's confrontation with the Orange Order in Portadown. Sadly, the same stance was adopted by many Catholic clergy who continued to portray the RUC as enemies of their congregations.

The February attack on Newry RUC Station had exposed tragically the weakness of many stations. Although commentators from outside Northern Ireland often portray these as fortified barracks this is far from true, as was shown by the destruction at Newry and on Chichester Road and Lisburn Road stations; the latter pair had been demolished by IRA bombs. However, the Newry attack had shown that the danger to buildings had been heightened with the development of the IRA's latest mortars, capable of causing extensive damage to a building and dubbed 'barrack busters'. Many stations had been built as oversized houses, especially in rural areas, while even the most modern were examples of 1960s' architecture with too much glass for safety and structures that could not absorb punishment from a large explosion. Stations had been given added protection in the form of fences or walls, with bullet-proof glass or armoured shutters fitted to windows. This work had been done on a priority basis with the most vulnerable stations dealt with first. Many remained with only simple defences and none was capable of offering adequate protection against the Mark 10 mortar. Strengthening station defences became a priority and, while complete protection could never be guaranteed, considerable improvements were made during the next four years by which time Sir John Hermon felt that he could relax in the knowledge that adequate strengthening was being carried out.

The building programme that ensued was no simple engineering project. Research had first to be carried out into the most effective means of protecting stations. Although this included drawing on existing knowledge, there was a need to test ideas and a series of explosions was carried out as part of this process at the Army's training area at Magilligan on the shores of Lough Foyle in County Londonderry. This caused an outburst of reaction from Nationalist politicians and even from the Irish government, since sound waves carried across the lough to County Donegal. Once again it appeared as if Nationalists cared little about the lives of RUC officers but were prepared to make political capital from measures intended to protect those officers. Such was the level of Nationalist objection to the research programme that one RUC officer involved in that programme told the author jocularly that he expected to be indicted in the 'Greencastle war crimes' proceedings' when the conflict ended.

The IRA went further than Nationalist politicians by declaring anyone working on the fortification programme to be a 'legitimate target'. This included employees of building contractors, the contractors themselves and anyone working in a police station or military establishment. In spite of condemnation from a wide spectrum, including Catholic Church leaders and SDLP politicians, the IRA were to take the lives of many who were simply trying to make a living.

At the same time the problem of sufficient and adequate accommodation throughout Northern Ireland was a long way from being solved. Such had been the expansion of the force in the 1970s that temporary accommodation had been brought into service in many areas. Some old police stations had been re-opened, such as that at Sion Mills in County Tyrone, but the problem remained. Even the Training Centre at Enniskillen, the heart of the force for almost fifty years, was stretched to bursting point with temporary classrooms on what had once been open space and the local divisional headquarters, which shared the former Army barracks site, overcrowded to a level that would not have been acceptable for a civilian employer. Specialist operational units were based in an Army camp outside Enniskillen but this was itself a temporary structure that was hardly adequate. The Hunt Report of 1969 had recommended establishing a new training centre and there had been much talk about this in the wake of the report with a number of local authorities in the province urging that it be established in their area. One of those was the Londonderry Development Commission, which had proposed that the centre be built at Culmore where the Foyle flows into Lough Foyle, close to the border. Nothing had materialized during those years in spite of Hunt's strictures and the entire training programme had about it an air of improvisation as a result of the obviously temporary nature of some facilities. However, the Police Authority had bought the former Belfast College of Domestic Science at Garnerville in east Belfast as a Further Training Centre and Hermon recommended that all recruit training be transferred there, a move that would improve security for recruits travelling between their homes and the Training Centre. Garnerville had been a residential college and had accommodation facilities that were superior to Enniskillen; these had been intended for females and the building lacked adequate toilet facilities for male officers. The Police Authority agreed in principle to transfer recruit training to Belfast but there were no moves towards providing a modern police college to cater for all levels of training. The Northern Ireland Office offered to make available recruit-training facilities in England but Hermon preferred that such training should remain in Northern Ireland. Experience with RUC Cadets in the 1970s had shown that, when the scheme had been based in England, many officers were lost to other forces. The RUC would finally move recruit training from Enniskillen to Garnerville after an IRA mortar attack on the former in September 1985; fortunately, there was no loss of life although thirty-five recruits and staff were injured. Hermon ordered that the first intake of recruits in 1986 would report to Garnerville rather than Enniskillen.

The political tension that had marked the year thus far continued throughout the rest of 1985. In spite of positive remarks from Garret FitzGerald on the RUC's handling of parades there was no significant improvement in Nationalist attitudes towards the force while many Unionists were describing the RUC as tools of Dublin, an attitude bolstered by FitzGerald's remarks. It seemed as if the force could not win. Nor had the terrorist campaign abated in any way.

On 31 August, Inspector Martin Vance was murdered by the IRA as he arrived at his Crossgar home after an evening at Downpatrick Golf Club. At least two gunmen were involved in the murder of the father of three, whose wife had to run over 400 yards to summon help because the family's phone was out of order. Martin Vance had moved from Downpatrick to Crossgar about a year before because of concerns about his family's safety. Inspector Vance was buried following requiem Mass in Downpatrick at which his parish priest, Dr Joseph Maguire, condemned the murder without reservation and challenged all 'those who think of the wanton and cruel killing of this young officer that policing is an essential service in any civilised society'. Bishop Cahal Daly, who presided at the service, also spoke, noting that the murder occurred at a time when more Catholics were joining the RUC. The SDLP's Eddie McGrady, later an MP, described the murder as the third of young police officers from Downpatrick whose 'sole purpose in life was to serve the community'. In contrast, two Sinn Fein councillors in Downpatrick objected to the adjournment of Down District Council's meeting as a mark of respect for Martin Vance.

The IRA continued targeting police officers and those they believed were helping or supporting the force in any way. Eleven days before they murdered Martin Vance, the IRA in Dublin murdered Seamus McAvoy, a Catholic businessman who supplied building materials and portacabins to the police, on the grounds that he was a collaborator 'with the occupation forces in the north'. And they also murdered a man in a Strabane bar, wrongly believing him to be a contractor who carried out work for the police and Army. In addition they, and the INLA, murdered several alleged informants, including a young Strabane man, Damien McCrory, who had difficulty in reading or writing and had a low IQ. The murder campaign against businessmen and alleged informants drew no condemnation from Sinn Fein whose representatives attempted to justify it. In November a German businessman, Kurt König, a former catering manager for the RUC, was murdered at his Londonderry home as part of this brutal campaign of murder and intimidation.

Near Crossmaglen, and about a mile from the Monaghan border, an IRA landmine took the life of David Hanson on 15 November. Constable Hanson was one of an eight-man group dropped off by helicopter to patrol the area. The explosion happened at about 10.20 a.m. and was triggered from high ground overlooking the scene. Another officer was seriously injured in the blast, which was caused by about 300lbs of explosive. An RUC spokesman said that the 'patrol walked into a trap'. David Hanson, the son of a former RUC officer, was buried in Clandeboye cemetery following a service in Hamilton Road Baptist Church in Bangor. He had joined the RUC in 1983.

Three hours after Constable Hanson's death, Margaret Thatcher and Garret FitzGerald signed the Anglo-Irish Agreement at Hillsborough Castle. In her subsequent speech Mrs Thatcher referred to the murder and said that it was sad that Constable Hanson should have died on the day that she and the Taoiseach were meeting to formalize an agreement that might help break the spiral of violence.

There had been much conjecture about the Agreement and many Unionists were incensed by suggestions that the Republic might be given a say in the running of Northern Ireland; Peter Robinson, Paisley's deputy in the DUP, said that this would be an act of war. On 2 November, some 6,000 members of the United Ulster Loyalist Front, including a newly formed Loyalist organization, the Ulster Clubs, had marched in Belfast to express opposition to the Anglo-Irish talks. Unionist fears appeared to be realized in the Agreement, although it is also noteworthy that Sinn Fein's leadership criticized the document on the grounds that it 'copper fastened partition'. How any document could hand Northern Ireland over to the Republic at the same time as it 'copper fastened' the border between them was a mystery to many. Ignoring Sinn Fein's opposition to the deal, Unionists began planning a campaign against the Agreement that was to push the RUC into the eye of the storm. Allegations were made that RUC handling of parades during the summer had been part of a deal with Dublin, as had the introduction of a force Code of Conduct.

The DUP even accused the Chief Constable of being a Quisling and demanded his resignation.

The first major demonstration of Unionist anger was made through a rally in Belfast on 23 November, attended by some 100,000 people. Under the slogan 'Ulster says No', Unionists also declared a boycott on Northern Ireland Office ministers and disrupted local council business by refusing to take part. All fifteen Unionist MPs at Westminster had already declared that they would resign their seats to fight by-elections to allow Unionists to demonstrate their rejection of the Agreement. Those by-elections were held in January 1986 and the Unionist vote increased over that of the general election of three years earlier but one seat was lost, Seamus Mallon taking Newry and Armagh to join Hume as one of two SDLP MPs at Westminster.

Against the background of the political turmoil in the wake of the Agreement, the IRA continued its campaign and, on 7 December, murdered another two RUC officers. This time the target was the RUC station in the quiet Tyrone village of Ballygawley. Reserve Constable William Clements, a native of Ballygawley, had swapped shifts with a colleague and was going off duty to attend a bible study meeting. Constable George Gilliland, from Clabby near Fivemiletown, opened the gates to allow his friend to drive out. As he did so, gunmen stepped out of the darkness and shot both men dead from close range. That did not end the terrorist attack, however, for the IRA then directed heavy gunfire on the front of the station to cover the planting of a 100lb beer-keg bomb that exploded ten minutes later, destroying the station. Three other officers survived by escaping through a back door. Constable Clements' Ruger revolver was stolen from his body and was used in three further murders.

Both murdered officers were married; George Gilliland had three children, while William Clements had five. The latter, who was fifty-two, had lived in South Africa for some years but returned with his family to Northern Ireland in 1969. He had joined the Reserve from a sense of duty to the community. As a Methodist lay preacher he had a strong Christian faith and, as his wife later said, 'saw himself as a policeman for all people, not just for the Protestants or the Catholics. He thought that as a Christian he could bring people together through Christ.'

For the RUC 1986 began badly, with the double murder of officers in Portadown just one minute into the New Year. Constable James McCandless and Reserve Constable Michael Williams were killed by a bomb in a litterbin that was detonated by remote control as they and another officer passed. Three IRA men had taken over a house on the corner of Dobbin and Ogle Streets some five hours earlier, holding hostage the family until they had carried out the murders. Although injured, the third officer was able to make his way to the local police station, having fired some rounds in the air to deter any possible follow-up attack. The murders were roundly condemned by the Irish foreign minister, Peter Barry, Cardinal O'Fiaich and Bishop Cahal Daly who said that the New Year had been 'ushered in by yet another heartless killing'. With four years' service in the RUC, Constable McCandless was married with two children. Reserve Constable Williams was also married but had no children. He had just over a year's service.

The year was to see another ten RUC officers lose their lives, all but one at the hands of the IRA; the exception was murdered by a Republican terrorist group calling itself the Irish People's Liberation Organization (IPLO). It was also a year in which officers and their families continued to come under pressure from Loyalists and, in May, the Northern Ireland Office admitted that 368 RUC personnel and their families had come under attack since the signing of the Anglo-Irish Agreement. During 1986 Loyalist opposition to that agreement continued with banners proclaiming 'Ulster Says No' across the province, and adorning several significant buildings. A programme of civil disobedience that included withholding rates was announced by Unionist leaders in April. The Assembly was finally dissolved, having failed to break the province's political impasse, although the Anglo-Irish Agreement seemed to have caused Sinn Fein to have a change of mind; the party abandoned its policy of abstention from Dáil Éireann and leadership of the Republican movement shifted towards the northerners such as Adams, McGuinness and Morrison. But the IRA continued to expand their list of 'legitimate' targets with anyone supplying vending machines to police stations or Army bases now included.

Derek Breen was a detective constable stationed in Lisnaskea, County Fermanagh who lived in nearby Lisbellaw. On the evening of 11 February, having finished duty, he stopped at the Talk of the Town bar in Maguiresbridge for a drink before continuing home for his evening meal. He was well known to customers and was a popular figure in the area. He was walking to the telephone to ring his wife to tell her that he was coming home when three masked IRA gunmen burst into the premises. The subsequent inquest was told that Detective Constable Breen called a warning to other customers: 'Get down, they know who they want.' In spite of knowing their target – and, had they been un-certain, Derek Breen had courageously identified himself to protect others – the terrorists simply opened fire indiscriminately, killing Derek Breen and barman John McCabe from Ballyconnell, County Cavan. A bomb was also left and exploded forty minutes later; the bodies had been recovered before the explosion.

Although the IRA later claimed that John McCabe's death was 'an accident' a statement in *Republican News* gave a more honest insight into their attitude: 'The safety of anyone who associates or socialises with these people cannot be guaranteed.' Derek Breen had one child, a nine-month-old girl. He was buried in Breandrum Cemetery, Enniskillen after a service in Lisbellaw Methodist Church. John McCabe had been married for seven months and had worked at the bar for six.

At this time the RUC was preparing for a one-day protest strike organized by Unionists on Monday, 3 March. Another Loyalist Workers' committee was formed and province-wide demonstrations were planned on the 'day of action'. The Civil Emergency Plan was implemented and all police leave was cancelled. A delicate balancing act was required of the force, accepting the right of people to protest peacefully on the one hand, and the right of others to be able to move freely. Thus liaison was to be maintained with protest organizers while 'maximum attention would be given to the Catholic community' to protect it from attack. On the evening of 2 March police officers were deployed tactically and found that small groups of Loyalist protestors were also out and about, preparing for the morrow.

With the new day those travelling to work found some roads clear while others were blocked. Several sharp encounters took place but in a number of areas there were insufficient police to keep roads open. Hermon felt that some subdivisional commanders did not deploy enough personnel initially and that there were occasions when police did not respond firmly enough. Some commanders agreed that they had begun the day with a 'softly, softly' approach, trying to persuade demonstrators to allow people to pass freely, but had found this did not achieve the agreement of demonstrators and so adopted a firmer policy with strict application of the rule of law by midday. Most major routes had been kept open but some less important roads were closed. Towards evening, as most workers had gone home, the police were able to 'deal more robustly' with the remaining blocks. By then, too, street disturbances had broken out, further straining police manpower, while there was also intimidation and attacks on Catholics. Fifteen police families suffered attacks on their homes during the day and made emergency rehousing a major problem for the force.

On the Tuesday a detailed analysis was made of the previous day's incidents. Over 1,000 roadblocks had been set up by Loyalists, of which police had cleared 441 quickly. The RUC had also policed eighty-four demonstrations that caused traffic disruption and led to some violence. Few civilian injuries were reported although forty-seven police officers were injured. In addition, there had been four gun attacks on police by Loyalists; some forty to fifty shots were fired. Officers had fired sixty-five baton rounds. In total, 329 cases of damage to property, including vehicles and buildings, were reported to police together with 237 complaints about intimidation. Cars had been hijacked and burned and a number of police vehicles petrol-bombed. Complaints about alleged police inactivity totalled 132, some of which were later withdrawn. Sir John Hermon refers to one he received from a senior civil servant, a Catholic, complaining about a two-hour delay in his thirty-mile journey home from his office. The Chief Constable responded, referring to the trials of Christian in Bunyan's *The Pilgrim's Progress*, to receive a second letter from the man a month later apologizing for having written in the first instance; having seen the abuse endured by RUC officers the civil servant confessed that he was ashamed to have allowed himself to be irritated by the delay in his journey.

Shortly after the day of action there were Loyalist demonstrations at Stormont and Maryfield, home of the Anglo-Irish Conference secretariat, but these were less violent than on previous occasions, although three DUP councillors were arrested for attempting to cut fencing at Stormont. Hermon attended meetings of the Conference and there were some who claimed that this made him a tool of the politicians. However, he was clear that he maintained his operational responsibility and that his attendance enhanced cross-border cooperation with the Garda 'to attack terrorist crime in all its forms, and from all directions'.[5]

Politicians continued to raise operational matters through the Conference while Hermon found that the UK government was not being entirely honest. Some months before the signing of the Anglo-Irish Agreement, he had established a study group to consider a force code of conduct and, in spite of the difficulties of the intervening months, that code became reality. It was issued through the House of Commons Library, thus preventing either government from taking political kudos from it. Some years later, Garret FitzGerald revealed in his autobiography that he had received undertakings from Westminster on the RUC Code of Conduct and the operational integrity of the Chief Constable.[6]

The summer months brought the usual marching season tensions and pressure on police families mounted with the re-routing of an Orange parade in Portadown on the 'Twelfth'. Intelligence had indicated that there were plans to extend Loyalist violence throughout the province in the aftermath of the banning of an Apprentice Boys' parade in Portadown at Easter and police operations had uncovered Loyalist arms caches that included Armalite rifles, explosives and small arms. Hermon had made the existence of the intelligence public in a TV interview and, realizing that these provided a direct means of communication, now chose to give media interviews in contrast to his earlier distrust of the broadcast media. Loyalist attacks on police families included one on Lady Hermon who was assaulted while leaving the home of a police family in Lurgan; she continued to make such visits, however,

197

demonstrating considerable personal courage and the dedication that marked the police family.

While politicians argued and sought the headlines, police officers continued to die. Inspector James Hazlett was taking his dog for a walk when he was murdered by the IRA on 23 April. His wife, Vera, heard the shots that killed her husband just outside their Bryansford Road, Newcastle, home. Jim Hazlett had been awarded the BEM for saving a man's life during a bomb attack on a Belfast store in 1974; he had also been commended seven times. With some thirty years' service, he was an outstanding officer who was happy in his job and completely without prejudice. Although accepted by Queen's University to study engineering, Jim Hazlett had decided to follow his father's footsteps and join the RUC to serve the people of Northern Ireland. He and Vera had four children.

A month after the murder of Jim Hazlett, the IRA took the lives of three men when they detonated a culvert bomb at Milltown Bridge in County Armagh, three miles from the border. Constables David McBride and William Smyth were killed instantly while Major Andrew French of the Royal Anglians died shortly afterwards. They had been part of an eight-man RUC/Army foot patrol. David McBride was buried in Breandrum cemetery near his Enniskillen home following a service in St Macartin's Cathedral. A single man, he was a brother-in-law of Sergeant Malcolm White, who had been killed in a similar attack near Omagh two years earlier. Constable William Smyth was also single and came from Cloughey, County Down. At his requiem Mass mourners were told that he had left instructions for all his possessions to be given to help the work of Mother Teresa of Calcutta. William Smyth was a talented Gaelic footballer but had to give up the sport when he joined the RUC because of the GAA's ban on RUC officers.

John McVitty, a father of three, was working on a farm at Drumady, near Roslea, County Fermanagh, on 8 July when he was shot by two IRA gunmen. His twelve-year-old son saw the two men as they murdered his father; they then made for the border. Constable McVitty's minister criticized the Catholic Church for presiding over the funerals of IRA men, some of whom had murdered members of the congregation, before reading out a list of men and women in Fermanagh who had been murdered by the IRA. John McVitty's home was at Cloncarn, Newtownbutler.

Less than three weeks later, on the 26th, three RUC officers were sitting in a patrol car in Newry's shopping district. Such was the heat that the men had left the armoured Cortina's doors open. Sergeant Peter Kilpatrick and Constables Karl Blackbourne and Charles Allen were shot by the IRA as they sat in the car. The two gunmen were dressed as butchers. They also threw a grenade into the car but it failed to explode since the pin had not been pulled out fully. Both constables died instantly while Sergeant Kilpatrick died shortly afterwards in hospital. Peter Kilpatrick had nine years' service and had been stationed in Newtownabbey and Larne before moving to Newry; he was married with an infant son. A native of Carrickfergus, Sergeant Kilpatrick was a Catholic. Constable Karl Blackbourne was only nineteen and had joined the RUC in January 1986. Following his son's murder, his father, Cedric Blackbourne, renamed his construction company Karl Construction. Eight of his employees were later murdered by the IRA at Teebane in 1992. Karl Blackbourne came from Antrim. Constable Charles Allen was married with two children. A Waringstown man, he had been in the RUC since 1983. One of the weapons involved in the triple murder was later used to murder Inspector Dave Ead in Newcastle in 1987.

More than two months passed before the next murder of an RUC officer. Reserve Constable Desmond Dobbin was on duty in the joint RUC/Army base at New Barnsley on 11 October when the IRA launched a mortar attack at about 10.00 p.m. Desmond Dobbin had left a sangar to walk to another when the 40lb bomb exploded above his head. The former art teacher was killed instantly and another reservist was injured; so, too, were two civilians, one of them a thirteen-year-old girl. The injured reservist, James Sefton, later left the force but was murdered with his wife by an IRA booby-trap in 1990. Reserve Constable Dobbin, who was married with two children, had been in the RUC for six years and was from Belfast. Several of his paintings adorn police stations.

Constable Derek Patterson was murdered on 10 November and was the first victim of the Irish People's Liberation Organization, an offshoot of the INLA formed after a split in that grouping earlier in the year. Derek Patterson was off-duty when he was murdered as he was getting into his car outside a friend's flat in Belfast. He died minutes later in hospital. The single gunman ran from the scene although he is believed to have later used a car. Constable Patterson was married with four children. He was the last police victim of 1986.

But the police had continued to suffer in other ways with attacks on the RUC at an Orange Order church parade in Portadown on 6 July when a Land Rover was overturned with its crew inside the vehicle. Attacks on homes continued and verbal attacks were also made by politicians. Not least of these was the SDLP which criticized Hermon's decision to allow an Orange parade along Portadown's Garvaghy Road. However, the Chief Constable had only given permission for the parade because it was on a main road with three housing estates set some distance back from the road – one estate was predominantly Protestant, the others Catholic – which meant that residents did not have to see the parade from close distance. With mutual respect and consideration, Hermon felt that this route could be maintained for the future. However, that respect and consideration were absent and he came in for criticism from both Nationalists and Unionists. The Twelfth parade was followed by attacks on Catholic homes in Portadown and police officers fired 150 baton rounds. Disturbances occurred across the province with twenty-eight officers injured, half of them in Portadown. In the latter, there were four further nights of violence with Loyalist mobs rioting, shots fired at police and a car bomb exploding close to police officers. The RUC was criticized by the Orange Order and the Ulster Unionist Party, who accused the force of causing the disorder and of indiscriminate brutality. Hermon thought that such condemnation from all sides probably meant that he had made the correct decision.

Pressure on police families continued with intimidation and attacks on homes. Anti-RUC graffiti appeared in Loyalist areas and in predominantly Protestant estates where there were police families. One notorious example read: 'Join the RUC and come home to a real fire.' However, condemnation by Protestant church leaders, the press and a number of politicians and members of the Loyal orders led to a diminution of this campaign, which began to reduce markedly in the latter part of the year. Even so, there were 564 incidents in which over 100 families had been attacked or threatened, some more than once; 120 families had to quit their homes. It was fortunate that the RUC casualty list for 1986 did not include members of officers' families.

As 1986 ended the RUC had policed almost 2,000 marches – 120 fewer than in 1985; the majority had passed without incident. Only sixty-seven parades had caused trouble, one of which was the first anniversary of the signing of the Anglo-Irish Agreement when police intervened to break up gangs of youths who were looting off-licences and other businesses; baton rounds were fired and the riot was quelled. Another incident linked to the Agreement had occurred in Keady on 8 August when police banned a march from the Catholic sector of the town and checked the rioting that followed; this was exacerbated by the return of the DUP's Peter Robinson who had been arrested in the Republic after a Loyalist mob had converged on the border village of Clontibret.

During 1987, sixteen officers lost their lives at the hands of the IRA in twelve terrorist incidents. The first of three incidents that each cost the lives of two officers occurred in Londonderry in March. On the 23rd, sixty-one year-old Leslie Jarvis, a prison service leatherwork instructor, had just got into his car in the grounds of Magee College, where he was studying for a degree, when he was shot by three masked terrorists who then walked away. Police arrived to investigate and as they removed Leslie Jarvis's briefcase from his car they detonated an explosive device.

The terrorists had substituted a booby-trapped case for their victim's. Two men died in the resultant explosion: Detective Inspector Austin Wilson and Detective Sergeant John Bennison. Both were married; Austin Wilson had two children and John Bennison was the father of one. Both also lived in Limavady. With seventeen years in the RUC, Austin Wilson had been commended or highly commended on thirty occasions. John Bennison was English and had served in the Grenadier Guards before joining the Avon and Somerset Constabulary, where he served alongside men who had worked with Sergeant David Dorsett, murdered less than a mile away fourteen years earlier. He had transferred to the RUC six years before and had four commendations for his police work. Leslie Jarvis was a Londonderry man, born in the Fountain area, known to and respected by a wide range of people in the city and with many friends. The triple murder was condemned widely.

Less than three weeks later, on 11 April, two officers were murdered while patrolling the streets of Portrush. Both were reserve constables, Frederick Armstrong and Robert McLean. They were shot dead about midnight by two gunmen who then escaped in a car that was later found abandoned at Portballantrae. Reserve Constable Armstrong, a father of three, was hit by four rounds in the back and shoulder while Reserve Constable McLean, who had two children, was struck three times in the neck and shoulder. Frederick Armstrong had been in the Reserve for six years while his colleague had seven years' service. At his family's request Robert McLean had a civilian funeral.

The final incident in which two officers died occurred in late summer when Detective Constables Ernest Carson and Michael Malone were shot dead in Belfast. With another officer, a detective sergeant, the two Special Branch men were in the Liverpool Bar opposite the ferry terminal at Donegall Quay on 26 August. Both died at the scene; the detective sergeant was also wounded, as was a civilian customer. The murdered officers were carrying out the normal Special Branch duties that are performed at all UK ports, checking both passengers and merchant seamen passing through. Ernest Carson, from Antrim, had been in the RUC for thirty years and was married with two children. At his funeral service in High Street Presbyterian Church in Antrim the Reverend Laurence Henry described him as 'a gentleman to his fingertips, a devoted family man and a brave and courageous officer'. Michael Malone was also married with two children. From Holywood, he had joined the RUC in 1971. Only family, friends and RUC personnel were permitted to attend his requiem Mass, the press being asked to remain outside the church grounds.

Reserve Constable Ivan Crawford was the first death of 1987. On 9 January he was on patrol on High Street, Enniskillen, when a bomb in a litterbin was detonated by remote control. He died almost instantly;

two other officers were injured slightly. After this attack all litterbins were removed from Enniskillen. Ivan Crawford was the father of three children and worked as a mechanic for the Post Office. From Brookeborough, he was buried following a service in St Ronan's Parish Church at Colebrooke.

The next police death was also a reservist who was killed by a booby-trap near the corner of Woodvale and Crumlin Roads in Belfast. On 10 March, Peter Nesbitt was responding to a call about a robbery in a confectionery shop when he was caught in the blast of a bomb hidden in a shop doorway. The call had been a hoax and the IRA had assumed, correctly, that police officers would take cover in the doorway next to the confectionery shop. Peter Nesbitt's father heard the explosion that killed his son who had been in the Reserve for twelve years. A single man, Peter was a draughtsman with the Belfast aerospace company, Shorts. He was buried at Roselawn cemetery following a service at Ballysillan Presbyterian Church. An hour before interment was due to take place, five officers were injured when a car bomb exploded at the cemetery entrance. According to the IRA, this was retaliation for 'RUC brutality' at the funerals of terrorists. For several hours, the city was disrupted by some forty bomb alerts.

Forty minutes before midnight on 3 April, Reserve Constable George Shaw was driving a police car out of Ballynahinch RUC Station when he was hit by gunfire from the grounds of the Church of Ireland church across the road. Another officer, who was opening the gates, was injured in the attack. George Shaw, a father of three, had seven years' service. He was buried with full police honours at Drumee Church, Castlewellan; he had lived all his life in the Castlewellan area.

On Easter Monday, 20 April, the seaside town of Newcastle was enjoying beautiful weather and was crowded with daytrippers. Inspector David Ead was walking back to Newcastle RUC Station after supervising foot patrols in the town when he was shot in the back by two terrorists who walked up behind him. Dave Ead was married with two children and lived in Newcastle. A former soldier, and native of Plymouth, he had joined the RUC in 1970, serving for several years in Londonderry where he married. He had escaped death in the Polytechnic bomb in 1983. The handgun used by Dave Ead's murderers had also been used in the triple murder of Peter Kilpatrick, Karl Blackbourne and Charles Allen in Newry in 1986.

Three days later a former N Division colleague of Dave Ead was murdered in Londonderry. Sergeant Tom Cooke had been on sick leave and was only days away from retirement when two gunmen shot him as he left City of Derry Golf Club at Prehen, just outside the city. He was hit by ten bullets and died almost immediately. Aged fifty-two, he was the father of three and lived at nearby Newbuildings. Tommy Cooke was buried at Altnagelvin cemetery after a service at Magheramason Presbyterian Church. Four years later his widow, a civil servant in Strand Road RUC Station, was shot and wounded seriously by the IRA as she left the station for home. One of the guns used to murder Tommy Cooke had also been used in the murder of Leslie Jarvis.

Constable Samuel McClean was stationed at Coalisland, County Tyrone. A Donegal man, he made regular visits to his parents' home and had been warned about his personal safety as a result of those visits. In the afternoon of 2 June he was working on his cousin's farm, some 400 yards from his parents' home, when he was shot and killed by two terrorists, one armed with a shotgun and the other with a revolver. On this occasion Sam had been home for a week because of his father's illness. With twenty years' service, Sam McClean had been awarded the BEM for gallantry and had five commendations. His funeral was held in Donegal and Sir John Hermon attended, as did the Garda Commissioner, Lawrence Wren, and 150 RUC officers.

Sergeant Robert Guthrie was shot dead as he arrived at Antrim Road RUC Station at 5.30 p.m. on 23 June. As he stopped to turn into the back of the station he was hit by rifle shots fired from the Waterworks park across the road. Robert Guthrie, a father of two, died later in the Mater Hospital. It was believed that the rifle used in the murder had been concealed in a pram. The gunman and an accomplice made off on a motorcycle which stalled, forcing them to run from the scene. Sergeant Guthrie, a Carrickfergus man, had joined the RUC in 1975. The son of an SDLP member was later convicted of the murder and sentenced to life imprisonment.

Constable Norman Kennedy was one of the officers forced to move by Loyalist intimidation. He and his family left Limavady and settled in Ballymena and it was in the family's new home that Norman was murdered on 27 July. As he and his wife watched television in their living room, two terrorists used a sledgehammer to smash down the front door before shooting him ten times. Their two children were asleep upstairs at the time. A member of Traffic Division, Constable Kennedy had served in the Reserve before joining the regular force.

Winston Finlay was a full-time reservist stationed in Cookstown who had joined the Reserve in December 1986, having previously served in the UDR and the Royal Air Force. On 30 August he and his wife were returning from visiting relatives and arrived at their Ballyronan home at about 10.30 p.m. Reserve Constable Finlay left the car to open the garage door and allow his wife to drive in. As he did so he was shot by gunmen who had been lying in wait; he died instantly. His family minister described him as 'a quiet, unassuming man and a loving husband'. Four years later, his brother Ronnie, a former UDR man, was murdered by the IRA in Castlederg.

The RUC's final fatal casualty of the year lost his life in one of the worst atrocities perpetrated by the IRA. Edward Armstrong, a reservist was one of eleven people killed by an IRA no-warning bomb at the Remembrance Sunday parade in Enniskillen on 8 November. He lived in Derrychara Drive in the town. In this instance the target was not specifically a member of the RUC but anyone who might be attending the service and parade. Another victim was Samuel Gault, a former RUC sergeant. The IRA's behaviour on that day illustrated the naked sectarianism of the organization and its atavistic hatred of anything associated with Britain. Not only was the Enniskillen service targeted but another, at Pettigo on the border, was also to be bombed. Fortunately the second bomb was discovered and made safe – by Irish Army bomb disposal experts who crossed the border to do so. There were no military or police targets at the second scene – only church organizations and children.

Since mid-1985 the IRA campaign had taken a new and even more evil twist with the intimidation of contractors working on police stations or Army barracks. In June 1985 contractors building a new police station at Lisnagelvin on the outskirts of Londonderry were told that they were 'legitimate targets' and would be shot. Work came to a standstill.

As this campaign of intimidation and murder increased there were bomb attacks on RUC stations that were intended to destroy them. The IRA's aim, having destroyed buildings, was to ensure, through fear, that they would not be replaced. Plumbridge station was destroyed by a bomb that also wrecked nearby homes while severe damage was caused to Ballinamallard station by a similar device. Toome and Ballygawley stations were also blown up – the station party in Toome still managed to have a lighted Christmas tree on the station wall – while there were attacks on the Training Centre at Enniskillen and stations at Carrickmore, Castlederg and Tynan.

Building work on new stations at Strabane and Larne stopped, as did the construction of a new prison at Maghaberry. Suppliers of materials were also being intimidated which disrupted even routine maintenance. Deputy Chief Constable Michael McAtamney recognized the IRA strategy for what it was: an attempt to drive the RUC out of its stations as had been done to the RIC in the 1920s. He issued a statement that the RUC would not be driven out, no matter what the IRA did.

The campaign continued throughout 1986 with Cloughmills and Coalisland RUC Stations among those bombed. Builders withdrew from Omagh RUC Station and, in that same town, Michael Murphy, Chief Executive of the Western Education and Library Board, was forced to resign from PANI after being named in a public threat against members. Murphy's resignation was a propaganda success for the terrorists, who had already murdered two Authority members, William Johnston and Oliver Eaton. A Catholic electrical contractor who had worked for the police was kidnapped and murdered in south Armagh. Terence McKeever's body was found close to the border; he had been bound and then shot in the head. The IRA claimed responsibility for this murder and that of quarry-owner John Kyle. Shortly after this the terrorists issued a fresh statement saying that their threat now extended to anyone working for or supplying the security forces. Several companies and contractors were named, including British Telecom. Such was the miasma of fear across Northern Ireland that bin men in Nationalist towns would no longer collect refuse from police stations.

This carefully developed strategy was endorsed by Martin McGuinness at the Bodenstown commemoration on 22 June when he claimed that all the 'resources and technology and weaponry available to the British government have not been sufficient to defeat our struggle'. He went on to say that killing contractors would cause the government serious problems and added that British forces in Ireland were sustained by 'those people who build interrogation centres and who service British Army camps and barracks which depend on protection and security'. According to McGuinness, the IRA had 'shattered that sense of security'. He was wrong, although the murder and intimidation campaign continued. But it was never to achieve what McGuinness and his Republican friends hoped for. Although there were problems in repairing damaged police stations these were not insurmountable. The Army could be used to some extent and military protection could also be provided for civilian contractors. But the IRA continued to murder, shooting dead Mervyn Bell, an electrician, as he sat in his car in Londonderry and murdering Kenneth Johnston, a manager of Jim Henry and Company, as well as Harry Henry, brother of Jim Henry. They had also carried out a spectacular attack on The Birches RUC Station near Portadown, ramming the station gates with an excavator to plant a bomb that destroyed the unmanned station. But an attempt to repeat this at Loughgall in May 1987 led to the IRA's most severe defeat when the terrorist gang drove into an SAS ambush and suffered the fate they had intended for the station party; eight IRA men were killed in an action that demonstrated that the security forces were not permanently on the defensive.

There had been another development in recent years as the problem of policing terrorist funerals had intensified. The car bomb at Reserve Constable Peter Nesbitt's funeral was in retaliation for what the IRA described as 'RUC brutality' at Republican funerals. This issue had been a persistent sore as the IRA attempted to give militaristic trappings to its members' funerals while police tried to prevent provocative displays.

Even the grounds of churches became battlegrounds in the Republican propaganda war. Since the early days of the terrorist campaign, the IRA had buried its dead following a funeral procession in which the coffin was draped in an Irish tricolour and shots were usually fired over the grave. Such displays had caused considerable anger not only in the Protestant community but also among many Catholics who disapproved strongly of the practice. Matters came to a head in late March 1987 when two IRA men fired shots over the coffin of another IRA man who had killed himself by the negligent discharge of a firearm. The 'salute' took place in the grounds of a Catholic church in Londonderry and there was considerable anger among the Catholic community in the city with many people seeing the incident as an act of desecration. Bishop Edward Daly proclaimed a restriction on requiem Masses for terrorists; in future, their funerals would have to take place before the requiem Mass was celebrated so that there would be no opportunity for similar displays.

Once again the Republican publicity machine had fastened on to a 'cause' that could be exploited to the benefit of the IRA and its political wing and to the detriment of the RUC. All that was needed was a high-profile Republican funeral and that came only a fortnight after the Londonderry incident when Laurence Marley was shot dead at his Ardoyne home by the UVF. Believed to have been one of the planners of the mass escape from the Maze prison in 1983, Marley was one of the most prominent Republicans in north Belfast. His funeral was certain to see a large-scale turnout of Republicans. Marley's death was followed by several days of rioting that presaged the confrontation that would occur over his funeral. Senior RUC officers knew that a display of IRA strength was inevitable and that the force faced a critical dilemma. To stand back would allow the IRA to exploit the funeral as they had done in Londonderry, but to police the funeral too robustly would allow Republican propagandists to score a PR victory. In short, it was a situation in which police could not win.

Marley's coffin was to leave his home on the morning of 6 April but, just as the cortege was due to move off, his family objected to the number of police officers near the house. A stand-off developed and, in spite of negotiations by local priests, the family decided to postpone the funeral until the following day; police believed that this was done at the behest of senior IRA members. Next morning there was a repeat of the stand-off and the situation was developing into a major crisis. Further negotiations took place with local priests acting as intermediaries between police and the family and, on the third morning, the police drew back from the house, but there was still a substantial presence. Although the funeral procession moved off to the local church for requiem Mass and thence to Milltown cemetery, there were clashes between police and mourners, whose numbers had increased to an estimated 5,000.

Republicans had had their high-profile funeral and confrontation and the resultant publicity had not favoured the police. Many Catholics who would not have supported the IRA were critical of the way the funeral had been handled. The propagandists had done their job well for it had not been obvious to the world, as it was to the police, that the funeral had been hijacked by the IRA to create a publicity showcase. Sir John Hermon conceded that the Marley funeral had been a disaster for relations between the RUC and Catholics.

In October two IRA members were killed by the premature explosion of their own bomb in Londonderry. Although Bishop Daly had announced that there would be no requiem Mass for terrorists until after a funeral had been held, the IRA defied his stance and appeared at St Eugene's Cathedral with the coffins of the dead men. They had timed their stunt to perfection. On a normal weekday it might have been possible for the church authorities to face down the terrorists and abandon services but this procession had appeared on All Saints' Day – 1 November – a day that is a holy day of obligation in the Catholic tradition on which the faithful are required to attend Mass. Thus it was that the confrontation at the cathedral between clergy and terrorists, with police in the background, saw many parishioners arriving for Mass caught in an unpleasant situation. In such circumstances the clergy decided to allow the coffins into the cathedral in an effort to maintain dignity. However, the terrorists did not have a complete victory since the Mass celebrated was that of the holy day and not a requiem. When the Mass had ended there were protests about the police presence, which resulted in a delay in the cortège moving away. This finally happened when police agreed to withdraw a short distance. Having made this concession in good faith the police then saw it exploited shamelessly when a masked man appeared from the crowd and fired shots over the coffins. As officers moved in to try to arrest the man there were clashes with mourners and baton rounds were fired. Once again the Republican publicity machine was in top gear and the RUC were painted as the villains of the piece. But the true villains were those who exploited the dignity of a church and the solemnity of a holy day to advance their cause; had they organized the deaths of their two members the IRA could not have timed things better. Terrorist funerals, with their pseudo-military trappings, were to remain an area of contention for years to come in spite of an IRA announcement a few months later that salutes would no longer be fired over coffins in the interests of the safety of mourners.

The IRA's statement on salutes at funerals was yet another round in the propaganda war. But while they fought the war of words, the IRA were also increasing their arsenal for the campaign of violence. The extent to which they were doing so became obvious at the beginning of November when the French authorities intercepted a freighter en route to Ireland with a cargo of explosives, weapons and ammunition. The ship, *Eksund*, had a consignment from Libya that included 150 tons of munitions. At first it was believed to be a one-off shipment and that the IRA were being denied a considerable addition to their stock but French interrogation of IRA men on board *Eksund* soon revealed that this was the latest of several shipments. There had been as many as four earlier consignments although this was probably the largest. From the French came the news that the IRA had already received over 150 tons of weaponry and explosives, including SAM7 air defence systems and Czech-made Semtex, a powerful and odourless military plastic explosive. Semtex had already been found in an unexploded IRA mortar bomb. By the end of the month both the RUC and Garda, supported by military units, were carrying out searches on both sides of the border. Nothing significant was found, other than storage spaces. However, in January 1988, an IRA arms dump was discovered at Five Fingers Strand, near Malin Head in Donegal. Just over a week later police stopped an ice-cream lorry at Sprucefield roundabout near Lisburn and found that it was carrying RPG7 launchers, warheads, hand grenades, Kalashnikov rifles – which had supplanted the American Armalite as the IRA weapon of choice – Webley revolvers, a general purpose machine gun (GPMG), magazines for the Kalashnikovs and some 10,000 rounds of ammunition. Nor was the IRA the only terrorist organization that was stocking up. Seizures of Loyalist weaponry were made in January and February; one of these was the largest-ever Loyalist arms haul, including sixty-one Kalashnikov AK47s, thirty Browning 9mm pistols and 150 fragmentation grenades as well as over 11,000 rounds of ammunition and grenade launchers for the AK47s. In the second seizure of Loyalist arms 40,000 rounds of ammunition were seized together with an RPG7, thirty-eight AK47s, fifteen handguns and rockets and boosters. At the end of February Gardai in Dublin discovered an IRA dump that included twelve RPG7s, almost 700lbs of Semtex, three tripods for GPMGs, sixty-four hand grenades, thirty rifles and over 30,000 rounds of assorted ammunition; some material was said to bear Libyan markings.

These arms finds were the result of intense activity by police and soldiers on both sides of the border, including stopping vehicles travelling into Belfast, searching buildings and farmland and seeking information from Republican and Loyalist sources. Cross-border operations between the seizure of *Eksund* and 1 April 1988 resulted in the seizure of 500 weapons, 165,000 rounds of ammunition and over 3,000lbs of explosives. By the end of 1988 it was estimated that RUC and Garda operations, as well as terrorist activities, had accounted for some five tons of the IRA arsenal, a fraction of what it was believed the terrorists possessed.

The RUC death toll from terrorism in 1988 reduced to six with all the officers murdered by the IRA. Their first victim was Constable Colin Gilmore who was killed when his Land Rover was ambushed on Belfast's Falls Road on 25 January. Homemade grenades were thrown at the vehicle from an upstairs window of a derelict house across the road from the Royal Belfast Hospital for Sick Children. The grenades were made from tin cans – the one that killed Colin Gilmore may have been a baked beans can – dropped on a small parachute and known as drogue bombs. His was the first death from this improvised weapon, which had the ability to penetrate the armour of police and military vehicles. Constable Gilmore was married with one child. A former Irish Guardsman, he was buried after a service in Seymour Street Methodist Hall at which Doctor Hedley Plunkett, onetime president of the Methodist Church, called on more Catholics to join the security forces.

Constable Clive Graham was murdered in Londonderry on 21 March. He was shot through the head when the IRA attacked a police checkpoint in Lislane Drive in the Foyle Hill area of the city. Three gunmen had taken over a nearby house in Benevenagh Gardens less than two hours before the shooting, which occurred in late morning. A man carrying his baby son was also struck in the leg by one of the terrorists' rounds. Constable Graham was single and had been in the RUC for two years, having joined from the Reserve in which he had served since 1982. His girlfriend revealed that they had been talking about emigrating.

Although there were many terrorist attacks on police it was 2 August before another officer was killed. Detective Constable John Warnock was a crime prevention officer in Lisburn where he had been stationed for three years. At 9 o'clock that morning he parked his car in Seymour Street, about 100 yards from Lisburn RUC Station. He returned to it at 3.30 p.m. and drove off, travelling some distance before a bomb exploded under the car. John Warnock died instantly. The explosion also injured at least eighteen people, including some children, a baby, an eighty-seven year-old man and a pensioner in a wheelchair. A single man from Knockbreda, Detective Constable Warnock was due to have announced his engagement on the day that he was murdered.

Two policemen died in October. Constable John Larmour was looking after his brother's ice-cream shop on Lisburn Road in Belfast while his brother was on holiday. He was working in the shop on the night of the 11th when two men walked in. One ordered an ice-cream while the other stood close to the door. As John Larmour turned to the counter both men opened fire. Two customers were wounded in the shooting. Constable Larmour was married and had one child. Both guns used by the killers had been used in previous murders. On the 26th Reserve Constable Hugh McCrone was leaving Kinawley RUC Station with another officer in an unmarked car. Both men were coming off duty. As they drove towards Enniskillen they came under fire and Hugh McCrone died instantly. Aged twenty, he had been in the Reserve for less than a year and had announced his engagement only six days before his death. At Reserve Constable McCrone's funeral in his native Stewartstown, the Presbyterian Moderator, Doctor Godfrey Brown, appealed to Catholics and their politicians to 'come clean on this issue' in order to isolate the men of violence. He commented that the failure of some constitutional politicians to support the police was both an abuse of their position and a morally indefensible stance.

The last RUC officer to fall victim to the terrorists in 1988 was another reserve constable. William Monteith was fifty-nine and a native of Castlederg. He was on duty at the security barrier in the town centre with another reservist, who was his nephew, on 21 November when he was shot and killed by a gunman who had arrived on a motorcycle and walked up to the barrier with another man. William Monteith's nephew was wounded but grappled with the gunman and tried to pursue him; he was unable to use his own weapon for fear of hitting civilians in the street. Reserve Constable Monteith was the father of five.

The year had seen two major attacks on the Army with the loss of thirteen lives. In June five soldiers perished in an explosion in Lisburn, following a fun run, when the IRA planted a bomb under their minibus while eight died when a bus carrying soldiers to Omagh's Lisanelly Barracks was blown up on the main A5 Ballygawley–Omagh road on 20 August. These deaths accounted for almost half the Regular Army's losses in 1988; a further twelve UDR soldiers also died. In addition to the Remembrance Sunday bombing in Enniskillen, the attacks prompted security reviews. After Enniskillen, Margaret Thatcher had called for a review of security policy in Northern Ireland, one result of which was the re-forming of 3 Brigade, based on Portadown. Neither Hermon nor the GOC, Lieutenant General Sir Robert Pascoe, supported this move but Pascoe was due to hand over and his successor, Sir John 'Muddy' Waters, was an enthusiast for the reborn 3 Brigade. The rationale behind the brigade's being re-formed was that it could assume responsibility for border security. This was the task assigned to it and it appeared to give the Army primacy in the border area. RUC/Army relations were not helped by this move. However, 3 Brigade was soon put on the same footing as 8 and 39 Brigades, especially when brigade boundaries were redrawn to correspond to the boundaries of the RUC's three regions: 39 Brigade aligned with Belfast Region, 8 Brigade with North Region and 3 Brigade with South.

This was also the year of the IRA's attempt to carry out a bomb attack in Gibraltar, which was prevented when SAS soldiers intercepted and

shot the bombing team. That was followed by the attack on the terrorists' funerals by Loyalist Michael Stone, which in turn led to further
funerals and the murders of two Royal Signals corporals, seen by the
world on television. One measure announced as an aid to police in their
fight against terrorism was the introduction of what was then described
as genetic fingerprinting but is now better known as DNA testing. But
such was the frustration being felt in the highest circles that year that the
Northern Ireland security minister, John Stanley, was removed from his
post during the summer. Following the Ballygawley bus bombing, there
was also pressure to bring back internment, which was resisted by
Hermon, his senior officers and the Army; it was eventually ruled out
by the politicians. However, Thatcher insisted on tough new measures
being implemented, including an end to the right to silence for an
accused, a reduction in the remission of prison sentences from half to a
third and powers to allow police to investigate the financial webs behind
terrorist organizations. In addition the Prime Minister, determined to
deny terrorist spokesmen the 'oxygen of publicity', announced a broadcast media ban on representatives of either Loyalist or Republican terror
groups.

The IRA damaged its own cause on a number of occasions during the
year. Two passers-by died in a bomb intended for police or soldiers while
a Londonderry man and woman, who were concerned about a neighbour, were killed by an IRA bomb when they entered the neighbour's
home; terrorists had kidnapped the man and were expecting police to
check his flat. Three members of one family, the Hannas, died on the
border near Newry in a bomb intended to kill Judge Eoin Higgins and
his RUC escort. And a young woman, Gillian Johnston, was murdered
in Fermanagh in the mistaken belief that she was a member of the UDR.
In spite of these incidents the IRA continued to pursue its campaign into
1989.

Nine RUC officers lost their lives in 1989 as well as twenty-six soldiers,
of whom two were members of the UDR. A former Reservist, Harry
Keys, a Fermanagh man, was murdered at Ballintra in County Donegal.
He had left the Reserve two years earlier. His girlfriend was with him
when he was shot in his car. As the killers left they were yelling and
cheering. The girlfriend later went to live in London where she died after
a fall in her sister's home. As a result of this murder, and that of Gillian
Johnston, the IRA claimed to have stood down one of its Fermanagh
units.

The first serving police officer to die was Constable Stephen
Montgomery who was killed by a drogue bomb in Sion Mills, County
Tyrone. He was in a patrol car that had stopped outside a bar when the
bomb was dropped on it. Stephen Montgomery died instantly and

another policeman was injured seriously. The third officer in the car was uninjured. Following the blast a crowd emerged from a disco in the bar and began jeering the police and laughing at what had happened. A soldier who attempted to help the injured officers was hit by a bottle. One young woman present said that she was disgusted by the crowd's behaviour and vowed never to return to the bar. Stephen Montgomery, a policeman for eight years, was buried in his native Omagh; he left a widow and one child.

Another former officer died on 27 February: Gabriel Mullaly who had retired as an inspector two years earlier, was killed by an under-car booby-trap that exploded at a road junction in east Belfast. A widower with six children he had been threatened many times by the IRA who claimed that he continued to have links with the RUC and with Loyalist terrorists. This story was dismissed as rubbish by his family who pointed out that Gabriel Mullaly, who was engaged to re-marry, had no interest in politics and had had no connection with security matters since his retirement.

On 20 March two senior RUC officers, Chief Superintendent Harry Breen, commander of H Division, and Superintendent Bob Buchanan, responsible for border security, travelled to Dundalk for a meeting with Gardai. Returning to Northern Ireland they were ambushed by the IRA near Jonesborough. It appears that Superintendent Buchanan, who was driving, attempted to J-turn the car when it came under fire; when found it was in reverse gear and his foot was pressing down on the accelerator pedal. Twenty-five rounds from a heavy machine gun had struck the unmarked Vauxhall Cavalier. Both men were married and each had two children. Harry Breen was the highest-ranking RUC officer to become a victim of the terrorists.

In the aftermath of the double murder there was considerable speculation that the men had been betrayed by a Garda officer. Hermon and Eugene Crowley, the Garda Commissioner, dismissed this speculation, which was also refuted by Superintendent Patrick McCullough, president of the RUC Superintendents' Association. Commissioner Crowley said that the murders would not stop the developing relationship between both forces, which were committed fully to finding the murderers. In spite of these rebuttals speculation continued that information had been provided to the IRA from a Garda source and the double murder was one of a series of incidents that retired Canadian judge, Cory, was subsequently asked to investigate.[7] His report suggests that a Garda officer was involved in the murder.

David Black, a full-time reservist stationed in Strabane, was killed by an explosive device under his car as he drove to visit his mother on the night of 27 June. Although he was taken by ambulance to Altnagelvin Hospital in Londonderry he died on the journey. The victim might easily have been his wife for he had chosen to drive her car on that fateful journey; their child might also have suffered. One of the bombers was jailed for life for the murder, although the judge said that the man had been exploited cynically because of his limited intelligence. As he was sentenced the convicted killer laughed and told the court that he had no regrets.

Four days after David Black's murder the IRA claimed another RUC victim. Constable Norman Arnett, a single man of fifty-six, was visiting his widowed mother, aged eighty-one, in her home between Maghera and Garvagh when two men shot him through her living room window. She was wounded in the abdomen as she pleaded with the killers to stop shooting. In spite of her injuries she crawled to the telephone to summon help. Norman Arnett, a Garvagh man, was due to retire in August, having served since 1955. Stationed in Musgrave Street in Belfast, he had survived a murder attempt in 1971.

A week later, on 7 July, three officers were seriously injured in an IRA bomb attack near Cushendall. The trio were in an armoured Ford Sierra that was blown up as it passed a Volvo parked at the Red Arch on the coast road. One of the injured, Reserve Constable Alexander Bell, was airlifted to hospital in Belfast but died on the 24th as a result of blood clots. He was single and came from Ahoghill. The explosive-packed Volvo had been stolen in Belfast three weeks earlier. In 1990 an Andersonstown man received a six-month suspended sentence for withholding information about the murder; he had been threatened to provide the IRA with the keys of a caravan near the Red Arch.

Two officers died in October, one of whom was Superintendent Alwyn Harris, a father of two and subdivisional commander in Newcastle, County Down. At the time of his murder he was on sick leave and suffering from heart problems. He was killed by a bomb under his car as he drove to church for a harvest service on 8 October; the bomb included two pounds of Semtex. His wife escaped from the explosion with minor injuries. Alwyn Harris had received complaints from Father Denis Faul that three Royal Marines were harassing a Catholic mother in Kilkeel and he had had the men removed from the area. The Reverend Faul paid tribute to him after his death. Constable Michael Marshall, a native of Markethill, died on the 20th when his patrol car was ambushed by an IRA gang using a 12.7mm heavy machine gun and rifles. The car was travelling between Camlough and Bessbrook when the shooting took place. Sixty-six rounds hit the vehicle which caught fire. Michael Marshall, a father of two, died behind the wheel while his colleague was seriously injured but survived. SDLP deputy leader Seamus Mallon MP condemned the murder as a 'grisly execution' of a young man who was also his neighbour. Some days later a Garda operation uncovered a Degtyarev heavy machine gun near Ballyshannon in County Donegal.

This weapon can fire armour-piercing rounds at a rate of 575 per minute up to a range of nearly five miles.

There was one further police death in 1989 when Constable Ian Johnston was shot accidentally by another officer during a plainclothes operation in the New Lodge area. A house was being raided by police at about 9.30 p.m. on 8 November and Constable Johnston was covering the back of the building when he was shot by a colleague coming through from the front. He was taken to the Mater Hospital where he died at 1.00 a.m. on the 9th in spite of emergency surgery. Ian Johnston was a member of E4 and was clad in casual clothing when he was shot; it is believed that the officer who opened fire was unaware of his identity. This incident led to the later arrest and trial of a leading Republican who subsequently received an eight-year sentence, although he was acquitted of conspiracy to murder. The raid had been mounted following information from a police agent in the IRA and Danny Morrison was later arrested during a further raid to rescue that agent from an IRA death squad.

Constable Johnston's death occurred in one of a series of operations against terrorist groups, both Republican and Loyalist. In late-November and early-December 1988, the RUC seized 3,500lbs of explosives and searched 700,000 vehicles and more than 1,000 build-ings. There were the usual cries of outrage about the inconvenience caused to the general public, especially when checks were carried out on early-morning traffic into Belfast, but the results more than justified that inconvenience and the efforts made by police.

In October 1988 Sir John Hermon announced his intention to retire in May 1989. There was much media debate about his successor but the choice lay with the Police Authority who advertised the post throughout the UK and received thirteen applications. Michael McAtamney, Hermon's Deputy and a policeman par excellence, did not apply. Four men were selected for interview and invited to Belfast at the end of February 1989. The candidates were Geoffrey Dear, Chief Constable of West Midlands, Brian Hayes, Chief Constable of Surrey, John Smith, an assistant commissioner with the Metropolitan Police and Hugh Annesley, also an assistant commissioner at New Scotland Yard. All were highly-experienced officers but Dear was considered the front-runner. When the interviews had been held PANI announced that the RUC's new chief officer was to be Annesley. He had not been the first choice. Dear had been ruled out because of his perceived lack of com-mitment to Northern Ireland: he was not prepared to relocate his family to Belfast. John Smith, a former Irish Guardsman with twenty-seven years' police service, was the Authority's preferred candidate but the security advisers at the Northern Ireland Office would not recommend his appointment to the secretary of state. And thus Annesley emerged as a compromise candidate. Born in Dublin, he appeared to have a good understanding of Northern Ireland and to be willing to relocate his family to Belfast. On 23 February the Police Authority announced that he would take up his post on 1 June.

This year of change also saw a number of particularly brutal murders, not least of which was the IRA bombing of the Royal Marines' School of Music at Deal in Kent in which ten men died and another succumbed to his injuries almost a month later. Service personnel and members of their families were murdered on the continent, including the German wife of a soldier and the infant daughter of an Indian RAF Corporal who was killed with her father; these deaths led eventually to the abandonment of the special vehicle registration system for British service personnel in Germany as these and other victims were identified because of the conspicuous BFG (British Forces, Germany) licence plates. At home sectarian murders continued, including that of solicitor Patrick Finucane who was shot dead by Loyalists as he ate a meal with his family in their Belfast home. Allegations were made that police or Army personnel were involved in the murder and the killing was one of those referred to Judge Cory.

When Hugh Annesley took over as Chief Constable it was against a background of continuing unrest, anti-RUC propaganda from Republicans and heightened security. However, his appointment was welcomed in many circles, including Dublin, and most RUC personnel were keen to see what he might do. He was certainly a very different personality from his predecessor and politicians seemed relieved that his style would be much less forceful than that of Jack Hermon. But the latter had made a significant mark on the RUC. He had inherited a force that had been through the trauma of the seventies in which Graham Shillington and Jamie Flanagan had ensured its survival and built the foundation for Kenneth Newman to mould it into one of the most professional forces in the world, especially in the realm of counter-terrorism. For his part, Hermon had instilled a tremendous sense of purpose in the force, enhancing its esprit de corps and ensuring that officers took pride in their impartiality and professionalism. He was not without his critics and he made mistakes – his attitude to female reservists was old-fashioned and led to the force being taken to an industrial tribunal; the end result was a financial settlement that cost the RUC £1,250,000 – but he had the good of the force at heart and was prepared to dismiss any officer whom he believed did not come up to the required standards and who let the RUC down. His place in the force's history is assured.

One of Hermon's aims had been to bring about a situation in

Northern Ireland where politicians might be able to sit down and talk about the province's problems. Behind the scenes there had been developments of which the public were unaware. Meetings had taken place between the SDLP and Sinn Fein, the IRA's political wing. The latter were aware that many of their actions were losing them support, especially the 'accidental' killings of civilians caught in bomb blasts or in booby-traps intended for security forces' members. In spite of the negotiations, however, words of war continued to emanate from the IRA and its political spokesmen. On 17 August *Republican News* carried an IRA statement that read

> At some point in the future, due to the pressure of the continuing and sustained armed struggle, the will of the British government to remain in this country will be broken. That is the objective of the armed struggle . . . there will be no ceasefire and no truces until Britain declares its intent to withdraw and leave our people in peace.

This followed a speech by Gerry Adams at Sinn Fein's annual conference in which he declared that the British government 'understands only the argument of force'. According to Adams this perception not only justified the 'armed struggle' but also demonstrated that Republican violence set the political agenda. But the RUC and Army were now better equipped than ever to deal with that violence – and both the IRA and Sinn Fein knew that.

In the early stages of the IRA campaign neither the RUC nor the Army had a detailed knowledge of members of the terrorist organizations. This was due to a number of factors. Many individuals with no previous involvement with violent Republicanism had joined the IRA and little was known about them; Special Branch, which provided the police with intelligence on subversives had been allowed to run down after the 1956–62 campaign and, therefore, did not possess an up-to-date and detailed knowledge of the IRA. The fracturing of the armed wing of Republicanism into Official and Provisional IRA had also had an adverse effect on intelligence gathering, as had the existence of 'no go' areas in late-1969 and again in 1971–2. But, throughout the seventies and into the eighties, the intelligence picture had changed dramatically. Intensive military patrolling had helped create this new picture and new and more sophisticated methods of intelligence gathering had also played their part. However, human intelligence remained the most important factor.

Part of the strategy pursued by the terrorists had been to dominate areas in which the population was predominantly Catholic. Protestants were made to feel unwelcome or were forced to leave by direct intimidation. In such manner most of the Protestant population on the west bank of the river Foyle in Londonderry quit the city and moved to the east bank or farther afield. Any Catholics who had chosen to join the UDR or RUC Reserve were subjected to intimidation and then to a campaign of murder. Families of police officers or UDR members in such areas were also targeted. The period after the introduction of internment in August 1971, which saw the creation of virtual 'no go' areas in Belfast and Londonderry, allowed a strengthening of the terrorist grip on these areas. However, some individuals refused to be cowed and were prepared to pass information to the RUC or the Army. This allowed the building of intelligence files based on the human factor and was reinforced by information from within the terrorist groups themselves; not every member was happy with the way in which these groups were operating. Others joined terror groups with the specific aim of passing information to the authorities. Their courage was admirable and they played a significant part in the campaign against terrorism.

Special Branch officers provided the contacts for these individuals but Branch officers also carried out their own work on the ground. Operations became more sophisticated as the years passed and the Branch increased in size as well as in importance. Surveillance on terrorists and suspects was carried out by the Branch through a unit known as E4A while the HMSU could then be deployed to act on intelligence gathered by E4A. Control of operations involving these units could be carried out through secure radio links from the Tasking Coordination Group (TCG). HMSU officers received special training in anti-terrorist operations from the Special Air Service, much of which was built on the experience of the regiment's Counter Revolutionary Warfare (CRW) wing. This training has been used as a propaganda weapon against the RUC by Republicans and also by many SDLP members. Their argument has been that this is not a police role, ignoring the fact that, in many other countries, the police carry out this very role. Both Germany and France, major European countries, place their police in the front line against terrorists; the former created GSG9 (*Grenschutze Gruppe 9*), a border police unit, in response to such terrorist groups as the Bader-Meinhoff Gang while France maintains the FIGN (*Force d'Intervention de la Gendarmerie Nationale*) within the *Gendarmerie*.

The nature of intelligence-gathering operations is such that little can be written about them without fear of compromising those involved. However, some examples of the nature of operations will suffice to illustrate the courage shown by Special Branch officers. Since two males in a car would immediately arouse suspicion in any area in which terrorists operated it was practice not to carry out surveillance in this manner but officers might drive through Republican or Loyalist areas alone; they might even walk through those areas, trying to look as nondescript as possible. In one case a male officer walked through a hard-line Republican area eating an apple as he did so. In another case, two female officers went on a shopping expedition in another Republican area, pushing trolleys through a supermarket as though they were a pair of local housewives about their weekly routine.

In tandem with such human intelligence gathering the RUC also employed modern electronic means of carrying out surveillance, either through listening, watching or tracking. The net result of this mix of intelligence work was that many terrorist operations were prevented, terrorists were arrested or intercepted while about to launch attacks and the level of activity by terrorists, either Loyalist or Republican, reduced significantly – to the benefit of all in Northern Ireland. The work of Special Branch played an inestimable part in wearing down the terrorist organizations, especially Republican, to the point where they began to realize that they could never achieve their aims through continuing violence.

Notes

1: When it was opened the home was under the control of the Welfare Department of Belfast Corporation but, in October 1973, with the re-organization of local government in Northern Ireland, it became the responsibility of the Eastern Health and Social Services Board.
2: Hermon, op. cit., p. 133
3: *Terry Report*, para 51
4: Hermon, op. cit., p. 169
5: Ibid., p. 195
6: FitzGerald, op. cit., pp. 552–3
7: Following allegations that security forces had colluded in the deaths of four individuals – Patrick Finucane, Robert Hamill, Billy Wright and Rosemary Nelson – the UK government appointed Judge Peter Cory in 2001 to investigate these killings to ascertain whether there might have been collusion. At the same time Cory was asked by the Irish government to carry out a similar investigation into allegations of Garda collusion in the deaths of RUC officer Harry Breen and Robert Buchanan and Lord Maurice Gibson and Lady Gibson.

Chapter Nine

Enter Annesley

Hugh Annesley inherited a force in the ascendant in the war against terrorism. In spite of all their exhortations of 'one last push', Republican leaders were also aware of the true situation but were caught in a dilemma of their own making. So often had they vowed that the 'armed struggle' would continue until the British withdrew that any sign of being prepared to end their campaign would be seen as weakness on their part and could lead to further splintering; it might also put the lives of senior Republicans at risk from their own followers. Jack Hermon's objective of creating a situation in which the politicians might begin to practise normal politics was coming close to reality.

There were also political moves taking place with the SDLP negotiating with Sinn Fein while the British and Irish governments kept a close watch. However, the violence continued and Annesley soon became familiar with the most wearing duty of the RUC's Chief Constable, attending funerals of murdered officers. Before his first six months were over he had lost five officers. The death toll for 1990 would be twelve, a seventh of the entire total for that year. A retired reservist was also among the victims of the year's violence. Most police deaths occurred in County Armagh.

Inspector Derek Monteith was the year's first police casualty, shot dead through the kitchen window of his own home on 22 January. Derek Monteith and his wife had been enjoying a cup of coffee while watching television with their three children at their Armagh home. At about 8.30 p.m. he lifted the cups and went into the kitchen and was shot through the glass door of the house by gunmen who had cut a hole in the hedge to enter his garden. Nineteen rounds shattered the door and Inspector Monteith died in the hail of gunfire. The murder was condemned by Cardinal O'Fiaich and by Seamus Mallon MP who described the murdered officer as 'a courteous and very helpful policeman who served all sections of the community'. Derek Monteith had been in the RUC for fourteen years.

In what was almost a carbon copy of Derek Monteith's murder, Reserve Constable George Starrett was shot dead in the kitchen of his Newry Road home on the outskirts of Armagh. Only recently discharged from hospital following treatment for injuries received in a car crash, he needed crutches to walk; these were found beside his corpse. With twenty years' service, George Starrett was the son of an RUC head constable; his younger brother, a UDR officer, had lost both legs in an IRA bomb attack in Armagh eight years earlier. At the time of the murder George Starrett's wife was out of the house; she returned a short time later. Their only son was in England. Once again the murder received widespread condemnation and Seamus Mallon accused the killers of trying to drive a wedge into the Armagh community.

On 6 June James Sefton, a retired reservist, was driving past Forthriver Primary School on Belfast's Ballygomartin Road when a Semtex bomb exploded under his car. The sixty-five year-old died immediately and his wife, Ellen, was injured so badly that she died next day. James Sefton, who had been injured in a previous IRA attack, had quit the force in 1986 after receiving further injuries in the attack on New Barnsley RUC Station in which Desmond Dobbin died.

On the last day of June, Constables Gary Meyer and Harold Beckett were on beat patrol in Chapel Lane, Belfast when they were gunned down from behind by IRA men. Both were shot in the head and the gunmen made off through the grounds of a nearby Catholic church. An off-duty officer pursued the killers but could not shoot for fear of hitting passers-by. The double murder was condemned by Dr Cahal Daly, Catholic Bishop of Down and Connor, who described the murdered policemen as being 'well known and greatly liked in that community . . . They gave the kind of policing that we want, that the Catholic community want, but which the IRA do not want. They were giving a peaceful service to the whole community.' Both Gary Meyer and Harold Beckett were married, the former with two children and the latter with one. Constable Beckett's wife died shortly after her husband's murder; the coroner at the inquest on the two policemen said that she probably died of grief. Constable Meyer's wife, Iona, became a member and later Chairperson of the RUC GC Widows' Association. In 2003 she was awarded the MBE for her work on behalf of police widows.

Three RUC officers and a nun died in an explosion on Killylea Road outside Armagh on 24 July. Constable William Hanson and Reserve Constables Cyril Willis and David Sterritt were travelling in an unmarked car that was blown up when the IRA detonated a bomb hidden in a culvert. The explosion gouged out a crater thirty feet wide and twenty deep and blew the car into a nearby hedge. Sister Catherine Dunne, assistant deputy director of St Joseph's Training School at Middletown, was also killed in the blast. She had been travelling in the opposite direction. A passenger in Sister Catherine's car escaped with a broken shoulder and other injuries. Martin McGuinness of Sinn Fein apologized for the nun's death but not for those of three policemen. William Hanson and Cyril Willis were married with four and two children; David Sterritt was single. Two men were convicted for the murders but were released under the terms of the Belfast Agreement. One was released on 24 July 2000, the tenth anniversary of the murders; this created even more pain for the families of those murdered.

Louis Robinson was a detective constable who lived in Newtownards and who had been on sick leave for three years. With a group of prison officers he travelled to County Kerry on a fishing trip but when their minibus was coming back across the border, on 16 September, it was stopped by what the occupants thought was either a British or Irish military patrol. In fact, the men who stopped them were IRA members and they kidnapped Detective Constable Robinson who was then murdered. His body was left near the village of Belleeks in County Armagh; his hands were bound and a bag covered his head. Politicians, both Unionist and Nationalist, made pleas for his release and an appeal was read out in Catholic churches; his wife also appealed for his safe return. However, Louis Robinson had already been murdered. At his funeral the minister commented that the murder of a sick man and the undignified dumping of his body had only magnified the pain of his family.

A month later, on 15 October, two RUC dog handlers were shot while they sat in an unmarked vehicle at security gates in High Street, Belfast. Constable Samuel Todd, a father of two, died in hospital. The other officer, although wounded badly, survived. The murder took place on a Saturday afternoon and the killer made off through crowds of shoppers. It was later established that a Browning pistol used by the murderer had been taken from Michael Stone, the Loyalist killer who had attacked a funeral in Milltown cemetery in 1988. A UDR soldier had also been killed with the same weapon.

Two more off-duty officers were murdered in County Armagh on 10 November. Detective Inspector David Murphy and Reserve Constable Thomas Taylor, together with Norman Kendall and Keith Dowey, were on a duck-hunting expedition at Castor Bay on the shores of Lough Neagh when all four were shot dead by the IRA. It was believed that David Murphy had struggled with the attackers. A Browning pistol and spent rounds were found at the murder scene. David Murphy was married with two children, and had received several commendations for his work; he was a member of Special Branch. Thomas Taylor, who had three children, was described by friends as 'a quiet inoffensive person'.

Armagh was also the scene of the murder of Reserve Constable Wilfred Wethers, shot by the IRA as he arrived at his Waringstown home just after midnight on 20 December. Reserve Constable Wethers had been a full-time reservist for fifteen years and was married with four children, one a boy of nine. At least eight rounds struck him at the gateway to his home. The killers, who had been lying in ambush, made their getaway in a car that had been stolen the previous day in Lurgan. One of Wilfred Wethers' relations told reporters that he had 'lived for his children'.

Hugh Annesley had no honeymoon period free from violence when he assumed command of the RUC. He did have a honeymoon period from his officers who were prepared to wait and see how this new broom would operate. Annesley's credentials were good. As an assistant commissioner in the Met he had been responsible for Special Branch and the Anti-Terrorist Unit as well as other specialized branches. In that capacity he had liaised with both the RUC and Garda and thus came to Belfast with an insight into the problems of fighting terrorism. Arriving in June he was soon into the marching season and impressed observers when he appeared on the streets in uniform and flak jacket to watch the marching phenomena at close hand. At the same time he visited police stations across the province, to make himself known to officers. His style of command differed dramatically from that of his predecessor, with much more authority being delegated. Senior officers' meetings were also an opportunity for Annesley to learn more and he encouraged exchanges of views.

The marching season of the summer of 1989 came with a higher threat of disorder than usual. This was the twentieth anniversary of the deployment of troops on the streets of Northern Ireland and Republicans were determined to use the occasion for propaganda purposes. From the IRA came the threat of increased activity, which was met with a heightened security profile that succeeded in preventing a number of major IRA operations, although one bomb that did get through caused major damage to the Belfast courts, close to the city centre. As had become customary, the major Republican marching occasion was the anniversary of internment on 9 August, which was usually used to stage a propaganda coup of some form, perhaps an appearance by a banned American supporter of the IRA or a major speech by an IRA leader. On this occasion, however, Republicans lost the publicity battle to Hugh Annesley who chose to walk down Belfast's Falls Road in full uniform in front of their march. It was a courageous display by Annesley that earned him much credit and underlined the fact that Republican west Belfast was not an area that the RUC feared to police.

But, having stolen the PR thunder from Republicans, Annesley almost immediately began spreading seeds of doubt amongst his own officers. He issued a special message to all members of the force in which he denied having had any direct talks with Sinn Fein or of having overridden the operational responsibilities of officers on the ground. It seemed an unusual denial to make and appeared to apologise for, or at least distance him from, the symbolism of having taken the initiative on Falls Road. Not for the last time would RUC officers ask questions about their new chief. Before his first summer in command was over, Annesley was faced with one of the most serious problems that beset him during his time in command. On 25 August, at 1.00 a.m., Loughlin Maginn, known as Locky, was shot and fatally wounded in his Rathfriland home by Loyalist terrorists. The murder was claimed by the UFF who said that their victim had been an IRA liaison officer, an accusation that the Maginn family refuted. Subsequently, the UFF claimed that they had intelligence material from security forces' sources and an internal RUC document was shown to a BBC reporter. When that information had been broadcast, the Maginn family then issued a statement saying that Loughlin Maginn had been harassed and threatened by security force members. Annesley decided to meet the allegations squarely and announced that there would be a full investigation led by a senior officer from a force in Great Britain. He intended to demonstrate to all that the RUC would not tolerate anyone within its ranks passing information to terrorists, whether Loyalist or Republican.

The officer selected to lead the investigation was John Stevens, then Deputy Chief Constable of Cambridgeshire Constabulary – formerly Mid-Anglia – who formed a team of detectives from several English forces and arrived in Northern Ireland in September to begin a rigorous investigation into allegations of what Republicans were calling 'collusion' between the RUC, UDR and Loyalists. Stevens' team established an incident room in Carrickfergus, with another in England, connected to the Home Office Linked Major Enquiry System, or HOLMES, the computerized system designed to assist in major enquiries. This had been introduced in the wake of the Yorkshire Ripper investigation, in which many flaws arising from human error were seen to have allowed the serial murderer Sutcliffe to remain on the loose when he might have been arrested earlier. Visits were made to police stations across Northern Ireland and to Army bases to interview RUC officers and military personnel. Loyalist terrorist organizations ran their own 'black' propaganda campaign aimed at discrediting the RUC. This campaign included an elaborate hoax about an alleged 'inner circle' within the force that was providing information to Loyalists. A reporter was shown information alleged to have come from this source and his newspaper carried a front-page story on the allegations. This provided an opportunity for a frenzy of anti-RUC propaganda from Republicans. But the internal intelligence team set up by Sir John Hermon some seven years earlier to guard against just such an eventuality was able to re-assure Annesley that the story was nonsense. Nonetheless, damage had been done to the RUC's reputation and there were those who argued that there was some truth in the story.

> The [Stevens] Enquiry was the most extensive of its type ever undertaken in the United Kingdom. In all Stevens' team had taken written statements from 1,900 witnesses; 2,000 investigations had been undertaken, and 2,600 documents of all types had been recovered from Loyalist paramilitary organizations, principally from the UDA. Some were original security forces documents, many were photocopies. All the documents were classified under the lowest security grading.[1]

Although the full report was not published, there was no evidence to suggest any widespread cooperation between members of the security forces and Loyalist terrorists. It was discovered that documents had been taken as souvenirs by many soldiers and a more rigorous accounting system was recommended for these. One soldier, a Gunner in the Royal Artillery, was convicted of providing photo montages of terrorist suspects to a newspaper and was fined £500. Some UDR personnel were arrested in an operation that caused friction between the RUC and UDR as it destroyed the cover of members of the regiment. Only three were convicted of serious offences. Another two UDR soldiers were convicted of passing on information that might have been used in the Locky Maginn murder; their convictions were due to the efforts of the RUC.

Additional security measures to protect documents, including using special paper that would not photocopy, were also recommended, as was tighter control of all intelligence material. Stevens suggested that the RUC should have a dedicated anti-terrorist unit, as was the case with the Met, but this was ruled out on the grounds of practicality; with so many incidents it was impossible to carry out similar work in Northern Ireland. However, a recommendation for the establishment of a Serious Crimes Squad was accepted, bringing several specialist groups into closer harmony. Stevens' investigations had been taken almost as an audit of procedures by the RUC and proved, yet again, that the force was prepared to take action against Loyalists as well as Republicans. Two RUC officers had been reported by Stevens but no charges were brought against them as the Director of Public Prosecutions ruled that there was insufficient evidence to bring them to court.

Six officers were murdered in 1991, all victims of the IRA. Spence McGarry was the first to perish, losing his life to an under-car bomb as he left his mother's home in Ballycastle, County Antrim on 6 April. The detective constable, who was married with three children, was based in Londonderry, although he lived in Limavady, and visited his elderly

224

mother on a regular basis. After the explosion, his car rolled downhill and struck another car but the female occupant of the second vehicle escaped without injury. Spence McGarry, with nineteen years' service, had survived a terrorist attack in which a colleague was murdered in 1976.

A week later Sergeant Ernest McCrum was shot dead in Lisburn. Aged sixty-one and close to retirement he was off duty and working in his wife's antique shop when he was murdered. The killers locked the door behind them and telephoned a radio station to report their deed. Ernest McCrum, with thirty-six years' service, had not even had an opportunity to draw his personal firearm, which was still holstered when his body was found. The gun used by the murderers was later found in a house search in west Belfast.

On 1 May Sergeant Stephen Gillespie, four times British Police 800 metres Champion, was travelling in a Land Rover along Beechmount Avenue in west Belfast when the vehicle was struck by a rocket. Sergeant Gillespie died the following day. He left a widow and two children. His athletic career had been cut short when he was injured during a Loyalist demonstration against the Anglo-Irish Agreement at Maryfield in 1985.

Just over a fortnight later, on the 17th, Reserve Constable Douglas Carrothers was killed near Lisbellaw when a bomb exploded under his car as he drove home from work at lunchtime. It was believed that the device had been planted while the vehicle was parked in a church car park. A timberyard worker, Douglas Carrothers had been a target of the IRA before and had moved house because of the threat. Those who killed him, and left three children fatherless, had crossed the border to do so and were guided to his home by a neighbour who was later jailed for life. He, and three other terrorists from south Fermanagh, received jail sentences totalling 1,000 years.

The next murder of a policeman followed just over a week later. On 24 May Constable Edward Spence was on patrol with three colleagues in the Lower Crescent area of Belfast when he was shot. He died on the 26th. Edward Spence was shot in the back five times and although nearby UDR soldiers opened fire, the killers escaped. The guns used in the murder had also been used in the killings of Detective Constables Ernest Carson and Michael Malone in the Liverpool Bar in August 1987, as well as in a number of other incidents including the murder of businessman Wallace McVeigh. Constable Spence was buried following a funeral service in First Larne Presbyterian Church. He had two children.

One other officer died in September. Constable Erik Clarke, a former member of the Royal Artillery, in which he had served for sixteen years, was killed when a horizontal Mark 12 mortar struck his Land Rover, the third of four patrolling in the Swatragh area of County Londonderry on 17 September. Three soldiers of 1st Battalion, King's Regiment were injured seriously. A native of Coventry, Erik Clarke had met his wife while serving as a gunner in Northern Ireland. They had three children.

As well as the six RUC officers, thirteen soldiers, of whom eight were UDR members, also died, as did sixty-three civilians and twenty members of terrorist organizations. The death toll had increased along with the overall level of violence and the government was making strenuous efforts to bring Northern Ireland's politicians together; they had not talked as a body for some sixteen years. Peter Brooke, the Secretary of State since 1989, succeeded in bringing them together at Stormont in May although the initiative ground to a halt due to the politicians' mutual distrust.

During the summer there was a spate of tit-for-tat sectarian murders that led some, including Cardinal Cahal Daly and Archbishop Robin Eames, to believe that civil war might break out. There were bombs, bomb scares and massive traffic disruption. Such was the tension in the community and the anger being expressed at the violence that Annesley suggested that internment might have to be considered, a concept that did not sit well with Nationalists or Republicans. Nor did Brooke help matters when he said that it was impossible to protect everyone all the time. His comment might have been nothing less than the plain truth but it was not political good sense to utter it, since this appeared to suggest that the security forces were losing the battle against terrorism. It also obscured some of the success achieved by the RUC, one example of which occurred in December when an HMSU patrol, acting on intelligence, intercepted and arrested a Loyalist murder gang at the junction of Falls Road/Waterford Street in Belfast. The terrorists had two AK47s, a sub-machine gun, a handgun and a radio receiver and probably intended to shoot at a group of Catholics in the vicinity.[2]

Annesley had one very delicate situation to deal with in October 1991 when Kevin McGovern, a student, was shot dead by a policeman in Cookstown. When it became clear that the young man had not been involved in terrorist activity, Annesley made a public statement in which he expressed sympathy for the McGovern family. He also called in the Independent Commission for Police Complaints and made it clear that the question of criminal prosecution or disciplinary action would be a matter for the DPP. The chief constable's sensitive handling of this tragic incident earned him considerable respect and, once more, gave the lie to the myth that police officers were beyond the law. There was another airing of a variation on this myth with a TV programme in October that rehashed the 'inner circle' story but without being any more convincing than the original hoax. Unfortunately, there were always those who were prepared to give credence to such allegations and, once the calumny of 'collusion' had been introduced, it proved to have a cloying presence.

The propaganda war against the RUC continued to be waged by Republicans at a high intensity, aided by the ambivalence of the SDLP, while, from time to time, Loyalist representatives would add their complaints to the mix. At the same time terrorists of each brand were waging war with bombs, bullets and rockets against the community in general and the security forces in particular. During 1992 the RUC death toll from terrorism fell to its lowest in over twenty years. Three officers lost their lives to the IRA while a fourth committed suicide after attacking a Sinn Fein centre in Belfast and shooting dead three men; another police officer was murdered by the IRA in Yorkshire.

Colleen McMurray came from Sixmilecross in County Tyrone and joined the RUC in 1976, shortly after leaving school. She was stationed in Newry and, on 26 March at 11.30 p.m., was on patrol with Constable Paul Slaine when their car was struck by a round from a Mark 12 mortar, fired horizontally. The weapon was hidden in a parked car and was fired through a hole in the side of the vehicle. Painted cardboard had been used to disguise the gap while the mortar was triggered from the opposite bank of Newry canal by a photographer's flash unit. Constable McMurray, who had been married to a policeman for a year, died some hours later in Daisy Hill Hospital. Constable Slaine lost both legs in the attack, although he later returned to duty and was the officer who received the George Cross from Her Majesty Queen Elizabeth II on behalf of the force.

This attack caused particular revulsion, with Cardinal Cahal Daly describing it as despicable and praising Colleen McMurray's dedication to her duty. 'She was herself greatly respected,' said the Cardinal, 'as a caring young woman who saw her policing work as a service to all sections of the community.' At the inquest on her death the coroner commented that 'A young woman from the island of Ireland with the name Colleen represents an ideal of Irish nationality worldwide. Colleen McMurray was brutally murdered by men who claim to be in pursuit of such an ideal.'

In the early hours of 7 June two IRA men were driving through North Yorkshire when they were stopped by police near the village of Tadcaster. The officers decided to radio their headquarters to make further checks on the car but as they did so one of the terrorists produced a gun and shot Special Constable Glenn Goodman twice, wounding him fatally. The other policeman was wounded and the gunmen sped off but were later pursued at up to 100mph by another police car, at which they fired with an AK47, hitting the vehicle nine times and causing it to crash. Both IRA men then approached the car but made off as a civilian car approached. They were subsequently arrested and one was convicted of murder. He had escaped from Crumlin Road gaol in Belfast while awaiting sentencing for the murder of SAS Captain Richard Westmacott in 1981. There can be little doubt that the terrorists would have had no compunction about murdering four North Yorkshire officers that day. Their actions underlined the danger that terrorism presented to the entire United Kingdom.

In early October Constable James Douglas was off duty and enjoying a drink in the Monico Bar in Belfast's Lombard Street when he was shot dead by two men wearing baseball caps. The killers ran off but later got into a car that they abandoned at Unity Flats where it was found. Earlier, James Douglas had told his brother that he had spotted a Republican whom he described as 'a bad bastard' but did not believe that the man had seen him. CID believed that Constable Douglas, a father of two, had been under observation by terrorists for some time; he had made a habit of drinking with relatives and friends in the same bar on Saturday afternoons.

Five weeks later, on 14 November, Reserve Constable Alan Corbett was manning a joint RUC/Army checkpoint at Belcoo in Fermanagh. At 11.30 p.m. he was shot by an IRA sniper, using a night-sight, from higher ground on the Cavan side of the border. The killer's weapon was an AK47 and he fired only one shot. Alan Corbett, who was single and came from Banbridge, County Down, had been stationed in Belcoo for less than a year.

On the night of 3 February, Constable Allen Moore drove to a cemetery where a friend had been buried earlier that day and, with his official-issue revolver, fired shots over the grave. As he reversed his car away from the cemetery entrance he was intercepted by police, responding to reports about the gunfire, and was taken into custody where he was examined by a doctor and found to have a blood alcohol level almost two and a half times the legal limit. Although the doctor said that he found no signs of psychiatric illness he also told police that Constable Moore might harm himself. Allen Moore's revolver was confiscated and he was released into the custody of another officer while arrangements were made for him to see the RUC medical officer at 12.30 p.m.

In the early hours of the morning Constable Moore telephoned a colleague whom he told that he was going to shoot Republican suspects. The colleague knew that Moore had a shotgun and alerted Newtownards RUC Station but the officer into whose custody he had been released was confident that all was in order since Allen was with him. Later that morning Allen Moore collected his car and drove to his own home in Bangor where he retrieved his shotgun. When he failed to turn up for his 12.30 p.m. medical appointment all RUC stations were alerted and asked to look out for him but were warned that he was armed and dangerous.

In the early afternoon he drove to Falls Road, having changed the number plates on his car, and entered the Sinn Fein building. He claimed to be a journalist with a prior appointment and was allowed access whereupon he shot dead three people in the centre and wounded another before driving away. He telephoned police stations to confess to the murders he had just carried out and then drove to Ballinderry, near Lough Neagh, where he shot himself. At his inquest a psychiatrist said that he believed that Constable Moore had been suffering from depression and that this, his drinking, the cemetery incident and his unrequited love for a married female colleague had combined to cause him to commit suicide – and to decide to take others with him. Subsequently, there was speculation that he had intended to kill Gerry Adams.

Although this was a tragic incident that demonstrated the stress under which police officers lived, there was the inevitable conspiracy claim from Republicans. This was given no credibility by the media and most people accepted that the incident had occurred because Allen Moore had been suffering from depression. Constable Moore was only twenty-four and had been in the force for almost six years. He had been awarded the Queen's Commendation for Brave Conduct in 1989. His parents lived in Ballymena, although his father had been born in County Donegal.

This incident illustrated the need for support for police officers and the necessity to study the problem of suicides in the RUC. One estimate put the suicide rate in the force at more than double the normal rate in society. Psychiatrist Dr Alec Lyons, speaking at Allen Moore's inquest, described as 'a disgrace' the fact that young officers were killing themselves and no one was examining the situation. He estimated that, between 1978 and 1993, there had been fifty-seven suicides and stated that the force was unwilling to admit this. Although an occupational health unit had been established in 1986 with two doctors and two nurses to provide a confidential health counselling service to officers there remained a reluctance among male officers to admit to suffering from stress.

By the end of 1992 over 3,360 had lost their lives as a result of the 'troubles'. While most died in Northern Ireland, others perished in the Republic, in Britain or on the continent. By now Northern Ireland had become more polarized than ever with the 1991 census indicating that most of the population lived in areas that were over 90 per cent Catholic or Protestant. There were, however, secret contacts between the IRA and John Major's government while 1993 saw the beginning of what became known as the 'peace process' with contacts between the SDLP's John Hume and Sinn Fein's Gerry Adams. The overall death toll for 1993 came to ninety with fourteen of those members of the security forces, including six RUC officers, all of whom died at the hands of the IRA. During the year Loyalist terrorists were responsible for more murders than Republicans while four Republican and three Loyalist terrorists were also killed. Sectarian tension was high throughout the year but increased in the autumn and early winter with some of the most horrific killings of the conflict occurring in Belfast and Greysteel in October. This was also the year of the Warrington bomb in which the IRA killed two children in an attack on a Cheshire shopping centre. It was a year in which many believed that Northern Ireland might edge over the line into civil war; a year in which a craving for peace became stronger than ever.

Michael Ferguson was a native of Omagh and the son of a policeman who had followed his father into the RUC. On the afternoon of 23 January, a Saturday, he was on duty in Londonderry's Shipquay Street, providing cover for officers carrying out an investigation in a shopping centre. As he stood near The Diamond, Constable Ferguson was approached by a lady who was a visitor to the city and was seeking directions. Michael Ferguson was giving her the information she needed when a teenager walked up behind him with a handgun and shot him twice in the head. The killer then ran off down Shipquay Street where he was struck a glancing blow by a passing car but still made his escape.

Michael Ferguson was the first officer to be murdered in the city since Clive Graham in March 1988. A Catholic, he was buried after a requiem Mass in his native Omagh. Bishop Edward Daly presided at the service and spoke of Michael's courage in joining the RUC; he added that his family should be proud of him. John Hume issued a statement condemning the murder as 'a reckless and ruthless act of brutality' and offered sympathy to the Ferguson family and to Michael's friends. Although he said that the murder offended every decent Christian standard of behaviour, he offered no support for the RUC. A month later, on what would have been her son's twenty-second birthday, his mother visited the murder scene and left a single red rose in his memory. A local priest conducted a short prayer service. It was a sign of changing attitudes in the city, of an appreciation of the work of the RUC and of disgust at the murder that the rose was left undisturbed. Ten years earlier it would have been destroyed as soon as Mrs Ferguson left the scene, if not in her very presence.

On 24 February the IRA carried out the first of two murders of police officers on successive days when they planted a bomb under the car of Reserve Constable Reginald Williamson. The father of two was separated from his wife and was having a drink with his girlfriend, a Catholic, in a bar in Moy. As they drove home, each in their own cars, the bomb exploded, blowing Reginald Williamson's car into a ditch. In October 1982 his brother Freddie, a corporal in the UDR, had also been murdered in Armagh in an ambush by the INLA.

Next day police and soldiers were establishing a checkpoint on the Castleblayney Road at Crossmaglen in south Armagh. Constable Jonathan Reid had been lying at the side of the road but got up to speak to a colleague. As he did so he was hit by a single shot from an AK47 rifle and fell onto the road. Although a colleague and a soldier began first aid Constable Reid died within minutes. He was the third policeman or soldier to be shot in a single-round attack along the border in a six-month period. Jonathan Reid was not wearing a flak jacket.

A single shot also killed Reserve Constable Brian Woods on 2 November. Married with one child, Brian Woods, who had joined the Reserve only in February 1993, was on duty at a checkpoint in Newry's Upper Edward Street on 13 October when he was hit in the neck. It was believed that the sniper might have been lying in a car boot. Reserve Constable Woods was taken to hospital and remained in a critical condition from which he never recovered. Shortly before the murderous attack a peace rally had ended in the town centre. The 100th reservist to lose his life in the conflict, Brian Woods and his wife had moved to a new house only a few months before. Sir Hugh Annesley described the murder as a reminder of the RUC's sacrifice arising from their service to the community.

Two officers died when their car was ambushed in Fivemiletown, County Tyrone, in the early hours of 12 December. Constable Andrew Beacom and Reserve Constable Ernest Smith were patrolling in an unmarked car that was struck by over twenty rounds at the Main Street/Cooneen Street junction. Drew Beacom lived nearby and his wife had just put her son to bed when she heard the shots. She was one of the first on the scene; the couple had two other children. Ernest Smith was from Augher and had two children. Canon Robert Riddle later described Drew Beacom as a 'gentle giant', an honest and friendly but shy man. He had almost twenty-four years' service while Ernest Smith had been in the Reserve for almost nineteen years. Both were stationed at Clogher.

The year had been marked by increased sectarian strife and, in Belfast, Loyalist terrorists were killing more people than Republicans. On 23 October ten people died when an IRA bomb exploded in a fish shop on Belfast's Shankill Road. Nine of the dead were Protestants, including the owner, John Desmond Frizzell, a sixty-three year-old father of two, and two children, seven year-old Michelle Baird and thirteen year-old Leanne Murray; four women were also killed and fifty-seven people injured, including two two year-old boys and a seventy-nine year-old woman. The tenth victim was one of the bombers, Thomas Begley, who died instantly when his bomb exploded. It seemed that the IRA believed that Loyalists were holding a meeting above the shop – the UDA had used the upstairs offices for many years – and that the bomb was intended to kill them. The second bomber was injured seriously and taken to hospital. A local Unionist politician told Belfast ACC, Ronnie Flanagan, that there was 'a Fenian' among the injured and police rushed to the hospital to protect the injured man from possible retaliation.

Retaliation came quickly. The UDA issued a threat, telling John Hume, Gerry Adams and the Nationalist electorate that they would pay a heavy price for the bombing. A series of attacks was then launched on Catholics: a taxi driver, a pensioner, two cleansing workers, and two brothers, an apprentice joiner and a lorry driver, were all murdered by Loyalist terrorists over the next few days. Then, on the 30th, Loyalist gunmen burst into the Rising Sun Bar at Greysteel in County Londonderry and shot dead seven people; an eighth died later. Among the dead were the bar owner's eighty-one year-old father and a fifty-four year-old Protestant man, whose wife was injured; the other victims were Catholics.

Northern Ireland was in one of the tensest periods of its history but the speedy and effective work of the RUC ensured that matters did not deteriorate further. The Greysteel killers abandoned their car a mile away. They had attempted to burn the vehicle but police were able to obtain forensic evidence from it. Raids on suspects' homes saw items that included a washing machine removed for forensic examination and detectives soon had a number of Loyalists detained for questioning. In February 1995 four men were jailed for the Greysteel murders and a number of other sectarian killings. One of the convicted laughed at relatives of the dead outside the court and later claimed to be proud of what he had done. Republican killers were apt to make similar comments. Although the officer in charge of the investigation commented that the suspect who decided that the Greysteel shootings should happen was not arraigned, there was considerable relief that the gang had been convicted. Sectarian killings did not cease but the horror of the weeks at the end of October was past, and most of the credit for that is attributable to the RUC's work. However, little credit was given to the police by Nationalists.

The people of Northern Ireland had little idea of what to expect from 1994. Although secret negotiations were underway to bring about a ceasefire, few were privy to this fact and as another year dawned, it seemed to augur yet more death and destruction. There had been hints from successive secretaries of state that the government was amenable to some form of settlement. One went so far as to say that the government accepted that the IRA could not be defeated militarily and a retired general was also brought out to present the same message. This was part of the government's window dressing for negotiations with Republicans, since it was already known that the terrorist organizations were under greater pressure than ever from the security forces and that, while they could still operate, they no longer presented the threat that they once had. However, the possibility of further attacks in Britain, especially in the City of London,[3] still existed and was a factor in a government desire to bring an end to the conflict. For the general public there seemed no reason for 1994 to be any different from previous years.

The RUC death toll from direct acts of terrorism reduced to three in 1994, all of whom were killed by the IRA in a nine-week period between February and April.

Constable Johnston Beacom, was the first to die on 17 February when his Land Rover was struck by a missile fired from a homemade rocket launcher in the Markets area of Belfast. Ironically, the attack occurred in Friendly Street. Johnston Beacom died in the arms of a local man who prayed with him as he breathed his last. Two other officers were injured. Priests from St Malachy's parish attended Johnston Beacom's funeral, as did Ian Paisley. Constable Beacom was buried the day before the first birthday of the youngest of his three children. On 10 March, Constable John Haggan, stationed at Willowfield in Belfast, was off duty and attending a greyhound-racing meeting at Dunmore Stadium in north Belfast. He was in the viewing lounge watching a race and talking with his wife, who was pregnant with their third child, and friends when a gunman walked up, shot him in the head and then shot him again as he lay on the floor. A second gunman fired shots into the ceiling as the pair made their getaway. Less than a year later a local man was jailed for aiding and abetting the killers. In alleged retaliation for the murder of Constable Haggan, the UVF later shot dead a Catholic newsagent, Jim Brown. Constable Gregory Pollock, from Shinn, County Down, was stationed in Lisnagelvin RUC Station in Londonderry and was driving a Land Rover along Spencer Road in the Waterside when it was hit by a horizontal mortar fired by a command wire that may have run from the nearby St Columb's Church. Greg Pollock died immediately and two of his colleagues were injured. The attack occurred outside the former Waterside RUC Station.

But the force lost some of its leading personalities in the battle against terrorism on 2 June when a Royal Air Force Chinook HC2 helicopter, travelling from RAF Aldergrove to Scotland, crashed into the Mull of Kintyre, killing all twenty-nine on board. Of these, ten were senior RUC officers, men with a vast range of experience in combating terrorism, a tremendous volume of knowledge on terrorists and their thinking, men that neither the RUC, nor the United Kingdom generally, could afford to lose. The RUC dead were: Assistant Chief Constable Brian Fitzsimons MBE, head of Special Branch, Detective Chief Superintendent Maurice

Neilly, who had escaped a murder bid in Londonderry over twenty years before, Detective Chief Superintendent Desmond Conroy BEM QGM, Detective Superintendents Ian Phoenix, William Gwilliam, Philip Davidson and Robert Foster, Detective Chief Inspector Dennis Bunting, and Detective Inspectors Andrew Davidson and Kevin Magee. Their loss to the RUC was incalculable. While information may reside in files and be available to others in that fashion, there is no electronic nor paper substitute for the knowledge built up by an experienced police officer. In his or her head repose the human elements of intuition, or feel, the ability to predict the behaviour of a target criminal or terrorist and the knowledge needed to know exactly when to act. The dead officers could be, and were, replaced by others but their particular skills and knowledge were lost forever. In Republican and Loyalist terrorist circles there must have been many who rejoiced at the tragedy. Among the wider public many questions were asked, not of least of which was: why put so many experts on one aircraft? For the other dead included Army intelligence personnel and MI5 officers, as well as the crew of the Chinook. The latter were among the elite of the RAF's helicopter crews, trained to Special Forces' standards and among the most professional flyers in the world. One has only to fly in their company on a night exercise practising the insertion of Special Forces to realize their great skill. All the more surprising, therefore, that such a crew should have flown into the Mull of Kintyre, especially as they had reconnoitred their route; standard operating practice. There were some suggestions of sabotage but no evidence surfaced to support these. But when the RAF board of enquiry produced its findings it laid the blame on the flight crew, claiming that they had made an error. Friends and relatives were aghast at this and questioned the findings, especially as it was known that there were concerns among aircrew over the FADEC software in the Chinook's avionics suite. The debate continues but what remains unchanged is the loss suffered that day, the greatest single loss incurred by the RUC in its history.

The bodies of the dead were flown back to RAF Aldergrove where they were met by Annesley and Sir Roger Wheeler, the GOC. Over the next few days the men were buried as their families and the RUC mourned. Those policemen who died as the Chinook ploughed into the hillside on the south of the Mull are not listed as victims of terrorism but yet they are victims just as surely as if their aircraft had been shot from the sky by terrorists or brought down by an explosive device. The final flight of Chinook ZD576 would never have taken place had it not been for the terrorist campaign in Northern Ireland; those who died, RUC, Army and MI5, were flying to attend a conference at Fort George on security and counter-terrorism.

The UK-wide threat posed by terrorists was demonstrated on 12 July when Lancashire police intercepted a lorry carrying explosives for an IRA bomb in London. Although the driver and his accomplice escaped, the explosives were seized by police officers.

On 31 August the IRA announced a ceasefire 'in order to enhance the democratic peace process'. The months of speculation had ended; Republicanism now appeared to be embarking on a political road and leaving violence behind. All IRA 'military operations' were to cease from midnight 31 August/1 September. There was mixed reaction to the announcement. While the *Irish News*, Northern Ireland's main Nationalist paper, welcomed it with the headline 'A New Era' and 'Time to build a peaceful future for all', the Dublin-based *Irish Times* was more cautious, suggesting that 'Northern Ireland [was] Hopeful and Uncertain' as the campaign of violence ended. For the *Guardian*, there was a 'Promise of Peace' and the opportunity to set about a resolution of Northern Ireland's troubles.

Many were indeed uncertain, as the *Irish Times* suggested, about what lay ahead. There was a spate of activity by Republicans with, for example, Martin McGuinness participating in a demonstration involving the removing of barriers on minor cross-border roads while some Unionists declared that the IRA had surrendered. But the organization had, as ever, been ambivalent. There was no clear declaration that the IRA would cease using violence or that it would stand down, as it had done in 1962. Sinn Fein's Gerry Adams saluted 'the IRA's bold and courageous decision', which increased Unionist suspicion of that decision. Nonetheless, on 13 October, Loyalists, through the Combined Loyalist Military Command (CLMC) announced that they, too, would be on ceasefire. Speaking for the Loyalists, Gusty Spence, jailed for the Malvern Street murder of Peter Ward in 1966, expressed sorrow for the hurt inflicted over the years.

The guns did not remain silent. In the course of an armed robbery, Republican terrorists murdered postal worker Frank Kerr in Newry in November but the IRA declared that its leadership had not sanctioned the robbery; the political manoeuvring continued. Both UK and Irish governments accepted the IRA disclaimer at face value; Frank Kerr's life seemed to have little value to politicians. The IRA ceasefire did not come as a surprise to the governments or to the RUC and Army. Plans had been in place for several years for an official reaction to such an announcement and, although both RUC and Army knew that the IRA was in difficulties, negotiators had let Republican representatives know of those plans, which included a reduction in the military presence and a 'softening' of the image of police officers.

But the ceasefire bought no respite in the Republican propaganda war against the RUC. Instead, this was increased. Posters calling for the disbandment of the force were displayed in Nationalist areas while some Belfast police stations had the RUC title painted out and 'Garda' painted in its place; one station even had an 'eviction notice' served on it by Republicans. In Nationalist areas of Belfast and Londonderry, attempts to introduce normal police beat patrols were met by Republicans with coordinated displays indicating that police were unwelcome. Allegedly, these were spontaneous protests but their occurrence in many areas while following a similar pattern was proof sufficient to indicate considerable planning. Sinn Fein was now leading a campaign intended to allow Republicans to police their own areas and to have the RUC disbanded. Unfortunately, the SDLP maintained its ambivalence, reiterating its policy of supporting the force in normal policing but not in its security role.

Before long the media were discussing a 'peace dividend', the benefits that might come from an end to the campaign of violence. A peaceful province was expected to attract more investment from across the world and a fatuous advertising campaign was launched by the Northern Ireland Office to convince people of the benefits of peace; using a song by Van Morrison, the fatuity of the campaign lay in the assumption that Northern Ireland's people needed convincing. Among the dividends expected from peace were reduced costs for security since it would be possible to decrease the number of troops committed to the province and close some bases. Further cost reductions might come from pruning the size of the RUC since the force was much larger than would be needed in a normal situation. Such speculation did not help morale, especially of full-time Reserve officers. The latter were employed on contracts that might not be renewed and so there were financial worries for many.

Within the RUC it was considered that the force would reduce and reorganize to meet the new situation in which it would be operating. Many officers felt some uncertainty, which was not helped by the concerted campaign against the force being launched by Republicans. At every opportunity Sinn Fein representatives were telling anyone who would listen that the RUC was the most discredited police force either in Europe or the world. And of course there were those outside Northern Ireland who were prepared to believe such propaganda. This was especially true in the United States where a strong Republican lobby commanded much attention in the media and on Capitol Hill. The RUC may have won the war against terrorism but it was now engaged in a war for its very survival, although it is doubtful if many appreciated that fact in 1994. Before long the anti-RUC campaign would be ratcheted up by Republicans with the appearance, again allegedly spontaneous, of groups of concerned residents in several areas across the province. The avowed aim of most of these groups was to bring an end to Loyal order marches through or close to their areas.

A number of marches became targets for 'concerned residents'. In Londonderry the Apprentice Boys hold two ceremonies each year, one on or near 12 August and the second on the Saturday closest to 18 December; the first commemorated the relief of the city at the end of the siege of 1689 while the latter commemorated the shutting of the city's gates against Jacobite troops in December 1688. The second event concludes with the ritual burning of an effigy of Robert Lundy, governor of the city at the beginning of the siege, and is commonly referred to as 'Lundy's Day'. Across the province in Belfast, Apprentice Boys marched along Ormeau Road on both days en route to boarding transport for the main parades. And in Portadown an Orange Order march to and from Drumcree Parish Church for a service to commemorate the 1916 Battle of the Somme also became a matter for dispute and, before long, the most serious of the confrontations.

Drumcree became a headline name in July 1995 but not before the RUC had mourned the death of an officer injured over two decades earlier. In May 1973, Constable Jim Seymour was on guard duty at Stewartstown RUC Station in County Tyrone when an IRA gunman fired on a patrol returning to the station. Jim Seymour was hit in the head and taken to hospital. Although paralysed, he remained conscious but unable to speak; he could smile and cry, however. For the next twenty-two years he remained in hospital, first in Belfast's Royal Victoria and then in South Tyrone Hospital in Dungannon, where his wife, May, kept a daily vigil by his bedside and told him of all that was happening in the world outside his room. Jim Seymour died on 2 March 1995 and was buried after a service at Killyman Parish Church, Dungannon, at which Archbishop Robin Eames spoke. The Archbishop spoke of the quiet dignity of Jim Seymour's suffering and of the love and attention he had received from his family and the staff of South Tyrone Hospital. He said that he had no words either to explain what the family had endured or to pay proper tribute to the hospital staff. Superintendent Basil Kerr, subdivisional commander for Dungannon, also paid his tribute to the Seymour family's courage and fortitude. Their suffering was an illustration of that of the entire RUC family, which includes the loved ones of those who served in the force.

This was a year in which the death toll reduced to single figures for the first time since 1968; seven were civilians, Jim Seymour was the sole RUC casualty, and a Loyalist terrorist also lost his life while one of the civilians was believed by police to be an IRA quartermaster. Both the UK and Irish governments were attempting to create a framework for discussions on Northern Ireland and issued the results of their deliberations in February. While Sinn Fein welcomed the proposed arrangements, and Loyalists said that these did not threaten them, Unionist politicians were loud in their criticisms. Meetings with politicians continued but, in June, Sinn Fein said that they would no longer meet British officials as they saw no sign of progress. Unionist suspicions and fears were exacerbated when Gerry Adams later addressed a Republican rally in Belfast and said of the IRA: 'They haven't gone away, you know.' That remark was made in July, by which time the first confrontation at Drumcree had occurred.

Garvaghy Road in Portadown was once a minor rural road but, with the expansion and development of the town, it had become a busy urban road serving a number of housing estates that stand some distance from the road. Since the end of the Great War, local Orangemen had used the road as their route when marching back from the Somme commemoration service in the parish church. While this had caused tension in the recent past it had never been a major problem, although two of the housing estates were mainly Catholic. Now, however, a Garvaghy Road Residents Association had been formed and it expressed opposition to the march on the grounds that it was provocative. To prevent an outbreak of disorder, police decided to stop the march from using the road. When the Orangemen refused to use an alternative route a stand-off began that lasted for three days before a deal was struck with reluctant residents that allowed the march through. When the marchers reached Portadown town centre there was a triumphal display by Ian Paisley and Unionist MP David Trimble, also an Orangeman, who headed the march with hands linked in the air to denote a victory. This caused considerable anger among Nationalists and Republicans and led to opposition to an Orange Order parade on Ormeau Road in Belfast on the 'Twelfth' itself.

Three years earlier a Loyalist terrorist gang had murdered five people in a bookmaker's shop on Ormeau Road and some Orangemen had later shouted offensive remarks as they passed the site during an Orange demonstration. Police officers had tried to arrange an agreement between residents and the loyal orders that limited the number of parades along the road but, following the Drumcree incident, Orangemen threatened to take the entire Belfast demonstration to Ormeau Road if they were not allowed to march along that road in the morning. Such an ultimatum carried the prospect of some 100,000 Orangemen converging on the district and creating an impossible public order situation. The decision was taken to allow local Orangemen to parade along the road with a large police escort and the outcome was a series of clashes with local residents. Once again the police were proclaimed by Republicans to be in the wrong and the outcomes of Drumcree and Ormeau Road were claimed to show an anti-Catholic and anti-Nationalist bias from the RUC and from government. Matters would be exacerbated by the Apprentice Boys' demonstration in Londonderry in August.

Part of the Apprentice Boys' tradition is that the parent clubs of the association march along the city walls on the morning of 12 August, or the Saturday nearest date. This element of the day's events was identified by protestors as their target for a counter demonstration. As they marched around the city walls, the Apprentice Boys found their way blocked by protestors among whose ranks were Sinn Fein's Martin McGuinness and the SDLP's Mark Durkan. The protest group in the city was the Bogside Residents' Group, led by a former IRA prisoner and son of a local Sinn Fein councillor. When the Apprentice Boys held their second demonstration of the year in December this, too, was marked by counter-demonstrations organized by the Bogside Residents' Group.

Although there were other points of conflict across the province these three, Drumcree, Ormeau Road and Londonderry, provided the main focus. Police were faced with a difficult, if not almost impossible task, of trying to ensure peace when many on both sides of the disputes did not want peace. Reconciliation efforts were made in all three cases but only in Londonderry did they meet with real success. There the Apprentice Boys managed to negotiate through local businessmen – John Hume had been involved in early negotiations – and to turn their August parade into the focus of a local festival. However, there seemed to be less willingness to reach agreement at Drumcree or on Ormeau Road although professional mediators were brought in. Over the years that followed, Drumcree would become a nightmare for police officers as the RUC tried to keep order and maintain a balance between the Garvaghy Road residents and the Orange Order. In 1996 the Drumcree confrontation caused widespread disorder throughout Northern Ireland and Sir Hugh Annesley made the fateful decision to allow the march along Garvaghy Road. In the aftermath of the summer marches of 1995 there was a spate of sectarian attacks with Orange Halls and Catholic churches suffering the attentions of arsonists. Tempers began to calm in the autumn and the fact that the RUC had contained the trouble without recourse to Army support was a matter for some satisfaction.

In spite of the difficulties of that summer there were still hopes that the overall situation could improve and that the work of mediators might bring about accommodations between marchers and their opponents. The RUC took a more sanguine attitude and prepared for further disorder in 1996 by planning the formation of additional DMSUs to deal with possible trouble. Such contingency planning was based on the knowledge that the IRA ceasefire was likely to break down and that the Loyal orders, especially in Belfast and Portadown, were adopting less compromising attitudes. Although Sinn Fein representatives argued that the IRA's guns were silent, and were supported in this claim by Hume, people were still dying at the hands of the IRA. Postal worker Frank Kerr had been the first, as we have seen, although both governments accepted the Republican explanation that the robbery in which he died had not been sanctioned by the IRA command. Other deaths followed. These included individuals labelled as drug dealers whose murders were claimed by a group calling itself Direct Action Against Drugs (DAAD). Although few believed this fiction, knowing that the title was another pseudonym for the IRA, it suited politicians to go along with it in the hope of keeping Sinn Fein in the political process.

In November 1995 the RUC had the task of protecting the first American president to visit Northern Ireland when Bill Clinton came on a tour described as not being a 'state visit'. He met, ostensibly by coincidence, Sinn Fein's Gerry Adams as his motorcade drove through Belfast. Working alongside the US Secret Service, RUC protection officers guarded their American visitor and learned something of the paranoia that has gripped presidential protection teams since the death of John F. Kennedy in 1963. It was not to be their last encounter with Clinton. However, as the President made his triumphal procession through Northern Ireland, the IRA was preparing another massive bomb in south Armagh that would be targeted at London. Clinton's staged meeting with Adams was supposed to keep Republicans from violence but the reality was very different.

The IRA ceasefire ended on 9 February 1996 when the 1,000lb bomb prepared during Clinton's visit, exploded in London's Docklands near Canary Wharf. Two men died, although the bodies of Inan Ul-haq Bashir and John Jeffries were not found until the next day, after their families reported them missing. Massive damage was caused to buildings in the area, including some of the City's financial institutions. Nine days later an IRA man was killed by the premature explosion of the bomb he was carrying on a London bus; a search of the bomber's London home uncovered Semtex, detonators, timers and ammunition. There were further bombs in London and, in late April, a Semtex device failed to explode under a flyover in the city. In June, Detective Garda Jerry McCabe was shot dead by the IRA during a robbery in County Limerick. Just over a week later, on 15 June, a large bomb severely damaged Manchester's Arndale shopping centre; over 200 were injured. It seemed that the hardliners had taken control of the Republican movement and were determined to go back to bombing and shooting. Republicans talked about the IRA's 'Tuas' policy, said by some to be a Gaelic word, by others to be an acronym meaning 'totally unarmed struggle' and by yet others to mean 'tactical use of [the] armed struggle'. There were claims that the political process had been sold to IRA members on the basis that the second acronym applied. Whatever the truth, it was obvious that peace was not just around the corner. This was emphasized with IRA attacks on an Army barracks in Germany and on the Army's headquarters at Thiepval Barracks in Lisburn in which a warrant officer in the Royal Mechanical and Electrical Engineers was killed. IRA activity in England led to the shooting of an IRA man by SO19, the Metropolitan Police specialist firearms unit, during a co-ordinated anti-terrorist operation in Britain.

Tension was probably at its highest level since the ceasefires as the marching season of 1996 got underway. It was expected that, once again, Drumcree would create problems and so it transpired with Orangemen determined to walk Garvaghy Road and the residents' group proclaiming that they would not. The dilemma facing the RUC was almost impossible: to re-route the parade would incur the wrath of members of the Loyal orders right across Northern Ireland and intelligence indicated that the mood of those members was one of anger; on the other hand, to allow the march to go ahead would anger not only the Nationalist residents along Garvaghy Road but also Nationalists across the province. It was a dilemma that required the wisdom of Solomon. Unfortunately, Hugh Annesley was no Solomon.

Efforts had been made by senior police officers and other mediators in the months, weeks and days before the march to reach a workable compromise but no one was prepared to compromise and, although discussions went on until almost the very last minute, it was to no avail. Annesley decided, on the advice of his senior officers, to halt the return march along Garvaghy Road. Mobile Support Units from across the province, including many of the newly formed additional units made up from personnel of various disciplines, were drafted into Portadown and when the Orangemen left Drumcree Church on 7 July they found Garvaghy Road denied to them by a wall of RUC officers, their Land Rovers barricading the road, backed up by soldiers who had erected barbed-wire barriers across nearby fields. Thus began a stand-off that lasted most of the following week. Across Northern Ireland support for the Drumcree Orangemen manifested itself in a series of demonstrations that threatened to rival the UWC strike of 1974. Roads were blocked, businesses forced to close and individuals and families intimidated. A prime target for intimidation was the RUC family. Police officers on duty heard their names and addresses being called out over a loudspeaker and attacks were made on the homes of police officers; many were forced to flee.

On the 8th a young Catholic taxi driver from Lurgan, Michael McGoldrick, was murdered by a UVF splinter group, the Loyalist Volunteer Force (LVF), whose leader, Billy Wright, was later murdered in prison by Republicans. This murder increased fear and tension across

241

the province. And yet the Secretary of State, Sir Patrick Mayhew, could urge a reporter to 'Cheer up'. Police morale was suffering as the pressure at Drumcree and on their families intensified. Officers were exhausted and there were concerns that there might be serious attacks on the police lines. It was believed that a slurry tanker had been brought in by Loyalists to lead an attack on those lines; the tanker was to be used as an improvised flamethrower to fire a petrol/sugar mix that would be as deadly as napalm. Army reinforcements were drafted into Northern Ireland in the form of 1st Battalion The Parachute Regiment. A Para recce group went to Drumcree and their assessment was that, should the Orangemen attack, the Paras could stop them only by opening fire. That the battalion involved in Bloody Sunday in Londonderry over two decades before might also shoot dead Orangemen was a prospect that appalled politicians and, apparently, Annesley. Aware of the police morale problem and of the danger of an attack on the RUC and Army at Drumcree, which could in turn lead to an attack on Garvaghy Road itself by thousands of Loyalists, Annesley decided to reverse his decision on the march. It was now to be allowed to go through on 11 July. Although the province's four main churchmen were trying to resolve the crisis, Annesley felt that they would not succeed and ordered the police to push the Orange march down Garvaghy Road.

Emotions had now run to such a pitch that it would be impossible simply to escort the march along the road. There was bound to be confrontation with residents and this is what happened. Police were forced to remove residents from the roadway and scenes of officers doing so were flashed across the world. Nationalist representatives, ever ready to condemn or criticize the RUC, were quick to speak to reporters from across the globe, alleging that the RUC were running true to form in using aggressive behaviour towards Nationalists whereas they had failed to confront Loyalists. That this was not true was ignored. Once again the Republican and Nationalist propaganda machine was in top gear and directed against the RUC.

They were aided by events on Ormeau Road in Belfast where police sealed off Lower Ormeau Road on the night of the 11th to allow Orangemen to march along it next day. Once more, there were confrontations that led to rioting in Belfast and Londonderry, where the worst disorder in over twenty years occurred over two nights during which about 4,000 petrol bombs were thrown at police. One man died when struck by an Army Saxon APC in Londonderry and many police and civilians were injured. Across the province some 6,000 baton rounds were fired, more than at any time since 1981, and 24,000 petrol bombs were thrown. The worst days of the seventies were echoed in that week.

In his book *The Fateful Split*, journalist Chris Ryder argues that this was the event that spelled the end of the RUC, that the perception of the force within the Catholic community was now such that it had to go. But this was a failure by politicians rather than by police officers. Certainly Annesley misjudged entirely the situation and did not make proper provision to protect his officers and their families, let alone the public; he had failed to ensure adequate Army support for the RUC in Portadown before the event. One cannot imagine a similar situation developing under Hermon, nor under Annesley's successor, Ronnie Flanagan. Even though it might be argued that the latter had the benefit of hindsight, it must be remembered that he had far greater insight into Northern Ireland's problems than Annesley ever had. The RUC did not fail Northern Ireland, although it can be argued that its chief officer did. Whatever the political correctness advocates claim, police forces must be led rather than managed and Annesley was a manager rather than a leader. The words of US General Colin Powell are apt: 'much more can be achieved through the art of leadership than can ever be imagined through the science of management'. Rarely was the truth of Powell's words better illustrated.

On 3 November Hugh Annesley retired from the RUC and from policing. Although he had hoped to move on to greater things, even proposing a national anti-terrorist force (of which, of course, he would be commander), that was not to be. On appointment he had suggested that he would be Chief Constable for five years but he held the post for over seven years and, in his final year, did mammoth damage to the force's image. After Drumcree 1996 anti-RUC propaganda was stepped up by Republicans and even Cardinal Cahal Daly commented that 'there was a crisis of confidence in the police' among Nationalists. Coming from a man who had been well disposed towards the RUC this was a severe criticism. At a stroke Hugh Annesley had undone the good work of decades. Perhaps the most pertinent description of Annesley and his style was the soubriquet bestowed on him within the force: 'The Eternal Flame', suggesting that he never went out.

For all the terrorist activity and unrest of 1996 there were no RUC deaths but, as the campaign continued into 1997 and the dying days of Conservative government, a young officer became a victim of the INLA. Constable Darren Bradshaw was drinking with friends in a Belfast city centre bar on the evening of 9 May when he was shot in the back by a gunman wearing a wig. Although the injured man managed to walk a few steps he was hit by two more rounds. A second gunman had threatened staff and both men escaped in a car that was later found burnt out. At his family's request there was no media presence at Darren Bradshaw's funeral. In what was an apparent retaliation for the murder, LVF terrorists shot dead a GAA official, Sean Brown, at Bellaghy, County Londonderry and dumped his body in County Antrim.

The day before Darren Bradshaw was murdered a young man died in

Belfast's Royal Victoria Hospital. Robert Hamill had been attacked and beaten by Loyalists in Portadown on 27 April while walking home with friends, one of whom said later that they had chosen to walk through Portadown town centre only because they could see a police Land Rover. Family members alleged that the officers failed to intervene in the attack although this was denied by police who stated that the officers in the vehicle had intervened but had been overwhelmed by the attackers, of whom there were about thirty, and had to call on reinforcements. This case was one of those referred to Judge Cory for investigation.

Annesley's successor as Chief Constable came from within the force. Ronnie Flanagan was a Belfast man who had graduated from Queen's University before joining the RUC in the wake of the Hunt Report. Moulded by the RUC and with a perceptive intellect and high regard for his fellow citizens, Flanagan adopted a totally different style that put him in the public eye and sought to seize the high moral ground for the RUC. He had already made his mark as an assistant and then deputy chief constable and had chaired a working group established by Annesley to consider future policing in Northern Ireland. Flanagan's group had recommended a number of dramatic changes, the most notable of which built on a Hermon initiative from a decade earlier. When Sir John Hermon had reduced the number of territorial divisions from sixteen to twelve one of his aims had been to bring the subdivisions into closer contact with the communities they served. Flanagan's group recommended taking this to its next logical level: abolish the divisions and re-align the subdivisions to coincide with local council areas; this would mean reducing the number of subdivisions and would also allow the creation of police/community liaison committees in each area. The removal of a command stratum would make personnel and financial savings. Each police district would be commanded by a superintendent; a national report on policing recommended the abolition of the rank of chief superintendent.[4] Another matter considered by the group was the strength of the force and it was suggested that while a reduction in size was possible there had still to be a capability of meeting any untoward situation. Since the terrorist ceasefires were not final, a force of about 7,500–8,500 officers was considered necessary. Once it was known that the ceasefires were real and that terrorist organizations had abandoned their weapons it would be possible to reduce to about 5,000 officers. The full-time reserve was to be phased out gradually while the part-time reserve would be retained as a means of enhancing police contacts with local communities. Thus it was that the man who took over from Annesley in November 1996 was one who not only had a deep knowledge of the RUC but also had given careful consideration to the force's future.

The years of death and destruction had not been consigned to the past, however, and during 1997 Ronnie Flanagan attended the funerals of four officers. That of Darren Bradshaw was the first, followed by Greg Taylor's funeral in June. Constable Taylor, a father of three, was beaten and kicked to death by Loyalist thugs after leaving a pub in Ballymoney where he had been drinking with friends, including another off-duty officer. Greg Taylor had been jostled and verbally abused in the bar by Loyalists who told him and his friends to go to Dunloy to drink; the RUC had re-routed an Orange march from Dunloy and there had also been local objectors, with Dunloy for a time becoming a flashpoint. Although Greg Taylor made a call from his mobile phone to seek police help the nearest patrol car was some miles away and could not assist him in time. He and the other officer were set upon with the second policeman being chased away and Greg singled out for what the Right Reverend James Moore, Anglican Bishop of Connor, later described as a 'wicked and savage in the extreme' attack. Between twelve and fifteen men kicked him, pushed him to the ground and stamped on his head. He died despite the efforts of a doctor. Fifteen people, including three women, were arrested and four Ballymoney men were charged with murder; one was the son of a reservist.

The United Kingdom now had a new government and Northern Ireland a new Secretary of State. For the first time in over eighteen years Labour was back in power and Prime Minister Tony Blair appointed Dr Mo Mowlam to the Stormont post. Shortly after Mowlam took up her new job, and with another Drumcree confrontation on the near horizon, Constable John Graham and Reserve Constable David Johnson were murdered on 16 June as they were on patrol in Lurgan, only yards from the police station. Two IRA men ran up and shot both officers in the head and, although doctors from a nearby surgery were quickly on the scene, John Graham and David Johnston were already dead. The two men were well-known as community policemen in Lurgan and there was much anger at the double murder. Although Gerry Adams claimed to be 'shocked' he failed to condemn the murders and was himself condemned by Fine Gael leader John Bruton who accused Sinn Fein of ransacking the dictionary to 'avoid condemning this brutal murder'. In Dublin the tricolour was flown at half-mast at Garda headquarters as a mark of respect, the first time this had happened. Although a Lurgan Republican was charged with the murders, charges were dropped and the man released. John Graham had three children and David Johnston had two.

And there was still Drumcree to contend with but Ronnie Flanagan proved himself more than equal to the task. Army support was built in to his plans for the parade but he had reached the decision that it was to be a case of pushing the march through Garvaghy Road as intelligence indicated that Loyalists planned to cause mayhem and destruction across the province should the marchers be stopped. Balancing the possibility of Loyalist attacks on Catholics against the reaction to the parade using Garvaghy Road, Flanagan considered the latter to be the option with less potential for serious consequences. In spite of efforts to reach an agreement between the opposing parties none was achieved and the march went through; in its wake followed four days of rioting and turmoil that saw police and soldiers fire 2,500 baton rounds while over 1,500 petrol bombs were thrown at them and many more attacks made. Some 400 vehicles were hijacked, 117 arrests were made and sixty police officers and fifty-six civilians suffered injury. Worse still was the sectarian murder of a young Catholic girl in the home of her Protestant boyfriend.

Against this background much pressure was being put on the IRA and Sinn Fein and the terrorist organization announced that its ceasefire would resume from midnight on 20 July. This allowed the negotiating process to go ahead with Sinn Fein invited to join the talks. Although Unionists boycotted the early sessions and IRA dissidents tried to sabotage the process with a large bomb in Markethill, County Armagh, it was not long before Unionists and Republicans were facing each other across a negotiating table for the first time in over seven decades. Negotiations were not straightforward and IRA dissidents, calling themselves Continuity IRA, launched a series of attacks across Northern Ireland; Gardai intercepted a bomb intended for Britain and the INLA murdered Cyril Stewart, a retired RUC Reservist, as he and his wife left an Armagh supermarket on 27 March 1998.

Shortly after the murder of Cyril Stewart, the political talks at Stormont came to a conclusion on 10 April with an apparent agreement for devolving power to a local assembly that would involve Unionists and Nationalists. Since that date happened to be Good Friday the media and Nationalists immediately dubbed the agreement 'the Good Friday Agreement', a title that smacks of blasphemy on a par with the Nationalist description of the 1916 rebellion as the 'Easter Rising'. However, the Agreement was not accepted by all Unionists; Ian Paisley's DUP had refused to participate in negotiations alongside Sinn Fein, while the latter at first refused to endorse the agreement. One prominent member of the Ulster Unionist negotiating team walked out of the talks as they neared their conclusion. This did not augur well for the future of the Agreement but did not prevent the British and Irish governments proclaiming it as a blueprint that would solve Northern Ireland's problems. It would certainly not solve the RUC's problems since the Agreement included a proposal to discuss the future of policing in the province and this led the way to yet another investigation into the force that was to spell the end of the title Royal Ulster Constabulary.

Notes

1: Potter, p. 338
2: Phoenix, p. 188
3: In April 1992 the IRA had caused some £1,000m worth of damage with two bombs in the City. This was more than any other bomb attack in their campaign.
4: Although this happened it was not long before the title chief superintendent was back in use, although those holding it were officers on the higher points of the superintendents' pay scale.

Chapter Ten

The End of an Epoch

On 3 June 1998, as a result of a recommendation in the Belfast Agreement, an Independent Commission on Policing in Northern Ireland was established under Chris Patten, last Governor of Hong Kong and a former junior minister at the Northern Ireland Office. The Commission's remit was to make recommendations for future policing in the province; it was to be 'broadly representative with expert and international representation amongst its membership'. It was to report to the UK government no later than summer 1999.

In addition to Patten, the Commission included: Kathleen O'Toole, Massachusetts Secretary for Public Safety and a former Boston police officer; Peter Smith QC, an eminent and highly regarded Northern Ireland barrister of over twenty years' experience; Sir John Smith, erstwhile Deputy Commissioner, London Metropolitan Police and HM Inspector of Constabulary; Dr Maurice Hayes, former senior Northern Ireland civil servant and later Ombudsman; Professor Clifford Shearing, Director, Centre of Criminology, University of Toronto, who had studied policing in Australia and South Africa as well as Canada; Dr Gerald Lynch, President, John Jay College, New York, who had developed courses on police and community relations for the US Department of Justice; and Lucy Woods, Chief Executive, British Telecom, Northern Ireland.

The Commission discharged its task through a series of visits to study policing methods in other jurisdictions and through public meetings in venues throughout Northern Ireland; submissions were also welcomed from individuals or organizations. Although this allowed the Commission to claim that the widest possible consultation had taken place, it had one fundamental flaw: Republicans, in a continuation of their 'disband the RUC' campaign, ensured that meetings in predominantly Nationalist areas were 'packed' with anti-RUC voices. This tactic had one clear aim: to present a picture of the RUC as a force totally unacceptable to the Catholic community in Northern Ireland and,

248

thereby, persuade the government to disband it and substitute something that would be more acceptable; Republicans had aspirations of convicted terrorists becoming police officers and thus perpetuating, by another means, the domination of Nationalist areas by terrorist groups.

As the Commission made its itinerant progress, life continued as normal in Northern Ireland. 'Normal' meant that terrorist groups continued to operate, individuals were intimidated, subjected to thuggish beatings called 'punishment' beatings, on the whim of terrorist kangaroo courts, and others were murdered. The murders, however, were usually carried out under cover names and victims were often people guilty of 'anti-social' activity such as drug dealing. This form of 'policing' was not peculiar to Nationalist areas; it was mirrored in Loyalist areas and the twin strands of terrorism often had tacit agreements on activities such as protection rackets, for which the building trade was one of their chief targets.

And tensions over marches continued. In Londonderry the Apprentice Boys were working towards accommodation with the Nationalist community but the sores of Drumcree and Lower Ormeau were no closer to resolution. By now the question of allowing marches to proceed, be re-routed or banned had been placed in the hands of a new Parades Commission, which ruled that Portadown Orangemen could not march along Garvaghy Road on their return from Drumcree Parish Church. The RUC's task was to enforce the Commission's ruling and, to that end, Flanagan prepared one of the largest police operations ever mounted in Northern Ireland. He made full use of the Army, drawing in Royal Engineers to build barriers to protect police and soldiers facing the demonstrators. Once again there was disruption across Northern Ireland and it appeared as if the annual 'Twelfth' celebrations might turn into a massive demonstration in support of the Drumcree Orangemen. But there was a change of mood following a sectarian petrol-bomb attack on a house in Ballymoney, County Antrim, in which three young children died. Richard Quinn, ten, and his brothers Mark, nine, and Jason, eight, perished when their Carnany Park home was set ablaze in the early hours of 12 July. The boys were Catholics living in a pre-dominantly Protestant area; they had been playing at a 'Twelfth' bonfire site the previous evening.

The triple murder caused revulsion throughout the province and there were strong words of condemnation from many quarters. In Ballymoney a senior RUC officer described the murders as 'the unbelievable result of sectarianism and naked hatred at its worst' but Ian Paisley chose to add a codicil to his condemnation, telling reporters that the IRA had carried out much worse murders on many occasions. Such an insensitive remark was at odds with a senior policeman's description of the attack as 'possibly the worst of its kind ever in the province'. The 'Twelfth' marches passed off in a strangely quiet manner while the protestors at Drumcree maintained a vigil beside the church throughout the summer months. That vigil was marked by sporadic outbreaks of violence, usually associated with protest marches, and ensured a steady drain on police personnel with other aspects of policing, such as Traffic and Community Relations, suffering. The violence at Drumcree also caused police casualties and among their number was the last RUC officer to die in the 'troubles'. Constable Frank O'Reilly, a Catholic, was on duty in Portadown on 5 September when a group calling itself the Red Hand Defenders threw a blast bomb at police officers. Frank O'Reilly suffered shrapnel wounds that resulted in the loss of an eye and severe head injuries. He was admitted to hospital in Belfast where, although his condition seemed to improve at one stage, he developed a chest infection and succumbed to his injuries on 6 October. Constable O'Reilly's wife, a Protestant, said that her husband considered himself a Christian rather than a Protestant or a Catholic while Sir Ronnie Flanagan described him as a 'decent family man, a decent public servant, a desperate loss to the community and a desperate loss to his family'. Sir Ronnie went on to describe his murderers as 'worthless cowards'. Although the Portadown Orangemen's press officer condemned the killing he went on to say that the protest would continue as Orangemen were standing up for their liberties and that 'sometimes the cost of those liberties can be very high'. This remark caused Pat Armstrong, Chairman of PANI, to describe as an insult to Frank O'Reilly's memory the suggestion that his death was somehow a price to be paid for civil liberties. Constable O'Reilly left three young children, the youngest a baby only a few months old.

The year had also seen the worst single atrocity in the thirty years of violence and disorder when another dissident Republican group, the Real IRA, exploded a car bomb in Omagh, County Tyrone, on 15 August. Thirty-one lives were lost, the youngest those of unborn twins due to have been born in October who perished with their mother; a baby aged twenty months also died. Those who were killed included Catholics, Protestants, a Mormon, visitors from Spain and three from the Republic, Nationalists and Unionists. For those who thought that peace might have descended on Northern Ireland the Omagh bomb was a terrible awakening and it created headlines across the world. Reporters from a range of countries arrived in Northern Ireland and among their reports were many tributes to the work carried out by RUC officers at the scene. Two warnings had been received and police were moving shoppers away from what was believed to be the location of the bomb. Unfortunately, the caller had said that the bomb was at the courthouse

250

and this area was evacuated with police officers shepherding people towards the far end of the main street, at the junction with Dublin Road. But the bomb, in a car stolen in County Monaghan, had been left close to that junction and when it exploded at 3.10 p.m. it caused devastation and left a scene comparable to a battlefield. One policeman spoke of using disposable nappies from a pharmacy to try to stop victims bleeding to death. The image of an RUC officer, his tie askew, his green shirt stained with blood, and shock and tears in his eyes flashed around the world. The Civil Emergency Plan was activated and local radio stations were asked to broadcast an appeal for medical help. Firefighters and ambulance crews raced to the scene, as did worried friends and relatives of people who had been in the town centre. Such was the press of those seeking news of relatives that police had to create a barrier of Land Rovers to seal off the rescue operations. Helicopters from the Joint Helicopter Force were flown to Omagh to evacuate casualties for treatment in Belfast and Londonderry. Throughout the emergency the work of RUC officers was critical. But the scene was also one of a major crime and had to be preserved as far as possible so that a search for evidence could be carried out. The search for the bombers was to lead to Ireland's largest ever manhunt with the RUC and Gardai cooperating as never before.

The Real IRA later claimed responsibility for the bomb but asserted that it had been aimed at a commercial target, that there had been no intention to take life and that adequate warning had been given. The terrorist group then offered apologies to the victims. In the wake of the attack two telephone boxes in south Armagh were removed for forensic tests; the warning calls had been made from those boxes which were sealed off after the bombing and subsequently removed by helicopter. Nearby County Louth in the Republic was the heartland of the Real IRA, which had carried out a bomb attack in Banbridge two weeks before and also made an unsuccessful bomb attack in Lisburn. Members of the Provisional IRA who did not accept their organization's move into politics had broken away to form the Real IRA and a parallel political group called the 32-County Sovereignty Committee. Reaction to the Omagh bomb led to the Real IRA declaring a ceasefire on 18 August.

The 'ceasefire' did not stop police efforts to find the bombers. In Omagh the scene of the atrocity was sifted through for evidence and what was left of the bomber's car was removed. Some sixty tons of rubble were lifted from the site where so many lives had been taken and shattered; and a total of some 400 tons of material was examined by forensic scientists. Anti-Terrorist Squad detectives from London joined RUC officers in Omagh to assist in this operation and many users of mobile phones were surprised to discover that their use of such equipment was traceable; this was the first occasion in Europe that police checked dialling records to uncover conversations between members of the bomb gang en route to Omagh; about 500 million calls had been made that day. Although almost eighty people were arrested by police on either side of the border – Gardai arrested fifty-five and the RUC a further twenty-three – all but one were later released without charge. The last individual was later tried in Dublin and convicted on charges of conspiracy and membership of an illegal organization.

While these events had played themselves out, the work of Patten's Commission was also underway. In the early days of the ceasefires it will be recalled that Annesley had established a team to look at policing developments in a more normal situation and that this team had been led by Ronnie Flanagan. From its deliberations had come many recommendations for change better to enable the RUC to perform its duties against a peaceful background. In all there were 189 recommendations dealing with the structures of the force and the way in which it would operate in the years ahead. However, the team's work was set aside by Flanagan lest there should be allegations that he was trying either to upstage or pre-empt the Commission's work. In the end, however, much that was in 'Patten' had been contained in Flanagan's review.

The Commission received the full support of the Chief Constable who even established a small team of police officers to work with it, supporting and assisting its work as well as making the professional police case on all issues. Following their first meeting in Belfast in June, Patten and his colleagues began their work, visiting police stations, meeting officers at work and seeing some of the normal summer work of the RUC. The latter, of course, included much policing of parades across the province. There were also visits to forces in Britain, the United States, Canada, South Africa and the Republic of Ireland. The programme of public meetings already noted began in October and some forty such were held in various locations across the province to enable the public to have their say; written submissions were also invited from the public. Significantly the Commission's programme of public meetings also provided an opportunity for a massive Republican anti-RUC campaign involving posters demanding the disbandment of the force, wall slogans supporting that demand or proclaiming 'SS RUC', and pickets outside police stations or along white lines on main streets. Sinn Fein members were prominent in these demonstrations and the party made clear its opposition to the RUC and its desire to have the force disbanded. With the Northern Ireland Assembly now operating, Sinn Fein had even more opportunity for its anti-RUC rhetoric and it was in the Assembly that Martin McGuinness claimed that the RUC was the most discredited police force in western Europe. More than ever the force became a political football with Unionist members coming to its defence and the SDLP continuing its ambivalent line but swinging towards Sinn Fein's stance. Ian Paisley's DUP took a very pro-RUC stand, oblivious to the paradox thus created, and, in so doing, hardened the views of many Republicans and Nationalists. Small wonder that many within the force worried about exactly what the future held.

The new secretary of state, Mo Mowlam, had also made a contribution to the policing debate. Many RUC officers were wary of the Labour government, suspecting that it might be prepared to make concessions to Republicans, and even more wary of Mowlam, who appeared to show antipathy towards the force almost from her arrival in Northern Ireland. Mowlam had promised to bring a new Police Bill for Northern Ireland before parliament and, in spite of work already underway at the Northern Ireland Office, a parliamentary committee chaired by former Secretary of State Peter Brooke and talks on policing then underway as part of the political negotiations, did so in December 1997. The Bill became law in summer 1998 and created what was described as the 'Northern Ireland Police Service', an umbrella title to encompass the RUC, RUC Reserve, traffic wardens, who already operated under police control, and civilian support staff. It also enabled government to establish a police ombudsman to investigate complaints against police and made the Chief Constable rather than PANI responsible for the force budget. In addition, the new Act abolished the oath of office that dated back to 1836, replacing it with a declaration that an individual would 'faithfully discharge the duties of the office of constable'.

While the Independent Commission was in the last stages of preparing its report, Northern Ireland went through yet another marching season. Once again Drumcree was expected to heighten tension and extensive arrangements were made to deal with any trouble. Additional MSUs were formed and officers undertook a programme of public order training while Flanagan arranged for the lease to the RUC of two water cannon from the Belgian national police; these vehicles would be available throughout the marching season. There were shades of 1969 in their deployment but the RUC was vastly more professional in dealing with public order than had been the case thirty years before. Few veterans of that summer were still serving but the conditions under which officers served at Drumcree would have stirred some echoes for them with hundreds accommodated in a tented camp at the Army's Mahon Barracks in Portadown where arrangements for washing were basic. Army support for the police operation at Drumcree included the provision of huge barriers that closed off Garvaghy Road and fencing that ensured separation of security forces and protestors. However, Drumcree passed off relatively quietly as did most of the marches in other areas. In Londonderry there was intelligence that Republicans intended to use the Apprentice Boys' march on 12 August to engineer a confrontation with the police, which would then be used for propaganda purposes; since this was the thirtieth anniversary of the so-called 'Battle of the Bogside', the nature of that propaganda requires little imagination. Although water cannon were deployed to the city these were not needed as the day passed off without full scale rioting. The Assistant Chief Constable, North Region, Alan McQuillan, had taken the initiative and announced that police were aware of the intention to create turmoil, thus undermining any possible claim that rioting was spontaneous or a result of police actions. McQuillan no doubt recalled a previous occasion when a human rights activist accused police of over-reacting to no more than about fifteen petrol bombs; on that occasion the lie had been given to the claim by television footage that showed at least that number of petrol bombs being thrown in less than half a minute. While no major rioting took place there were attacks on city centre business premises with a number being burnt out.

Thus the marching season of 1999 passed without creating serious problems, although Northern Ireland's tourist industry undoubtedly suffered. But the Republican propaganda assault on the police continued without any let up. On the tenth anniversary of the murder of solicitor Patrick Finucane claims were again made that there had been security force collusion in his death. Then, on 15 March, another solicitor, Rosemary Nelson, was murdered in Lurgan when a Loyalist booby-trap exploded under her car. Her death also opened a connection with another recent case in which six men had been accused of murdering Robert Hamill in Portadown. Hamill, a Catholic, had been kicked and beaten to death by a group of about thirty. Murder charges against five of the six had been dropped after witnesses withdrew statements and the sixth was finally convicted of causing an affray. Allegations had been made that a police patrol had failed to intervene to save Robert Hamill but, in September 1999, the DPP decided not to bring charges against any of the officers. Rosemary Nelson had been the Hamill solicitor and had complained that police officers were harassing her and had insulted and threatened her. Further complaints arose from her representation of the Garvaghy Road Residents' Association in 1997. In that year also Nelson had defended a man who was acquitted of the murder of a former UDR soldier. Her client was later arrested for the double murder of Constable John Graham and Reserve Constable David Johnston in Lurgan but those charges were dropped.

In September 1999 the report of the Independent Commission was published. Reaction was predictable: Unionist politicians condemned the document while Nationalists welcomed it. Sinn Fein differed from the SDLP by rejecting it initially. While much of what was contained in the report had also been in the internal review, the report went further and recommended a change of name and the adoption of a system of recruiting that demanded that the force accept one Catholic applicant for every Protestant applicant; no mention was made of recruits of other, or no, faiths; but Northern Ireland's peculiar definitions of equality define anyone who is not 'Catholic' as 'Protestant'.

While the debate about the Patten Report continued, an announcement was made from Buckingham Palace that The Queen had decided to award the George Cross, the highest civilian award for courage, to the Royal Ulster Constabulary in only the second collective award of the Cross 'to honour the courage and dedication of the officers of the Royal Ulster Constabulary and their families who have shared their hardships'. Although Chris Ryder asserts that only 'some forty individuals' have been awarded the George Cross since its inception this is not true: 401 George Crosses have been awarded, including the Malta and RUC GCs, which makes it one of the rarest decorations (it is not a medal). On 23 November the *London Gazette* carried the citation, which read:

> For the past 30 years, the Royal Ulster Constabulary has been the bulwark against, and the main target of, a sustained and brutal terrorism campaign. The Force has suffered heavily in protecting both sides of the community from danger – 302 officers have been killed in the line of duty and thousands more injured, many seriously. Many officers have been ostracised by their own community and others have been forced to leave their homes in the face of threats to them and their families. As Northern Ireland reaches a turning point in its political development this award is made to recognise the collective courage and dedication to duty of all of those who have served in the Royal Ulster Constabulary and who have accepted the danger and stress this has brought to them and to their families.

From the date of that announcement the force was entitled to the name Royal Ulster Constabulary GC. Many messages of congratulations were received by the force and the SDLP's deputy leader, Seamus Mallon MP, commented that:

> The announcement reflects the reality that, whatever differences exist over the role and conduct of the RUC, many members of the RUC and their families have suffered greatly and demonstrated courage over many years. The award of the George Cross should be seen as recognition that the concerns of those who most value the RUC have been acknowledged and appreciated.

Mallon's comments were generous in view of the SDLP's attitude to the force over the years but his party leader, Hume, was less generous. Hume's attitude to the Independent Commission's report brought a stinging rejoinder from Mowlam's successor, Peter Mandelson, who suggested that it was time for Nationalist leaders, both political and religious, to back the police and call on their community to follow suit.

Her Majesty did not leave the award of the George Cross to a simple announcement and an investiture at Buckingham Palace, at which the Cross would be presented to a representative of the force, but chose to pay personal tribute to the courage and sense of duty of the members of the Royal Ulster Constabulary. She did so by investing the force with the award at Hillsborough Castle on 12 April 2000 in the presence of 1,500 RUC officers, civilian support staff and family members. The Queen told them:

> This award is an exceptional recognition of the outstanding contri-
> bution made by the RUC to peace in Northern Ireland. It is a singular
> acknowledgement of the gallantry and courage shown and in all too
> many cases, the ultimate sacrifice paid by the members of the
> Constabulary during the past 30 years of terrorism and civil unrest.
>   I want to take this opportunity to pay tribute to all members of the
> RUC – the regular officers of all ranks, the members of the full-time
> and part-time Reserve, and former members who have served so
> loyally over the years. I salute your courage and your sense of duty.
> I admire your determination to maintain the rule of law, and to
> provide a police service for all the people during some of the most
> difficult times in the history of this Province.
>   A terrible price has been paid for this brave and resolute stand.

And she spoke of the 'very special contribution' made by families who had 'been a constant source of support, and have had to endure fear, intimidation and, worst of all, the pain of bereavement'. That Northern Ireland was now a more peaceful and stable place to live was, said Her Majesty, due in no small measure to that bravery and dedication shown over the years by the men and women of the Royal Ulster Constabulary.

The George Cross was not presented to the Chief Constable on behalf of the force but to a young constable who, eight years before, had been maimed in the horizontal mortar attack in Newry in which Constable Colleen McMurray had been murdered. Constable Paul Slaine had lost his legs in that incident and it was he who received the George Cross from the Queen. Constable Slaine was escorted by Constable Susan Wright, the last recruit to the RUC, and Assistant Chief Constable Bill

Stewart MBE, the longest-serving member of the force; the Cross was then paraded through the ranks of the assembled officers.

Replying to Her Majesty on behalf of the RUC GC, Sir Ronnie Flanagan said that each individual present recognized the 'signal honour' that had been bestowed upon their 'most proud' organization and went on to say that he saluted

> all those individuals, organizations, agencies and community groups without whose partnership we simply could not function. But there is not one of us who is not reflecting today on the tremendous sacrifice of the past; on those officers whose lives were so cruelly taken; on those officers who have been so grievously injured in the course of their duty; they and their families are today, and constantly, in our thoughts.

The Chief Constable concluded that the RUC GC now looked forward 'to a new and exciting future' built on the traditions of the past and the 'wonderful foundations' laid by officers past and serving.

> This most gracious award is not only therefore a recognition of outstanding past achievement, but also the most tremendous incentive to us all, now and in the years to come, to draw on our experience; to work in partnership with all of the people of Northern Ireland; to build a better future for us all and for generations to come.

As Sir Ronnie Flanagan spoke the experience of the force was being drawn upon to help in another country that had suffered from internal strife but to a much greater degree than Northern Ireland.

In June 1999 NATO troops had entered the former Yugoslav republic of Kosovo in a major peacekeeping operation. To maintain the peace in Kosovo a United Nations international police force was being established to which the UN sought the secondment of RUC GC personnel, recognizing that the skills and experience of the force over thirty years would be invaluable in building a new police force in the Balkan state. This international recognition of the professionalism of the RUC GC gave the lie to McGuinness' calumny that the force was western Europe's 'most discredited'; rather this was an endorsement of the high regard in which it was held throughout Europe and beyond.

At home the 'Patten Report' continued to provide much opportunity for debate but the government was determined to implement the report's recommendations, including the change of name. The initial recommendation was that the force would become the Northern Ireland Police Service but this soon changed to Police Service of Northern Ireland

(PSNI). A campaign was begun to save the RUC name and the support of many prominent individuals was enlisted. MPs sought to have the name of the RUC incorporated in the new title and Monsignor Denis Faul, a trenchant critic of the force in the past, lent his support to this concept on the grounds that it would give official recognition to the suffering and sacrifice of the RUC and the families of those who had lost their lives. Monsignor Faul pointed out that some Army regiments had two titles, an example that could be followed by the police. It might have produced a force entitled The Royal Ulster Constabulary GC (Northern Ireland Police Service) or vice versa, but this was not to be and the best that could be achieved was to have the RUC's name incorporated in the 'title deeds' of the Police Service of Northern Ireland. The new name was to be adopted from Sunday, 4 November 2001. With the eightieth anniversary of the RUC due in June 2002 the decision to implement the name change in late-2001 can only be described as petty. The same may be said of the way in which RUC crests were removed from police stations across the province, although indecent haste might be a more apt description. At RUC GC Headquarters the process of removing the crest and title began before the name change and under cover of darkness. By 4 November most stations had had their crests removed in what appeared to be a determined attempt to remove a proud title from history.

However, there was no change in the uniform and badges worn by police officers on 4 November, since a decision on a badge had not been reached. New recruits, the first for the PSNI, were due to report to the Training Centre at Garnerville and were advised that there they would meet staff wearing RUC uniforms and badges although they themselves would wear uniforms without insignia. In other words an apology was being made to them for that fact. The new name would be in use for five months before new uniforms and badges became available since these had to be agreed by the Policing Board, also established following the 'Patten Report' to supersede PANI.

But before the new title was adopted there were significant changes in the policing map of Northern Ireland with what are best described as a 'back to the future' redrawing of operational boundaries. The divisions created in 1970 were to disappear and subdivisions were to re-align along the boundaries of the twenty-five local council areas outside Belfast, which would be divided into four districts; there would thus be ten fewer such areas. It seemed that the best model for policing Northern Ireland had, after all, been that inherited from the RIC. These new police areas were styled district command units (DCUs) and, usually, adopted the title of the local council with the exceptions of those in Belfast and Londonderry; the former's became North, South, East and West while the latter became Foyle. The regional system was to be retained with Urban (or greater Belfast) covering Antrim, Carrickfergus and Lisburn as well as Belfast, North covering from Fermanagh through Londonderry to Larne, and South including most of Tyrone, Armagh and Down. Urban Region had the largest population with about 696,000, followed by North with some 511,000 and South with around 482,000. Each region continued to be commanded by an assistant chief constable.

Other changes since the first ceasefire were more obvious to the casual onlooker. Many of the RUC's fleet of Land Rovers had been repainted in white while patrol cars were fitted with signs and 'liveried' with fluorescent stripes along the sides and on the rear. Officers on patrol did not wear flak jackets to the same extent as before and, although rifles and sub-machine guns remained in the force armoury, these were not seen in public as often. New vehicles were delivered with police signs and blue lights fitted and RUC crests were also added, usually on the front door panels. In line with many forces in Great Britain, the RUC adopted the 'Battenberg' scheme for its vehicles, with the sides of those vehicles finished in a checkerboard blue-and-yellow scheme; similar schemes using green or red in place of blue were adopted by ambulances and fire service vehicles. By the end of 2000 new vehicles were taking to the road without the RUC crest on the sides. When this was commented upon the official answer was that it was a question of health and safety: the crest allegedly compromised the vehicle's conspicuity and, therefore, had to go. This was nonsense: the Battenberg scheme was based on bad science, and even poorer research, and the presence of a crest made no difference.[1] Elsewhere in the UK, many forces that adopted the scheme had no problem with placing a force crest on the sides of cars, or even the word 'police' in large letters.

Nationalists wanted the changes in policing to reflect a 'new beginning' and thus any vestige of the RUC GC became unacceptable. This included the badge, the crowned harp that had served from RIC days. The full RUC GC crest, based on the badge of the Order of St Patrick, also included a wreath of shamrock but despite the overwhelmingly Irish appearance of badge and crest, these had to go and new insignia, free of any symbols of either the British or Irish states, would have to be introduced. Thus one would expect some completely neutral design to be adopted. However, what was introduced in April 2002 included symbols of both states and failed to meet that particular criterion so beloved of Nationalists. Chris Ryder has described the PSNI badge as a 'sunburst' containing a six-pointed star inside which is a cross of St Patrick.[2] Ryder's description, also used by other commentators, is wrong. The badge is not a 'sunburst' but a disproportioned adaptation of the star of the Order of St Patrick. The 'sunburst' is a very Irish symbol, being the traditional badge of the Fianna and now used as the official badge of Oglaigh na hEireann, the Irish Defence Forces. Perhaps the most obvious feature of a 'sunburst' is that the rays are curved.

The proportions of the star were modified to allow the title 'Police Service Northern Ireland' to be borne on a circular band that, in turn, surrounds the six-pointed star within which is the Cross of St Patrick. The star is nothing other than the old symbol of Northern Ireland turned through 90 degrees so that the single points of the star point horizontally rather than vertically. Between the points are a series of small symbols: a set of scales, a harp, a torch, a laurel leaf, a shamrock and a crown. The scales are those of justice, the symbol of the judiciary, thus contradicting the tradition that police and judiciary are totally separate; the harp, also poorly proportioned, is the ancient symbol of Ireland and a variation of the symbol of the Republic; the torch is that of knowledge, now a rather obscure symbol but used until the mid-1960s as the road sign for a school; the laurel leaf apparently symbolizes reconciliation, although it has traditionally been used as the symbol of victory; the shamrock is another Irish symbol; and the crown represents the British link. It is noteworthy, however, that an SDLP spokesman described the crown as not necessarily being 'the Crown'; the symbol on the crest bears more resemblance to that used on a Claddagh ring. The new crest and uniform were in place for the first PSNI passing-out parade, now referred to as a graduation ceremony, in April 2002. Officially the symbols in the crest reflect 'diversity, hope, parity and inclusiveness'. In reality, the badge is one of the worst examples of the badge designer's art that this author has ever seen and suggests that it was designed by a committee rather than by someone with an artistic eye. That it is basically the star of the Order of St Patrick seems to have escaped most commentators and thus they fail to appreciate the irony of the badge of the same Order being replaced by a poor twenty-first century redesign of the Order's main insignia.

RUC officers were on duty as usual across Northern Ireland on the evening of Saturday, 4 November 2001. At Shakespeare's 'witching hour' they became officers of the Police Service of Northern Ireland. There were no outward signs that the change had occurred, other than in the names of those stations that had already lost their RUC symbols. The uniforms of officers had not changed and RUC badges and insignia were still on display. Part of the reason for this was the creation of PANI's successor, the Policing Board of Northern Ireland; the setting up of the Board had been delayed by the politicking over the Police Act and the Board did not have its first meeting until 7 November 2001. Until the Policing Board was functioning nothing could be done about badges or uniforms. However, this emphasizes the improper haste with which the name change was applied and supports the argument for delaying what was described as the 'transition' from RUC GC to PSNI until June 2002. To its credit the Board managed to have a new uniform – still in bottle green – and badges in place by April when the first PSNI recruits were due to pass out from the Training Centre although the badge was the aberration already described and there were many problems with the uniforms. (Health and Safety legislation required that safety boots be supplied but some officers, especially women, found that boots could not be provided in their size. Complete sets of the new uniform were also issued to officers retiring within days of the change; in at least one case an officer whose normal duty was performed in plain clothes and who was to retire at the beginning of April received a new uniform.)

Thus it was that the change, or transition, was handled very badly and this added undoubtedly to the pain of those who regretted the passing of the RUC title. The proper handling of the process would have involved a formal ceremony, possibly including a parade, at which the new badges would have been issued and officers in both RUC GC and PSNI uniforms might have taken part. There was no excuse for this not happening since the example was already there from the Army and, especially, from the infantry regiments recruited in Northern Ireland. Twice in twenty-four years, on 1 July 1968 and 1 July 1992, these regiments have undergone amalgamations but the pain of loss was lessened in each case by a ceremonial farewell to former titles and welcome to the new, whether Royal Irish Rangers in 1968 or Royal Irish Regiment in 1992. Just as the traditional wake and funeral assist grieving families and individuals, so the use of ceremony might have helped RUC GC members to accept change. As it was, however, the change was botched and the impression given that officialdom was glad to be rid of the RUC GC. Certainly there was the impression of subterfuge in the process and this has left an indelible stain in the memories of many.

The Police (Northern Ireland) Act 2000 had included a provision that would ensure that the RUC GC would not be allowed to fade from memory. This provision created the Royal Ulster Constabulary George Cross Foundation with the aim of 'marking the sacrifices and honouring the achievements of the Royal Ulster Constabulary'. Under the chairmanship of Jim McDonald, the Foundation was set the task of creating a memorial garden in the grounds of Brooklyn. The concept of the garden was to allow visitors to see each aspect in their own way and take away different impressions. An existing formal terraced garden was chosen to locate the memorial, the form of which represents a journey past various symbols to a private 'area of peace' where those who died as a result of terrorism and those who died in service would be remembered. To enter the garden, visitors would pass through a 'history trail', outlining the story of policing; the start and end of the 'trail' would be marked by sculptures of the RUC crest and the George Cross, the final design of which would be the subject of a competition.

HRH The Prince of Wales had agreed to be Patron of the Foundation and, on 2 September 2003, performed the official opening of the Memorial Garden in the presence of family members of officers who had lost their lives, the Secretary of State, Mr Paul Murphy, the Security Under-Secretary, Jane Kennedy, the PSNI's Chief Constable, Hugh Orde, Professor Desmond Rea, chairman of the Policing Board and the Foundation Trustees. Also present were Sir John Hermon, Sir Ronnie Flanagan and Sir Hugh Annesley with their wives, as well as Lady Kennedy, widow of Inspector General Sir Albert Kennedy. Members of the emergency services were also among the 700 guests as were representatives of police forces in Britain, the Deputy Commissioner of the Garda Síochána and the US Consul General, Barbara Stephenson. Representatives of the four main churches in Northern Ireland, The Most Reverend The Lord Eames, Church of Ireland Primate, The Most Reverend Dr Sean Brady, Roman Catholic Archbishop of Armagh and Primate of All Ireland, The Right Reverend Dr Ivan McKay, Moderator of the Presbyterian Church in Ireland, and The Reverend James Rea, President of the Methodist Church in Ireland, were present to conduct the service of dedication, which was led by The Reverend David Coulter, the Senior Chaplain of HQNI.

Following the service, Prince Charles spoke to some of the guests who represented the broad RUC GC family, including members of the RUC GC Widows' Association, Disabled Police Officers' Association, RUC GC Parents' Association, Northern Ireland Retired Police Officers' Association, the Superintendents' Association, the Police Federation and the RUC GC Benevolent Fund. His Royal Highness described the Garden as an 'appropriate tribute to the individual dedication, determination, resilience, courage and stamina of the thousands of RUC officers who have defied real and constant danger, on and off duty, and continued the struggle to defeat terrorism, thus giving locally elected representatives the opportunity to govern Northern Ireland within new and mutually agreed structures'. For his part, Chief Constable Hugh Orde remarked that the ceremony 'reflects the courage and dedication of all of the officers who have gone before and recognises that their professionalism provided the solid foundation on which today's police service is being built'.

Almost two years after the name change the dedication of the Garden, in the presence of the Prince of Wales, was a sign of assurance that the name and achievements of the Royal Ulster Constabulary GC would not be allowed to fade from memory. Irrespective of the attitudes of politicians, and politically-correct senior officers who see the RUC title as something to be swept under the carpet, the crest of the force and the memory of those who lost their lives in the eighty years of its existence shall not be blotted out.

Notes
1: At a conference in the University of Kent at Canterbury in 2001, the head of investigations at the Transport Research Laboratory revealed that a new colour scheme for police vehicles had been based on a survey of motorists at a motorway service area where two police vehicles, one in the 'old' livery and one in the 'new' were parked. Each motorist was asked to state a choice for the more conspicuous scheme and most chose the 'new' livery. When questioned by the author, the speaker confirmed that the 'new' livery was the Battenberg scheme.
2: Ryder, *The Fateful Split*, pp. 322-3

Chapter Eleven

Reflections

What contribution did the RUC GC make to Northern Ireland? The answer to that question will vary depending on the individual to whom it is addressed. A Republican will claim that the RUC was part of the problem, that members of the force, especially of Special Branch, were anti-Nationalist and anti-Catholic. One Republican source once proclaimed that the RUC was ninety-two per cent Protestant and 100 per cent Unionist, a sneering reference to the Catholics in the force who were all classed as enemies of their community. (The number of Catholics then in the RUC exceeded 1,000, which would have constituted one third of the force in 1969.) A clear example of Republican antipathy occurred when a fire broke out in a house on the outskirts of Londonderry in November 1997 and a young policewoman had to drive an ambulance carrying child victims to Altnagelvin Hospital. The response of one Sinn Fein politician was not to praise the officer but to demand to know if she was insured to drive the ambulance.[1] In the Republican view of life there remains no scope for good words about the RUC GC.

Over the past three decades the voice of Nationalism in Northern Ireland has been expressed by the SDLP, a party that, since the departure of founding members Gerry Fitt and Paddy Devlin, has had an ambivalent attitude towards the police. Under the leadership of John Hume this hardened into a preparedness to accept the force while performing 'ordinary' duties but not those duties related to terrorism. The SDLP was often trenchant in its criticism of the police but took little time to develop an understanding of the problems faced by the RUC, or to cultivate empathy for it. Thus it was that Chris Ryder was able to comment that the leading SDLP spokesperson on policing was not even familiar with the force rank structure.[2] One can understand politicians being critical of police and there have been many examples of this in Britain and, in more recent times, in the Irish Republic. However, such criticisms have never become deeply embedded policy. Thus Labour,

264

while criticizing police handling of the 1984 miners' strike, did not become an anti-police party. Nor did examples of corruption in various forces – a fault from which the RUC GC suffered hardly at all – lead to politicians calling for their disbandment. One wonders how many name changes might have been imposed on the Metropolitan Police had politicians in Britain adopted SDLP thinking? However, some SDLP politicians have occasionally been generous in making tributes to the force, Seamus Mallon's words on the occasion of the award of the George Cross being an example. While the SDLP has adopted a more positive attitude towards policing since the 'Patten Report', suddenly throwing up a host of experts on policing, and this more positive attitude is also displayed towards the PSNI, there is still the feeling that the 'Hume view' holds good for many SDLP members. One Catholic RUC GC Chief Superintendent, now retired, opined that the party's initials indicated that they 'still don't like police'.

On the other end of the spectrum, many convinced Unionists, whether UUP or DUP, will argue that the force was almost without fault. That is an argument no sensible police officer would accept, since they know that no organization composed of human beings can be perfect. When criticisms of the force, or of individual members, were voiced by the SDLP or Republicans this led often to a war of words from Unionists. And yet there were times when Unionists could be every bit as vociferous as their political rivals in their complaints about police, as with the regular stand-offs at Drumcree. There were many other occasions, often linked to political protests or marches that drew the ire of Unionists on the RUC GC. Yet many of these politicians would claim the force as their own, giving a perceived justification to Nationalists and Republicans for further criticism.

Any analysis of the contribution made by the RUC GC to Northern Ireland, especially between 1969 and 2001, has to be based on objective assessment. For much of its existence the force was a small body from which much was demanded; over many years RUC officers performed duties that ought to have been carried out by Customs officers or by other agencies; these included preventing livestock smuggling, weights and measures inspections, collation of agricultural statistics, enforcement of regulations on the control of weeds and acting as census enumerators. Police officers were even called upon to provide credit ratings for farmers who applied for loans to the Ministry of Agriculture and fishermen who had made similar applications to the Ministry of Commerce. Those duties have long passed to other agencies but many remained within the remit of the force for many years, in the case of census enumeration until 1971; this task placed a particular pressure on manpower. However, such duties brought the force into close and regular contact with members of the public and, invariably, had a positive effect on public perceptions of the police. There was also the burden of security duties brought about by the existence of the border and a terrorist organization that wanted to destroy Northern Ireland. While this burden increased at various times during the first half-century of the force, it was not until the 1970s that it became the greatest burden on the RUC GC. In earlier times the Ulster Special Constabulary had taken much of the burden of security duties although its contribution to routine policing outside Belfast and Londonderry was small.

Yet throughout all those years the RUC GC had discharged its responsibilities well, providing an effective deterrent against crime and having an excellent detection rate, so much so that even in the worst years of the 'troubles' the crime clearance rate in Northern Ireland was higher than that of many forces in Great Britain. Until the early 1970s, single officers also patrolled throughout Northern Ireland and were a familiar sight to everyone in the province, whether in town or country. The 1960s had seen the rural policeman give up his bicycle for a patrol car while many small stations in villages and remote areas closed down, thereby reducing contact between police and public. But the reassuring presence of an officer on the beat was something that helped maintain good order in the community. That the officer often knew many of those who lived on his beat – and certainly knew most of those few who were likely to cause trouble – was an added bonus, enhanced by the fact that many police officers lived in the communities they policed. Some parents even used the policeman as a mild form of 'bogey man' to ensure that their children behaved; but there were officers who were as likely to stand and chat to a group of young people as to admonish them for playing football in the street or hanging around corners. The author recalls one policeman, whom he later came to know well, who would even join in a 'kick about' street football session with local boys; he was practising neighbourhood policing long before the term had been coined. Many officers were invited into homes or businesses for a cup of tea, although this would have been frowned upon by senior officers. If spotted by a head constable, the officer would often have a story about being asked for advice by a homeowner or businessman; needless to say, the Head had probably used a similar story himself in his younger days.[3]

At times the years before 1969 are portrayed as some form of Elysian age in which all was either good or becoming good. Of course, that is not the truth as Northern Ireland was beset with many problems, mixed with an unhealthy dose of abnormal politics. But it is not true to claim that the police were part of the problem or in any way estranged from the community. Officers mixed with the community – although there must always be restraints on the company an officer keeps – and took part in local activities, were members of local groups and clubs and often became prominent in these activities.[4] There were criminals in Northern Ireland but there was little serious crime. Murders were infrequent and became major news events when they did occur. Even an attempted murder could become a 'nine day wonder'. Serious assaults were also rare, as were rape and other major sexual crimes. Prostitution existed, although some would try to deny this, especially in the ports of Belfast and Londonderry, and this problem was dealt with and kept under control by the small but very effective Women's Police Branch. Although the IRA mounted a campaign during the Second World War and again from 1956 to 1962, their activities had little impact on day-to-day policing, in marked contrast to what happened in the campaign that began in 1970. Police stations might have been sand-bagged and surrounded by Dannert wire and officers might have been armed but ordinary policing continued and normal patrols were carried out in border areas. Police officers visited schools to talk to children about road safety – or, as it was known in the 1950s, 'safety first' – and might later be called upon by some of those children to 'cross' them over a road.[5] It is fair to say that the RUC GC was an effective force, in spite of the manpower and financial restrictions imposed by the Ministry of Home Affairs, and that the vast majority of Northern Ireland's people appreciated its work.

All that appeared to be 'changed, changed utterly' in the final three decades of the force's history. This is the era on which much of this book has concentrated and in which the majority of RUC GC casualties were sustained. But was the change so great as to suggest that this was an entirely different force? Was there policing as an officer from the 1930s, the 1950s or the 1960s might have understood it? The answer to that question has to be positive. In spite of the horrific background of a terrorist campaign being waged, in large part, against them, the men and women of the RUC GC continued performing the ordinary duties of police officers everywhere. Some might try to argue otherwise, as did Denis Bradley, vice chairman of the Policing Board, on BBC's *Spotlight* programme on 2 March 2004, when he claimed that the 'terrorist war' made police ignore other issues and that the force was 'spoiled' by concentrating on the 'war'. Bradley's comments were far from accurate.

The RUC GC never lost sight of the many problems facing Northern Ireland although the shadow of the terrorist was always present. Throughout this book there have been many examples of police officers carrying out an everyday service to the community and being murdered whilst so doing. The case of Sergeant Patrick Maxwell of Dungannon in 1975 is a perfect example. It will be recalled that Sergeant Maxwell's patrol was on an errand of mercy, carrying a message of a cross-border bereavement to a family with no telephone. At least that is what the officers believed, as did the Gardai in Monaghan who had passed the message to the RUC. However, the message was the bait for a coldly planned ambush that led to the brutal deaths of Sergeant Maxwell and Reserve Constable Samuel Clarke.

In February 1973 Constable Charles Morrison was administering first aid to a woman injured in a car crash in Dungannon when he was shot in the back by an IRA terrorist using a sub-machine gun. He died almost immediately. Three local ministers condemned the murder as 'the devil's work', and asked how humanity could sink so low as to murder a man carrying out an errand of mercy. More recently, Michael Ferguson was giving directions to a female visitor to Londonderry when he was shot in the back of the head by a teenage gunman in January 1993. Constable Ferguson was the softest of targets as he pointed out to the lady the route she needed to take. In many other cases, officers carrying out foot patrols in local communities were targeted and murdered or seriously injured. Efforts to maintain normal beat patrols in much of Belfast and Londonderry in the early 1970s led to many attacks on police officers.[6]

All through the dark years of death and destruction, police officers were still helping the public in many ways. Some of these, as always, were beyond the normal call of duty. When a Londonderry postal worker, Harry Forbes of Argyle Terrace, was called to the Renal Unit of Belfast City Hospital on an August Sunday afternoon in 1975, he needed to be there as quickly as possible to improve the chances of a successful kidney transplant. His work colleagues at the local GPO sorting office got in touch with the police. N Division headquarters in Londonderry contacted Sergeant Neil Falkingham, of Traffic Division, who was off duty but volunteered to drive the patient, his wife and a family friend to Belfast in a Traffic patrol car, a Ford Escort Mexico with a 2-litre engine. A second police officer accompanied the party on the journey, which, from Victoria RUC Station to Belfast City Hospital, took only sixty-five minutes.[7]

Stewart Tosh went to Belleek as station sergeant in the late 1970s. Soon after his arrival he discovered that the station party did not venture into the village on market day as it was felt that this might lead to trouble. Sergeant Tosh thought otherwise and decided that there should be a police presence on the main street during the weekly market. Going out on patrol himself he stopped to chat to market-stall holders and found that one stall was tended by nuns selling handicrafts from their convent. Not only did Tosh stop to talk to the nuns but he also bought some of their products as a gift for his mother. While he remained in Belleek the market patrol was a regular feature of the duty roster. On another occasion, a young man from the district was killed in a car crash on the Enniskillen–Belleek road and Sergeant Tosh acted as a family liaison officer – as the role would be described today – in keeping the family informed of developments in the case, including the coroner's enquiry. That some members of the wider family circle were known to have Republican sympathies did not deter him from his task as he believed that everyone deserved such a service from the force. During his time as station sergeant in Belleek, there were no attacks by Republican terrorists on RUC personnel.[8] Was this a direct result of a young sergeant's efforts at establishing a rapport with the local community?

We have seen how Traffic Division was all but disbanded in the wake of the internment operation in August 1971 and how 1972, when Traffic patrols operated only on motorways, was the worst year ever for death on Northern Ireland's roads. Although patrolling was restored, it was at reduced strength but officers assigned to Traffic were conscious of the responsibilities they faced and over the following decade worked diligently to reduce the toll on the roads. In this they succeeded so that by the late 1990s the numbers killed on the roads had returned to the figures of the 1950s, in spite of the massive increase in traffic volumes. This was one instance of how RUC GC officers continued to deal with the everyday matters of policing.

At the Northern Ireland Road Safety Congress in Newcastle, County Down, in February 2001, Dr Jim McCabe, Vice-Chairman of the Road Safety Council of Northern Ireland, representative of Londonderry Road Safety Committee – and onetime Nationalist councillor on Londonderry Corporation – praised the work of the RUC's Traffic Branch, saying that the force's contribution to saving lives on Northern Ireland's roads was 'a bright shining star in the firmament of the RUC'. In 2003, a senior Traffic (now Road Policing) officer, Chief Inspector Douglas Hogg BEM, was awarded an Honorary Fellowship of the Institute of Road Safety Officers in recognition of the outstanding contribution that he had made to road safety over three decades. An initiative by other Traffic officers, a dramatic roadshow aimed at sixth formers, earned a Prince Michael Road Safety Award – although this was presented after the name change.[9]

A similar story could be told of the Community Relations Branch, which underwent several name changes, and of its work with the public through schools, community groups and other organizations. The Branch involved many young people in its activities and, at times, incurred the wrath of Republicans and their political representatives who resented the fact that those young people were seeing a side to the RUC GC other than the adverse propaganda image presented by Republicans.

Although the Women's Police Branch had ceased to exist, policewomen continued to make a strong contribution to policing in Northern Ireland with involvement in all the specialist branches and their continuing work with children and women who were the victims of sex offences. The 1980s saw a period of increasing concern about the abuse of children and led to the creation of a specialist course for child sex abuse victims and rape victims. This was the CARE (Child Abuse and Rape Enquiry) course, the first of which was held in September 1985. Thereafter, CARE units and CARE suites were opened across the province, staffed by trained officers, both female and male, while the force appointed Liaison Inspectors for each of the four health and social services board areas and Chief Inspector Hilary Cockett was appointed as force CARE Coordinator. Women officers also took the lead in other initiatives, such as Juvenile Liaison, a scheme designed to 'prevent children and young persons from drifting into crime through lack of parental authority, bad environment or undesirable associations'.[10]

Sister Carina Muldoon, Director of St Joseph's Training School at Middletown, County Armagh, paid tribute to the professionalism and sensitivity of the RUC GC's women in a contribution to Margaret Cameron's history of the women police. Sister Carina wrote that policewomen had often been in 'the front line of preventative work' by helping to resolve difficult family situations and 'supporting "at risk" adolescents' and that:

> Despite the very changed and tragic circumstances . . . over the past twenty plus years the women officers have tried to maintain this special relationship. In the past decade we have all experienced in our differing professions the evolution of new processes, policies and emphases. Words like 'productivity', 'achievement yardsticks', 'prioritising financial controls' have not always led to the provision of people orientated service. However, I feel that the women officers have always managed to maintain the necessary balance and develop their skills and expertise in very sensitive areas.
>
> The ever-growing problem of child sexual abuse is just one area where women officers contribute in a unique and very professional manner. I want to pay tribute in particular to women officers who have worked with us on very difficult sexual abuse cases. The spirit of the early pioneers in the Women's Branch continues in these young women. Their dedication, thoroughness, commitment and care has often been an inspiration to us as is their generous giving of their time – even their off duty time. In areas such as these there are no yard sticks for measuring achievement. I say thank you to all the women over the years who been so caring, courteous and understanding of very difficult adolescents. Their patience, tolerance and sympathy have often rescued young people from despair.[11]

And Sister Carina went on to pay special tribute to the women officers who had lost their lives, especially those who were murdered in Newry in 1985, who had been 'most supportive and caring towards young people who were the victims of sexual abuse and/or drug abuse'.[12]

Performing their duties in Northern Ireland called for many sacrifices from police officers. Sadly, in too many cases, officers were called on to make the ultimate sacrifice. Every police officer knows that his or her job involves the risk of death or injury but, in other forces, that risk is usually low. Not so for the RUC GC where the risk of injury or death was the highest in any European police force and one of the highest in the world. In the eighty years of the force's history, 314 officers lost their lives to those who believed in using violence for political ends; all but twelve died between 1969 and 1998. The number of officers injured between 1968 and 2001 was about 9,000 and injuries ranged from cuts and bruises to loss of limbs, brain damage and other trauma leading to lifelong disability. Few officers served in the RUC GC in those years without sustaining some injury.

But there was another, almost invisible, price to pay for policing Northern Ireland that was measured in terms of stress on officers and their families. It has been estimated that about seventy officers committed suicide between the early 1970s and 2001. In addition, many others have suffered from the stress of being a police officer with all the risks involved in the profession in the decades since 1969. Officers have also had to live with memories that, as Winston Churchill once commented, no human being should have to endure. These have included witnessing the murders of colleagues as well as those of innocent bystanders. Among the more horrific memories are those of trying to recover body parts after explosions, carrying the lifeless and shredded body of an infant from the scene of a bombing, and arriving at the scene of a murder to find the victim's body in the driving seat of his car but with the top of his skull blown off and his brains lying in the pocket of the driver's door. All these, and more, have been experienced by many officers, some of whom have also become victims themselves.

Of course, even in normal circumstances, police officers are likely to have very unpleasant and, at times, terrifying experiences, arising from armed robberies, assaults and traffic collisions; the latter can have consequences as horrific as explosions. In one crash in central Belfast in 1980, five RUC officers lost their lives when their Land Rover was struck and shattered by an articulated lorry.

Conveying the news of a traumatic death to a family has its own horror. This is one of the most unpleasant duties a police officer has to carry out and most hope that they never experience it. Perhaps one of

271

the worst examples of this experience fell to the lot of a mobile patrol in Londonderry on 21 November 1964 following a collision between a lorry and a minibus carrying a local showband, the Statesiders, home from a dance in County Antrim. In that collision, at a crossroads near Cloughmills, most of the band were killed but the worst aspect was that four of the six dead were brothers, all but one of whom were unmarried; James, Bill, Jackie and Jerry Mallett were aged between twenty-seven and twenty-two. It fell to the lot of the two officers in the district mobile patrol in Londonderry that night to take the news to the families. But telling one family of the true extent of their loss was not something that they felt able to do alone and so they called at the local parochial house to enlist the help of a priest in their sad duty.

Stress was not always confined to the officers themselves since their families also suffered. Life for a police family in Northern Ireland was never straightforward in the years after 1968 and especially after the murder campaign against RUC personnel began. Officers' families found that they had to be selective in who they befriended and who was allowed to know that the family included a police officer. Police wives even found that hanging out the family washing could disclose that the father of the family was in the RUC: the distinctive pale-green shirts of constables and sergeants were rather obvious signals while the white shirts of senior officers were also noticeable. Even a simple telephone call might be laden with danger. Terrorists had a practice of trying to discover the home telephone numbers of officers and ringing to establish that they had identified positively a policeman or woman. This could be achieved quite easily if a young child answered the phone and said that his or her father was out, a response that could be followed by a question such as 'Oh, he's at the barracks, is he?' which was intended to ascertain the identity and home address of an officer. Thus children had to be discouraged from answering phones or coached not to reveal that daddy or mummy was a police officer. This tactic was also used against families of UDR personnel.

Although the greatest danger came from Republican terrorists, Loyalist terrorists also attacked officers – they were responsible for the first murder of the most recent 'troubles' in October 1969 – and posed a constant threat that intensified in the mid 1980s. During that period, when Sir John Hermon chose to take a tough line with Loyalist demonstrations, there were many attacks on police homes and families suffered a very high level of intimidation. This prompted Sir Eldon Griffiths to comment:

> the crux of the matter is that the RUC is now required to police against the demonstrated will of a majority in Northern Ireland while simultaneously waging a war, for which it is neither trained nor

equipped, against an international terrorist offensive . . . . The wonder is that the RUC has not cracked under the strain of being shot in the back by the IRA and being spat at, or intimidated out of the police houses, by mobs of loyalist hooligans.[13]

Griffiths had encapsulated the RUC's predicament while paying tribute to the doughtiness of the force in standing up to aggression from so many sectors. In doing so, the force had the support of the wider RUC family, including the immediate families of officers, those who worked for and with the force and those who recognized the importance of the work being carried out by the force and its value to the community. But, as already mentioned, the price paid was high and few know that as well as the widows of officers, the parents and families of young officers who were murdered and those officers who survived terrorist attacks but sustained permanent injury. It is in the nature of media reporting that the stories of such victims are headline news for a short time before being allowed to fade into memory. For the victims themselves, the comfort of fading memory does not exist. The families of those murdered in the 1956–62 campaign feel their loss as acutely as those bereaved more recently; the pain of a widow who lost her husband in 1972 is as great as that of she who was bereaved in 1992; those who lost a father while children themselves will always have many unanswered questions that will frustrate them until their dying days. For young men, the memory – or, perhaps, only photographs and stories – of a lost father have provided role models and an ideal to live up to but they will still feel deprived of the example and friendship of a father as they grow into manhood. Sadly, some became embittered by the experience; one murdered officer's son joined a Loyalist terrorist organization. For girls, the memories, photographs and stories will also serve the same role but the questions remain and the pain will be felt most acutely when the daughter of a murdered officer walks up the aisle on her wedding day without her father at her side. For the bride's brother or uncle, who acts as surrogate father on that day, the pain will also be felt; and one can only imagine the feelings of the bride's mother.

Those who lost a son or daughter serving in the RUC GC feel that something unnatural has happened to them since it is in the normal order of life that children bury their parents. When Willie John Hunter was murdered at Jonesborough in 1961 (See Chapter Four) his father was devastated and his family are convinced that he never recovered from the loss of his son; he died less than nine years later in 1970. For Robert Hunter, selecting his son's grave and choosing his coffin were tasks he had never expected to have to do; and they seemed only to emphasize the terrible pain that had been inflicted upon him and his family.[14]

The old axiom that 'time heals' the pain of bereavement is only partially correct. While the immediate shock caused by the brutal murder of a loved one may diminish in intensity as time passes, the pain of that loss remains forever. That initial shock can have different manifestations: for some it is comparable to a numbness of both body and spirit; for others it is akin to having one's insides torn out; for yet others it brings on a sense of disbelief. In most cases the time following a murder took on a surreal air, as if time was either suspended or measured in some abnormal fashion with hours, minutes and seconds seemingly mixed up. It was also a time of speaking to so many people that the disorientation was exacerbated and recalling a chronology of events would be all but impossible.

As time passes a widow may appear to outsiders to be living life normally but there are always reminders. Even decades after a murder, she may find it difficult to cope with the day of the week on which her husband lost his life; she may find it impossible to visit the site of the murder; if someone was convicted of the murder – and most murders of police officers remain unsolved – there is always the dread of meeting the killer in the street, or of seeing him, or her, on television, while some have even been elected to the Northern Ireland Assembly or to local councils throughout the province. Many found the early release of convicted terrorists following the Belfast Agreement to be especially painful, a pain often exacerbated by the desire of media outlets to seek the views of relatives of murdered RUC officers on those releases – or, worse still, on the release of the particular terrorist who had murdered a husband. The Patten Report was another occasion for pain, leading many to ask what their loved ones had served and died for and if there was any gratitude at all in the establishment in either the United Kingdom or the Irish Republic. The loss of the name Royal Ulster Constabulary was especially painful and one that few felt was necessary, a view supported by Catholic priest, Monsignor Denis Faul, once a critic of the RUC but a man who showed an ability to understand the pain of the RUC family in the wake of Patten.

There is another family that has been affected by every murder of a police officer and that is the RUC family itself, the officers who make up the force, their kin, their friends, those who work for and with the force. On too many occasions that family has suffered trauma and grief and borne those with dignity. Occasions such as the mortar attack on Newry RUC Station in 1985, the crash of the Chinook on the Mull of Kintyre in 1994, the loss of five officers in a traffic collision in central Belfast in 1980, the deaths of seven policemen in the German bombing of Belfast in 1941 have all struck at the fibre of the police family. But those occasions have also shown the strength of the bonds within that family. Comradeship, mutual trust and respect have helped the force though such dark days when morale might have been affected. Good leadership also helped and the RUC was fortunate, especially in the recent past, to have many good senior officers who helped their men and women bear the burden that fell to the force.

Throughout the weeks, months and years of grief, the bereaved of the RUC GC found a constant support in the RUC Benevolent Fund. Every bereaved member of the RUC family knows that the Fund is there to help and that advice or assistance is available at the end of the telephone line. The Fund was established in 1970, in which year it paid out £894, and every serving member of the force has contributed to it while many voluntary donations have also been received from without the RUC. One of the recommendations of the Hunt Report in 1969 was that the force should appoint a civilian welfare officer and this was acted upon in 1970, leading to the creation of a welfare department that would work in close harmony with the Benevolent Fund and the Police Federation of Northern Ireland. (See Appendix Three.)

The need to support the injured and bereaved led to the creation of a number of groups that include the Disabled Police Officers' Association, the RUC GC Widows' Association and the RUC GC Families' Association. Each group provides its own particular form of support to victims and their families and by bringing individuals and families in similar situations together each is a valuable asset to dealing with the pain that continues to afflict those victims and families.

Following the change of name to Police Service of Northern Ireland, a number of retired RUC officers decided to create an association for former officers. This was named the Royal Ulster Constabulary George Cross Association, which was created initially as separate groups in different parts of Northern Ireland but now has an umbrella body to which the area groups send representatives. The Association allows former officers to meet together for a wide range of activities and outings. It also ensures that the name of the force will live on for many years.

Another group that ensures the continuation of the RUC name is the RUC GC Foundation, created specifically for that purpose by the Police Act (2000). (See Appendix Four.) The Foundation has already been responsible for overseeing the creation of the RUC GC Memorial Garden at police headquarters at Brooklyn and it has also designated the first Sunday of June as RUC GC Sunday; this is marked by an inter-denominational church service to which representatives of the various bodies representing the RUC family are invited. The 2004 RUC GC Sunday service was held in Armagh and was attended by representatives of the VC and GC Association, which was visiting Northern Ireland as guests of the Foundation.

Thus there is a determination that the name of the Royal Ulster Constabulary will not be allowed to fade away and will not be consigned, as some would wish, to the history books. Which brings us back to the question posed at the beginning of this chapter: what contribution did the RUC GC make to Northern Ireland? Will the verdict of history support the views of Martin McGuinness and his fellow Republicans or come down in favour of the RUC GC?

In spite of the many efforts being made to airbrush the RUC GC from history, the true value of the force is much more likely to be appreciated by future generations. Between 1969 and 1994 there were several occasions when Northern Ireland seemed about to plunge into civil war and, with the murderous activities of both Republican and Loyalist terrorists feeding off each other, there was the prospect of a Balkans-type conflict that would have destroyed the province and caused death and destruction on a much greater scale than was actually experienced over those years. This was especially so in 1972 and again in the mid-to-late 1980s and, for a brief spell, in late 1993. At each of these times one of the most vital factors in ensuring that the horror did not intensify was the work of the RUC GC. Contrary to the arguments put forward by many Nationalist politicians, it should be remembered that the force's success rate against Loyalist terror groups was higher than that against Republicans and it was the dedicated work of the special squad under Detective Chief Inspector Jimmy Nesbitt that brought an end to the killing campaign of the 'Shankill Butchers'. It was the speedy work of RUC officers in bringing to justice the Loyalist Greysteel murderers that helped defuse one of the most tension-laden periods in recent history. And the even-handedness of the force was demonstrated time and time again: during the UWC strike in 1974, in the attempted repeat of that in 1977, in the policing of the hunger strike period in 1981, in dealing with disputed Orange marches in Portadown and with the protests against the Anglo-Irish Agreement in the mid 1980s, and, most of all, in the general handling of the Drumcree situation, in spite of Hugh Annesley's maladroitness.

In its dealing with a society in which there were too many guns the RUC GC also showed commendable restraint. Once again this gives the lie to the image painted by Republican propagandists and many Nationalist politicians. One Dublin-based commentator, who admitted that in 1958 the IRA were heroes and the RUC fascists in his eyes, wrote that his view began to change in the 1970s as news bulletins brought reports of RUC officers murdered on duty or at home and of the 'daily butcher's bill' of the IRA. He went on to comment that people in the Republic felt 'degraded by what was being done in our name and we felt growing respect for the RUC'.[15] That growing respect meant that many people in the Republic saw the RUC 'as by and large a decent body of men and women', a view that was mirrored in the ranks of the Garda Síochána.

276

One could argue that Republicans have no right to comment on the effectiveness of a force that they were trying to destroy. But it is also a surreal compliment to that effectiveness that those whose hands are stained with the blood of murdered officers should try to demean the force through propaganda when they failed to destroy its morale and ability to do its duty. And it must also be remembered that the RUC GC was given a duty that is outside the ambit of ordinary policing: to contain terrorist organizations intent on destroying the society in which they operated. Republicans are apt to declaim about the number of people killed by the RUC while ignoring the numbers killed by Republican terrorists. Between 1968 and 2000 the RUC GC was responsible for fifty-one deaths; one of the dead was a police officer and a second a soldier, leaving a total of forty-nine civilians. Of those, some were innocent but some were not. In the same years the principal Republican terrorist group, the Provisional IRA, killed 713 civilians, seventy-three of whom were children. All of those dead were innocent and very many were Nationalist or Catholic. In the years of the 'troubles' a Northern Ireland Nationalist faced greater danger from Republicans with guns and bombs than from any other source – and those Republicans were people who claimed to be protecting the Catholic community.

A brief comparison with police forces in the United States is also enlightening. US Department of Justice figures, compiled by the Federal Bureau of Investigation (FBI), indicate a 'justifiable homicide' rate of over 400 per year in the early 1990s. In other words, American police officers killed more than 400 people each year. And yet those officers, although facing a criminal underclass that routinely carried guns, did not face a terrorist threat. That American annual death rate of 400-plus compares starkly with the forty-nine civilians killed by the RUC GC over three decades – a rate of 1.7 each year. At the same time an officer in the RUC GC was seven times more likely to be murdered than was a police officer in the United States.[16]

It would be untrue to claim that every single police officer in Northern Ireland did his or her full duty at all times; but to exaggerate the failings of a few is to be dishonest; officers were arrested, arraigned and convicted for serious crimes, including murder and kidnap, having been detected by their comrades who felt betrayed by those few who decided to take the law into their own hands. Columnist Eoghan Harris, writing in *The Sunday Times*, commented that:

No doubt on a daily basis many nationalists met bad apples. I met a few myself at checkpoints down the years. But the Garda has gurriers too. And what are a few bigoted bad apples when measured against the raw courage of the RUC, the sheer professionalism – look at how fast the Greysteel killers were put behind bars – and the sheer restraint shown by the RUC while standing in the front line, facing one of the most ferocious terrorist groups in the world.[17]

In spite of having to contend with terrorists of both Republican and Loyalist persuasions, the RUC GC had also to provide a normal policing service to Northern Ireland. As noted earlier in this chapter they succeeded in doing this and earned tributes from many for the quality of that service. Carrying out these twin roles placed an enormous strain on the men and women of the force and on their families and, at times, almost all available resources were committed. The RUC GC held the line between law and order on the one hand and anarchy on the other. At times that line was stretched to the very limit but the thin green line never broke; and not only Northern Ireland but also all of the United Kingdom and the Republic of Ireland owe a great debt to the dedication of the men and women of the Royal Ulster Constabulary GC. Rarely has an award for gallantry been better earned than was the George Cross awarded to the force by Her Majesty The Queen in 1999.

Notes
1: The fire claimed the lives of four members of the McCauley family; the parents and two children.
2: Ryder, *The Fateful Split*, p. 310
3: A number of police officers who served in this period recalled similar experiences.
4: Inspector Norman Duddy, murdered in Londonderry in 1982, had been an active member of Londonderry Amateur Operatic Society and of City of Derry Golf Club. Other officers had been involved in youth groups and coaching for several sports, as well as being members of local sports teams. In spite of the ban on membership imposed by the Gaelic Athletic Association, several RUC officers continued to play Gaelic games until the end of the 1960s; some even played after that.
5: This experience was also recalled by a number of officers.
6: These beat officers were targeted on a number of occasions and several were wounded before the practice was abandoned.
7: *Derry Journal*, 19 August 1975.
8: Stewart Tosh MBE to author.
9: The author was present at the conference when Doctor McCabe made the comment and was present when the Institute of Road Safety Officers decided to recognize Chief Inspector Hogg's service. As Chairman of that Institute he also commended the RUC GC for a Prince Michael Award but, as noted, the Award was not made until after the name change.
10: Cameron, *Women in Green*, p. 92
11: Ibid., p. 159
12: Ibid., p. 160
13: *Irish News*, 2 April 1986

14: Mrs Agnes Adair BEM (formerly Sergeant A. E. Adair) to author.
15: Eoghan Harris, *Sunday Times*, 12 September 1999
16: Ibid; www.fbi.gov Federal Bureau of Investigation, Washington DC, USA
17: Harris, op. cit.

Appendix One

Gallantry Awards to individual members of the Royal Ulster Constabulary GC

Empire Gallantry Medal (exchanged for George Cross)	1
George Medal	16
Member of the Order of the British Empire (MBE) for Gallantry	1
Bar to British Empire Medal (BEM) for Gallantry	1
British Empire Medal for Gallantry	40
Bar to Queen's Gallantry Medal	1
Queen's Gallantry Medal	115
King's Police Medal for Gallantry	3
King's Police and Fire Service Medal for Gallantry	4
Queen's Police Medal for Gallantry (posthumous)	5
Queen's/King's Commendation for Brave Conduct	163

This list has been compiled by Mr Roy Black, a member of the RUC GC Historical Society and is reproduced here with his kind permission.

Appendix Two

Roll of Honour

Lest We Forget

Blessed are the dead who die in the Lord,
for their works follow them.

Name	Where killed	Date
Constable James O'Neill	Co. Londonderry	1924
Constable John Ryan*	Belfast	1933
Constable George Thompson		1933
Constable Charles Anderson*	Belfast	1933
Constable Frederick Clarke	Belfast	1935
Constable James Mahoney	Co. Londonderry	1936
Constable Thomas Halliday	Co. Tyrone	1937
Constable Andrew Duncan		1938
Sergeant Peter O'Reilly	Co. Londonderry	1939
Constable George Brown	Belfast	1939
Constable Harold Anderson	Co. Down	1939
Head Constable Thomas Dempsey*	Londonderry	1940
Constable William Armstrong		1940
D/Sergeant Robert Wilson	Belfast (Blitz)	1941
Constable James Meaklim	Belfast (Blitz)	1941
Constable Martin Armstrong	Belfast (Blitz)	1941
Constable Hugh Campbell	Belfast (Blitz)	1941
Constable William Lemon	Belfast (Blitz)	1941
Constable James McKenna	Belfast (Blitz)	1941
Constable Robert Reid	Belfast (Blitz)	1941

Name	Where killed	Date
Constable Christopher Crawford		1941
Constable John Cunning		1941
Constable William Hasson	Co. Fermanagh	1941
Constable Thomas Forbes*	Dungannon, Co. Tyrone	1942
Constable Patrick Murphy KPM*	Belfast	1942
Constable James Laird*	Co. Tyrone	1942
Constable Patrick Mageean	Londonderry	1942
Constable Samuel Armstrong	Londonderry	1943
Constable Patrick McCarthy*	Belfast	1943
Constable James Phillips		1943
Constable William Ellison	Belfast	1944
Constable Robert McLaughlin	Belfast	1944
Constable Walter Bond	Belfast	1944
Constable John Rankin		1947
Constable Samuel Baird	Belfast	1948
Constable Robert Lindsay		1951
D/Constable Michael Small		1952
Constable John Clifford	Belfast	1955
Constable John Murphy		1955
Constable John Scally*	Derrylin, Co. Fermanagh	1956
Constable Thomas Clarke	Co. Antrim	1957
Constable Cecil Gregg*	Forkhill, Co. Armagh	1957
Sergeant Arthur Ovens*	Coalisland, Co. Tyrone	1957
Constable Patrick Joseph Duignan	Co. Down	1957
Constable Henry Ross*	Forkhill, Co. Armagh	1958
Constable Cecil Cunningham	Co. Londonderry	1958
Constable George Elliott	Co. Down	1960
Constable Norman Anderson*	Roslea, Co. Fermanagh	1961
Constable William John Hunter*	Jonesborough, Co. Armagh	1961
Constable Nathaniel Davidson		1962
Constable Kenneth Armstrong		1962
Constable John Brown	Co. Fermanagh	1963
Constable Patrick Kerr	Co. Londonderry	1968
Head Constable Robert Murdoch	Belfast	1968

Name	Where killed	Date
Constable Victor Arbuckle*	Belfast	1969
D/Head Constable John Hunter	Belfast	1969
Constable Samuel Donaldson*	Crossmaglen, Co. Armagh	1970
Constable Robert Millar*	Crossmaglen, Co. Armagh	1970
Constable Robert Buckley*	Belfast	1971
D/Inspector Cecil Patterson*	Belfast	1971
Sergeant William Hall	Co. Down	1971
Constable Robert Leslie*	Strabane, Co. Tyrone	1971
Constable Cecil Cunningham*	Belfast	1971
Constable John Haslett*	Belfast	1971
Sergeant Ronald Dodd*	Toome, Co. Antrim	1971
Inspector Alfred Devlin*	Belfast	1971
D/Constable Stanley Corry*	Belfast	1971
D/Constable William Russell*	Belfast	1971
Sergeant Dermot Hurley*	Belfast	1971
Constable Walter Moore*	Belfast	1971
R/Constable Raymond Denham*	Belfast	1972
Sergeant Peter Gilgunn*	Londonderry	1972
Constable David Montgomery*	Londonderry	1972
Constable Raymond Carroll*	Belfast	1972
Sergeant Thomas Morrow*	Camlough, Co. Armagh	1972
Constable William Logan*	Coalisland, Co. Tyrone	1972
Constable Ernest McAllister*	Belfast	1972
Constable Bernard O'Neill*	Belfast	1972
Constable David Houston QPM*	Newry, Co. Down	1972
Constable Robert Laverty*	Belfast	1972
R/Constable Robert Gibson*	Belfast	1972
D/Constable Robert Nicholl	Belfast	1972
Constable Gordon Harron QPM*	Belfast	1972
R/Constable Joseph Calvin*	Enniskillen, Co. Fermanagh	1972
Constable Robert Keys*	Belleek, Co. Fermanagh	1972
Constable James Nixon*	Belfast	1972
Constable George Chambers*	Lurgan, Co. Armagh	1972
Sergeant David Dorsett*	Londonderry	1973
Constable Mervyn Wilson*	Londonderry	1973
R/Constable Henry Sandford*	Co. Tyrone	1973
Constable Samuel Hyndman	Co. Armagh	1973
Constable Charles Morrison*	Dungannon, Co. Tyrone	1973
Constable Raymond Wylie QPM*	Aghagallon, Co. Armagh	1973
Constable Ronald McCauley QPM*	Aghagallon, Co. Armagh	1973
Constable David Purvis*	Enniskillen, Co. Fermanagh	1973

Name	Where killed	Date
R/Constable William McElveen*	Armagh, Co. Armagh	1973
R/Constable William Campbell*	Belfast	1973
D/Constable John Doherty*	Nr Lifford, Co. Donegal	1973
Constable Robert Megaw*	Lurgan, Co. Armagh	1973
D/Constable Maurice Rolston*	Newcastle, Co. Down	1973
Constable Michael Logue*	Belfast	1973
	— — —	
R/Constable John Rogers*	Glengormley, Co. Antrim	1974
R/Constable William Baggley*	Londonderry	1974
Constable Thomas McClinton*	Belfast	1974
Constable Cyril Wilson*	Craigavon, Co, Armagh	1974
Sergeant Frederick Robinson*	Greenisland, Co. Antrim	1974
Constable Thomas McCall*	Newtownhamilton, Co. Armagh	1974
Constable Brian Bell*	Finaghy, Co. Antrim	1974
Constable John Ross*	Finaghy, Co. Antrim	1974
Constable John Forsythe*	Lurgan, Co. Armagh	1974
R/Constable William Rea	Belfast	1974
Sergeant Daniel O'Connor*	Belfast	1974
D/Inspector Peter Flanagan*	Omagh, Co. Tyrone	1974
Inspector William Elliott QPM*	Newtownabbey, Co. Antrim	1974
R/Constable Arthur Henderson*	Stewartstown, Co. Tyrone	1974
Constable Robert Forde*	Craigavon, Co. Armagh	1974
Constable David McNeice*	Killeavey, Co. Armagh	1974
	— — —	
Sergeant George Coulter*	Donaghmore, Co. Tyrone	1975
R/Constable Mildred Harrison*	Bangor, Co. Down	1975
Constable Albert Saunderson	Belfast	1975
Constable Paul Gray*	Londonderry	1975
Constable Noel Davis*	Maghera, Co. Londonderry	1975
Constable Norman McDowell	Co. Antrim	1975
D/Constable Andrew Johnston*	Lurgan, Co. Armagh	1975
Constable Robert McPherson QCB*	Dungiven, Co. Londonderry	1975
Constable Adrian Johnston	Co. Tyrone	1975
D/Constable David Love*	Nr Limavady, Co. Londonderry	1975
R/Constable Andrew Baird*	Portadown, Co. Armagh	1975
R/Constable Joseph Clements*	Sixmilecross, Co. Tyrone	1975
R/Constable Cherry Campbell	Maydown, Co. Londonderry	1975

Name	Where killed	Date
Sergeant Patrick Maxwell*	Nr Dungannon, Co. Tyrone	1975
R/Constable Samuel Clarke*	Nr Dungannon, Co. Tyrone	1975
Constable Francis Sullivan	Co. Armagh	1975
R/Constable Clifford Evans*	Nr Toome, Co. Londonderry	1976
Inspector George Bell*	Belfast	1976
Constable Neville Cummings*	Belfast	1976
Sergeant James Blakely*	Belfast	1976
Inspector William Murtagh*	Belfast	1976
R/Constable Victor Hamer*	Claudy, Co. Londonderry	1976
R/Constable William Crooks*	Coalisland, Co. Tyrone	1976
R/Constable Thomas Evans*	Co. Fermanagh	1976
Sergeant James Hunter*	Warrenpoint, Co. Down	1976
R/Constable Francis Kettles*	Belcoo, Co. Fermanagh	1976
Sergeant Harry Keys*	Belcoo, Co. Fermanagh	1976
R/Constable Kenneth Nelson*	Nr Dungannon, Co. Tyrone	1976
Constable John McCambridge*	Dungannon, Co. Tyrone	1976
R/Constable Linda Baggley*	Londonderry	1976
D/Inspector William Heasley	Co. Down	1976
D/Constable Ronald McAdam*	Belfast	1976
Constable Thomas Cush*	Lurgan, Co. Armagh	1976
R/Constable James Armour*	Maghera, Co. Londonderry	1976
Constable James Heaney*	Belfast	1976
Sergeant Albert Craig*	Portadown, Co. Armagh	1976
R/Constable Arthur McKay*	Kilrea, Co. Londonderry	1976
D/Constable Noel McCabe QGM*	Belfast	1976
R/Constable Joseph Scott*	Dungannon, Co. Tyrone	1976
Constable Norman Campbell*	Portadown, Co. Armagh	1976
D/Sergeant Ronald McMahon	Co. Armagh	1976
R/Constable James Greer*	Portglenone, Co. Antrim	1977
D/Constable Patrick McNulty*	Londonderry	1977
R/Constable Robert Harrison*	Gilford, Co. Down	1977
R/Constable Samuel McKane*	Cloughmills, Co. Antrim	1977
Inspector Harold Cobb*	Lurgan, Co. Armagh	1977
Sergeant Joseph Campbell*	Cushendall, Co. Antrim	1977
Constable William Brown*	Nr Lisnaskea, Co. Fermanagh	1977

Name	Where killed	Date
Constable John McCracken*	Nr Magherafelt, Co. Londonderry	1977
Constable Kenneth Sheehan*	Nr Magherafelt, Co. Londonderry	1977
R/Constable Robert North*	Benburb, Co. Tyrone	1977
Constable Samuel Davison*	Ardboe, Co. Tyrone	1977
Constable Norman Lynch*	Ardboe, Co. Tyrone	1977
R/Constable Hugh Martin*	Ardboe, Co. Tyrone	1977
D/Sergeant Adam McPherson	Co. Antrim	1977
D/Constable Colin Graham	Co. Antrim	1977
R/Constable David Morrow*	Aughnacloy, Co. Tyrone	1977
Constable James Hill	Co. Antrim	1978
R/Constable Gordon Crothers*	Castlereagh, Co. Down	1978
Constable Charles Simpson*	Londonderry	1978
R/Constable John Moore*	Armoy, Co. Antrim	1978
Constable Millar McAllister*	Lisburn, Co. Antrim	1978
Constable Thomas Nesbitt		1978
R/Constable Robert Struthers*	Londonderry	1978
Constable Hugh McConnell*	Nr Camlough, Co. Armagh	1978
Constable William Turbitt*	Nr Camlough, Co. Armagh	1978
R/Constable Jacob Rankin*	Castlederg, Co. Tyrone	1978
R/Constable John Lamont*	Ballymena, Co. Antrim	1978
R/Constable Howard Donaghy*	Nr Loughmacrory, Co. Tyrone	1978
— — —		
Constable Richard Baird*	Nr Newry, Co. Down	1979
Constable Paul Gray*	Nr Newry, Co. Down	1979
R/Constable Robert Lockhart*	Nr Newry, Co. Down	1979
Constable Noel Webb*	Nr Newry, Co. Down	1979
D/Constable Norman Prue*	Maguiresbridge, Co. Fermanagh	1979
R/Constable Stanley Wray*	Londonderry	1979
R/Constable Alan Dunne*	Armagh, Co. Armagh	1979
Superintendent Stanley Hanna*	Clonalig, Co. Armagh	1979
Constable Kenneth Thompson*	Clonalig, Co. Armagh	1979
R/Constable John Scott*	Ardboe, Co. Tyrone	1979
Constable George Walsh*	Armagh, Co. Armagh	1979
Constable Derek Davidson*	Belfast	1979
Sergeant William Pollock*	Belfast	1979
Constable Gerry Davidson	Belfast	1979
R/Constable Stanley Hazelton*	Glasslough, Co. Monaghan	1979

Name	Where killed	Date
R/Constable Robert Crilly*	Newtownbutler, Co. Fermanagh	1980
R/Constable David Purse*	Belfast	1980
Constable Joseph Rose*	Lisnaskea, Co. Fermanagh	1980
Constable Winston Howe*	Lisnaskea, Co. Fermanagh	1980
R/Constable Bernard Montgomery*	Belfast	1980
Constable Stephen Magill*	Stewartstown, Co. Tyrone	1980
R/Constable Fred Wilson*	Belfast	1980
R/Constable Wallace Allen*	Newtownhamilton, Co. Armagh	1980
Constable William Anderson	Co. Down	1980
Constable Thomas Dickson	Co. Armagh	1980
R/Constable Ernest Johnston*	Magheraveely, Co. Fermanagh	1980
Constable Joanne Best	Belfast	1980
Constable Francis Collins	Belfast	1980
R/Constable Brian Harris	Belfast	1980
Constable Paul Mason	Belfast	1980
Constable Norman Montgomery	Belfast	1980
Constable James Drennan	Co. Londonderry	1980
R/Constable Lindsay McDougall*	Belfast	1981
R/Constable James Stronge*	Tynan, Co. Armagh	1981
R/Constable Charles Lewis*	Belfast	1981
R/Constable Alexander Scott*	Belfast	1981
Constable Kenneth Acheson*	Bessbrook, Co. Armagh	1981
Constable Gary Martin*	Belfast	1981
Constable Philip Ellis*	Belfast	1981
Constable Samuel Vallely*	Belfast	1981
Constable Mervyn Robinson*	Whitecross, Co. Armagh	1981
R/Constable Colin Dunlop*	Belfast	1981
R/Constable Christopher Kyle*	Nr Omagh, Co. Tyrone	1981
Constable Neal Quinn*	Newry, Co. Down	1981
Constable Martha Harkness	Co. Londonderry	1981
Constable John Smyth*	Nr Loughmacrory, Co. Tyrone	1981
Constable Andrew Woods*	Nr Loughmacrory, Co. Tyrone	1981
Constable Mark Evans*	Nr Pomeroy, Co. Tyrone	1981
Constable John Montgomery*	Nr Pomeroy, Co. Tyrone	1981
R/Constable John Proctor*	Magherafelt, Co. Londonderry	1981
Constable George Stewart*	Killough, Co. Down	1981

Name	Where killed	Date
Constable Alexander Beck*	Belfast	1981
Constable Hugh Lewis	Co. Down	1981
R/Constable Silas Lyttle*	Ballygawley, Co. Tyrone	1981
Constable William Coulter*	Belfast	1981
Inspector Norman Duddy*	Londonderry	1982
Sergeant David Brown*	Belfast	1982
Constable Gordon Anderson	Co. Armagh	1982
Constable Mable Cheyne	Co. Armagh	1982
Constable Denis Maguire	Co. Armagh	1982
Constable Alan Caskey*	Londonderry	1982
D/Constable Reginald Reeves*	Londonderry	1982
R/Constable John Eagleson*	Cookstown, Co. Tyrone	1982
R/Constable Charles Crothers*	Londonderry	1982
Sergeant John Quinn*	Lurgan, Co. Armagh	1982
Constable Alan McCloy*	Lurgan, Co. Armagh	1982
Constable Paul Hamilton*	Lurgan, Co. Armagh	1982
Constable Garry Ewing*	Enniskillen, Co. Fermanagh	1982
R/Constable Ronald Irwin*	Markethill, Co. Armagh	1982
R/Constable Snowdon Corkey*	Markethill, Co. Armagh	1982
Sergeant Eric Brown*	Rostrevor, Co. Down	1983
R/Constable Brian Quinn*	Rostrevor, Co. Down	1983
R/Constable John Olphert*	Londonderry	1983
R/Constable Edward Magill*	Warrenpoint, Co. Down	1983
Sergeant Gordon Wilson*	Armagh, Co. Armagh	1983
Constable Lindsay McCormack*	Belfast	1983
R/Constable Frederick Morton*	Nr Newry, Co. Down	1983
Constable Gerald Cathcart*	Belfast	1983
R/Constable Colin Carson*	Downpatrick, Co. Down	1983
Constable John Wasson*	Armagh, Co. Armagh	1983
R/Constable William Finlay*	Downpatrick, Co. Down	1983
R/Constable James Ferguson*	Downpatrick, Co. Down	1983
Constable John Hallawell*	Londonderry	1983
Constable Paul Clarke*	Carrickmore, Co. Tyrone	1983
Inspector John Martin*	Jordanstown, Co. Antrim	1983
Sergeant Stephen Fyfe*	Jordanstown, Co. Antrim	1983
R/Constable John McFadden*	Rasharkin, Co. Antrim	1983
R/Constable William Fitzpatrick*	Kilkeel, Co. Down	1983
R/Constable William Fullerton*	Newry, Co. Down	1984
Sergeant William Savage*	Nr Newry, Co. Down	1984
Constable Thomas Bingham*	Nr Newry, Co. Down	1984
Constable Michael Dawson*	Belfast	1984

R/Constable Trevor Elliott*	Camlough, Co. Down	1984
Constable Neville Gray*	Camlough, Co. Down	1984
Constable Michael Todd QPM*	Belfast	1984
Sergeant Malcolm White*	Nr Gortin, Co. Tyrone	1984
Sergeant William McDonald*	Jordanstown, Co. Antrim	1984

Chief Inspector Alexander Donaldson*	Newry, Co. Down	1985
Constable Rosemary McGookin*	Newry, Co. Down	1985
R/Constable Geoffrey Campbell*	Newry, Co. Down	1985
R/Constable Denis Price*	Newry, Co. Down	1985
R/Constable Paul McFerran*	Newry, Co. Down	1985
R/Constable Sean McHenry*	Newry, Co. Down	1985
Constable David Topping*	Newry, Co. Down	1985
Sergeant John Dowd*	Newry, Co. Down	1985
Constable Ivy Kelly*	Newry, Co. Down	1985
Sergeant Hugh McCormac*	Enniskillen, Co. Fermanagh	1985
R/Constable John Bell*	Rathfriland, Co. Down	1985
R/Constable Michael Kay*	Newry, Co. Down	1985
Inspector William Wilson*	Killeen, Co. Down	1985
Constable David Baird*	Killeen, Co. Down	1985
Constable Tracy Doak*	Killeen, Co. Down	1985
R/Constable Steven Rodgers*	Killeen, Co. Down	1985
Sergeant Francis Murphy*	Drumsallon, Co. Armagh	1985
R/Constable Willis Agnew*	Kilrea, Co. Londonderry	1985
Constable William Gilliland*	Kinawley, Co. Fermanagh	1985
Inspector Martin Vance*	Crossgar, Co. Down	1985
Constable David Hanson*	Crossmaglen, Co. Armagh	1985
Constable George Gilliland*	Ballygawley, Co. Tyrone	1985
R/Constable William Clements*	Ballygawley, Co. Tyrone	1985

Constable James McCandless*	Armagh, Co. Armagh	1986
R/Constable Michael Williams*	Armagh, Co. Armagh	1986
D/Constable Derek Breen*	Maguiresbridge, Co. Fermanagh	1986
Inspector James Hazlett*	Newcastle, Co. Down	1986
Constable David McBride*	Crossmaglen, Co. Armagh	1986
Constable William Smyth*	Crossmaglen, Co. Armagh	1986
R/Constable John McVitty*	Roslea, Co. Fermanagh	1986
Sergeant Peter Kilpatrick*	Newry, Co. Down	1986
Constable Karl Blackbourne*	Newry, Co. Down	1986
Constable Charles Allen*	Newry, Co. Down	1986
R/Constable Desmond Dobbin*	Belfast	1986
R/Constable Edward McFarland	Co. Tyrone	1986
Constable Derek Patterson*	Belfast	1986

Name	Where killed	Date
R/Constable Ivan Crawford*	Enniskillen, Co. Fermanagh	1987
R/Constable Peter Nesbitt*	Belfast	1987
D/Inspector Austin Wilson*	Londonderry	1987
D/Sergeant John Bennison*	Londonderry	1987
R/Constable George Shaw*	Ballynahinch, Co. Down	1987
R/Constable Robert McLean*	Portrush, Co. Antrim	1987
R/Constable Frederick Armstrong*	Portrush, Co. Antrim	1987
Inspector David Ead*	Newcastle, Co. Down	1987
Sergeant Thomas Cooke*	Prehen, Co. Londonderry	1987
Constable Samuel McClean*	Drumbeen, Co. Donegal	1987
Sergeant Robert Guthrie*	Belfast	1987
Constable Norman Kennedy*	Ballymena, Co. Antrim	1987
D/Constable Michael Malone*	Belfast	1987
D/Constable Ernest Carson*	Belfast	1987
R/Constable William Finlay*	Magherafelt, Co. Londonderry	1987
R/Constable Sydney Roxborough	Co. Armagh	1987
R/Constable Edward Armstrong*	Enniskillen, Co. Fermanagh	1987
Constable Colin Gilmore*	Belfast	1988
Constable Clive Graham*	Londonderry	1988
D/Constable John Warnock*	Belfast	1988
Constable John Larmour*	Belfast	1988
R/Constable Hugh McCrone*	Kinawley, Co. Fermanagh	1988
R/Constable William Monteith*	Castlederg, Co. Tyrone	1988
Constable John Smith	Co. Down	1989
Constable Stephen Montgomery*	Sion Mills, Co. Tyrone	1989
Chief Superintendent Harry Breen*	Nr Jonesborough, Co. Armagh	1989
Superintendent Robert Buchanan*	Nr Jonesborough, Co. Armagh	1989
Constable David Cooper	Co. Londonderry	1989
R/Constable David Black*	Nr Strabane, Co. Tyrone	1989
Constable Norman Annett*	Garvagh, Co. Londonderry	1989
R/Constable Alexander Bell*	Nr Cushendall, Co. Antrim	1989
Superintendent Alwyn Harris*	Lisburn, Co. Antrim	1989
Constable Michael Marshall*	Belleek, Co. Fermanagh	1989
Constable Ian Johnston	Belfast	1989
Inspector Derek Monteith*	Armagh, Co. Armagh	1990
R/Constable George Starrett*	Armagh, Co. Armagh	1990
Constable Harry Beckett*	Belfast	1990
Constable Gary Meyer*	Belfast	1990

Name	Where killed	Date
R/Constable Cyril Willis*	Nr Caledon, Co. Armagh	1990
Constable William Hanson*	Nr Caledon, Co. Armagh	1990
R/Constable David Sterritt*	Nr Caledon, Co. Armagh	1990
D/Constable Louis Robinson*	Nr Killeen, Co. Armagh	1990
D/Constable Wilfred Good	Co. Antrim	1990
Constable Samuel Todd*	Belfast	1990
D/Inspector David Murphy*	Lough Neagh, Co. Armagh	1990
R/Constable Thomas Taylor*	Lough Neagh, Co. Armagh	1990
R/Constable Wilfred Wethers*	Lurgan, Co. Armagh	1990
D/Constable Spence McGarry*	Ballycastle, Co. Antrim	1991
Sergeant Samuel McCrum*	Lisburn, Co. Antrim	1991
Sergeant Stephen Gillespie*	Belfast	1991
D/Constable Douglas Carrothers*	Lisbellaw, Co. Fermanagh	1991
Constable Edward Spence*	Belfast	1991
Constable Erik Clarke*	Swatragh, Co. Londonderry	1991
Constable William Evans	Belfast	1991
Constable Colleen McMurray*	Newry, Co. Down	1992
Constable James Douglas*	Belfast	1992
R/Constable Alan Corbett*	Belcoo, Co. Fermanagh	1992
Constable Michael Ferguson*	Londonderry	1993
Constable Reginald Williamson*	Nr Moy, Co. Tyrone	1993
Constable Jonathan Reid*	Crossmaglen, Co. Armagh	1993
R/Constable Brian Woods*	Newry, Co. Down	1993
Constable William Beacom*	Fivemiletown, Co. Tyrone	1993
R/Constable Ernest Smith *	Fivemiletown, Co. Tyrone	1993
Constable Johnston Beacom*	Belfast	1994
Constable Jackie Haggan*	Belfast	1994
R/Constable Mark Collins	Londonderry	1994
Constable Gregory Pollock*	Londonderry	1994
Assistant Chief Constable Brian Fitzsimons MBE	Mull of Kintyre, Scotland	1994
D/Chief Superintendent Maurice Neely	Mull of Kintyre, Scotland	1994
D/Chief Superintendent Desmond Conroy BEM QGM	Mull of Kintyre, Scotland	1994
D/Superintendent Ian Phoenix	Mull of Kintyre, Scotland	1994
D/Superintendent William Gwilliam	Mull of Kintyre, Scotland	1994
D/Superintendent Philip Davidson	Mull of Kintyre, Scotland	1994
D/Superintendent Robert Foster	Mull of Kintyre, Scotland	1994

Name	Where killed	Date
D/Chief Inspector Dennis Bunting	Mull of Kintyre, Scotland	1994
D/Inspector Andrew Davidson	Mull of Kintyre, Scotland	1994
D/Inspector Kevin Magee	Mull of Kintyre, Scotland	1994
Constable Jim Seymour*	Dungannon, Co. Tyrone	1995
Constable Alan George Thompson	Omagh, Co. Tyrone	1995
Constable Michael Gamble	Killadeas, Co. Fermanagh	1997
Constable Darren Bradshaw*	Belfast	1997
Constable Greg Taylor*	Ballymoney, Co. Antrim	1997
Constable John Graham*	Lurgan, Co. Armagh	1997
R/Constable David Johnston*	Lurgan, Co. Armagh	1997
Constable Frank O'Reilly*	Portadown, Co. Armagh	1998
R/Constable William Norman Thompson	Belfast	2000

Note
*Murdered by terrorists.

Others

Police Authority of Northern Ireland members
Councillor William Johnston – 1972
Colonel Oliver Eaton TD DL - 1976

The following officers of the RUC GC were murdered by terrorists after retiring or resigning from the force.

D/Constable Ivan Johnston	1973
R/Constable William Meaklin	1975
R/Constable John Morrow	1975
Sergeant Cecil Shaw	1977
R/Constable John Anderson	1977
R/Constable Frederick Lutton	1979
R/Constable James Wright	1979
R/Constable Robert Shields	1980
Constable Thomas Harpur	1981
Inspector Albert White	1982
R/Constable John Martin	1982
Sergeant Samuel Gault	1987
R/Constable Harold Keys	1989
Inspector Gabriel Mullaly	1989
R/Constable James Sefton	1990
R/Constable Steven Craig	1990
R/Constable Cullen Stephenson	1991
R/Constable Robert Orr	1991
Constable John Murphy	1993
R/Constable Cyril Stewart	1998

Each man's death diminishes me,
For I am involved in mankind.
Therefore, send not to know
For whom the bell tolls,
It tolls for thee.

Appendix Three

The Royal Ulster Constabulary GC Benevolent Fund

Founded in 1970, the RUC Benevolent Fund is the force charity and is administered by the Police Federation of Northern Ireland from its headquarters at Garnerville, in Belfast. The Fund is run by a management committee that represents all ranks of the force and which is chaired by an assistant chief constable. Close links are maintained with the force occupational health and welfare departments.

The services and support of the Benevolent Fund are available to all members of the police family who might be in need. This is the principal criterion used by the Fund which thus covers all serving officers, police pensioners, widows, children and disabled officers. Serving officers may apply to the Fund for assistance in case of illness or intimidation, among other reasons. In the case of intimidation – often as a result of being targeted by terrorists – an officer may obtain a loan to permit a change of car. Needless to say, the Fund also provides a listening ear when such is needed.

Grants may be awarded to members of the police family and these have covered items such as the purchase of domestic equipment for widows, the provision of holidays for widows and children, educational costs for children, computers, wheelchairs and other equipment for the disabled. The Fund has also bought fifteen modern apartments that are available to widows, dependants and pensioners for week-long breaks throughout the year; these apartments are maintained by the Fund.

In addition, the Fund makes grants to local voluntary welfare groups that hold regular meetings for retired officers, widows and dependants. This assistance also includes grants to provide holidays.

The Fund receives much of the money that it disburses from monthly contributions from serving officers. At present the contribution from a regular officer or a full-time reservist is £7.99 while a part-time reservist pays £2.60 each month. As noted in Chapter Eleven the Benevolent Fund also receives many donations from outside bodies and individuals, most of which are unsolicited. RUC GC widows, children and disabled have also benefited from more than £500,000 which has been donated by the Police Dependants' Trust and, for this reason, the Benevolent Fund makes a contribution of 25p from each membership fee to the Trust.

The RUC Benevolent Fund's Representative is responsible for the preparation and completion of applications for assistance from the Fund and these are presented to each monthly meeting of the Fund's management committee which decides on the grants and other assistance to be made. Over more than thirty years the RUC GC Benevolent Fund has done outstanding work for the police family. In the words of one police widow, the Fund has always been there and its representatives have provided the finest support possible. No greater tribute could be made to the Fund's work.

Appendix Four

The Royal Ulster Constabulary GC Foundation

One of the clauses of the Police (Northern Ireland) Act 2000 allowed for the creation of The Royal Ulster Constabulary GC Foundation 'to mark the sacrifices and honour the achievements of the Royal Ulster Constabulary'.

The Foundation's trustees were appointed in late 2001 under the Chairmanship of Mr Jim McDonald LVO MBE JP DL and they were to be responsible for a range of activities that included:

the creation of a memorial garden and a new museum alongside the garden;

supporting the development of officers and innovations in policing through bursaries, exchange programmes, research funding and other means;

undertaking joint initiatives with the RUC GC Widows' Association, Disabled Police Officers' Association and other individuals or groups within the RUC GC 'family';

arranging and encouraging appropriate RUC GC Day events.

Development of the garden actually began in February 2000 under the guidance of a working group, the members of which were drawn from across the police family. With the appointment of the trustees of the Foundation the working group became the advisory group that brought the memorial garden to completion.

On 2 September 2003, HRH The Prince of Wales, who had accepted the position of Patron of the Foundation, opened the memorial garden in the grounds of Brooklyn, which has been the headquarters of the RUC GC and PSNI for some forty years. Over 700 guests, representing families and support groups from within the RUC GC family, attended. Representatives of the principal churches – Lord Eames, the Church of

Ireland Primate, Archbishop Sean Brady, the Roman Catholic Primate, the Right Reverend Dr Ivan McKay, Moderator of the Presbyterian Church, and the Reverend James Rea, President of the Methodist Church – conducted a religious ceremony that marked the formal opening of the garden.

One of the most poignant moments in a very moving service was the reading of a 'Prayer for the Royal Ulster Constabulary GC', derived from the symbols of the RUC GC crest, the shamrock, harp and crown:

O Holy Trinity, as symbolized by the humble shamrock, we give thanks for the love of the Father, the sacrifice of the Son and the indwelling of the Holy Spirit. As Jesus Christ has shown us that the reward of love may be a cross, so we praise you O God for your faithfulness through times of prosperity and of adversity.

Like a harp that sounds forth in glorious tunefulness, so we give honour and thanks to those in the policing family who served gallantly and sacrificed dutifully for the harmony of our communities. Steadfast to their legacy and mindful of continuing needs, may our eyes shine with the light of hope as we embrace the future.

Lord, grant us the perseverance to faithfully finish the race, that we may receive the crown of righteousness to which we have been called heavenward. Equip us with the spirit of peace, an abundance of your grace and the wisdom and strength to meet the challenges that may lie before us.

All this we ask in the precious name of Jesus Christ, our Lord and Saviour.

Amen.

Following the opening of the garden, Prince Charles spoke to many of the guests, and relatives of murdered officers were especially pleased to meet him.

There are four sculptures that are central to the garden. These include the **RUC GC Crest**, by Ned Jackson Smyth, which is based on a sentinel guarding both the garden and the name of the Royal Ulster Constabulary GC; the **RUC George Cross** by Eleanor Wheeler and Alan Cargo, which honours the many acts of gallantry performed by the force and the sacrifice of its members and their families and includes words from the Queen's speech at Hillsborough when she presented the Cross to the force; **Serving the Community**, by Bob Sloan, which depicts hands supporting other hands to create a column and symbolizes how the police support the community but also need the support of the community; and **Remember Those Who Suffer Physical and Mental Injury**, also by Bob Sloan, which is based on turbulent water bubbling from a granite base with six birds appearing to be blown upwards and outwards but which also has at its core the DNA double helix captured in the conical form of two flights of birds soaring as they achieve inner peace.

The Foundation has already organized RUC GC Sundays, as noted in Chapter Eleven and this will be an annual feature of its work, providing an opportunity for remembrance of the many officers who lost their lives on duty with the RUC GC between 1922 and 2001.

Bibliography

Abbott, Richard, *Police Casualties in Ireland 1919–1922*, The Mercier Press Ltd., 2000

Allen, Gregory, *The Garda Síochána*, Gill & Macmillan, 1999

Allen, Mary, *The Pioneer Policewoman*, Chatto & Windus, 1925

Bardon, Jonathan, *A History of Ulster*, The Blackstaff Press, 1992

Breathnach, Seamus, *The Irish Police from Earliest Times to the Present Day*, Anvil Books, 1974

Brewer, John, *Inside the RUC: Routine Policing in a Divided Society*, Clarendon Press, 1991

Bruce, Steve, *God Save Ulster: The religion and politics of Paisleyism*, Oxford University Press, 1986

Cameron, Margaret, *The Women in Green*, RUC Historical Society, 1993

Carroll, Frederick G, *The Register of the George Cross*, This England Books, 1985

Carver, Michael, *Out of Step. The Memoirs of Field Marshal Lord Carver*, Hutchinson, 1989

Devlin, Paddy, *Straight Left*, The Blackstaff Press, 1993

Dewar, Michael, *The British Army in Northern Ireland*, Arms & Armour Press, 1996

Doherty, Paddy, *Paddy Bogside*, The Mercier Press, 2001

Doherty, Richard, *Irish Volunteers in the Second World War*, Four Courts Press, 2002

Duncan, Ivan F, *From Insult to Injury. My Life of Fun, Mayhem and Murder in the Royal Ulster Constabulary 1955–1988*, Figments Publishing, nd

Dunn, Seamus (ed), *Facets of the Conflict in Northern Ireland*, Macmillan, 1995

Ellison, Graham & Smyth, Jim, *The Crowned Harp: Policing Northern Ireland*, Pluto Press, 2000

English, Richard, *The Armed Struggle*, Macmillan, 2003

Evans, Peter, *The Police Revolution*, George Allen & Unwin Ltd., 1974

Faulkner, Brian, *Memoirs of a Statesman*, Weidenfeld & Nicolson, 1978

Fevyer, W. H., (ed), *The George Medal*, Spink, 1980

Foster, R. F., *Modern Ireland 1600–1972*, Allen Lane, 1988

Gorman, Sir John, *The Times of My Life,* Leo Cooper, 2002

Hall, Michael, *20 Years. A Concise Chronology of Events in Northern Ireland from 1968–1988,* Island Publications, 1988

Haythornthwaite, Philip J., *The Armies of Wellington,* Arms & Armour Press, 1994

Herlihy, Jim, *The Royal Irish Constabulary. A Short History and Genealogical Guide,* Four Courts Press, 1997

The Royal Irish Constabulary. A Complete Alphabetical List of Officers and Men, 1816–1922, Four Courts Press, 1999

Hermon, Sir John, *Holding the Line,* Gill & Macmillan, 1997

Hezlet, Sir Arthur, *The 'B' Specials. A History of the Ulster Special Constabulary,* Tom Stacey, 1972

Holland, Jack, *Hope Against History: The Ulster Conflict,* Hodder & Stoughton, 1999

Holland, Jack & Phoenix, Susan, *Phoenix: Policing the Shadows. The secret war against terrorism in Northern Ireland,* Hodder & Stoughton, 1996

Jordan, Hugh, *Milestones in Murder. Defining moments in Ulster's terror war,* Mainstream Publishing, 2002

Kennedy, Colonel William V., *The Intelligence War,* Salamander Books, 1983

Latham, Richard, *Deadly Beat. Inside the Royal Ulster Constabulary,* Mainstream Publishing, 2001

Lee, J. J., *Ireland, 1912–1985: Politics and Society,* Cambridge University Press, 1989

McKittrick, David; Kelters, Seamus; Feeney, Brian & Thornton, Chris, *Lost Lives. The stories of the men, women and children who died as a result of the Northern Ireland troubles,* Mainstream Publishing, 1999

McKittrick, David & McVea, David, *Making Sense of the Troubles,* The Blackstaff Press, 2000

McNiffe, Liam, *A History of the Garda Síochána,* Wolfhound, 1997

Mooney, John & O'Toole, Michael, *Black Operations. The Secret War against the Real IRA,* Maverick House, 2003

Morton, Peter, *Emergency Tour: 3 PARA in South Armagh,* William Kimber, 1989

O'Connor, Stephen, *More than a Uniform,* Kesh, 1999

O'Doherty, Malachi, *The Trouble with Guns. Republican Strategy and the Provisional IRA,* The Blackstaff Press, 1998

O'Halpin, Eunan, *Defending Ireland. The Irish State and its enemies since 1922,* Oxford University Press, 1999

(ed), *MI5 and Ireland, 1939–1945. The Official History,* Irish Academic Press, 2003

O'Neill, Terence, *Ulster at the Crossroads,* Faber & Faber, 1969

O'Sullivan, Donald J., *The Irish Constabularies 1822–1922,* Mount Eagle Publications, nd

Potter, John, *A Testimony to Courage. The History of The Ulster Defence Regiment 1969–1992,* Leo Cooper, 2001

Ripley, Tim & Chappell, Mike, *Security Forces in Northern Ireland 1969–92*, Osprey Elite series No. 44, 1993

Ryder, Chris, *The RUC. A force under fire*, Methuen, 1989

——*The Fateful Split. Catholics and the Royal Ulster Constabulary*, Methuen, 2004

Urban, Mark, *Big Boys' Rules*, Faber & Faber, 1992

Sinclair, R. J. K., & Scully, F. J. M., *Arresting Memories*, The Royal Ulster Constabulary Diamond Jubilee Committee, 1982

Smith, Jeremy, *Making the Peace in Ireland*, Longman, 2002

Smith, M. L. R., *Fighting for Ireland? The military strategy of the Irish republican movement*, Routledge, 1995

Stewart, A. T. Q., *The Narrow Ground. The Roots of Conflict in Ulster*, Faber & Faber, 1977

The Shape of Irish History, The Blackstaff Press, 2001

Wilson, James, *Varieties of Police Behavior*, Harvard University Press, 1968

Articles

Breen, Anthony M., 'Policing the English', *Irish Roots*, no. 44 (2002 Fourth Quarter), pp. 30–31

Dean, Colin, 'Time Heals?', *Wel-Com, the magazine of the Bristol Avon and Somerset (Police) Comrades Association*, Spring edition 1982

Malcolm, Elizabeth, 'From Light Infantry to Constabulary: the military origins of the Irish police, 1798–1850', *The Irish Sword*, vol xxi, no. 81 (Winter 1998), pp. 163–175

Reports

Interim report on policing in Northern Ireland (Belfast 1922)

Report on policing in Northern Ireland (Belfast 1924)

Disturbances in Northern Ireland (The Cameron Report) (Belfast 1969) Cmd. 532

Report of the Advisory Committee on Police in Northern Ireland (The Hunt Report) (Belfast 1969) Cmd. 535

Report of the enquiry into allegations against the Security Forces of physical brutality in Northern Ireland arising out of events on the 9th August, 1971. (The Compton Report) (London 1971) Cmd 4823

Violence and Civil Disturbances in Northern Ireland in 1969 (The Scarman Report) (Belfast 1972) Cmd. 566

Report of the Committee of Inquiry into Police Interrogation Procedures in Northern Ireland. (The Bennett Report) (Belfast 1979) (Cmd. 7497)

Report of the Independent Commission on Policing, 'A new beginning: Policing in Northern Ireland' (The Patten Report) (Belfast 1999)

Newspapers, journals and magazines

The Belfast Telegraph
The Irish News
The Newsletter
The Northern Whig
The Impartial Reporter
The Fermanagh Herald
The Londonderry Sentinel
Wel-Com
The Irish Sword

The Daily Telegraph
The Times
The Sunday Times
The Irish Times
The Irish Independent
The Derry Journal
The Constabulary Gazette
Irish Roots

Websites

www.rucgcfoundation.org Royal Ulster Constabulary GC Foundation
www.psni.police.uk/museum Police Museum, Belfast
www.psni.police.uk Police Service of Northern Ireland
www.garda.ie/angarda/home An Garda Síochána
www.esatclear.ie/~garda/ Garda Síochána Historical Society
www.fbi.gov Federal Bureau of Investigation, Washington DC, USA
www.lancashire.police.uk Lancashire Constabulary
www.btp.police.uk British Transport Police
www.met.police.uk Metropolitan Police

Other sources

Documents from the series, ADM, AIR, CAB, DEFE, HO, WO and PREM
from The National Archives, Ruskin Avenue, Kew.
Some documents were also examined at the Public Record Office of Northern
Ireland, Balmoral Avenue, Belfast.

Index

RUC ranks before 1970 are abbreviated as:
H/Con.   Head Constable
Dist. Insp.   District Inspector
Co. Insp.   County Inspector
C. Comm.   City Commissioner
The rank of Commissioner in An Garda
Síochána, the City of London Police and the
Metropolitan Police is abbreviated as
Comm. In the RUC the rank of Constable is
abbreviated to Con.

Bradley, Co. Insp. (later ACC) Sam, 86, 88, 129
Bradshaw, Con. Darren, 243, 245, 292
Brady, Sgt. John, 34
Bramshill Police College, 88
Breen, C/Supt. Harry, 212, 218, 290
Breen, D/Con. Derek, 195–6, 289
Brett, Con. William, GM, 45–6
Bridewell RUC Station, Newry, 34
Brock, W/Con. Florence May, 48
Brookeborough RUC Station, 60
Brooklyn, 69, 89, 172, 296
Brown Square RUC Station, 95–6
Brown, Con. George, 281
Brown, Con. John, 282
Brown, Con. William, 136, 285
Brown, Sgt. David, 168, 288
Brown, Sgt. Eric, 173, 288
Browne, Con. W., 101
Bruce, W/Con. Annie May, 48
Buchanan, Supt. Bob, 212, 218, 290
Buckley, Con. Robert, 98, 283
Bunting, D/Ch. Insp. Dennis, 234, 292
Byrnes, Con. Patrick MM, 53–4, 63
Byrnes, Con. Richard, 54, 63
Byrnes, WPC Elizabeth, 54

C Specials, 13–14, 24
Caledon RUC Station, 75
Calvin, Con., 72
Calvin, R/Con. Joseph, 109, 283
Campbell, Con. H., 45, 281
Campbell, Con. Norman, 133, 285
Campbell, R/Con. Cherry, 120–1, 284
Campbell, R/Con. Geoffrey, 185, 289
Campbell, R/Con. William, 112, 284
Campbell, Sgt. Joe, 136, 285
Carrickmore RUC Station, 177, 180, 204
Carroll, Con. Raymond, 104, 283
Carrothers, R/Con. Douglas, 225, 291
Carson, D/Con. Ernest, 201, 290
Carson, R/Con. Colin, 175–6, 288
Carson, Sgt. Thomas, 34–5
Caskey, Con. Alan, 167–8, 288
Caskey, D/Ch. Insp. George, 181–2
Castlederg RUC Station, 145, 204
Castlereagh RUC Station, 82, 150–1
Cathcart, Con. Gerry, 175, 288
Chambers, Con. George, 109, 283
Chermside, S/Con. William, 18
Cheyne, Con. Mabel, 288
Chichester Road RUC Station, 102, 190
Clarke, Con. Erik, 225–6, 291
Clarke, Con. Frederick, 281
Clarke, Con. Paul, 178, 288
Clarke, Con. Thomas, 282
Clarke, R/Con. Samuel, 119–20, 268, 284
Clements, R/Con. Joseph, 119, 284

Clements, R/Con. William, 194, 289
Clifford, Con. John, 282
Cloughmills RUC Station, 204
Coalisland RUC Station, 204
Cobb, Insp. Harold, 136, 285
Cockett, C/Insp. Hilary, 270
Collins, Con. Francis, 287
Collins, R/Con. Mark, 291
Connor, Co. Insp. H., 35
Conroy, D/Ch. Supt. Desmond BEM QGM, 234, 291
Constabulary Act (NI) 1922, 16, 20
Constabulary Act (NI) 1963, 69
Constabulary Act, 5
Constabulary Bill (NI), 16
Constabulary Gazette, 31, 34, 36–7, 49, 71
Constabulary of Ireland, 5–6
Cooke, Sgt. Thomas, 202–3, 290
Cooper, Con. David, 290
Corbett, Cadet David (later Co. Insp), 52
Corbett, R/Con. Alan, 228, 291
Cordner, Sgt. Kenneth BEM, 60–1
Corkey, R/Con. Snowden, 169, 288
Corr, Con., 44
Corry, D/Con. Stanley, 102, 283
Coulson, Dist. Insp., 34
Coulter, Con. William, 162–3, 288
Coulter, Con., 72
Coulter, Sgt. George, 118, 284
Craig, Sgt. Albert, 132, 285
Crawford, Con. Christopher, 282
Crawford, Con. Ian, 71
Crawford, R/Con. Ivan, 201–2, 290
Crilly, R/Con. Robert, 152, 287
Crooks, R/Con. William, 123–4, 285
Crossmaglen RUC Station, 95
Crothers, R/Con. Charlie, 168, 288
Crothers, R/Con. Gordon, 142, 153, 286
Crowley, Comm. Eugene, 212
Crozier, Co. Insp. Tom, 69
Crozier, Con. Bob QCB, 123
Cubitt, W/Con. Madge, 61
Cullingtree Road RUC Station, 30
Cummings, D/Con. Neville, 123, 285
Cunning, Con. John, 282
Cunningham S/Con. Thomas, 18
Cunningham, Con. Cecil, 102, 282, 283
Cush, Con. Thomas, 131, 285
Cushendall RUC Station, 136

Davidson, Con. Derek, 147, 286
Davidson, Con. Gerry, 147, 286
Davidson, Con. Nathaniel, 282
Davidson, D/Insp. Andrew, 234, 292
Davidson, D/Supt. Philip, 234, 291
Davies, Con. Cecil, 110
Davis, Con. Noel, 119
Davison, Con. Samuel, 138, 286

Dawson, Con. Michael, 183, 288
Dear, Ch. Con. Geoffrey, 214
Dempsey, H/Con. Thomas, 33, 44, 281
Denham, R/Con. Raymond, 103–4, 283
Derry City Force, 17, 278
Derrylin RUC Station, 57, 60
Devlin, Insp. Alfred, 102, 283
Dickson, Con. Thomas, 287
Disabled Police Officers' Association, 262, 275, 296
Doak, Con. Tracy, 187, 289
Dobbin, R/Con. Desmond, 199, 220, 289
Dodd, Sgt. Ronald, 102, 283
Doherty, D/Con. John, 112, 284
Dolan, Con. Eddie, 89
Donaghy, R/Con. Howard, 145
Donaldson, C/Insp. Alex, 96, 185–6, 289
Donaldson, Con. Samuel, 95–6, 283
Donegall Pass RUC Station, 42, 123
Donemana RUC Station, 55
Dorsett, Sgt. David, 110–11, 126, 201, 283
Douglas, Con. James, 228, 291
Dowd, Sgt. John, 185, 289
Drennan, Con. James, 287
Drennan, W/Con. Gertrude, 48
Dublin Metropolitan Police (DMP), 5–6, 11, 16–17, 20
Dublin Metropolitan Police Act, 4
Dublin Metropolitan Police District, 4
Duddy, Insp. Norman, 167, 278, 288
Duignan, Con. Patrick, 282
Duncan, Con. Andrew, 281
Duncan, Sgt. Ivan, 75–6, 84–5, 90–1
Dungannon RUC Station, 119
Dunlop, R/Con. Colin, 160, 287
Dunne, Con. William, 34
Dunne, R/Con. Alan, 146–7, 286

Ead, Insp. David, 199, 202, 290
Eagleson, R/Con. John, 168, 288
Elliott, Con. George, 282
Elliott, Insp. William QPM, 114–5, 284
Elliott, R/Con. Trevor, 183, 289
Ellis, Con. Phillip, 158, 287
Ellison, Con. William, 282
Evans, Con. Mark, 161, 287
Evans, Con. William, 291
Evans, R/Con. Clifford, 122, 285
Evans, R/Con. Thomas, 129, 285
Ewing, Con. Gary, 169, 288

Falkingham, Con. (later C/Insp.) Neil QPM, 54, 268
Ferguson, Con. Michael, 230, 268, 291
Ferguson, R/Con. James, 176, 288
Ferris, Con., 34
Finlay, R/Con. William QCB, 176–7, 290
Finlay, R/Con. Winston, 203, 288

Fitzpatrick, R/Con. William, 177–8, 288
Fitzsimons, ACC. Brian MBE, 233–4, 291
Flanagan, D/Insp. Peter, 114–15, 284
Flanagan, Sir Jamie, 50, 110, 112–13, 117–18, 121–4, 127–8, 173, 215
Flanagan, Sir Ronnie, 232, 243–6, 250, 252–3, 257, 262
Forbes, Con. Thomas J., 42, 282
Forde, Con. Robert, 115–6, 284
Forsythe, Con. Alex, GM, 62
Forsythe, Con. John, 115, 284
Foster, D/Supt. Robert, 234, 291
Fullerton, R/Con. William, 182–3, 288
Fyfe, Sgt. Stephen, 177, 288

Gamble, Con. Michael, 292
Garda Síochána (Gardai), 5, 17, 34, 39, 58, 60–1, 66–7, 98, 106, 112, 119, 121, 154, 164–5, 172–3, 187, 197, 208, 212–3, 221, 236, 245–6, 251–2, 262, 268, 276–7
Gault, Con. (later Sgt.) Samuel, 66, 204, 293
Gibson, R/Con. Robert, 107, 283
Gilgunn, Sgt. Peter, 103
Gillespie, Sgt. Stephen, 225, 291
Gilliland, Con. George, 194, 289
Gilliland, Con. William, 188, 289
Gilmore, Con. Colin, 209, 290
Gilmore, S/Con. Hugh, 66
Good, D/Con. Wilfred, 291
Goodman, S/Con. Glenn, 227
Gorman, Cadet John, MC (later Dist. Insp.), 52, 58, 63
Gorman, Co. Insp. J. K., MC, 41
Graham, Con. Charles (Carol), 84–5
Graham, Con. Clive, 209, 230, 290
Graham, Con. John, 245, 254, 292
Graham, D/Con. Colin, 286
Gray, Con. (later Sgt.) David, 110–1, 126
Gray, Con. Paul, 118, 284
Gray, Con. Paul, 145, 286
Greer, R/Con. William, 134, 285
Gregg, Con. Cecil, 58–9, 68, 282
Gregg, Sgt., 72
Gregg, W/Con. Carrie, 58, 68
Grey, Con. Neville, 183, 289
Guthrie, Sgt. Robert, 203, 290
Gwilliam, D/Supt. William, 234, 291

Haggan, Con. John, 233, 291
Hall, Sgt. William, 283
Hallawell, Con. John, 177, 288
Halliday, Con. Thomas, 281
Halligan, Con. Robert, 59
Hamer, R/Con. Victor, 123, 285
Hamill, Con. Norman, 102
Hamilton, Con. Paul, 168–9, 288

305

Hamilton, S/Con. Samuel, 42
Hanna, Supt. Stanley, 147
Hanson, Con. David, 193, 289
Hanson, Con. William, 220–1, 291
Harkness, Con. Martha, 287
Harkness, Con. Martha, 287
Harris, R/Con. Brian, 287
Harris, Supt. Alwyn, 213, 290
Harrison, R. D. W., Belfast City
    Commissioner, 47–8, 50
Harrison, R/Con. Mildred, 120, 285
Harrison, R/Con. Robert, 135, 285
Harron, Con. Gordon QPM, 108, 283
Haslett, Con. John, 102, 283
Hasson, Con. William, 282
Hay, Con. Ian, 32
Hayes, Ch. Con. Brian, 215
Hazelton, R/Con. Stanley, 148, 286
Hazlett, Insp. James BEM, 198, 289
Heaney, Con. James, 132, 285
Heasley, D/Insp. William, 285
Henderson, R/Con. Arthur, 115, 284
Hermon, Sir John, 56, 93, 110, 121, 124,
    126, 128–9, 138–40, 148, 151–5, 159,
    163, 165–6, 168–73, 178–82, 185,
    187–90, 192, 196–7, 199–200, 203,
    207, 210–12, 214–15, 218–19, 223,
    243–4, 262, 272
Heuston, H/Con., 33
Higginson, Sgt., 34
Hill, C/Supt. Wilson, 93
Hill, Con. James, 286
Hogg, Con. (later C/Insp.) Douglas BEM,
    269, 278
Houston, Con. Samuel QPM, 106–7, 283
Howe, Con. Winston, 153–4, 287
Hunter, Con. Willie John, 65–7, 90, 273–4,
    282
Hunter, D/Con. John, 283
Hunter, Sgt James, 130, 285
Hunter, W/Con. Agnes (see also Adair,
    Agnes), 66, 68
Hunter, W/Con. Hazel, 106
Hurley, Sgt Dermot, 90, 102, 283
Hyndman, Con. Samuel, 283

Independent Commission for Police
    Complaints, 226
Independent Commission on Policing in
    Northern Ireland, 248, 254
Inspectorate of Constabulary, HM, 182
Institute of Road Safety Officers, 126, 269,
    278
Irish Constabulary Act, 6
Irwin, R/Con. Ronnie, 169, 288

Johnson, R/Con. David, 245, 254, 292
Johnston, Con. Adrian, 284

Johnston, Con. Ian, 214, 290
Johnston, D/Con. Andrew, 118, 284
Johnston, R/Con. Thomas, 154, 287
Joint Helicopter Force, 251
Jones, W/Con. Rebecca, 48–9

Kay, R/Con. Michael, 187, 289
Kelly, Con. Ivy, 185, 289
Kelly, H/Con., 33
Kennedy, Con. Norman, 203, 290
Kerr, CI. George Paul, 72, 76
Kerr, Con. Patrick, 282
Kerr, Supt. Basil, 237
Kettles, R/Con. Francis, 129–30, 285
Keys, Con. Robert, 109, 283
Keys, Sgt. Henry, 129–30, 285
Kilpatrick, Sgt. Peter, 198–9, 202, 289
Kilrea RUC Station, 132
Kinawley RUC Station, 209
King, Con., 46
Kyle, R/Con. Christopher, 160, 287

Lagan, C/Supt. (later ACC.) Frank, 104,
    113, 121
Laird, Con. James, 42, 282
Lamont, R/Con. John, 145, 286
Larmour, Con. John, 209, 290
Laverty, Con. Robert, 107, 283
Lemon, Con. W J, 45, 281
Leslie, Con. Roy, 101–2, 283
Lewis, Con. Hugh, 288
Lewis, Dist. Insp. F W, 34
Lewis, R/Con. Charles, 157, 287
Lindsay, Con. Robert, 282
Lindsay, Con., 52
Lindsay, W/Con. Joy, 106
Lisburn Road RUC Station, 190
Lisburn RUC Station, 209
Lisnagelvin RUC Station, 204, 233
Lisnaskea RUC Station, 57
Lockhart, R/Con. Robert, 145, 286
Logan, Con. Billy, 104, 110
Logue, Con. Michael, 113, 135, 284
Londonderry, 5, 17, 23, 24–5, 33, 35, 37,
    40–1, 44, 47, 50, 56–8, 61–3, 66, 70–2,
    74, 76–8, 81–2, 84, 88–90, 94–5, 99,
    101–4, 107, 111, 113–14, 118, 120,
    131–2, 141–2, 146, 158, 164, 167–8,
    174, 177, 193, 200, 202, 204–7, 209,
    211–12, 217, 224, 230, 232, 234,
    236–7, 239, 242, 249, 251, 258–9, 264,
    266–8, 272, 278
Loughgall RUC Station, 205
Love, D/Con. David, 119, 284
Lucy, Con. Norman (later Sgt.), 55
Luney, Con. Lyn QCB, 136
Lurgan RUC Station, 109

306